Better Ways to Achieve Good Governance in Nigeria: A Critical Look at Governance in Nigeria

CHRISTIAN C. ONWUDIWE

First Published in 2016
Published by:
FORTE Publications
#12 Ashmun Street
Snapper Hill
Monrovia, Liberia

FORTE Publishing
7202 Tavenner Lane
208 Alexandria
VA, 22306

FORTE Press
76 Sarasit Road
Ban Pong, 70110
Ratchaburi, Thailand

http://fortepublishing.wix.com/fppp

ISBN:
ISBN-13: 978-0-9945347-7-4

DEDICATION

This work is dedicated to tens of thousands of Nigerians dying annually because of acute starvation and chronic diseases that would have been prevented if it weren't for the misguided policies of the Nigerian governing elite.

Dr. Christian Onwudiwe's tough-love stance flows from his deep, unwavering concern for his beloved country, Nigeria; his belief that uplifting change, is always possible IF you genuinely want it!

Jane Ogunro, Author- *Psalm 23: An Interpretation*

Contents

UNITY AND FAITH, PEACE AND PROGRESS

List of Abbreviations

ABU	Ahmadu Bello University
ACE	African Centres of Excellence
ACF	Arewa Consultative Forum
ACN	Action Congress of Nigeria
ACSTWU	African Civil Service Technical Workers Union
AD	Alliance for Democracy
AEA	Academic Earned Allowance
AG	Action Group
AGCWU	African General Clerical Workers Union
AGF	Accountant General of the Federation
AGWU	African General Workers Union
AMF	American Mineral Fields
AMWU	African Mercantile Workers Union
ANC	African National Congress
ANPP	All Nigerian Peoples Party
APC	All Progressive Congress
APEC	Asian Pacific Economic Cooperation
APGA	All Progressive Grand Alliance
APP	All People's Party
ASEAN	Association of South East Asian Nations
ASUU	Academic Staff Union of Universities
AU	African Union
AYF	Arewa Youth Forum
BCCI	Bank of Credit and Commerce International
BCBP	Bureau of Customs and Border Protection
BICE	Bureau of Immigration and Customs Enforcement
BOFIA	Bank and Other Financial Institutions Act
BOP	Bureau of Prisons
BNHS	British National Health Service
BP	British Petroleum
BPE	Bureau of Public Enterprises
BRICS	Brazil, Russia, India, China, and South Africa (BRICS Nations)
CAC	Corporate Affairs Commission
CBN	Central Bank of Nigeria
CBP	Customs and Border Protection
CD	Campaign for Democracy
CEOs	Chief Executive Officers
CIA	Central Intelligence Agency
CIS	Commonwealth of Independent States
CMIR	Currency or Money Instrument Report
CNOOC	China's National Offshore Oil Corporation

COLA	Cost of Living Allowance
CORE	Congress of Racial Equity
CPC	Congress for Progressive Change
CS	Customs Service
CTR	Currency Transaction Report
CWU	Colliery Workers Union
DEA	Drug Enforcement Administration
DHS	Department of Homeland Security
DNC	Democratic National Convention
DNI	Director of National Intelligence
DOJ	Department of Justice
DPW	Dubai Ports World
ECA	Economic Commission for Africa
ECOWAS	Economic Community of West African States
EDs	Executive Directors
EEO	Equal Employment Opportunity
EEOC	Equal Employment Opportunity Commission
EFCC	Economic and Financial Crimes Commission
EU	European Union
FAAN	Federal Airport Authority of Nigeria
FBI	Federal Bureau of Investigation
FCPA	Foreign Corrupt Practices Act
FCT	Federal Capital Territory
FEMA	Federal Emergency Management Agency
FNLA	National Front for the Liberation of Angola
FRSC	Federal Road Safety Corps
GCI	Global Competitive Index
GOC	General Officer Commanding
HRVIC	Human Rights Violations Investigation Commission
IAEA	International Atomic Energy Agency
IBRD	International Bank for Reconstruction and Development
ICC	International Criminal Court
ICPC	Independent Corrupt Practices and other Related Offenses Commission
ICT	Information and Communication Technologies
ICT	International Criminal Tribunals
ICTY	International Criminal Tribunals for the Former Yugoslavia
IGC	Interim Governing Council
IMF	International Monetary Fund
IMC	Implementation Monitoring Committee
INEC	Independent National Election Commission
INS	Immigration and Naturalization Service
IOM	International Organization for Migration

JAMB	Joint Admission Matriculation Board
JNI	Jama'atu Nasril Islam
KBR	Kellogg Brown and Root
LIEO	Liberal International Economic Order
MAD	Movement for the Advancement of Democracy
MASSOB	Movement for the Actualization of the Sovereign State of Biafra
MDAs	Ministries, Departments, and Agencies
MDs	Managing Directors
MDCN	Medical and Dental Council of Nigeria
MEND	Movement for the Emancipation of the Niger Delta
MNCs	Multinational Corporations
MNOCs	Multinational Oil Corporations
MOSOP	Movement for the Survival of the Ogoni People
MOU	Memorandum of Understanding
MPLA	Popular Movement for the Liberation of Angola
MTEL	Mobile Communications/GSM
NAACP	National Association for the Advancement of Colored People
NADECO	National Democratic Coalition
NAFTA	North American Free Trade Agreement
NANS	National Association of Nigerian Students
NAPTIP	National Agency for Prohibition of Trafficking in Persons
NARD	National Association of Resident Doctors
NATO	North Atlantic Treaty Organization
NCAA	Nigerian Civil Aviation Authority
NCBWA	National Congress of British West Africa
NCNBE	National Committee on the Nationalization of Business Enterprise
NCNC	National Council of Nigeria and Cameroon
NCNC	National Council of Nigerian Citizens
NCOS	Non Commission Officers
NCP	National Council on Privatization
NCS	Nigerian Customs Service
NDFI	Northern Development Focus Initiative
NDLEA	National Drug Law Enforcement Agency
NEC	National Economic Council
NEMA	National Emergency Management Agency (Nigeria)
NEPA	Nigerian Electric Power Authority
NEPD	Nigerian Enterprises Promotion Decree
NESG	Nigerian Economic Summit Group
NFIU	Nigerian Financial Intelligence Unit
NIL	National Institute for Legislative Studies
NITEL	Nigerian Telecommunications Limited
NIS	Nigerian Immigration Services

NJC	National Judicial Council
NLC	Nigerian Labor Congress
NLDB	Nigerian Local Development Board
NLNG	Nigerian Liquefied Natural Gas
NMA	Nigerian Medical Association
NNDP	Nigerian National Democratic Party
NNOC	Nigerian National Oil Company
NNPC	Nigerian National Petroleum Corporation
NPA	Nigerian Ports Authority
NPC	Northern People's Congress
NPN	National Party of Nigeria
NPP	Nigerian People's Party
NPRC	Nigerian Petroleum Refining Company
NRC	National Republican Convention
NRWU	Nigerian Railway Workers Union
NSACC	Nigeria-South Africa Chamber of Commerce
NSC	National Security Council
NSCDC	Nigerian Security and Civil Defense Corps
NSE	Nigerian Stock Exchange
NTRC	Northern Traditional Rulers Council
NUC	National Universities Commission
NUT	Nigerian Union of Teachers
NYM	Nigerian Youth Movement
NYSC	National Youth Service Corps
OAS	Organization of American States
OAU	Obafemi Awolowo University
OAU	Organization of African Unity
ODNI	Office of the Director of National Intelligence
OHCSF	Office of the Head of Civil Service of the Federation
OIC	Organization of the Islamic Conference
OML	Oil Mining Licenses
OPC	Oodua Peoples' Congress
OPEC	Organization of Petroleum Exporting Countries
OPL	Oil Prospecting Licenses
PAF	Presidential Air Fleet
PARSLEAF	Past Rivers State Students' Leadership Forum
P&O	Peninsular and Oriental Steam Navigation Company
PDP	People's Democratic Party
PHCN	Power Holding Company of Nigeria
PIB	Petroleum Industry Bill
PPP	Public Private Partnership
PPPRA	Petroleum Products Pricing and Regulatory Agency

PRESSID	Presidential Scholarship Scheme for Innovation and Development
PRT	Pension Reform Task Team
RMAFC	Revenue Mobilisation Allocation and Fiscal Commission
SADC	Southern African Development Community
SAP	Structural Adjustment Program
SARA	Scanning, Analysis, Response, Assessment (SARA Model)
SAR	Saudi Arabian Riyal
SCIA	Supreme Council for Islamic Affairs
SCN	Supreme Court of Nigeria
SCLC	Southern Christian Leadership Conference
SDP	Social Democratic Party
SMC	Supreme Military Council
SNCC	Student Nonviolent Coordinating Committee
SNPA	Southern Nigeria Peoples Assembly
SSS	State Security Service
STEM	Science, Technology, Engineering, and Mathematics
TRC	Truth and Reconciliation Commission (South Africa)
TSA	Transportation Security Administration
UAC	United African Company
UAE	United Arab Emirates
UBA	United Bank for Africa
UN	United Nations
UNESCO	United Nations Educational, Scientific and Cultural Organization
UNIA	United Negro Improvement Association
UNICEF	United Nations International Children's Educational Fund or United Nations Children's Fund
UNITA	National Union for the Total Independence of Angola
UNN	University of Nigeria Nsukka
UNO	United Nations Organization
UNODC	United Nations Office on Drugs and Crimes
UNOCAL	Union Oil Company of California
UNSC	United Nations Security Council
UPE	Universal Primary Education
UPN	Unity Party of Nigeria
USD	United States Dollar
USSR	Union of Soviet Socialist Republics
WOCLEF	Women Trafficking and Child Labor Eradication Foundation
WHO	World Health Organization
WTO	World Trade Organization

List of States

NIGERIAN STATES, CAPITALS, AND YEAR CREATED

STATES	CAPITALS	YEAR CREATED
ABIA	UMUAHIA	1991
ADAMAWA	YOLA	1991
AKWA IBOM	UYO	1987
ANAMBRA	AWKA	1991
BAUCHI	BAUCHI	1976
BAYELSA	YENOGOA	1996
BENUE	MAKURDI	1976
BORNO	MAIDUGURI	1976
CROSS RIVER	CALABAR	1967
DELTA	ASABA	1991
EBONYI	ABAKALIKI	1996
EDO	BENIN CITY	1991
EKITI	ADO EKITI	1996
ENUGU	ENUGU	1991
GOMBE	GOMBE	1996
IMO	OWERRI	1976
JIGAWA	DUTSE	1991
KADUNA	KADUNA	1976
KANO	KANO	1967
KATSINA	KATSINA	1987
KEBBI	BIRNIN KEBBI	1991
KOGI	LOKOJA	1991
KWARA	ILORIN	1967
LAGOS	IKEJA	1967
NASARAWA	LAFIA	1996
NIGER	MINNA	1976
OGUN	ABEOKUTA	1976
ONDO	AKURE	1976
OSUN	OSHOGBO	1991
OYO	IBADAN	1976
PLATEAU	JOS	1976
RIVERS	PORT HARCOURT	1967
SOKOTO	SOKOTO	1976
TARABA	JALINGO	1991
YOBE	DAMATURU	1996
ZAMFARA	GUSAU	1996
FCT	(ABUJA)	1992

Six Geopolitical Zones In Nigeria And Their Number Of States

NORTH-CENTRAL ZONE

BENUE
KOGI
KWARA
NASARAWA
NIGER
PLATEAU
FCT (ABUJA)

NORTH-EASTERN ZONE

ADAMAWA
BAUCHI
BORNO
GOMBE
TARABA
YOBE

NORTH-WESTERN ZONE

JIGAWA
KADUNA
KANO
KATSINA
KEBBI
SOKOTO
ZAMFARA

SOUTH-EASTERN ZONE

ABIA
ANAMBRA
EBONYI
ENUGU
IMO

SOUTH-SOUTH ZONE

AWKA IBOM
BAYELSA
CROSS RIVER
DELTA
EDO
RIVERS

SOUTH-WESTERN ZONE

EKITI
LAGOS
OGUN
ONDO
OSUN
OYO

Foreword

Dr. Christian C. Onwudiwe has, in my sincere opinion, written a masterpiece. "Better Ways To Achieve Good Governance In Nigeria" is an extremely well researched, highly captivating and informative book. By providing us with an excellent overview of the history of colonialism and neo-colonialism in Nigeria and an understanding of the attitudes and mentality of the typical Nigerian, Dr. Onwudiwe has done a most thorough job of dissecting Nigeria's socio-economic and political problems by revealing the root causes of them.

The book describes quite elaborately the adverse social, economic and political effects of bad governance in Nigeria with emphasis on the effects of corruption on the energy sector, public education, health care, infrastructure, security, standard of living and the law enforcement community. These consequences are traced to: 1) colonialism which brought together various tribes with different cultures without adequately unifying the ethnic groups as one nation, a situation that caused tribalism and has negatively affected the political development of Nigeria; 2) neo-colonialism by global financial institutions and Western multi-national corporations resulting in the control of Nigeria's economy primarily for the benefit of these organizations; and 3) the unpatriotic and materialistic attitude of average Nigerian which has manifested as a high level of corruption, the country's biggest problem, in both the private and public sectors of the economy.

Finally, "Better Ways To Achieve Good Governance In Nigeria" provides present and future governments in Nigeria well thought out and pragmatic proposals, recommendations and suggestions on how to improve governance in Nigeria to tackle poverty, unemployment, crime, insecurity, corruption and other socio-economic and political problems.

I very strongly recommend this book to every Nigerian. "Better Way To Achieve Good Governance In Nigeria" will undoubtedly help Nigerians understand the causes of the social, economic and political problems of the country and the governance challenges of the ruling class. I strongly advise present and future Nigerian governments to seriously consider the policy proposals and recommendations presented in this book for the improvement of governance in the country.

Finally, this book would also be invaluable to all non-Nigerians who have a passion for learning about governance issues in countries.

Dike Obih, MBA, CPA, ACA, ACTI
Senior Adviser, Corporate Finance
Summa Guaranty and Trust Company Ltd.
Lagos
Nigeria

Preface

This timely study is a reaction to the man-made problems that are plaguing Nigeria today. The study is conceived to further explore and advance on Professor Chinua Achebe's famous theme "*The Trouble with Nigeria,*" an era of massive corruption in Nigeria, to which many Nigerians have come to conclude was far better than what is presently taking place in the country since the birth of Nigeria's Third and Fourth Republics (1993-present). To bring this exercise to a logical conclusion, efforts are made to identify the underlying causes of the Nigerian endemic problems.

An examination of this magnitude has offered the author of this discourse the opportunity to place blame squarely where it belongs. By the same token, such an in-depth examination has also given the author the opportunity to articulate adequate and effective proposals that, if implemented, will minimize further damage to the Nigerian project. The author's main concern is that the government of the day may not implement these sound proposals, as Nigerian governing elite are known for not implementing ideas or policies that are not beneficial to them.

Like most countries, Nigeria is confronted with numerous problems caused by poor governance, which has hampered the country's development and progress. For example, Nigeria had undergone a Civil War (1967-1970) and was governed by a military dictatorship for several decades before returning to a representative democracy. Currently, the corporate existence of the country is seriously threatened by armed militants seeking to rectify the alleged wrongs done to their regions and people by the country's central governing authorities. Other problems facing the country include: endemic poverty and illiteracy; massive unemployment and corruption; inadequate health care; inadequate and dilapidated infrastructure; election fraud; religious and ethnic intolerance; lack of visionary leadership; lack of national identity and cohesiveness; political assassinations and other violent crimes like armed robbery, kidnapping, money laundering, as well as drug and human trafficking.

In addressing these problems, vital questions are raised, some of which include the following: Why have these problems persisted, given the country's enormous wealth? Why have these problems remained unresolved after the country celebrated its fifty-five years of independence? Why are these problems still lingering, when the country has backed away from military dictatorship to a representative democracy and free market economy? And why is the country not developing as fast as other countries of its size with the same resource capacity? Let it be known that Nigeria's national security interests are seriously threatened by these unresolved problems. The grave consequences emanating from these unsolved problems have led to the following unhappy events in the country:

o The corporate existence of Nigeria is once again threatened by some group of people in the country who feel their ethnic interests and wellbeing are marginalized and ignored by the Federal Government of Nigeria. The activities of these armed groups have made some parts of the country ungovernable, and the alarm of the country breaking up, is sounding loud and clear;

o The prevailing uncertainty in the country, which includes insecurity, massive unemployment, poverty, and crime are forcing many Nigerians both skilled and unskilled to leave the country in record number for other countries in search of a better life. Given this trend, Nigeria is losing a huge number of its brilliant minds to several foreign countries, such as the United States of America, United Kingdom, Canada, Sweden, France, Germany, Ireland, Italy, Spain, Poland, Israel, Saudi Arabia, and even South Africa. Nigerians consider these countries as "countries of opportunities." Nigeria's losses have, indeed, become these countries' gains, because Nigerians are gifted, innovative, and industrious people;

o Nigeria is facing isolation from some countries of the world because of the insecurity, which has engulfed the country. Some major Western countries, including the United States of America, Canada, France, and the United Kingdom, have repeatedly warned their citizens of the risks of traveling to Nigeria. Such risks include kidnapping by armed groups for ransom, robbery, and other armed attacks. Citizens of these countries have been told repeatedly to stay away entirely from certain states in Nigeria. Such states include Bayelsa, Delta, Edo, Plateau, Gombe, Adamawa, Yobe, Bauchi, Borno, and Kano.

These warnings have had enormous economic implications for Nigeria, as foreign investors and tourists are forced to stay away from the country. Such travel warnings will definitely hamper investment plans foreign investors may have had for the country. Absence of foreign investments and tourists means loss of revenues and employment opportunities. These are resources Nigeria desperately needs, in order to address its huge unemployment pool of young men and women.

In responding to the vital questions raised above, two theoretical frameworks are utilized here to guide the discussions. These theoretical frameworks are historical and comparative in nature. The historical analysis assists the author in examining holistically Nigeria's past and present. It provides explanations as to why the country was put together by a foreign power and the impact such a foreign rule had on the indigenous people in terms of their history of existence, development and socio-political institutions, and what it did to their cultural values and psychology. The historical analysis also helps the author to analyze other experiences the indigenous people endured while living under a foreign domination. It provides answers and cues or hints as to why the indigenous people sought self-determination and, the way the country is governed after independence. Most importantly, the historical framework helps the author to organize his thoughts in a more chronological order and helps him draw logical conclusions.

On the other hand, the comparative analysis assists the author to examine ways other countries of the world dealt with their own national problems. With comparative analysis, the author is able to look at various policies some countries have articulated to overcome their own problems. Naturally, social problems are the result of human behavior and activities rooted in human nature. Human nature, therefore, is said to be muddled up with several human vices, such as greed, hatred, the passion to oppress and exploit others, bullying and domineering attitudes, racism, ignorance, arrogance, and xenophobia (the fear of the unknown). The application of these human vices may at times lead to human conflict and wars. Generally, human conflicts or disputes are healthy when they are properly managed and contained, but they become unhealthy and destabilizing when they are allowed to go on for too long without being resolved amicably, as we have seen in many cases throughout human history. Failure to resolve national problems in a timely manner often leads to unpleasant situations, such as war and violence, as is the case in Nigeria today, where government officials do not address problems of national significance from the outset until they get out of hand.

The comparative framework, therefore, helps the author conclude that war and violence have always led to catastrophe, when it comes to human loss and suffering, and the disruptions of social order, as we saw during the following wars: Iran-Iraq War (1980-1988), the invasion of Iraq by the Bush-Blair Administrations (2003-2011) and the invasion of Afghanistan by the US and its North Atlantic Treaty Organization's (NATO) allies (2002-2014), the two Sudanese Civil Wars (1955-1972 and 1983-2005), the Nigerian Civil War (1967-1970), the current Syrian Civil War (2011 to present), the Arab Awakening or Arab Spring (2011 to present), the Israeli-Palestinian conflicts (1948, 1967, 1973, 2000, 2004, 2006, 2008, 2009, 2012, and 2014), and other World Revolutions, such as the American Revolutionary War of 1775-1783, the French Revolution of 1787-1799, the Haitian Revolution of 1791-1804, the Russian Revolution of 1917-1918, including World War 1 (1914-1918) and World 11 (1939-1945).

War and violence in these countries decimated their social fabric, claimed many lives, and destroyed many properties worth tens of billions of dollars if not more. Such destabilizing forces negatively affected countries' economic growth and inflicted untold hardship on a number of innocent people who, in most cases, were women and children. These people were often displaced from their homes and some would flee to neighboring countries, where they became refugees, while those who stayed were rendered homeless.

It is important to underscore here that the articulation of this discourse would not have come to fruition without the voluminous information gathered from various sources, mainly secondary sources. A majority of these sources came from the Nigerian press, whose aggressive reporting revealed exactly the true nature of the country's problems and their root causes. The Nigerian press must be congratulated for its efforts in keeping Nigerians adequately informed about the governance of the country and its enduring challenges. Such aggressive reporting has made the Nigerian press the most independent and freest on the continent of Africa. By the same token, the Nigerian government officials must be congratulated for keeping the press free and independent since the Fourth Republic (1999 to present).

The author's several trips to Nigeria and his discussions with many Nigerians from all social classes, especially from the poor, have given credibility to the accuracy and authenticity of the information provided in this discourse. Those trips afforded the author the opportunity to evaluate Nigeria's problems holistically by listening to various viewpoints and sentiments expressed by those Nigerians whom the author met at various locations in the country. The author also recalls a remark made by one of his former history professors during his college years in the United States of America. What the professor said was so profound that, such a remark remains with the author till this day. The history professor is quoted as saying that, "for one to discover the truth about how a country is doing in fulfilling its obligations to its citizens is for one to go to the victims of the system who, in honesty, are the poor, uneducated, and dispossessed. Knowing the conditions under which these poor people live, becomes the best and available measuring yardstick that tells one how exactly government policies affect the daily lives of the poor." The newly elected Catholic Leader, Pope Francis also echoes this obvious fact, when he said that, "a country is judged by how it treats its poor." This is what the author's trips to Nigeria have revealed. Most of the people, whom the author spoke with, were the poor who had nothing positive to say about the country's ruling class and its adherent supporters, while the few, the governing elite or (system maintainers), whom the author contacted spoke highly of the government's programs and their efforts to govern well. It is not surprising that these "system maintainers" would speak highly of the government because they are the beneficiaries of the system, to whom most government policies and programs are designed to favor.

Acknowledgments

First and foremost, I would like to use this medium to thank the Bitonte College of Health and Human Services of Youngstown State University for organizing a platform (a research colloquium), where this research project was initially presented. The interests generated from this presentation and words of encouragement from several of my colleagues in the College prompted me to further explore the research topic, which now has led to a book publication.

Let it be known that this magnitude task of human endeavor wouldn't have come to fruition if it weren't for the efforts of a fine team of dedicated and committed scholars assembled from two continents (Africa and North America) who assisted tremendously in the preparation and presentation of this book. Indeed, I owe a great deal of gratitude to this team of African professionals and my American colleagues from Youngstown State University, Youngstown, Ohio, USA, for making my dream a reality.

I am deeply grateful to these noble men and women, including Marius Ajelo, Darlington Ibe, Emmanuel Duru, Kenneth King, Jane Ogunro, Dr. Christopher Bellas, Dr. John Hazy, Dr. Abel Waithaka Gitimu, and Dr. Priscilla Gitimu for reading the entire manuscript and providing useful suggestions and constructive criticisms, which helped in strengthening the overall quality of the book. My special thanks and profound gratitude also goes to Dike Justin Obih for writing such an impressive and well-articulated foreword. By the same token, I am highly grateful to my editor, D. Othniel Forte. Lastly, much appreciation to Butterfly Designs, for the magnificent design of the book cover, the typing setting and formatting.

I cannot thank you all enough for providing the time to do this, not minding your busy schedules. It is true that we all did this together, but I am solely responsible for the authenticity and accuracy of the facts presented in this book.

INTRODUCTION

Nigeria, a country of about 170 million people, and known as Africa's most populous nation, is located on the West coast of Africa. It gained its political independence from Great Britain in 1960. The country is endowed with vibrant human capital and a lot of strategic natural resources. It is the seventh largest oil producing nation within the Organization of Petroleum Exporting Countries (OPEC), the ninth largest producer of Liquid Natural Gas in the world, and the world's thirteenth largest oil producer. Nigeria is a diverse country with over 250 ethnic groups and dialects. It is a federation of 36 states with 774 local government areas and 9572 political wards, excluding Abuja, the Federal Capital Territory (FCT). Currently, Nigeria is said to be Africa's largest economy, surpassing that of South Africa which, for many years, was regarded as Africa's biggest economy (Aljazeera, 2014; and The Economist, 2014).

In spite of the country's strategic natural resources and its booming economy, Nigerians are the poorest among OPEC's member-states and the country ranked third on world poverty index. This unfortunate situation has forced many Nigerians to flee the country in search of a better life abroad, but these Nigerians are not finding things easy in their new host countries, as many of them thought it would be. It is difficult for these Nigerians, especially the unskilled ones, to find jobs in their new host countries because of the massive unemployment plaguing most of these countries—unemployment brought about by the 2008-2009 global economic meltdown. Lack of employment opportunities in these host countries, especially in the Western World, has forced some Nigerian migrants to involve themselves in illegal activities and those caught are usually thrown into jails, where they are kept until their deportation arrangements are finalized. Other Nigerians are facing death penalty in some Asian countries, especially in Indonesia, where three Nigerians (Sylvester Obiekwe Nwolise, Okwudili Oyatanze, and Raheem Agbaje Salami) were summarily executed with other nationals from Australia, Brazil, Ghana, and France on April 29, 2015 by a "firing squad" for drug trafficking. In South Africa, for example, Nigerian and other South Saharan African migrants were targeted and subjected to unprecedented group violence led by young black South Africans who accused the African migrants of taking their jobs and being responsible for most of the heinous crimes committed in the country.

Another dilemma facing Nigerian migrants in Europe and North America, in particular, is the on-going anti-immigration sentiments being expressed throughout these two continents. Although the anti-immigration feelings in these regions of the world are not something new, recent expressions have become more intense, loud and clear, after the September 11, 2001 incidents, when the United States and some cities in Europe were attacked by what has become known to many around the world, as global terrorism. Nigerians would not be encountering these ugly human experiences abroad, such as job discriminations, personal humiliations, and prison torture if the Nigerian governments (federal, state, and local) had created similar economic opportunities at home.

Given the above claims, Nigeria is not the only country facing endemic national problems resulting from its bad governance, war and violence, but one major difference between Nigeria and some other countries, especially those in the Western world, is that Nigerian leadership does not confront national problems head-on, as it should. Nigerian leaders always pretend that all is well and will not act until problems get out of hand or out of control. Nigerian leaders prefer to seek foreign assistance rather than confront the country's crises directly. For example, the country cannot tackle the Boko Haram menaces in the country independently without seeking help from the United States of America, the United Kingdom, France, or China. This kind of attitude does not speak well of a country. Nigerian leadership has always cited lack of resources and logistics as reasons for inviting foreign countries to meddle in the country's domestic problems. It is very unfortunate that the Nigerian leadership cannot solve the country's problems without calling on other nations, including some of the UN Specialized Agencies like the World Health Organization (WHO), the United Nations Children Fund (UNICEF), and the United Nations Educational, Scientific and Cultural Organization (UNESCO) to intervene in matters it can handle squarely.

There are times when countries can ask for assistance from friendly countries or from world bodies, but not all the time. A country should only seek outside help when it encounters a natural disaster of enormous proportion—a disaster that the country's natural resources, revenues, and manpower cannot cope with or sustain. Nigeria is, indeed, capable of addressing crises like those created by Boko Haram or other ethnic militants without seeking outside help, given its enormous wealth, number of men and women in military uniform, including the huge number of Army Generals, Air Force Marshals and Vice Marshals, Navy Admirals and Rear Admirals, and Inspectors-General of Police the country has produced.

Nigeria has an abundance of natural resources and manpower to confront some of its domestic crises, but the biggest problem is that most of the country's revenues and resources are often looted and end up in foreign offshore bank accounts of the looters. Given this obvious fact, Nigeria is not addressing its internal crises the way it should because the country's ruling class is mismanaging the country's resources and transferring its funds to foreign countries where they boost the economies of those countries. When it comes to dealing with incidences of natural disasters or tackling their domestic economic problems, the United States, the United Kingdom, and France, for example, have never sought help from Nigeria. These countries deal squarely with their internal problems without expecting any help from Nigeria or from other countries. The United States sought help from its NATO allies and from some Third World countries like Jordan, Egypt, Yemen, Pakistan, and Kenya in its war effort against international terrorism; however, that is as far as that country has gone to seek foreign assistance in dealing with its internal crises.

Although the author of this discourse cites the success stories of Brazil, China, Japan and India in his book, the United States of America is the main focal point in his analysis. The comparison of Nigeria with the US is worth examining, given United States' accomplishments on the world stage. The author recognizes the fact that what works in one country may not necessarily be the case in another country, because countries' histories, cultural values, and other human characteristics may not be the same everywhere. In spite of the above claim, countries do borrow ideas from one another. In solving problems associated with multi-ethnic, multi-cultural and multi-religious issues in Nigeria, it is apparent and imperative that Nigerians learn and understand how the United States of America dealt with its own history of racial discrimination and its cultural diversity.

The United States of America is chosen as a reference point for several reasons. One of the reasons is that the Nigerian political structure and Constitution are modeled after those of the United States with few variations. Nigerians abandoned the British model of Parliamentary System when the system was unable to cope with the emerging trends and complexities the country had been experiencing up to 1999. In response to the failure of the British model to adequately address the issues facing the country, the Nigerian intelligentsia community and other stakeholders in the country quickly adopted the United States' Presidential System, as the viable model for the country. While the Nigerian elite class favored the American model, they failed to embrace those essential parts of the United States' political structure that created more room for mass political participations. The omission of these parts of the US political structure forms the bases for our comparison.

Other reasons for choosing the United State of America for comparison stem from certain fundamental characteristics the two countries have in common. These characteristics cannot be overlooked by any stretch of the imagination. They include the following: First, Nigeria and the United States of America have always viewed each other as strategic trading partners. For example, Nigeria is America's largest African trading partner and fifth largest oil supplier, until July of 2014, when the Obama administration completely ended his country's oil importation from Nigeria, said to be at a peak of 1.3 million barrels per day (Akande, 2014). Second, Nigeria has embraced the American brand of democracy and its free market economy and has been sending its lawmakers to the US Congress to learn the US legislative process. Third, the US security apparatus has been providing training, sharing intelligence and logistics with their Nigerian counterparts, especially since the violent activities of Al Qaeda and Boko Haram have become noticeable in the West African region. This effort has co-opted Nigeria to join the United States in its War against what the US government described as Al-Qaeda's terrorist activities in the Maghreb or Western Saharan region of North Africa.

Other similarities between the two countries are: 1) they are both former British colonies; 2) both countries' criminal justice systems including their judicial philosophy are deep-rooted in the British Common Law and tradition; 3) the two countries have federal systems of government and executive presidency; 4) they have a diverse population and deep-seated history of racial discrimination; and 5) both countries have fought bloody Civil Wars: the US Civil War was fought between 1861 and 1865 ; while Nigeria's Civil War was between 1967 and 1970.

While these similarities exist between the two countries, there are also enormous differences existing between them. The United States of America, for example, is an advanced country with an advanced economy and is the world's strongest military, while Nigeria is a Third World country with a weak economy and military. The United States of America is the oldest nation-state; obtaining her independence from Great Britain on July 4, 1776, much earlier than Nigeria whose independence was won on October 1, 1960, from Great Britain. This means that the United States is two hundred and thirty nine years old on July 4, 2015, while Nigeria is fifty five years old on October 1, 2015. Americans are more nationalistic than their Nigerian counterparts. A few Nigerians would sacrifice their lives in the defense of the country while a huge majority of Americans would die in the defense of their country. This is due in part because the United States government offers more opportunities to its citizens than its Nigerian counterpart that offers little or no opportunities to its own citizens. Although Nigeria is said to be a Third World country, it has vast natural resources to enhance the quality of life of its citizens, but she is currently not doing so. As previously stated, many Nigerians are fleeing the country in large numbers to seek a better life elsewhere, because the Nigerian ruling class has failed to invest adequately in its people.

Plan of the Book

To expand on the questions raised and to determine how the comparison presented truly reflects on the country, deeper analyses of issues affecting Nigeria are offered in five parts and in nine chapters. **Part One** focuses on the political history of the Nigerian State. To analyze this section comprehensively, Chapter One discusses the nature and purpose of modern governments, reasons why they are created, and the instruments they have at their disposal to discharge their functions. Chapter One also touches on the chronological order of Nigerian political history. This aspect of the work enables the author to examine the relationships that existed between Europeans and the indigenous Africans (Nigerians) during their early contact and what followed thereafter, and why Nigeria became a British colony and not a French or Portuguese colony? Chapter Two of the study touches on the challenges the Nigerian State endured and continues to endure after independence was attained. In this section, issues such as the retention of colonial legacy, Civil War in Nigeria, military dictatorship, leadership problems, and election fraud are discussed in detail as they adversely affect the country's development efforts.

Part Two of the discourse focuses on the Privatization Scheme in Nigeria. Chapter Three of the book deals specifically on the role played by the World Financial Institutions and Foreign Multinational Corporations in Nigeria. The Chapter reveals how the policies of the World Bank (IBRD) and the International Monetary Fund (IMF) helped in strangulating the Nigerian economy and how they coerced the governing elite to embark on a massive borrowing exercise from the Bank and the Fund. In addition, the Chapter demonstrates how this massive borrowing and the accrued huge interests from the IMF's loans have impoverished the Nigerian people. It discusses how the IMF's Structural Adjustment Program (SAP) induced the Nigerian ruling class to auction away the Nigerian government property and parastatals to the benefit of foreign subsidiaries doing business in the country. Parastatals were sold for little or nothing compared to the amounts the Nigerian government invested in acquiring them. Chapter Three also beams its focus on how foreign multinational corporations, especially those in the oil and communications sectors corrupted the Nigerian government officials in their attempts to gain access to the country's natural resources. Money laundering schemes are another area of focus in this chapter. The chapter analyzes how foreign banks profited from this criminal enterprise; how they encouraged capital flight (money laundering) from Third World countries; and how this criminal enterprise has fueled corruption in Nigeria, leading to the impoverishment of the Nigerian people.

Chapter Four takes an in-depth look at the nature and scope of corruption in Nigeria and how it adversely affects the public and private sectors of the country's economy, especially in the banking and oil industries. Chapter Five explores the consequences of corruption and how this immoral behavior negatively affects the development of the country. The Chapter also documents the effects of corruption and how it decimated the country's electric energy, the communications infrastructure, and the country's social institutions like public education and public health care sector. It also reveals how corrupt practices in Nigeria have increased poverty and crimes in the country.

Part Three deals specifically with insecurity and public safety in Nigeria. In this section, efforts are made to identify those actors directly responsible for the instability of the country. Thus, Chapter Six takes an in-depth look at the causes of violence and insecurity in Nigeria. The failure of the Nigeria Founding Fathers to unify the country is identified as one of the major factors responsible for the present day violence in the country. Other factors include the prevailing defective political institutions in the country, religion, and the unpatriotic attitudes of some Nigerian politicians who are bent on getting their way regardless of how their selfish behavior may have affected the country's national unity. To sustain Nigeria's nascent democracy, the chapter recommends strongly that formidable social movements should be made part of the country's political calculus and should be seen as a balancing force in the pursuit of democracy in Nigeria.

Part Four explores ways and means of achieving good governance in Nigeria. In this regard, Chapter Seven articulates a new vision for the country. It outlines what must be done if the Nigerian project is to be preserved and nurtured for the generation unborn. The chapter introduces sets of criteria that will ensure good governance and enhance Nigeria's national unity. These sets of criteria call for new thinking, new orientations, new core values, new attitudes and new framework on how Nigerians can relate to each other amicably with love and respect.

Part Five focuses on a blueprint for action. Chapter Eight lays out how the new vision for Nigeria can be achieved and translated into public policy. Whilst Chapter Nine draws the curtains on the policy proposals addressed in the chapter before and offers concluding thoughts on the way forward for Nigeria.

PART ONE

THE POLITICAL HISTORY OF THE NIGERIAN STATE

Chapter 1

NATURE AND PURPOSES OF GOVERNMENTS

Governments are instituted to balance the various interests and values existing in societies, to secure the safety of their citizens, and to enhance their citizens' socio-economic well-being. On the other hand, citizens are obliged to obey their countries' laws, enlist in their countries' armed forces, pay their taxes, and perform other legitimate services that their governments may deem proper and necessary. Governments derive their existence, legitimacy, and authority from the "General Will" of their people through what political philosophers like Jean-Jacques Rousseau, John Locke, and Thomas Hobbes termed as "Social Contract." Without citizens' consent (loyalty and support), and without deriving legitimate powers from their countries' Constitutions, governments will not be able to discharge their ascribed duties and responsibilities effectively.

Various forms of governments exist today. Some countries, for example, operate under a unitary form of government whilst others operate under a military form of government, a confederate form of government, or a federal form of government. Each of these forms of government has its own unique characteristics, merits and demerits. Equally, there are different political ideologies (e.g., democracy, aristocracy, and totalitarianism) and different economic ideologies (e.g., capitalism, fascism, socialism, and communism).

A lot of people today are confused about the nature and scope of these ideologies. Laymen, for example, think that these ideologies are one and the same, not knowing that they are two different things altogether. It is a common belief among those in the Western world that totalitarianism goes hand in hand with the socialist or communist economy and that the communist economy does not encourage economic growth and prosperity, however, China and the Russian Federation have proven this to be false.

Today, these countries have successfully combined their totalitarian political philosophy with the capitalist economy and their economies are doing much better than the economies of most Western capitalist nations.

Demonizing or vilifying nations whose political and economic systems are different from what is practiced in the Western world is not the right approach to international relations. Countries should be free to adopt any politico-economic ideologies of their choice and should be free to make changes when those ideologies are no longer serving their needs. Sovereign nation- states should not be coerced to embrace political and economic ideologies that violate their histories and traditions.

They should be allowed to make changes within their own political and economic systems, whenever they deem that such changes are proper and necessary, without foreign dictation or intervention. Nations have the right to make mistakes and learn from such mistakes without being told what to do by outside forces. "Rome was not built in a day," and nations should be allowed to correct their mistakes no matter how long it takes them to do so. These are experiences that most western nations know all too well.

Governments worldwide use various instruments to achieve their countries' laudable missions, visions, and their core values. The most significant instrument of any government is its Constitution, which reflects the history, tradition, and cultural values of the country in question.

This document is essential to all governments for various reasons: it outlines a country's political framework and institutions; defines what types of political system and ideologies a country should embrace; and describes the nature and scope of the country's body polity.

For example, should elections be held and, if so, how frequently and how should they be conducted? How many political parties should be formed? Should a country be governed under a single-party system, a two-party system or a multiple-party system? Should the people be allowed to express their opinions freely and publicly? Should freedom of the press be allowed to prevail in the country's body polity? Should states be created and if so how?

The Constitution also determines how a country's revenues and political powers should be shared. It establishes whether or not political powers should be centralized or decentralized, and whether or not the nation's revenues should be shared between central and state governments; and how such revenues should be generated and shared.

Constitutions outline how much power should be assigned to the central and state governments, including their limitations. They establish the roles and functions of the legislative, the executive, and the judicial branches, including checks and balances, and the tenure of office holders. Constitutions articulate the rights of citizens including their limitations, and how constitutions can be amended and ratified.

Additionally, each government uses its country's military to execute its ascribed goals and objectives. Most countries' military consists of such units as the army, the navy, and the air force whose responsibilities are the protection of the countries' borders—land, air, and sea—from external enemies.

On the other hand, a country's criminal justice institutions like the police, courts, prisons, and other specialized law enforcement agencies, such as the State Security Service (SSS), the Immigration and Naturalization Service (INS), and the Customs Service (CS) are used for protecting citizens within the country's borders from internal enemies and criminal elements. A country's intelligence community is also a vital tool used in protecting a country from both foreign and domestic enemies.

Governments in general, depending on needs and circumstances, may create commissions or tribunals like Nigeria's Economic and Financial Crimes Commission (EFCC), South Africa's Truth and Reconciliation Commission (TRC), and United States of America's 9-11 Commission, as additional tools to tackle specific national problems that demand urgent attention or solution.

International, regional, and sub-regional organizations are other mechanisms governments around the world use in their relationship with one another. They use these instruments for various purposes:

1) Promoting unity and solidarity among themselves;

2) Building military and economic alliances; and

3) Maintaining world peace and stability.

These organizations have become necessary and useful to governments everywhere because they realize that they cannot live in isolation, no matter how powerful they may be. Nations need each other for their survival. Governments achieve their foreign obligations when they work together and respect each other's sovereign rights, national interests, and cultural values. The following are examples of international, regional, and sub-regional organizations which most countries of the world belong to, including Nigeria:

- United Nations Organization (UNO)
- International Bank for Reconstruction and Development (IBRD)
- International Monetary Fund (IMF)
- International Atomic Energy Agency (IAEA)
- World Trade Organization (WTO)
- African Union (AU)
- Economic Community of West African States (ECOWAS)
- Southern African Development Community (SADC)
- European Union (EU)
- Organization of Petroleum Exporting Countries (OPEC)
- North Atlantic Treaty Organization (NATO)
- Organization of American States (OAS)
- Association of South East Asian Nations (ASEAN)
- North American Free Trade Agreement (NAFTA)
- Asian Pacific Economic Cooperation (APEC)

These organizations are created by treaties whose protocols are binding on consenting members. The above named organizations came into existence through multilateral treaties. States also use bilateral treaties to engage one another on issues that matter to them the most. The Federal Republic of Nigeria uses the above-named instruments and other constitutional means to govern those persons residing within its geographical boundaries.

In this discourse, efforts are made to analyze how the government of Nigeria utilizes these instruments of power to achieve its ascribed missions, visions, and core values. However, before evaluating the Nigerian government performance thus far, the political history of the Nigerian nation will be examined in a chronological order.

History of the Struggle against Colonial Rule in Nigeria

The Nigerian society did not evolve in the same way as Europe. Like most Third World countries, Nigeria was a creation of a foreign power. It did not have the same opportunities that countries in the western world had in transforming itself from one experience to another without being dictated to by foreign entities, as to what political and economic ideologies it should adopt. During the early years of nation building in Nigeria, the country's traditional values and methods of governing were disrupted by outside forces. This disruption did not allow the Nigerian society to make mistakes and learn from such mistakes. The Nigerian people were forced against their will to embrace political and economic ideologies that were alien to them.

When one looks back to what transpired during the pre and post-colonial era, one would agree that there were two divergent opinions held by Nigerians. Some Nigerians like some Africans, viewed the coming of the Europeans to the African continent as an impediment to the development of the continent; while others viewed such a contact as a blessing.

To digest what happened during those dark days in Nigeria and elsewhere in Africa, a brief political history of the Nigerian nation is provided to educate the public on the enormous challenges the indigenous people of Nigeria encountered and endured.

Nigeria, as we all know, was a mere geographical expression before the territories that constituted it were carved out from the famous Songhai Empire by Great Britain before and during the Scramble for Africa. The partition of Africa was conceived in Berlin, Germany, in what has become known as the Berlin Conference of 1884/1885, where major European powers, including the United States of America, met and established grand rules that would partition the African continent forever.

Before the Berlin Conference, Europeans had several contacts with the Africans, including Nigerians. The first European nation to make such an early contact with the Nigerians was Portugal when its explorers led by Vasco da Gama landed in West Africa in 1460, during their sea route to India in search of gold, ivory, and spices. Another Portuguese sailor and explorer who landed in Africa en route to Indies (India), but could not continue the journey to India was Bartholomeu Dias (known then as Bartholomew Diaz). Dias' crew was said to have landed at the Cape of Good Hope in South Africa in 1486, but did not continue because of the difficulty the voyage encountered. Diniz Dias, a family member of Bartholomeu Dias, was said to have discovered Cape Verde Islands off the coast of West Africa before Bartholomeu Dias' expedition to India.

Great Britain was another European nation that set its footprints on Nigerian soil. The British explorers, especially Mungo Park and his crew, were sent out to explore the source of the River Niger and possibly to establish trade with the natives. Mungo Park and his crew took off from Timbuktu in Mali in 1805 for their expedition. Unfortunately, Mungo Park died at the rapids of Bussa and could not complete his mission.

To complete Park's work, Hugh Clapperton, in the 1820s, tried to reach the point where the Niger River ended. Before his death, Clapperton's dairy revealed that the river flowed from Guinea, Mali to Niger passing through the Hausaland. It was Richard Lemon Lander and his brother (John) who, in 1830, finally traced River Niger to where it joined with River Benue.

From there, the Lander brothers followed the river down to the Niger delta where it flowed into the Atlantic Ocean. From the Lander brothers' assessment, the River Niger was proclaimed to be one of the longest and most promising trading rivers in the world (Falola and Heaton, 2010). River Niger is the third longest river in Africa after the Nile and the Congo River. Sadly, Richard L. Lander "died on his third West African trip; he was said to have been killed along the Niger River by African tribesmen on February 6, 1834."

In 1861, the British authorities took control of Southern Nigeria, when it annexed Lagos as its Colony. The country was later brought together under one political umbrella in 1914, when Southern and Northern Protectorates were amalgamated or unified under the leadership of Sir Frederick John Dealtry Lugard, who was born in Madras now Chennai, India in 1858 to British parents. Lugard died in 1945. Before his death, he was appointed as the British High Commissioner of Northern Nigeria Protectorate (1900-1906). He later became the Governor-General of the combined Colony of Nigeria and served in that capacity from 1914 to 1919, after having served as the Governor of Hong Kong from 1907 to 1912 (*Wikipedia, the Free Encyclopedia,* 2014). The Jonathan Administration has designated 2014, as the year to celebrate the country's one hundred years (bicentennial) of existence.

From 1914 till 1960, the realm of power did not return to the indigenous people. They were ruled and dominated by foreigners who had no business to be there. The acquisition of this massive territory from West Africa was the turning point of the ugly things to come. The early relationships between the natives and Europeans centered on trade of goods and materials, then after a while, shifted to a trade in human cargo (slavery). During this period of slavery, came the Christian Missionaries, and before anyone could figure out what was happening, all the territories known today as Nigeria, were overrun and occupied by British settlers (colonizers). Most of Britain's intrusion was accompanied by violence.

To justify their unconscionable and immoral acts perpetrated against the indigenous people of Africa, the colonial authorities including the British, the French, the Portuguese, and, to a certain extent, the Germans, claimed that their objectives were to bring Christianity to the unbelievers (pagans) and to civilize the backward people of Africa. The acceptance of foreign ideas was a sharp departure from the way Nigerians and other indigenous Africans were governed before the coming of European settlers to the continent of Africa.

In furthering its dominance of this vast territory known as Nigeria, the British government came up with a strategy known to historians as "Divide and Rule." This strategy was designed solely to sow a seed of discord among the various ethnic groups in the colony to prevent them from forging a united front against British imperialism (colonialism) in the country. The implementation of this strategy meant preventing an organized revolt; and drawing boundaries arbitrarily without giving considerations to the different cultural and ethnic groups residing in those areas. Because of this design, over 250 ethnic groups with distinctive histories, traditions, and cultural values were forcefully brought together to create an entity called Nigeria.

These groups of natives were never given the opportunity to express their support for or against foreign rule. They were never consulted, before they were brutally brought together as one political entity, as to whether or not they would support the dissolution of their traditional institutions and their way of life. After bringing these divergent indigenous people under one nation (the Nigerian nation), they were denied the right to determine their own destiny and were also denied the right to participate in the governance of their new nation until they fought and won their political freedom from the British.

Although there are many ethnic groups in Nigeria today, the Igbos, the Yorubas and the Hausa-Fulanis are the predominant ones. Islam and Christianity are also the most predominant religious sects in the country. Ethnicity and religion as they are known in Nigeria today, have become the most divisive and destabilizing forces in the country since their injection into the Nigerian body polity. This is one of the several legacies of British rule in Nigeria. During its one hundred years of colonial rule in Nigeria (1861-1960), the British government neither introduced democratic processes nor respected the rights of the indigenous people. Instead it ruled by reign of terror. It subjected the indigenous people to all forms of humiliation and torture. In sustaining British colonialism in Nigeria, compulsory taxes were imposed on the indigenous people and those who failed to comply with the tax policy were subjected to forced labor and other forms of punishment.

Because colonial rule in Nigeria and elsewhere in Africa was oppressive and disruptive, Nigerians, as well as other oppressed Africans, resorted to violence as a means to achieve their freedom. During British rule in Nigeria, no freedom was granted to the Nigerian people. They had to fight for it themselves. Those who dared oppose the legitimacy of the colonial authorities were labeled as trouble-makers and thugs and such individuals were detained in prison indefinitely and without trial.

Others would be intimidated, tortured, and sometimes killed. Nigerian nationalists like Herbert Macaulay, Nnamdi Azikiwe, Michael Imuodu, and others are examples of those who were tortured and imprisoned for speaking out against the evils of British imperialism in Nigeria.

To ensure the smooth running of the colony, the British colonial administration added another strategy into its arsenal. The added strategy was known as indirect rule. Indirect rule was instituted in the colony because the colonial administration did not have enough British administrative personnel to control the entire country. It used traditional rulers in areas where such institutions existed to govern the indigenous people, however, in places where traditional rulers were not well entrenched, the British colonial authorities handpicked such persons and imposed them on their people.

In Southeastern Nigeria, for example, individuals who were handpicked by the colonial authorities became known as "Warrant Chiefs." Traditional rulers and Warrant Chiefs were used as middlemen or surrogates of British interest and they had no voice within the colonial administrative circles.

Traditional rulers, at the time, were only viewed as a line of communication between the colonial administration and the indigenous people. They made the governance of the colony much easier for British authorities.

The Nigerian intelligentsia and its counterparts in other parts of Africa did not condone or accept foreign rule on the African continent. Their mindset and attitude reflected on the activities of a group of nationalists drawn from the English Speaking West Africa (the Anglophone) nations of Nigeria, Gold Coast (Ghana), Sierra-Leone, and Gambia, who came together in 1920 to form a social movement called the National Congress of British West Africa (NCBWA).

The founding members of this organization included personalities like: Thomas Hutton-Mills, Sr., J.E. Casely Hayford, Edward Francis Small, F.V. Nanka Bruce, A.B. Quartey-Papafio, H. Van Hein, A. Sawyer, and Kobina Sekyi. The NCBWA members saw themselves as representatives of Africans in the fight against British colonialism.

The NCBWA was a conservative movement that wanted to gradually dismount British colonialism in the region through constitutional means and cooperation with the colonial authorities. Gershoni (2001) articulated the group's objectives to include the following:

- African participation in the colonial government;
- British West Africa to maintain its dependencies with the British Empire;
- British West Africa to maintain unreservedly all and every right of free citizenship of the Empire;
- British government to ensure within her borders the government of the people by the people and for the people; and
- Equal opportunity for all and to preserve the lands of the people for the people

The NCBWA's platform was not welcomed by many other Western educated Africans who were heavily influenced by the Marcus Garvey's United Negro Improvement Association (UNIA). Like the NCBWA, the UNIA had branches in Freetown, Sierra Leone and Lagos, Nigeria. As a pan-African organization, the UNIA promoted racial pride and called for the creation, by force if necessary, of an independent black republic over the entire continent of Africa. The UNIA's platform called for the declaration of the rights of the Negro peoples of the world. It promoted the mass emigration of African-Americans to Africa to serve in the building of the independent black republic. Like the NCBWA, UNIA was of the opinion that Africans must take control of their social, economic, and political destiny in order to control the instrument of nation building.

The common vision shared by both the NCBWA and UNIA spurred Herbert Samuel Heelas Macaulay to oppose British rule in Nigeria. As the founding father of Nigerian nationalism, Macaulay did everything he could to discredit the colonial authorities. For example, he exposed British hypocrisy and corruption in the handling of the railway finances in 1908.

In the London Privy Council, Macaulay successfully defended local Chiefs whose lands were forcefully taken away from them by the British colonial authorities. In that case, British colonial authorities were forced to pay compensations to the local Chiefs. Macaulay was jailed twice in retaliation for his opposition to British rule in Nigeria.

In 1923, Macaulay created a political platform from where he attacked colonial policies and from where he prepared Nigerians for what was to come after colonialism was defeated. The political platform was the Nigerian National Democratic Party (NNDP), which historians described as the first Nigerian political party ever created. After the demise of the NNDP in 1938, Macaulay and Dr. Nnamdi Azikiwe founded the National Council of Nigeria and Cameroons (NCNC). As a patriotic organization, the NCNC brought Nigerians of all stripes together to demand the independence of the country from the British. When Macaulay died in 1946, Azikiwe became the Party's leader. Because of Nnamdi Azikiwe's political activism during the struggle for independence, he was unanimously chosen as the country's first indigenous Governor General and President after Nigerian independence in 1960.

Another group of Nigerians, who also played an important role in the emancipation of the country from British colonial rule, was the Nigerian Youth Movement (NYM). The movement was known to Nigerian historians as the first genuine nationalist organization in the country. It was founded in Lagos in 1933. Its founding members were James Churchill Vaughan, Hezekiah Oladipo Davis, and Samuel Akinsanya, Ernest Ikoli, Kofo Abayomi, Adeyemo Alakija, and Nnamdi Azikiwe.

Like the Macaulay's group (NNDP), the NYM was dedicated to liberating the country from British colonial rule. The NYM opposed "Indirect Rule" and set out a goal that would unify the people to work towards a common objective. Its other goals included the mobilization of public opinion to develop a national consciousness needed to achieve the objective and a complete autonomy within the British Empire, based on equal partnership with other member-states.

The Nigerian women also became a formidable force against colonial rule in Nigeria. For example, women in the Southeastern Nigeria played a pivotal role in dislodging British rule in the country. In what historians termed as the "Aba Women's Riot" or "Women's War" of 1929, the women in this region mobilized themselves into a mass movement to address what they perceived as injustices aimed at them by the colonial administration.

The hatred for Warrant Chiefs and Native Courts in Southeastern Nigeria for their corrupt practices and unfair sentences they imposed on the people was one of the reasons the women mobilized against colonial authorities for creating such oppressive institutions. Other reasons women in the Southeastern region vehemently protested against British colonial rule in Nigeria were the fear that British authorities would impose taxes on women separately from men, and the dissatisfaction emanating from British threats of lowering prices placed on local produce (palm kernels and edible oil) while prices of imported goods were kept artificially high.

In 1929, when the women formed street demonstrations, the colonial repressive forces (the Police) turned on them. The riot took the lives of twenty-one women and injured many more in Calabar province, at Abak and Utu Etim Ekpo and twenty more women were killed in Opobo (Falola, 2009).

The Women's agitation forced the British colonial administration to halt some of its oppressive policies. Consequently, the system of Warrant Chiefs was abandoned and the native court system was reorganized to include women as members. Although the riot turned violent, the political activism of the Southeastern Nigerian women (Igbo, Ibibio, and Opobo) became an unprecedented morale booster for the empowerment of women throughout Nigeria and beyond.

In addition to efforts made by Nigerian nationalists and women activists to dislodge British rule in Nigeria, there were two other fundamental events that helped to speed up the decolonization process, and these events were of global significance. One of the events, was Clause III of the Atlantic Charter of 1941, which declared as follows: That the signatories to the charter (Franklin D. Roosevelt, President of the United States of America and Winston Churchill, Prime Minister of Great Britain) would "respect the right of all people to choose the form of government under which they will live; and wish to see sovereign rights and self-government restored to those who have been forcibly deprived of them."

This was an encouraging statement that mobilized national liberation movements throughout Africa and elsewhere in the world to fight colonialism until it was defeated and eliminated.

The second event that helped to dislodge British rule in Nigeria and elsewhere was the impact that World War II had on British government and its people. Although the Germans did not win the war, they weakened British resolve to keep maintaining its overseas colonies. British infrastructures were decimated by the German war machines, which brought the government to the verge of collapse before the American military might and its economic Marshall Plan came to the British government's rescue. Because of the unanticipated massive destruction of infrastructures and the weakening of the "British military superiority and might," the British government was unable to withstand the insurmountable pressures coming from its overseas' colonies, especially those pressures from India, Ghana, and Nigeria.

During World War II, many Nigerians were forced against their will to fight on the side of the British. The war experiences of the Nigerian returning soldiers, helped to intensify the struggle for Independence. Before the war, there were some mythical beliefs held by many Nigerians at the time that, "white people" were superhuman and could not be destroyed. In some quarters, they were perceived as God. But, in the battle fields, a different picture emerged. Returning Nigerian soldiers from the war claimed that they were shocked to see thousands of dead white soldiers whom they once thought were indestructible.

The scene of these dead white soldiers changed the mindset and perception that the returning soldiers had of the white man. The war scene made many of these returning soldiers realize that white people were just as human as they were. They came to the realization that the only differences between them and their white counterparts were skin color and, perhaps language. This obvious fact prompted the returning soldiers to query the legitimacy of colonialism and they demanded to know why they were subjugated to a foreign rule. The tale of stories from the returning soldiers inspired many other groups in Nigeria such as the Nigerian Labor Union to be confrontational with the British authorities.

The Nigerian Labor Union was also a major partner in the struggle for the country's independence. It played a pivotal role in dislodging British rule in Nigeria, just as the Nigerian nationalists and Women activists did. The history of Labor Union in Nigeria, according to Falola (2009), began in 1912, when government employees formed a Civil Service Union. In 1914, the name changed to "Nigerian Union of Civil Servants following the amalgamation of the protectorates of Southern and Northern Nigeria." Consequently, two major labor unions emerged: the Nigerian Union of Teachers (NUT) in 1931; and the Nigerian Railway Workers Union (NRWU) in 1932. Members of NUT comprised of both public and private school teachers. In 1941, NRWU persuaded nine trade unions representing technical employees to form the African Civil Service Technical Workers Union (ACSTWU). This umbrella organization was formed to address the needs of Nigerian workers who, at the time, were exploited by British imperialism. Using their numeric strength the Nigerian workers, including the returning military servicemen, mounted heavy pressure on the British colonial administration. Such pressures led to the passage of a series of legislations: The Trade Disputes and Arbitration Ordinance and Workmen's Compensation Ordinance, 1941; the Nigerian General Defense Regulations, 1941; and the Employment of Ex-Servicemen's Ordinance, 1945 (Falola, 2009).

The Trade Disputes and Arbitration Ordinance and Workmen's Compensation Ordinance was an attempt by the colonial administration to encourage the establishment of labor unions in the colonies. It was also an attempt to resolve conflict by dialogue in order to minimize the use of strikes. The General Defense Regulations enacted under the Emergency Power/Defense Act of 1939 and 1940 was meant to suffocate the Nigerian Labor Unions by making strikes and lockouts illegal in the country. The Employment of Ex-Servicemen's Ordinance authorized the colonial government to restore veterans to civilian life and called for the establishment of the Nigerian Ex-Servicemen's Welfare Association (Falola, 2009).

The Nigerian Labor Unions were not intimidated by the draconian labor laws the colonial administration put in place. They pressed on for more demands and in 1945, a group of labor leaders led by Michael Imuodu organized protests around the issue of increased wages and cost of living allowance (COLA). The colonial administration responded by making an offer, which was turned down by the Unions; they rejected the offer because it was not enough and when the administration did not yield further to Labor Unions' demand, workers began to plan for direct action, which came to fruition on June 21, 1945. This activity became the first general strike ever undertaken by Nigerian Labor Unions.

The Labor Unions' famous victory would not have been achieved if it were not for the support they received from political activists (like Margaret Ekpo, and Jaja Nwachukwu, etc.), political organizations, especially from the NYM and the Zikist Movement, and the print media, such as the West African Pilot and the Daily Comet. Nnamdi Azikiwe was the founder of these two famous newspapers in the country, which the Zikist Movement and NCNC used effectively to criticize the British colonial administration for creating conditions that led to the 1945 general strike, the first of its kind in the country. The West African Pilot and the Daily Comet were banned by the British colonial administration, because the two printing media were, according to the administration, promoting anti-government activities in the country (Falola, 1929).

The 1945 labor victory attracted more membership to the Unions. Labor Unions became more relevant; they became powerful instrument agitators used to bring pressure on the colonial government. The success of the 1945 general strike led to more labor strikes in Nigeria: the 1947 strike at Burutu in Warri Province and the 1949 Coal Miners' strike in the Iva Valley in Eastern Nigeria (Falola, 2009). The two strikes came as a result of demands for better wages and better working conditions. Taking a cue from government workers who won a labor victory in 1945, workers in private commercial firms like the United African Company (UAC) and the coal mining company in Enugu began forming unions to address their economic needs.

The effort of these indigenous workers who were acutely exploited by British private companies and other foreign corporations led to the formation of more labor Unions, such as the African General Clerical Workers Union (AGCWU), the African Mercantile Workers Union (AMWU), the African General Workers Union (AGWU), and the Colliery Workers Union (CWU). When the management of these industries and their indigenous workers could not work out a compromise, riots ensued and security agents were always brought in to disperse the crowds. During both incidences (the 1947 and 1949 strikes), security agents used excessive force on the workers, which resulted in more violence and deaths of the workers. Police brutality did not intimidate the striking workers who continued the strikes until the colonial government caved in to their demands. The Nigerian Labor Unions' victories were huge; they helped to speed up the dislodgement of British rule in Nigeria.

With these unprecedented waves of unity and solidarity exhibited by Nigerian workers and political activists, the British colonial administration had no other choice than to find a way to end its domination of the country. When it realized it could no longer govern the country effectively, the colonial administration began proposing a series of constitutional reforms to include Nigerians in its governing effort of the country and to gradually prepare them for independence.

The first of such constitutional reforms was instituted in 1947, known to many in Nigeria, as the Richards Constitution. The Constitution assumed the name of the sitting colonial governor at the time, Sir Arthur Richards. It was instituted to right the wrongs the Clifford Constitution of 1922 created when it excluded Northern Nigeria from the Legislative Council. In unifying the country, the Richards Constitution included the Northern Region in the central legislature for the first time. It also established Regional Houses of Assembly in each of the three existing regions—East, West, and North. Analysts, at the time, concluded that the Richards Constitution was the first instrument created by the British colonial administration that opened the door to making Nigeria a federated state, with a unitary legislative apparatus coupled with separate and individual legislative bodies at a regional level (Falola and Heaton, 2010).

The second constitutional reform that was instituted was that of Macpherson Constitution of 1951. Many Nigerians, especially the nationalists, favored the 1951 Constitution for several reasons: Sir John Macpherson's administration included Nigerian leaders in the drafting of the Constitution, which was a sharp departure from his predecessors (Sir Frederick Lugard, Sir Hugh Charles Clifford, and Sir Arthur Richards). The 1951 Constitution had a provision for Council of Ministers whose members included twelve Nigerians, four from each of the three regions, and six British officials.

The Macpherson Constitution had a provision for a central legislative body. The House of Representatives was the only law making body for the central government, whose composition included a president, six ex-official members, and 136 representatives elected from the Regional Assemblies "with half of the representatives allotted to the North while the remaining half was divided between Southwest and Southeast regions," and six special members appointed by the Governor to represent interests not adequately represented in the House (Falola and Heaton, 2010; Citizens for Nigeria, 2007). The Macpherson Constitution also expanded Regional Assemblies by turning Western and Northern Regional Assemblies into bicameralism. Both Regional Assemblies had two Houses: House of Assembly and House of Chiefs. The Regional Assembly in the Eastern Region remained unicameral. The three Regional Assemblies (Northern, Western, and Eastern) had both legislative and executive bodies. The Macpherson Constitution granted greater legislative and financial powers to regional assemblies and provided the first general election in the country's history.

The third constitutional reform, which broadened Nigerians' participation in the governance of the country, was instituted in 1954 under the name of the Secretary of the Colonies, Oliver Lyttelton. The Lyttelton Constitution was another important victory for Nigerian nationalists. The Constitution strengthened the powers of the central government by making Nigeria a federation of three regions (Northern, Western, and Eastern). It designated Lagos as a Federal Territory to be administered by the central government (Falola and Heaton, 2010).

The central government retained its unicameral legislature which, at this time, consisted of 184 members. Ninety-two of these members came from the North, forty-two came from the West, forty-two came from the East, six came from the British Cameroons, and two came from the Federal Territory of Lagos. The Constitution gave the Federal House of Representatives the supreme authority to pass legislations regarding issues placed on the exclusive legislative lists. This meant that the Federal House of Representatives had the power to pass legislations on all issues, but not on those lists devolved to the regional legislatures. By designating the "supremacy clause" to the central government, it meant that "Federal laws always overrode regional laws in case of legislative overlap."

The composition of the Federal Council of Ministers included the Governor–General, three officials (Chief Secretary, Financial Secretary and the Attorney General), and three Ministers from each Region and one from the Cameroons appointed by the Government on the advice of the Regional Executive Council (Citizens for Nigeria, 2007). The Constitution also made provisions for regional self-governing by instituting a clear division of powers between the Central Legislature and the Regional Legislatures. It is important to note here that although these constitutional reforms helped pave the way for independent Nigeria, they did not resolve the lingering issues and concerns many Nigerian nationalists had at the time. These unresolved issues (national unity and identity) later came to be the biggest obstacles hampering the nation building efforts being made ever since the country achieved its political independence from Great Britain. This line of reasoning will lead us to the analyses of the enormous challenges facing Nigeria since its independence.

Chapter 2

POLITICAL CHALLENGES OF THE NIGERIAN STATE: PAST AND PRESENT

The Effects of Colonial Legacy on Nigerian National Identity

Many Africans, including Nigerians, thought that the concept of "sovereign independent nation-state" meant absolute freedom and independence. They also thought that democracy meant "the right to choose," but it did not take too long after independence for these Africans to realize that political independence is not the same thing as economic independence, and that democracy does not always mean what it says. These were hard lessons the Africans learned and had to live with.

Before independence, Africans had expected their newly emerged leaders to turn things around in their favor, if and when, independence was achieved. This expectation became a huge challenge to the newly emerged African leaders, as George B.N Ayittey eloquently expressed in his book, *Africa Betrayed*. The book examined in part, the damage done to the Africa indigenous political institutions by colonial rule and efforts made by the newly emerging African leaders, if any, to reverse the trend. In his analysis, Ayittey (1992), made the following observations:

> It is true that colonial rule was marked by atrocities, plunder, and neglect. But Africa's indigenous institutions were largely left intact by colonial rule. From this perspective, the task facing African leaders after independence was clear: to develop the tradition sector that the colonialists had neglected, to restore the tradition authority that the chiefs and kings had lost under colonialism, and to rebuild the native political structures that the colonialists had tried to destroy (p.94).

From all indications, the African leaders after independence did not do much to reverse the damage of colonialism; rather they embraced and legitimatized foreign political institutions and cultures at the expense of their own. They became custodians and defenders of foreign values, and helped to perpetuate colonial legacies in their respective countries.

After independence was won in 1960, Nigeria retained virtually every aspect of political structure the British colonial administration left behind. It retained the federal structure, which was introduced in 1954 by the Lyttelton Constitution; adopted a multi-party system that has perpetuated ethnic politics in Nigeria; adopted a parliamentary democracy that yielded no positive results; and a mixed economy, which enabled the Nigerian government to compete with the private sector economy on key issues ranging from education, transport and telecommunication to health care. Nigeria also retained the English language and made it the country's official language and a language of instruction in schools and in the public service. In most recent time, the country has abandoned the British parliamentary system to adopt the United States of America's political model, which calls for an Executive Presidency. These are major reasons why the Nigerian political culture and institutions have not stabilized.

The modern political culture in Nigeria is alien to the country's indigenous political institutions, which consisted of the following: 1) Traditional Rulers; 2) Inner or Privy Council of Advisers; 3) Council of Elders; and 4), Village Assemblies. Each of these bodies has its own distinctive functions and responsibilities. Although the traditional rulers (Emirs, Obas, or Ezes) wielded vast powers in the day-to-day administration of their kingdoms and how legislations were made, they rarely made policies. The traditional rulers' governing role was not autocratic but consultative. Their foremost concerns were the preservation and protection of their kingdoms' interests and people. Traditional rulers, at the time, acted as umpires to ensure fair play and equal justice for all. In mediating disputes, they were expected to weigh all sides impartially. Native courts existed to assist traditional rulers in dispensing justice fairly. As judges, traditional rulers were not infallible; their decisions in court could be reversed or invalidated in parts by Council of Elders and, in most cases, by Village Assemblies (Ayittey, 1992). These were checks and balances that existed between the traditional rulers and other constituted bodies found in the indigenous African political institutions.

When Nigeria became independent, the people jubilated and celebrated for various reasons, but largely due to the following:

- Defeating British colonial rule in the country;
- Obtaining the power and authority to control the country's sovereignty and destiny without foreign interventions;
- Obtaining the power to govern the country amicably without acrimonies;
- Obtaining the power to improve the people's socio-economic status;
- Obtaining the authority to promote peace, unity, tolerance, and harmony amongst the divergent segments of the society; and
- Obtaining the authority to provide effective and trusted leadership that will lead the country to prosperity by creating opportunities to its citizenry.

This was wishful thinking and dreaming that did not come to fruition, because of the caliber of leaders that emerged after independence and those that came after them. A majority of these leaders were characterized at best, as power hungry, selfish, overbearing, and sectionalists. As soon as independence was won, many of these leaders took the opportunity to deepen the division of the country by promoting ethnic politics at the expense of national unity. On the other hand, they saw politics as a means of enriching themselves. Thus, the socio-economic well-being of average Nigerians was relegated to the back burner.

The quest for regional politics and the temptation to get rich quickly exacerbated the "class struggle" that marred the country's body polity, and continues to do so till today. Such behaviors also prevented the modifications of indigenous political institutions. The poor performance of these leaders has become a huge disappointment to many Nigerians. Their poor performance in office betrayed the national struggle against colonialism and foreign occupation of the country. It also betrayed the trust and mandate the Nigerian people bestowed on them. With few exceptions, leaders in Nigeria have acted in the worst form than those they replaced—their British counterparts. In addition, many African countries and people of African descent in the Diaspora had similar hopes and expectations that Nigeria could provide the able leadership needed to liberate the Black World from the yoke of slavery and colonialism, given the country's immense natural resources and human capital. Unfortunately, these hopes and expectations dissipated quickly when Nigerians leaders failed to provide such needed and able leadership that would energize and mobilize the rest of the continent for such a good cause. With some exceptions, the Nigerian leaders, both past and present, have not fully delivered the dividend of independence and democracy the people had expected after five decades of independence.

The failure to infuse some elements of African traditions into the country's modern political structures and institutions is a rejection of who we are. It shows that Nigerians are not proud of themselves; their histories and traditions. This is a true reflection of what is happening today in the country. Nigerians are witnessing the demise of their indigenous cultural values because they are gradually disappearing in certain parts of the country. As a result of this obvious fact, some Nigerian local languages are becoming extinct--a conclusion reached by a group of Nigerian distinguished scholars, who were assembled by the Nigerian Institute of International Affairs (NIIA) to discuss how to save Nigeria's indigenous languages. In his own contribution to the discussion, Professor Samuel Aje, who chaired the event, numerated some efforts made by the government to encourage the use of local languages in Nigeria's schools, but admitted that "beyond learning, language defines the customs and traditions of its people."

On the other hand, the coordinator of the Abuja-based Goodluck Ebele Jonathan Foreign Language Institute agreed, claiming that the neglect of local languages by most African countries had contributed to their struggle globally. He was quoted by the *Guardian Nigeria Newspaper* on March 4, 2014, as saying:

> The lip service being paid to the language industry in Nigeria had led to the extinction of many languages. The neglect of language has really come to fore and it is for all of us to accept responsibility for this problem. We should all know that language is more than a means of communication as it defines the customs and traditions of the people. It is also a product of many generations and it is its neglect that had contributed to the struggle being faced by many African countries. We need to rescue our local languages from extinction to be able to compete favourably with others. Despite the adoption of the English language as the official language, we have not been able to master it well, as the results from the school certificate examinations have shown this. We need to develop our language by empowering researchers to provide a good ground for it to prosper.

In his own contribution to the language saga, the former Director of Economic Commission for Africa (ECA), Ambassador Olusola Sanu, stated that "language has been at the vanguard of everything we do and we should do everything possible to promote our languages." He called on parents and guardians to encourage their wards to embrace their local languages rather than compelling them to make use of foreign languages. He blamed parents for contributing to their wards' incapability of speaking indigenous languages, noting that "it is essential that our children understand our language."

The Igbo language, for example, is fast disappearing because many Igbo families prefer their children to learn and speak English rather than their native language. In today's world, bilingual education should be encouraged; none of the spoken languages in the area should take preference over the other. The languages should be studied and spoken jointly; and same values should be attached to each other. To reject one's own indigenous cultural values means rejecting one's existence and history. It is very sad that Nigerians are fond of condemning their cultural values out rightly, instead of modifying them to suit their purpose, as is done elsewhere in the world. The above scenario explains why many Nigerians are not proud of their country. Nigerians, in general, are lovers of foreign values whether good or bad, at the expense of their own cultural values and norms. For example, they love foreign made goods more than those manufactured at home. This helps explain why Nigeria and, indeed, the entire African continent has become a dumping ground for foreign made goods and cultures.

Military Dictatorship in Nigeria

Military rule in Nigeria had been a major challenge to the Nigerian project. It abruptly ended the First Nigerian Republic (1960-1966) and ushered in a Civil War, which lasted three years (1967-1970). It also ended the Second Republic (1979-1983), and the Third Republic (June 12, 1993-November 17, 1993). Since Nigeria's post-independent history, the military had dominated the political landscape of the country. Nigeria has had eight military regimes during the era of military intervention in the country's polity. They included: the Ironsi's regime; the Gowon's regime; the Mohammed's regime; the Obasanjo's regime; the Buhari's regime, the Babangida's regime; the Abacha's regime, and the Abudusalami's regime. Of these regimes, six of them were orchestrated and headed by Northern Military Generals, while the remaining two regimes were headed by Southern Military Generals—Maj. Gen. Aguiyi-Ironsi and Gen. Olusegun Obasanjo.

On the other hand, Nigeria has had six civilian administrations since its independence: the Balewa's Administration (1960-1966); Alhaji Shehu Shagari's

Administration (1979- 1983); Olusegun Obasanjo's Administration (1999-2007); Umaru Musa Yar'Adua's Administration (May 29, 2007-May 5, 2010); Goodluck Jonathan's Administration (May 6, 2010- May 29, 2015) and Muhammad Buhari (May 30, 2016-present). Of these administrations, only two were headed by Southerners while the remaining four were headed by Northerners.

These are the political realities of the country when it comes to the question of what region of Nigeria has dominated the leadership of the country since independence. President Jonathan is the first minority individual ever elected as Nigerian president. He hails from the former Southeastern region, known today in the Nigerian political lexicon as the South-South Political Zone of the country.

Here are the analyses of what transpired during those days of military dictatorships in Nigeria. The first military regime in Nigeria is traceable to Maj. Gen. J. T. U. Aguiyi-Ironsi (January 15, 1966-July 29, 1966). General Ironsi was the beneficiary (heir) of the failed military coup of January 15, 1966 led by a group of young Army Majors: Maj. Patrick Chukwuma Kaduna Nzeogwu; Maj. Emmanuel A. Ifeajuna; Maj. D. Okafor; Maj. C. I. Anuforo; and Maj. A. Ademoyega (Falola and Heaton 2010; Osaghae, 1998). General Ironsi was faulted on two key issues by Northern military elites. First, he was accused of sheltering the January 15 coup plotters from facing military justice; thereby, allowing them to escape to the Eastern Region, where they were later released by the then military governor of the region, Col. Chukwuemeka Odumegwu Ojukwu. Second, the Northern military elite accused General Ironsi of unilaterally imposing a Unification Promulgation Decree on Nigerians without giving the Supreme Military Council (SMC) the opportunity to debate on the issue. The Decree was said to have abolished the federal and regional structures that gave the North greater autonomy.

Ironsi's Northern critics accused him of favoring the Igbo military officers more than officers from other ethnic groups. They used the military promotion he enacted before his demise as a basis for their argument. His critics claimed that out of the twenty one (21) people he promoted from the rank of major to Lieutenant Colonel, eighteen (18) of them were of Igbo extraction.

His critics were also suspicious of the urgency in setting up a tribunal of inquiry to investigate the mass killing of the Igbos and other Easterners in the North that occurred most recently, while his regime had not brought the January 15 coup plotters to justice six months after the fact (Osaghae, 1998; Siollun, 2009). These suspicions culminated into the notion and suggestions that General Ironsi was part of the Igbo conspiracy or agenda to dominate the entire country. To the Northern elite, these conspiracies or agenda were unacceptable. Consequently, on July 29, 1966, General Ironsi was brutally murdered and his regime toppled in a countercoup hatched by his Northern military detractors.

Gen. Yakubu Gowon assumed the Nigerian military leadership after Ironsi's regime was toppled on July 29, 1966. The Gowon regime (July 29, 1966- July 29, 1975) executed the Civil War that erupted after the Eastern Region seceded from Nigeria to create a sovereign state of Republic of Biafra. It was the mishandling of the Nigerian crisis, which resulted in the massacre of many Easterners (Civilians, Military officers and men) in Northern cities, and the wanton destruction of their properties, and the failure to implement the true principles of the Aburi (Ghana) Accord, that forced Igbos to seek secession from the Nigerian Union.

The Coup of July 1966 was a retaliation of the January 1966 coup—a pogrom (an organized massacre of helpless people) in which Northern elites felt was designed by the Igbo military officers to conquer and colonize the North.

Many Nigerians believed that the military would return to barracks once the Civil War was over, but they were wrong. Gen. Mohammed and his men overthrew Gowon's regime for two major reasons: failure to hand over power to civilian government as promised; and the exclusion of some key battle field officers from the corridors of power and patronage.

For these reasons, Gen. Mohammed and his men struck while Gen. Gowon was in Kampala, Uganda, attending the annual summit of the Organization of African Unity (OAU), now known as the African Union (AU). The failure of Gowon's regime to address these issues to the satisfaction of the Nigeria military oligarchy, at the time, led to the escalation of military dictatorship in Nigeria, as the country witnessed more coups and countercoups.

Like Maj. Gen. Aguiyi-Ironsi's regime, Gen. Murtala Ramat Mohammed's regime (July 29, 1975-February 13, 1976) was short-lived. Mohammed's regime was very popular among Nigerians because, within the few months he was in power, his regime initiated a series of sweeping reforms, which included the compulsory retirement of thousands of military officers and civil servants, and he established a time table to return the country to a civilian rule. His regime also initiated the relocation of the Federal Capital Territory from Lagos to Abuja; however, this idea was implemented in 1991 under General Babangida's regime.

General Mohammed's regime made many enemies both domestic and foreign: On the international stage, he was despised by some Western governments, especially the United States of American and Great Britain, for his unwavering support for the Popular Movement for the Liberation of Angola (MPLA) and the African National Congress (ANC).

At the time, the ANC was in a fierce armed struggle against the Apartheid White Minority regime in South Africa while the MPLA was also in armed struggle against Portugal, South Africa White Minority regime, the United States, and their local surrogates—the National Front for the Liberation of Angola (FNLA) and, later the National Union for the Total Independence of Angola (UNITA).

Because of his unwavering support for the African Liberation Movements in Southern Africa during the peak of the Cold War, and because of his regime's uncompromising attitude against corruption and indiscipline in Nigeria, General Mohammed did not live long to see the demise and collapse of colonialism in Angola and South Africa. His life was cut short at the age of thirty-eight (38) by his fellow Northern military colleagues. Prominent among these Northern military elites were Lt. Col. Buka Suka Dimka, and Maj. Gen. Iliya Bissalla. General Gowon, who ended up in Warwick University in England after he was ousted from power, was also implicated in the February 13, 1976 coup that overthrew the Mohammed regime. Gowon was perceived by many people in the country as the main architect of the coup, but that perception went nowhere. After his studies in London, he came back to the country to resume his normal life-style.

Gen. Olusegun Obasanjo's regime (February 13, 1976-October 1, 1979) continued the policy agenda of his immediate predecessor, Gen. Murtala Mohammed, after he was brutally assassinated in a failed military coup. General Obasanjo was the first military leader in the history of Nigeria to voluntarily "hand over power to a civilian government" and, by his brilliant and patriotic act, the Nigerian Second Republic (1979-1983) was born. Unfortunately, the Republic did not last too long before it was crushed by another military coup. As luck would have it, Obasanjo was twice elected to lead the country decades after he handed over power to a civilian government. His presidency ushered in the "Fourth Nigerian Republic" (1999-2007), and he served two consecutive terms in office where he made a smooth transition of power from one civilian administration to another, in spite of the fact that he tried as much as he could to elongate his stay in power by trying to amend the Constitution to accommodate his political desire for a third term. Nigerians did not fall for that and, such a positive reaction ended his presidential ambition for his third time presidency.

Maj. Gen. Muhammadu Buhari's regime (December 31, 1983-August 27, 1985) emerged after Buhari overthrew Alhaji Shehu Shagari's administration (October 1, 1979-December 31, 1983). Shagari's administration was democratically elected thirteen years, after the Nigerian First Republic (1960-1966), which was headed by Alhaji Tafawa Balewa. Military dictatorship in Nigeria disrupted the smooth transition of one democratic government to another until the Nigerian Fourth Republic (May 29, 1999 to present). The election of Shehu Shagari under the political banner of the National Party of Nigeria (NPN) marked the beginning of Nigeria's Second Republic. Shagari was elected for a second term in July of 1983, but his administration was ousted in a military coup before he could complete his second-term in office. General Buhari claimed that the reason he and his cohorts took the realms of power by military means was to combat indiscipline and corruption that perverted the country's social fabric at the time. A claim, military regimes in Nigeria had always used, as justifications for their interventions into the country's polity. Nigerians knew better. They knew that military rule in Nigeria was an instrument for a big grab of the oil money. These regimes could not fool Nigerians with their rhetoric of fighting corruption and indiscipline, when their hands were dirty with corruption.

Gen. Ibrahim Badamasi Babangida (August 27, 1985-August 27, 1993) overthrew General Buhari's regime in August 1985. General Babangida was not well known outside the military until February 1976, when he squashed the abortive coup hatched by Lt. Col. B. Suka Dimka, the coup that took the life of General Mohammed. Babangida's regime was responsible for many things that impacted the country negatively. His regime instituted the International Monetary Fund (IMF) Structural Adjustment Program (SAP) that brought economic hardship to many Nigerians.

The IMF conditionalities imposed on Nigeria usurped the country's sovereign rights from providing for its citizens' well-being. Literally, this meant that Nigerian domestic and foreign policies were dictated by the World financial institution and its Western allies. The IMF conditionalities were said to have rendered the country as a subservient nation to Western capitalist economy.

The Babangida regime nearly brought the country to the brink of another Civil War when his regime annulled the result of the June 12, 1993 presidential election, an election which many Nigerians claimed was won by Chief Moshood Kaskimawo Olawale Abiola. The annulment of the election and the public anger that followed thereafter forced Babangida to resign from his position, as the Commander in Chief of the Nigerian Armed Forces.

His regime could not withstand the pressure brought to bear against it by many Nigerians who felt that the military had over played its hand. To defuse the mounting pressure, the regime established an Interim Governing Council (IGC) to handle the affairs of the nation pending when a solution to the crisis could be reached.

To fill the void, Chief Ernest Shonekan was appointed by Babangida to head the Council. The legitimacy of IGC was challenged by the Abiola camp and the issue went up to the Lagos High Court, where the Court ruled in favor of Abiola by declaring the Council illegal and unconstitutional.

The Court reasoned that since the election was successfully conducted, Babangida should hand over power to M.K.O Abiola, the purported winner of the election. Under the 1989 constitution, Babangida had no legislative authority to govern the country since a new Head of state had emerged. These claims, however, were disputed by the IGC, which later filed an appeal (Falola and Heaton, 2010).

Gen. Sani Abacha's regime (November 17, 1993-June 8, 1998) picked up the pieces that were left behind by General Babangida's regime. General Abacha took over the leadership of the country by toppling the IGC's leadership, Chief Shonekan, and declaring himself the Head of state and Commander in Chief of the Nigerian Armed Forces. It was a known fact that the IGC and Chief Shonekan were setup to fail. The abrupt removal of Chief Shonekan by General Abacha, and the poor handling of the June 12, 1993 presidential election, compounded the Nigerian problem even more. These activities infuriated many Nigerians, especially the Yorubas who saw what transpired as a plot to deny them the leadership of the country, a presidency which one of them had won convincingly and legitimately.

A majority of Yoruba intelligentsia and grass root organizations, and other progressive-minded Nigerians saw the annulment of the June 12 presidential election as a great setback to the Nigerian democracy. Consequently, these groups of Nigerians tagged as Pro-democracy movement, operating under a label known as the National Democratic Coalition (NADECO), mounted vigorous criticisms and a campaign against Abacha's regime.

The group mobilized support for Abiola and wanted him to be inaugurated as the president of the country. Abacha's regime saw the activities of the Pro-democracy movement as an affront to his regime and the regime started to clamp down on the group by arresting and imprisoning its leadership indefinitely, as a way to intimidate the group and others. To justify his regime's tough and brutal stance against the Pro-democracy movement, he claimed that some of its members were planning coups to overthrow him from office and to undermine his regime.

The regime saw Chief M.K.O Abiola, the former Head of state, Gen. Olusegun Obasanjo, and his former deputy, Maj. Gen. Shehu Yar' Adua, as chief architects of the Pro-democracy movement. These men were arrested and thrown into prison, where both Yar' Adua and Chief Abiola died mysteriously. Many senior military officers of the Yoruba extraction lived under fear of being accused by Abacha's regime of plotting coups against the regime.

For example, Lt. Gen. Donaldson Oladipo Diya and other Yoruba military officers were implicated in a coup, where Diya was sentenced to death. Given the circumstances surrounding Abacha's sudden death and the intervention of the international community over the secrecies of the trial, Diya's death sentence was commuted by Gen. Abubakar Abdusalami, Abacha's successor.

In his newspaper interview with the *Nigerian Vanguard Newspaper* reporter, Adefaka (2011), Chief Olabode Ibiyinka George who was the former Commodore of the Nigerian Navy, the ninth Governor of old Ondo State, and former Chairman, Board of the Nigerian Ports Authority (NPA), lamented bitterly about his ordeal in Abacha's regime. Bode George claimed that General Abacha instituted a policy to exclude Southern military officers from his regime, describing such a policy as the "new Southern cleansing." He saw his unexplained firing from his position as the principal staff officer and the arrest of some top Yoruba military officers, like Diya, as an example of the implementation of Abacha's ethnic cleansing agenda. The regime also went into a massive hunt for NADECO's members, which forced many of them to flee the country. Some went to Europe, others ended up in the United States and from those places they mounted intensive campaigns against the regime until its abrupt end in 1998, following Abacha's mysterious death.

Another dark history of Abacha's regime was the execution of Ken Saro-Wiwa and eight other individuals from the Ogoni land. For years, the people of the Delta region, from where the Nigerian government derives its vast oil revenue, had been complaining about the eco-terrorism committed against the region by Western Multinational Oil Corporations (MNCs), especially the Shell Oil Company, but no Nigerian administration had ever taken the complaints seriously. The oil pollutions in that region were grave and had enormous economic and health consequences for the region and national security, which had been ignored for too long by both the Nigerian government and foreign oil companies responsible for the pollutions. No meaningful and responsive government in the world would tolerate such environmental destruction and allow it to go on for too long without a solution.

Take for example, the incessant reactions of the Obama administration and the American people when the Gulf Coast (Gulf of Mexico) of the United States of America was polluted in May of 2010 by the British Petroleum (BP) oil blowout that destroyed the eco-system and lifestyle of the people of that region. The government and the people reacted quickly by holding BP and other subsidiaries (Transocean Ltd., and Halliburton) involved in the oil spill accountable for their negligence and forced them to clean up the spill. The Obama administration demanded that BP should provide $20 billion (Twenty billion USD) to clean up the area and compensate the victims, which the oil company agreed to. The opposite is the case in Nigeria, where leaders are handsomely bribed to shield and protect foreign oil companies from prosecutions for polluting the environment.

The Abacha regime, like its predecessors, was too slow to act and because of the regime's inaction to force foreign oil companies to clean up their oil spills and comply with the pollution-friendly environment, the Ogoni and other riverine people in the Delta region, whose lands were heavily polluted by oil spills decided to take the law into their hand. The people of the region saw no option other than to sabotage and vandalize oil companies' installations and, at times, threatened to shut down their operations. When it was obvious that the Nigerian government had failed to protect the region and its people from the environmental degradation, the people organized themselves into militant groups, such as the Movement for the Survival of the Ogoni People (MOSOP) and the Movement for the Emancipation of the Niger Delta (MEND), to end oil pollutions in the region and empower their people to control their God given natural resources.

Instead of tackling the issue at its very root, the Abacha regime went after the messengers, and consequently, Saro-Wiwa and his lieutenants were tried in a Kangaroo tribunal, where they were charged and convicted of illegal activities against the state—activities the regime claimed threatened the peace and stability of the region and national security. Consequently, Saro-Wiwa was hanged and the execution of these men was widely condemned by various international human rights and environmental organizations. The execution further isolated Abacha's regime from the comity of nations before his sudden death.

Gen. Abdulsalami Abubakar's regime (June 9, 1998-May 29, 1999) is the last military regime Nigeria has had so far. After the sudden death of General Abacha on June 8, 1998, General Abdusalami was chosen by top military officials to spearhead the affairs of the country. As the Commander in Chief of the Nigerian Armed Forces, General Abubakar showed no intention of staying in power for too long like his predecessors. This new thinking and change of heart within the military circle came because of the following issues in the country: 1) Nigerians have had it with military dictatorship; 2) the country was about to disintegrate due to the unresolved issue of the June 12 presidential election; and 3) the controversies generated by Abacha's intrigues and intention of succeeding himself in office as a Nigerian civilian president.

To calm the situation, General Abubakar pledged to return the country back to a civilian rule, a pledge he kept. The regime oversaw the country's transition of power from a military rule to a civilian government. The regime took several steps in achieving this feat. It created a multiparty system and registered three political parties out of the "twenty six (26) organizations that applied for recognition." These three major parties included the Alliance for Democracy (AD), the All People's Party (APP), and the People's Democratic Party (PDP) (Falola and Heaton, 2010). The regime also created an electoral body known as the Independent National Election Commission (INEC) to execute the electoral process, and Justice Ephraim Akpata, a former Nigerian Supreme Court Justice, was appointed to head the Commission.

Prospects for another Civil War in Nigeria

The misguided policies of the newly emerged elite in Nigeria further deepened the division of the country and plunged the country into a Civil War (1967-1970). The War was costly and devastating. It took many lives from the warring parties, destroyed private properties and public infrastructure, costing tens of billions of Naira. The Civil War was also fueled by the fact that before the war, many Nigerians felt they were not part of the Nigerian success story; they felt marginalized and were often referred to as "minority groups." As demonstrated in the section dealing with the chronological order of Nigeria's political history, the country was initially partitioned into three major regions (Northern, Western, and Eastern), and within these regions, there were groups of Nigerians who felt they were not part of the mainstream. Their struggle for inclusion into the country's political process paved the way for the creation of states in Nigeria, beginning with the creation of the Midwestern region in 1963.

Today, there are thirty-six (36) states in Nigeria, excluding the Federal Capital Territory (FCT) in Abuja. There are still many groups in the country agitating for more states. States creation has become the order of the day; it is viewed as a vital means of redistributing the country's economic resources equitably; and it gives voices to the voiceless by encouraging mass participation in the country's body polity. It is a way of addressing the political and economic imbalances that have existed in the country for far too long.

Regrettably, the current leaderships in Nigeria have not learned from the mistakes of their predecessors—the mistakes that triggered the Civil War in Nigeria. Similar mistakes are being repeated and, once again, the country is drifting towards another catastrophe. Today, the country is engulfed with an endemic violence that has no end in sight. This violence emanates from criminal behaviors that were not common in Nigeria in those early days. Since independence, Nigerians have witnessed various forms of sectarian violence, political assassinations, kidnappings, armed robbery, drug trafficking, human trafficking, money laundering and the list goes on.

The country is also witnessing unprecedented ethnic militant groups in the horizon with high intensity of violence. The activities of Boko Haram, MOSOP, and MEND are well documented and known to Nigerians, including those outside Nigeria. The actions and rhetoric of these groups have the potential of destabilizing the country if adequate measures are not taken to address the groups' concerns and agitations. There are other similar ethnic militant groups lying in wait. These are the Oodua Peoples' Congress (OPC), and the Movement for the Actualization of the Sovereign State of Biafra (MASSOB). Each of these groups has their own grievances against the federal government, but has chosen to remain peaceful for the time being. From all indications, these groups have the potential of becoming violent at any time of their choosing. They have the organizational structure, the manpower, support and logistics, and other instruments of violence at their disposal. They are only waiting for the right moment before they strike.

Leadership Problems in Nigeria

Nigeria has a problem in producing leaders who have qualities of Plato's philosopher King—qualities such as virtues, visions, and wisdom. Philosopher kings are moral and transformational leaders who govern by good examples. They are God fearing and always want to leave good legacies behind for the next generation to emulate. They operate within and not around the rule of law. These are selfless leaders who always view themselves as servants of the people and not masters of the people.

These are leaders who understand that their countries' national interests supersede personal interests. With the exception of a few, Nigeria has not produced leaders who think less of themselves and more of the country. Borrowing a page from John F. Kennedy's famous slogan, Nigeria has leaders who always think of what the country can do for them and not what they can do for the country.

Since its independence, Nigeria has produced leaders who are selfish, shameless, overbearing, arrogant, sectional, power hungry, and more so, leaders who do not care about the needs of average Nigerians.

The issue of poor and underperforming leadership in Nigeria was well articulated by Prof. Chinua Achebe in his 1983 work, titled *The Trouble with Nigeria*, where he briefly examined those social ills that have inhibited the progress of the country. Some of these social ills included the following: failure of leadership; tribalism; false image of ourselves; lack of patriotism; social injustice and cult of mediocrity; indiscipline; and corruption. In digesting Nigeria's problems, Professor Achebe claimed that the trouble with Nigeria lies squarely in the failure of leadership. He recounted that,

> There is nothing basically wrong with the Nigerian land or climate or water or air or anything else. The Nigerian problem is the unwillingness or inability of its leaders to rise to the responsibility, and to the challenge of personal example which are the hallmarks of true leadership. (Achebe, 1983:.1).

The Professor Emeritus "called on all thoughtful Nigerians to rise up today and reject those habits which cripple our aspiration and inhibit our chances of becoming a modern and attractive country." He went further to ask the following moving and thought provoking questions: "Nigeria has many thoughtful men and women of conscience, and large numbers of talented people. Why is it then that all these patriots make so little impact on the life of our nation? Why is it that our corruption, gross inequities, our noisy vulgarity, our selfishness, and our ineptitude seem so much stronger than the good influences at work in our society? Why do the good among us seem so helpless while the worst are full of vile energy?"

On tribalism, Achebe of "blessed memory" and other well-meaning Nigerians see tribalism as the most divisive element in the building effort of a united Nigeria. He queried why most Nigerians are more loyal to their ethnic origin than they are to the country as a whole. In his work, Achebe (1983) described how Nigerians have accepted and continued to perpetuate tribalism in their daily lives; tribalism in Nigeria has become a way of life in the country. Here is why:

> A Nigerian child seeking admission into a federal school, a student wishing to enter a College or University, a graduate seeking employment in the public service, a businessman tendering for a contract, a citizen applying for a passport, filling a report with the police or seeking access to any of the hundred thousand avenues controlled by the state, will sooner or later fill out a form which requires him to confess his tribe (or less crudely and more hypocritically, his state of origin) (p. 8).

The Professor Emeritus admitted that there were manifestations of tribal culture which could not be condemned or disregarded in their entirety; these are: peculiar habits of dress, food, language, music etc. For him, these manifestations were positive and desirable values which confer richness on national culture, but rejected the notion of preventing a citizen from living or working anywhere in his country or from participating in the social, political, and economic life of the community in which he chooses to live.

The seed of tribalism was sown when the British colonial authorities brought divergent groups with unique traditions and histories together to create the Nigerian state and did little or nothing to unify the country. The local leaders who emerged after independence did not do much either to correct this erroneous mistake. Instead, they perpetuated such misguided policy by promoting tribal interests at the expense of the unity of the country. The formation of political organizations in Nigeria during the pre and post-independence was based on tribal lines and the fallout from such an experiment impacted the country's political development and government processes negatively. This fallout is still being felt today. The Nigerian project cannot be sustained if this mindset is not discontinued.

In his own analysis of leadership in Africa, Prof. Bedford Umez indicted post-independence African leaders for contributing immensely to the suffering of millions of their people. He made a strong case against these leaders (military and civilian), whom he described as "leaders without shame." In critiquing these leaders' lifestyles, Professor Umez, a Nigerian illustrious son and renowned Political Scientist, eloquently but painfully described the political environment and climate created by these shameless leaders:

> Africa is sick and tired of being ruled mostly by narrow minded, egotistical, selfish and twisted brains of individuals who find it only fashionable to rob their own brothers and sisters with impunity, with pride and without mercy, only to feed Swiss people and other foreigners through their investments in those countries. Africa is sick and tired of being mostly led by leaders who do not know the importance of education. Africa is sick and tired of being ruled by over ninety percent [90%] of her leaders whose priority in life is conspicuous lavish lifestyle, tragically rooted in the mentality that my gold bathtub has more gold than yours, or my Mercedes is bigger than yours, when hunger and malnutrition are claiming, without mercy, so many innocent lives in Africa, when African hospitals are abandoned, schools closed for months, roads filled with endless pits, graduates jobless, armed robbery rampant (*Excerpts from Professor Umez's critique of African leaders, 2002*).

In pursuing the above line of thought, Professor Umez provided critical, but yet vital, analyses of what really went wrong in Africa and why many African leaders have not been a productive force on the continent; and why they are part of the problem and not part of the solution:

> Something is definitely wrong with a leader, or any man who hates himself and his people only to love outsiders. Something is definitely wrong with a leader, or any man who is totally inferior to anything foreign. Something is definitely wrong with a leader who is so comfortable in his gold bathtubs, dozens of private cars bought with the money he has embezzled, when his people are dying daily of starvation, malnutrition and Kwashiorkor due to his demented mentality of piling up his country's money in foreign countries. Something is definitely wrong with a leader who is constantly subjecting his people, his country and his continent to pure laughing stocks. Something

is definitely wrong with a leader, or any man who simply refuses to think. A leader without shame is as good as a dead body. A leader without pride is completely empty and useless. It does not take a course in logic for one to understand that the primary cause of our problems today is that so many dead brains are ruling us (*Excerpts from Professor Umez's critique of African leaders, 2002*).

The above analyses summed up the characteristics of most African leaders and why they rigged themselves into positions of power. They are in government only to loot the people's money and wealth and not to do the people's business.

Election Fraud

Elections are the hallmark of democracy. They give citizens of voting age the opportunity to express who should represent them in a Representative Assembly. In a society, where democratic values are revered and cherished, citizens are free to elect a body of men and women who should govern their affairs. Because societies are becoming more complex, a few people are chosen through publicized elections to represent divergent opinions and interests that exist in those societies. When people cast their votes for a particular candidate, they are simply expressing their consent or giving their mandate to that candidate/s to represent their interests. This is logical since modern governments are not like Towns' or Villages' Assemblies, where every adult is free to attend and partake in the decision making processes of their respective towns and villages.

There are four essential elements in modern electoral processes: 1) there must be organized political parties with different ideologies willing to compete against one another in order to determine the party that takes over the leadership of the country for a specific time period. It is the ruling party that controls the country's resources and detects public policies that affect the entire country; 2) there must be candidates representing each party's ideology and willing to compete for various political offices or positions; 3) elections must be conducted under secret ballots, as a means of determining the party that wins the majority vote cast; and 4) the conduct of elections must be free and fair to ensure the integrity of elections and legitimize duly elected candidates.

When an election is rigged or bought, it undermines the integrity of such an election and delegitimizes the party and candidates who rigged themselves into power. Election fraud denies the legitimate party's candidates the opportunity to represent the interest of majority voters who cast their votes on the party's behalf. Election fraud is also viewed in certain quarters, as a "crime against humanity" because it robs the popular party and deserving candidates the opportunity to implement their popular programs that attracted most of the voters to their course.

Election fraud is, indeed, an anti-democratic process—one that leads to social unrests in places where it occurred. The eruption of violence in some part of Northern Nigeria, where many Nigerians including some election officers were killed after the presidential results of 2011 elections were released, is a typical example of what happens when an election is rigged.

We saw similar violence erupting in Kenya after that country's election in 2007, where many Kenyans were killed because of a stolen election. Cote d'Ivoire underwent similar post-election violence in 2010, when the former Ivoirian President, Laurent Gbagbo, refused to cede power to Alassane Outtara, the winner of the presidential election. By failing to transfer power to Outtara, who received the majority votes cast and by Gbagbo declaring himself the president-elect, supporters of both camps engaged in fierce violence that took the lives of many Ivoirians. As a result of this carnage and, to stop the waste of human lives, the French troops invaded the country and Gbagbo was captured and transported to The Hague, where he is now facing charges of war crimes and crimes against humanity, at the International Criminal Court (ICC).

Election fraud has become one of the many challenges confronting many countries today, including Nigeria. The history of election fraud in Nigeria could be traced to the Nigerian First Republic (1960-1966), where partisan electoral processes were new to most Nigerians. The allocation of resources in Nigeria, like in many other countries, has also been identified as the leading cause of the country's political tensions. The distribution of resources among various segments of the Nigerian populace and among other political actors fuels these tensions. Lasswell (1948), an American Political Science icon, who defined politics as the determination of "who get what, when, and how," claimed that the reason government was instituted was to allocate the country's resources equitably in order to avoid conflict among the various competing groups in society. He also noted that it was government's role to breach imbalance in the system if conflict was to be avoided. But, unknown to him, at the time, he did not realize that the maneuvering or the scramble for resource allocation (who benefits and who loses) would lead to massive corruption and other political intrigues we are witnessing today in many countries, including Nigeria.

Falola and Heaton (2010) reechoed this sentiment in their work, *A History of Nigeria,* where they noted that the scramble for resource allocation had culminated into fear of domination of one region by another, and it was this fear of domination that clouded the moral and social psyche of the leaders of the Nigerian First Republic. Here is how the leaders, at the time, described the situation:

> Southerners feared that an NPC (Northern People's Congress) controlled government representing the interests of the Northern Region would divert resources to the North, cut Southerners out of their positions in the administration and the military, and gradually Islamize the country. Northerners feared that Southerners "domination" by Awolowo's Action Group and Azikiwe's newly renamed National Convention of Nigerian Citizens (NCNC) would allocate resources to the more developed Western and Eastern Regions, which would prevent the North from ever developing in a competitive way. They also feared that Southern "domination" would mean that Southerners would come to control the civil service and educational institutions of the North, since Northerners would continually be denied the resources to develop an educated class to compete on merit with Southerners (p. 165).

Falola and Heaton went further to postulate that it was this "fear of domination that clouded any sense of national unity in Nigeria in the 1960s, as residents in each region increasingly came to fear that other regions intended to use the political system to enrich themselves at the expense of their Nigerian "brothers" in other regions."

It was their (Falola and Heaton) conclusion that "under such conditions, it became imperative for the parties once in power to stay in power and for those out of power either to ally with the majority party or to wrest control of the government away from that party in the next election, as opposition parties faced the prospect of perennial marginalization." With this expressed fear of domination, the seed of disunity, ethnic, regional and religious rivalries was sown. The urge to remain in power in perpetuity and the urge to be in control of the nation's resources have become the chief source of election fraud in the country. Since Nigeria's Fourth Republic (1999 to present), the People's Democratic Party (PDP), the country's ruling party, has been in power for sixteen years (1999-2015) and has been vigorously accused by the opposition parties of rigging itself into power and staying in power for that number of years.

Being in control of the country's resources and its public policies are things that attracted many people to politics. As noted previously in one of the sections of this study, many people are in politics for the wrong reasons. They are in politics simply to use their political positions and influence to amass personal wealth for themselves and to reward their family members, and cronies alike. These are individuals who are intoxicated with power and will do anything humanly possible to stay in power as long as they live. Many banks in Nigeria failed because their owners embezzled depositors' money simply to contest for political offices. Part of the embezzled money was used in rigging elections and bribing elections' Tribunal Court Judges to render decisions in their favor.

Holding public office in Nigeria has paid handsomely. It enables politicians to loot public funds for their future political aspirations or ambition. Politicians are never satisfied with serving only one term in office. Knowing the reward of being in politics, these people may start off with the Local Government Chairman position (an equivalent of a city mayor in the United State) and, in the next election, he/she may end up becoming a state governor. In another situation, a candidate may start off as a state governor and, in the next election, he/she may end up becoming a vice presidential aspirant or maybe running for the nation's Senatorial seat. The irony of this saga is that, initially, most of these politicians did not have money of their own to contest for these elections.

They depended solely on wealthy individuals known within the Nigerian political circles as "political godfathers," who would like to use these vulnerable candidates to loot states' treasuries at the expense of the general well-being of the people. Once elected, candidates' first priority would be to repay their borrowed campaign loans to their political godfathers with public funds. After paying off the loan, the remaining looted funds would be used to seek for a higher political office and, when he/she won the election, embezzlement of public funds would continue unabated, and by the time you knew it, this one-time poor politician had become a billionaire by stealing public funds.

Prof. Bolaji Akinyemi's lecture eloquently described the above stated facts more adequately—a lecture he delivered in Akure, the Ondo State Capital during the second term inauguration lecture of Governor Olusegun Mimiko. In that lecture, the eminent scholar of International Relations and Diplomacy, former Director General of the Nigerian Institute of International Affair (NIIA), and former Minister of External Affairs was quoted as saying:

> It is not possible for any Nigerian to be a billionaire without being corrupt. No one can be a billionaire today without being corrupt. If you are a businessman, you would have evaded tax or other levies like import duties with the active connivance of those in charge. Your entire income as political office holder, either elected or appointed, cannot make you a billionaire without indulging in corrupt practices. It is also not possible for you to work and retire as a civil servant in whatever capacity and become a billionaire without being corrupt.... Unless our leaders tackle the issue of

corruption and offer selfless service to the people, our democracy may not produce the desired development we are all expecting. Politics of development was replaced by politics of looting (Aborisade, 2013).

The seasoned Professor further lamented that "Nigerians had sacrificed value systems on the altar of greed, indiscipline, selfishness and insatiable craze for material wealth acquisition." That "there are no more values to hold on to, parents not only encourage their children to cheat in order to beat the system, but also aid and abet them in their nefarious activities." He queried why no one is asking for the source of this ill-gotten wealth. "People in jail, accused of murder run for, and win elections. More than a score of members of the Senate have EFCC court cases hanging against them. Only in Nigeria do you steal billions and escape with less than a million naira fine." Practices of this kind will continue unless something drastic is done to curb it. This is why a body of work of this kind is of essence, to alert the reading public of the immense problems the country is enduring and will continue to endure if positive actions are not taken to address them.

PART TWO

PRIVATIZATION SCHEME AND ENDEMIC CORRUPTION IN NIGERIA

Chapter 3

THE CORRUPTING ROLE OF THE WORLD FINANCIAL INSTITUTIONS
AND FOREIGN MULTINATIONAL CORPORATIONS IN NIGERIA

The Global Intent of the World Financial Institutions and their Corporate Partners

The activities of the world financial institutions and their multinational corporate partners are well known in Nigeria. This high visibility is due to the country's enormous natural resources, its regional significance, and its market potential. Unfortunately, this relationship has not been cordial and has not been based on equal reciprocity. The world financial institutions and their corporate partners would want average Nigerians to believe that their relationship with Nigeria has been beneficial to all parties involved. But, this is a relationship solely orchestrated to exploit Nigeria's natural resources and to undermine the country's sovereignty, as Hiatt (2007) eloquently noted in his work where he pointed out that the world financial institutions, which include the International Bank for Reconstruction and

Development (IBRD), otherwise known as the World Bank and the International Monetary Fund (IMF), have become a Web of Control, which Western governments are using to dominate the developing world following the demise of colonialism. The Bank and the Fund have a policy of lending money to weak and vulnerable nations for capital intensive ventures whether or not these nations actually need the money. If they don't want the money, there is an unwritten policy to pressure them to accept the loans, as is the case in Nigeria. For instance, many Nigerians of all persuasions disapproved Gen. Ibrahim Babangida regime's acceptance of the IMF loans, but his regime did not yield to public opinion because of the intense pressure brought to bear by the lenders.

During the formation of the two sister banks, which were founded through the Bretton Woods system in 1944, the world community was told by their founding fathers (the US and UK), that the IMF and the World Bank, were primarily conceived to reduce the barriers to free flow of trade and capital in order to promote today's interdependent world political economy. Perkins (2006) has refuted this claim, arguing that the World Bank and the IMF were created to build a global empire where capitalism would flourish and reign supreme, and not to save the world from the evil clutches of communism, as their founders claimed and wanted the world to believe (p. 199). Kegley, Jr. and Wittkopf (1996), also drawing from many sources, argued that, "the postwar Liberal International Economic Order (LIEO), which resulted from the establishment of the IMF and World Bank, rested on three political pillars or bases:

1) The concentration of power in a small number of states;
2) The existence of a cluster of important interests shared by those states; and
3) The presence of a dominant power willing and able to assume a leadership role" (p. 207).

These three political pillars supported Perkin's assertion that the creation of the Bank and the Fund was to boost capitalism and not to deter the spread of communism. Since their creation in 1944, the Western world has dominated the two Banks. For example, the World Bank has always been headed by a nominee of the United States of America, while the IMF has been headed by a nominee of Europe. Perkins (2006) goes on to say that because modern wars are more costly in both monetary and human terms and because military coups and social unrests are more destabilizing, western corporate elites and their political allies in government (the anti-government school) now view the IMF and the World Bank as an important corporate instrument of soft power that can be used to consolidate their quest for empire hegemony.

As a result, western corporate elite have used these global financial institutions to advance their neocolonial agenda throughout the developing nations. The agenda call for continuous plundering of the Third World natural resources and the weakening of the sovereign rights of these countries, which so far, has been very successful.

To strangulate the economies of Third World countries, especially those countries that received World Bank or IMF's loans, and to force debtor nations to pay their loans, the Bank and the Fund instituted draconian policies known to scholars of the world political economy, as conditionalities or austerity measures. These policies have subjected these countries, including Nigeria to:

> Abandoning state-led development policies, including tariffs, export subsidies, currency controls, and import-substitution programs. Their approved model of development instead focuses on export-led economic growth, using loans to develop new export industries—for example, to attract light industry to export-processing zones (firms like Nike have been major beneficiaries of these polices). Membership in the World Trade Organization also requires adherence to the IMF's free trade orthodoxy (Hiatt, 2007, p.21).

Other such policies include the removal of government subsidies from education and health care programs, the privatization of government parastatals, devaluation of currency, and the abolition of labor and trade unions. These policies, according to the Bank and the Fund, were aimed at promoting a "free market economy" throughout the Third World, but in reality, these policies created situations where western multinational corporations would be able to penetrate and control these debtor nations' economies for the benefit of western corporations.

Coercing weak and vulnerable nations to accepting these loans has become one of the ways to boost Western economies, especially when these countries' corporations are contracted by the Bank or the Fund to execute those capital intensive projects that the borrowing countries have articulated. These long and short-term loans attract huge interests, which increase the initial principal amounts borrowed. The accruing interests place a huge burden on the borrowing nations, which in most cases are unable to pay off those debts at the stipulated time-frame and, for this reason, the debts keep quadrupling.

Because many Third World countries were unable to meet their debt payments, which resulted from the boom in lending to these countries, the Bank and the Fund resorted to a "series of disguised defaults, rescheduling, rolled-over loans, new loans, debt plans, and programs, all with the goal of helping the debtor countries get back on their feet," but from all indications, this was not the case.

Under this arrangement, the debtor nations were made to pay more than they bargained for. Hiatt (2007) states in his work that the "Third World debt increased from $130 billion in 1973 to $612 billion in 1982 to $3.2 trillion in 2006." He further noted that, in the end, "Third World countries pay more than $375 billion a year in debt service, twenty times the amount of foreign aid they receive. This system has been called a 'Marshall Plan' in reverse, with the countries of the Global South subsidizing the wealthy North, even as half the world's population lives on less than $2 a day" (p.19).

Nigeria is a typical example of this intrigue. "The country's debts in the early 1980s ballooned to more than $35 billion due to penalties and late fees during the 1990s" (*BBC News*, 2006). In spite of the huge revenue derived from oil and gas sales, the Nigerian government, at the time, was unable to pay off its World Bank loans and other loans the country borrowed from other private sources like the Paris Club and London Club until in 2006, when the Olusegun Obasanjo administration renegotiated the terms of the loan and "paid almost $20 billion to two giant international syndicates: Paris Club and London Club of Creditors to settle her foreign debts." Chiakwelu (n.d.), in his article, noted that "this transfer of wealth by a relatively poor nation contradicts the entire prudent financial judgment and rudimentary economic disposition preached to Nigeria by the rich donor nations that babbles about the ills of capital flight in developing nations." For him, this was the largest transfer of wealth in modern time. As the *BBC News* reported, Nigeria's plan to pay off its debts and restructure its economy was approved by the IMF, and the debt repayment was a key part of the economic reform plan of President Olusegun Obasanjo, who was also planning a string of privatizations, tax reform, and greater transparency in order to boost the economy and attract foreign investors.

The monetary policies of the World Bank and the IMF are deeply rooted in the idea of free market economy (Laissez-Faire), or the monetarist school, which is associated with the Department of Economics at the University of Chicago--a Department popularly known within the conservative economists' circles, as the Chicago School of Economics.

This anti-government school, formerly led by Milton Friedman (1912-2006), has four basic assumptions or tenets, which suggest that 1) markets allocate resources more efficiently than any government, 2) monopolies are created by government's attempt to regulate an economy, 3) governments should avoid trying to manage aggregate demand, and 4) government should focus on maintaining a steady and low rate of growth of money supply. The School is said to rely heavily on mathematical models for its analyses, which its critics claim, gives it the leverage to prove anything it wants to (*BusinessDictionary.com*, 2010).

The economic philosophy of the Chicago School of Economics is in contrast with that of the Keynesian government-led or the guided economic development. The Chicago School of Economics favors corporate-inspired movement and tries to restore the measure of laissez-faire (neoliberalism). This economic ideology was later put into practice through public policy initiatives advanced by some Western leaders like Ronald Reagan, a former US President, Margret Thatcher, a former British Prime Minister (Hiatt, 2007, p.19), and their cronies in the Third World, such as Chile's former military dictator, Augusto Pinochet, and Nigeria's military henchman, Gen Ibrahim Babangida, to name just a few. Many of these Third World governments were coerced to embrace this neoliberal economic philosophy and one of the vehicles or instruments this anti-government school has used in advancing its conservative economic ideology and bringing Third World economies under its "Web of Control," is the World Financial Institutions, namely, the World Bank and the IMF, as was previously noted.

The architects of IMF's Structural Adjustment Program (SAP), many of whom were protégés or students of the Chicago School of Economics, have used these world financial institutions to drum up policies that brought enormous hardships to 99.9% of ordinary Nigerians and in other countries, where IMF's draconian policies were implemented. These conservative economists and their allies in government circles advanced the following views: "that suffering will occur whenever countries readjust their economies; that this suffering is a necessary part of the pain countries have to experience on their way to becoming a successful market economy; and that these measures will, in fact, reduce the pain the countries will have to face in the long run."

This is a view, which Stiglitz (2003), the former World Bank Chief Economist and Senior Vice President of the Bank (1997-2000), has debunked and refused to accept. In his penetrating and insightful book titled *Globalization and Its Discontents,* the world renowned economist stated the following:

> Undoubtedly, some pain was necessary; but in my judgment, the level of pain in developing countries created in the process of globalization and development as it has been guided by the IMF and the international economic organizations has been far greater than necessary. The backlash against globalization draws its force not only from the perceived damage done to developing countries by polices driven by ideology but also from the inequities in the global trading system. Today, a few—apart from those with vested interests who benefit from keeping out the goods produced by the poor countries—defend the hypocrisy of pretending to help developing countries by forcing them to open up their markets to the goods of the advanced industrial countries while keeping their own markets protected, policies that make the rich richer and the poor more impoverished—and increasingly angry (pp. xiv-xv).

The supply-side or trickle-down economic theory espoused by the Chicago School of Economics has been discredited and blamed for the income disparities being experienced worldwide, as critics claimed that such economic theory is responsible in making the rich richer and the poor poorer. For example, the Obama Administration and the Vatican Papacy have become the most adherent critics of the Chicago School of Economics. Pope Francis, through the *Apostolic Exhortation*, has published the most powerful critique ever of modern capitalism. On issues bordering on the importance of remembering those who are less fortunate, on the failure of traditional economic dogmas, and on exploding inequality, the Pontiff was quoted as saying the following:

> We can only praise the steps being taken to improve people's welfare in areas such as health care, education and communications. At the same time we have to remember that the majority of our contemporaries are barely living from day to day, with dire consequences....Some people continue to defend trickle-down theories which assume that economic growth, encouraged by a free market, will inevitably succeed in bringing about greater justice and inclusiveness in the world. This opinion, which has never been confirmed by the facts, expresses a crude and naïve trust in the goodness of those wielding economic powers and in the sacralized workings of the prevailing economic system. Meanwhile, the excluded are still waiting....While the earnings of a minority are growing exponentially, so too is the gap separating the majority from the prosperity enjoyed by those happy few (Apostolic Exhortation Evangelii Gaudium of the Holy Father Francis, 2013; Weisenthal, 2013).

In furthering the critique of capitalism, its dynamics and intrigues, Kern (2007) illuminated in her work the devastating human cost of cheap cell phones, resulting from the plundering and exploitation of Third World resources. In her illustrations, she claimed that

> [The] civil strife in the Democratic Republic of Congo has cost 4 million lives in the last ten years, as militias and warlords fight over the country's resources. The atrocities have been funded, at least indirectly, by some of the biggest Western corporations. They see the country as only a source of cheap coltan—vital to making semiconductors—and other minerals (p. VI).

She revealed in her work how western corporations and their governments, especially the United States of America, United Kingdom, Switzerland, Belgium, Denmark, and Canada, and corporations like Brown & Root, a subsidiary of Halliburton, the Bechtel, the American Mineral Fields (AMF), Citibank NY, the

Belgium company Cogecom, and the Canadian mining firm, Barrick Gold company, had encouraged, instigated, and funded the violence (destabilization) that had overwhelmed the Great Lake Region or the Congo Basin (Kern, 2006, pp. 99-100).

The activities of these entities included: the sponsoring of the removal of the former Congolese military dictator, Mobutu Sese Seko, and the installation of Laurent Kabila into power; the building of a military base on the Congolese/Rwandan border, where the Rwandan army has trained; the military training of the Rwandan President, Paul Kagame, by the US military at Fort Leavenworth in 1990 and providing him with $75 million in military aid after he took control of the country following the genocide of 1994; and turning a blind eye when Uganda and Rwanda invaded the Eastern part of Congo. These efforts were instituted solely to allow western corporations to gain free access and to control the Congolese strategic natural resources, which include gold, diamonds, copper, zinc, uranium, cobalt, cadmium, coltan, and timber (Kern, 2006, pp. 98-99).

These strategic natural resources have, indeed, brought more harm than good to the people of the Great Lake Region. The reason for the carnage and destruction of human lives and property, which have been raging throughout the Congo since the country gained her political independence from Belgium on June 30, 1960, is mainly due to the country's huge deposits of natural resources—resources, which outsiders have taken full advantage of in improving their socio-economic well-being of their citizens, at the expense of the indigenous people. While Western governments are preaching free market economy and liberalism in trade and commerce, they still maintain their mercantilist ideology that calls for economic independence and self-reliance. From this and other observations, a free market economy benefits the West, as Stiglitz and other critics have noted. It benefits the West because non-Western corporations have not been allowed to do business in the West, as their Western counterparts do in the developing nations.

This disparity explains why there is no reciprocity between the Global North and the Global South, when it comes to trade and other economic relations. This is the kind of behavior that has sustained an economic ideology known to most Western economists as "Economic Nationalism or Protectionism"—a system that allows Western governments to use their natural resources exclusively in assisting their local industries. Given the rhetoric of free trade and economic liberalism, one would think that this kind of economic ideology is no longer in existence (obsolete) and no longer the driving force in national public policy making. Unfortunately, this is not the case; the mercantilist economic ideology is alive and well.

For example, in 2005, the US Congress denied China's National Offshore Oil Corporation (CNOOC) the opportunity to acquire Union Oil Company of California (UNOCAL), America's seventh biggest Oil Corporation. The Chinese oil giant was prepared to buy UNOCAL, a private corporation, for a sum of $18.5 billion in cash—the highest bidder so far, but its effort was blocked. Various reasons were advanced as to why the deal could not go through. Drawing from many sources, Zhang (n.d.) gave the following summations as reasons why the CNOOC-UNOCAL deal fell apart:

- The CNOOC bid simply is not a market-based transaction because China is not a market economy;

- The Chinese government would not allow an American company take over such a Chinese company;

- The CNOOC is the corporate vehicle of a communist dictatorship; and

- CNOOC's bid for Unocal will threaten American energy security, national security, and economic independence.

Those in support of the deal saw the Congressional debate differently. They argued that "We handed China the money they are using to try to buy Unocal, and now we are telling the Chinese, please keep investing in our bonds but you can't invest in what amounts to a sliver of surplus in an oil company."

In 2006, the US Congress also denied the Dubai Ports World (DPW), a state owned company in the United Arab Emirates (UAE), the opportunity to acquire and manage six major US seaports slated for sale. The ports were said to be run and managed by Peninsular and Oriental Steam Navigation Company (P&O), a British firm. The P&O had agreed to sell these ports and other US ports that were under its authority to DPW and the sale contract was completed in March of 2006. The Bush administration even approved the deal and vigorously argued that a delay by US Congress to approve the deal would send the wrong message to US allies. This warning, however, fell on deaf ears as the US Congress and its domestic allies (special interest groups) blocked the transaction, claiming that such takeover would compromise US port security and, thereby endanger the country's national security. These are just a few examples to demonstrate that the West will preserve and protect its vital and strategic industries for its own citizens, but will like to manipulate and exploit the vital natural resources of other nations, especially the Third World nations, such as Congo and Nigeria. There is nothing wrong in protecting one's national interests, but what is wrong is when one uses a policy (free market economy and economic liberalism) s/he claims to be suitable for all nations of the world to exploit and undermine the national interests of others, especially those of weak and vulnerable nations.

Privatization Scheme: An Instrument of Neo-colonialism in Nigeria

By bowing to World Bank and IMF pressures, the Nigerian military government headed by Gen. Ibrahim Babangida plunged the country into the Western economic orbit and the privatization of government owned ventures (parastatals) became the order of the day. From that moment, the Nigerian government abandoned its responsibility of making sure that the four existing oil refineries in the country were functional, as they should. The privatization of the country's oil sector and other government parastatals became the center of attraction; it attracted all attentions to itself; and brought untold hardships on the lives of millions of Nigerians.

The Nigerian leadership must be held accountable for not looking out for the interests of the Nigerian people like its Western counterparts always do. The Nigerian ruling elites, like their counterparts in most African countries, have chosen to defend privatization—a slogan known in the United States as "Reaganomics" or trickle-down economy—a theory that stipulates that "financial benefits given to big business will in turn pass down to smaller businesses and consumers" (*Webster's Ninth Collegiate Dictionary,* 1984). As noted above, it is a theory that has failed to deliver what it promises.

The privatization of the country's strategic natural resources is not benefiting the people; rather, it is making them poorer and poorer and more dependent on foreign governments and corporations. Privatization cannot make Nigeria a self-sufficient and reliant nation; instead, it opens the country up to more exploitation and manipulation. It is an obvious fact that Africa is the richest continent in the world in terms of strategic natural resources, but her people are the poorest in the world. These strategic natural resources include Cobalt, Oil, Iron-ore, Uranium, Bauxite, Manganese, Platinum, Gold, Valium, Chromium, Col-tan or Columbite-tantalite, and Diamond just to mention a few. These are resources the Western world and others are exploiting for their own economic development and well-being. This is being done at the expense of Africa's development and progress. The reason this is happening is because most African leaders are busy accumulating personal wealth and simply don't care about what happens to their countries and people. By failing to protect their nations' national interests, these African leaders are viewed as agents and surrogates of foreign powers, whom the foreign powers are using to undermine the sovereignty of the African states.

Nwachukwu (2000), in his publication, points out that the supporters of privatization (free market economy) in Nigeria have made similar arguments advanced by their European and North American counterparts. The central arguments of this anti-government school of thought are as follows:

[That] privatization came from a combination of disillusionment with the result of state ownership and from the belief that private ownership would bring substantial economic benefits. Government and state owned enterprises were viewed as highly inefficient, slow at developing and introducing new technologies, subject to over-frequent and damaging political intervention. Privatization seemed to offer a means of ridding government of the financial burden of loss making activities, while at the same time, spreading the share ownership to private individuals and investors (pp. 13-15).

Drawing from other sources, Nwachukwu further defined privatization as "the sale of government owned enterprises to private individuals which represents the private sector. The idea behind the privatization programme is to transfer the burden of financing and sustaining these enterprises (a load which was too heavy on the government to shoulder) to private individuals. In essence, government shifted the risks associated in the running and management of these enterprises to the private sector."

Supporters of privatization have always maintained that privatization will be sustained if built on Reaganomics' four economic pillars, which according to Ferrara (2011), included: 1) cutting tax rates to restore incentives for economic growth; 2) reducing government spending to eliminate deficits and national debt burden; 3) promoting anti-inflation monetary policy to maintain a strong and more stable monetary value; and 4) deregulating government's policies that hinder productivity. Proponents of this school of thought (the Chicago School of Economics) felt that government over-spending philosophy on social issues inhibit economic growth. They viewed government as being too big and intrusive in people's lives and freedom. They see government as creating lazy and unproductive citizens by providing such people with "free government handouts." Ironically, what these corporate elite (the anti-government group) have failed to acknowledge is that their corporations benefited the most from government programs (subsidies) than the poor and the powerless they always vilify and demonize.

Based on these false notions that privatization of government businesses is the way forward and the cure for the economic woes plaguing Nigerian economic growth, the Babangida regime, subsequent military regimes, and civilian administrations implemented the IMF Structural Adjustment Programs by embarking on a massive privatization scheme of the country's strategic industries and government's parastatals, such as the Iron and Steel Industry, the Oil Industry, the former Nigerian Electric Power Authority (NEPA), whose name was later changed to Power Holding Company of Nigeria (PHCN), the Nigerian Ports Authority (NPA), the Banking and Insurance Industry, the Nigerian Telecommunications sector, Education and the Health Care industry, and the list goes on.

The Olusegun Obasanjo administration did not halt the privatization scheme in his eight years in office as the Executive President of the country; rather, his administration intensified the implementation of the IMF policy. The administration brags today that its effort to privatize the Nigerian Telecommunications has paid off, and that most Nigerians have more access to cell phones than ever before. The questions that must be raised to address these issues are: at what cost? Who are the beneficiaries of this venture? The privatization of the Nigerian Telecommunications has not benefited most Nigerians because of the costs involved in making the calls. In spite of the draw backs of privatization, the policy continues to be enforced without examining its adverse effects on the Nigerian economy and people. Privatization may be good for the Western economy, but bad for the Nigerian economy. It has neither improved the Nigerian economy nor enhanced the quality of lives of the Nigerian people, as promised by supporters of SAP. Today, normal life in Nigeria has become a "living hell" for most Nigerians.

In the United States, for instance, whenever large private corporations run into financial difficulties (like the Great Depression of 1929-1939, the 2008-2012 recessions, and the September 11, 2001 terrorist attacks on the American soil) they have always sought for government's assistance because, within the government circles, most of these corporations are considered as being "too big to fail." On the issue of the 2008-2012 recession, those US corporations (the Wall Street Bankers and Insurance Companies and their clientele, including the Auto industries), that were directly responsible for the recession, which resulted from corporate greed and bad policies, asked for and received billions of US dollars in government bailouts to keep themselves afloat.

The same principle applies to the airline industry and its clientele, which received billions of US dollars from the economic stimulus package for the 9-11 terrorist attacks on the US soil. The airline industry was devastated as a result of the attacks, because all airlines were grounded for days and that meant heavy losses for the industry. The rationale for these bailouts is based on a notion that, if government allows corporations to go under, the economic impact of such a collapse will be devastating to the country's economy and there will be, for instance, a massive layoff of workers. No government operatives can sustain a huge unemployment rate without being forced out of office. This is one singular factor that induces governments to consider instituting a bailout package to corporations if and when the country's economy experiences distress.

National disasters, such as hurricanes, tornados, massive floods and wild fires are other areas that get the attention of most governments. The US government, for example, has always assisted companies and individuals who lost their homes and businesses due to these natural disasters. For example, Hurricane Andrew (1992) cost $26 billion in damages;

Hurricane Katrina (2005), cost $110 billion in damages; Hurricane Isaac (2012) was estimated to have cost $2 billion; and Hurricane Sandy (2012) was said to have cost $60 billion in damages (FAQs n.d., Buhayar, 2012; Business Time, 2012, and Padgett, 2012). In these cases and in other similar cases, the US Federal Emergency Management Agency (FEMA) assisted those who were directly affected by these natural disasters in numerous ways, to rehabilitate them. Through FEMA, the US government provides the victims with a variety of vital assistance.

For example, the agency provided temporary shelters to those individuals who lost their homes due to hurricanes, flooding or tornados. It assists victims in wreckage removal, providing guidelines on how to avoid disaster scams, guiding victims on how to rebuild, providing food assistance, providing business loans to those eligible through the Small Business Administration, and providing vital contact telephone numbers of other federal agencies like the Federal Public Health Response and the Red Cross (USA.gov, 2012). Folks, this is just one of the many ways government has become essential and relevant.

These are types of assistance that private corporations cannot provide to the masses, and the provision of these services by governments makes them unique institutions. Corporate greed (corruption), and lack of accountability and transparency, resulting from the removal of the regulative regime by the Reagan administration in the 1980s, and the Bush tax cuts for millionaires were directly responsible for the US economy meltdown in 2007/2008. The two major wars the US government is currently waging in Iraq and Afghanistan, costing trillions of US dollars, are also directly responsible for the collapse of the US economy which, in itself, has adversely affected the economy of the world.

The 2008 US government massive bailouts to US ailing corporations is not something new in the history of the United States of America. On December 20, 1979, President Jimmy Carter signed into law the Chrysler Corporation Loan Guarantee Act. This Congressional Act forestalled the collapse of Chrysler Corporation, the country's third largest automaker, whose crisis emanated from corporate greed and mismanagement. As usual, the working class was blamed for the near-collapse of the industry, while no blame was leveled at the administration and management of the company, or the Chrysler Chief Executive Officer (CEO), Lee Iacocca, "who soon after the bailout, was making millions of dollars even as he ruthlessly axed tens of thousands of jobs" (Eley, 2008).

Another government bailout occurred in 1989 under President George Herbert Walker Bush. This time, it was the Savings and Loan industry that was resuscitated with taxpayers' money for the mismanagement and plundering of the industry's assets by the very corporate elite who have always claimed that corporations are far better and efficiently administered than government owned businesses. Zepezauer and Naiman (1996) outlined, in their book, a series of subsidies US corporations had received from the US government. These subsidies range from nuclear, aviation, mining, oil and gas, export, synfuel, timber to ozone tax exemptions, and the list goes on. As we have seen, it is not the token amount of money the US government spends on its middle class and the poor that brought the US economy to a brink, as the anti-government pundits would have you believe. The trickle down economic philosophy is the source of the US economic meltdown, which also affected the world economy.

The trickle-down ideology has not worked and will never work as long as the greedy nature of the corporate class is not curtailed. As noted by Zepezauer and Naiman, the US government has always provided these corporations with enormous incentives they need to create jobs, but instead of creating more jobs, they ship jobs overseas, where labor is extremely cheap.

The greedy nature of the corporate class in the West has spurred the growth of anti-capitalist movements throughout Europe and North America. The 2007/2008 recession, resulting from massive corporate greed, has forced many Americans to lose their homes and leaving millions of them unemployed, thereby, creating the "new poor." In examining the consequences of the 2007/2008 economic downturn in the US, brought about by corporate greed and prevailing anti-government sentiments, which dominated the American moral psyche, Smiley and West (2012) revealed that too many middle class Americans are now becoming new members of the poor class.

> The "new poor" find themselves standing shoulder to shoulder at the welfare office, food pantry, or thrift store with people they used to disregard [the poor]. As the politicians they elected predict a doomed "entitlement nation" and boast of shredding the poor's safety nets, the former middle class tries to reconcile these contradictions by clinging to the belief that this is a temporary destination, that somehow "they" are still better than "those people" (pp. 8-9).

The "new poor" (Middle class) have always seen themselves as doing well in the society due to their work ethics. They demonized and vilified the poor whom they often described as "lazy people" who solely depended on government handouts. Members of the middle class also blamed the poor for being the source of their problems.

Today, middle class America is learning the hard facts that the problems of the poor are systemic and not by personal choice. The 2007/2008 recession has really changed middle class America's thought process. Middle class America has now realized that "poverty is no longer confined by class or color; like an unrestrained and deadly virus, it doesn't discriminate," and that "the faces of poverty are no longer solely relegated to the easily maligned black, red, or brown people. Poverty of all colors abounds unchecked in our cities, suburbs, and rural communities with ever-growing shameful numbers of impoverished children joining its ranks" (Smiley and West, 2012: 10).

Despite the recession, Americans are learning that still "one percent of the nation's richest individuals control 42 percent of the country's wealth." This is an attestation that "America was a corporation before it was a country." Smiley and West also conclude that "because economic injustice in America has been overshadowed by greed; because unequal taxation benefits the rich at the expense of everyone else; and because our political system has become so paralyzed and acquiescent to a culture of greed and moral decay—the people are fighting back." The rise of the "Occupying Wall Street," a movement which overtook many American cities in 2011/2012 and the massive protests in Greece, Spain, Italy, Portugal, and Ireland during these periods are attestations to the previous assertions and a typical example of what ordinary Europeans and Americans are thinking about privatization and the austerity measures being imposed on them by their government operatives who happen to be surrogates of the corporate class and the IMF/World Bank institutions.

The US corporate elite have never complained about the numerous incentives they receive from their government, but they are quick to condemn other government programs meant to enhance the quality of lives of the poor and the less privileged. In addition, Western governments, especially the US government, spent billions of dollars annually in military armaments for the defense of Western corporations overseas. For instance, most of the US wars in the developing world, such as Africa, Asia, Middle East, Latin America, and South America are fought in the defense of US corporations, especially those corporations that are in the oil and gas and mining sectors. Defending corporations abroad has become a major part of the national interests' rhetoric of the US foreign policy (Stone and Kuznick, 2012).

Whenever wars could not be used to advance western interests abroad, covert or clandestine activities, such as military coups and social unrests would be used, as an alternative means of removing Third World leaders (regime change) whom western governments perceived to be harboring anti-western sentiments or whom they perceived to be members of the Communist movement, or terrorist sympathizers. For example, Kwame Nkrumah of Ghana, Patrice Lumumba of Congo, Saddam Hussein of Iraq, Gen. Murtala Mohammed of Nigeria, Muammar al-Gaddafi of Libya were all viewed as working against western interests in their respective countries and, consequently, decisions were made in Washington D.C. and in other European capitals to eliminate these leaders from the world scene through military coups, or direct military invasions and, in most cases, these assassinations were often executed by local cronies of foreign powers.

Hiatt (2007) listed several methods Western corporations and their governments have used to maintain control in the global system, which they created as an empire of theirs. These methods include: divide and rule; private or semi-official military force; exploring ethnic or religious division within a country; terrorism; eliminating uncooperative or ambitious Third World leaders; coup d'état; civil war by proxy, using a combination of terrorism and guerrilla warfare to overthrow the government or to wear down the population through a war of attrition that can only be ended by electoral defeat or negotiations; and direct military intervention (pp. 25-28).

The US foreign military bases are also established around the world to sustain US hegemony. (Paul, 2008; and Bennis, 2006), meaning the dominance of the world economy to enable US Multinational Corporations (MNCs) and the corporations of its Western allies gain access to the strategic natural resources found in every part of the globe, especially in the developing world. The invasion of Iraq in 2003, for instance, was executed for the singular purpose of controlling Iraq's oil reserves, but not the propaganda the Bush-Blair administrations advanced in ousting Saddam Hussein from power.

It was not the democratization of Iraq as they claimed, but the control of Iraq's oil that spurred the invasion. It was a similar story in Iran in 1953, when the Eisenhower-Churchill administrations ousted a democratically elected government headed by Prime Minister Mohammad Mossadegh through a military coup, because the Iranian government nationalized its oil, once controlled by the British Petroleum (Stone and Kuznick, 2012).

The primary intent of SAP, according to Stiglitz and other critics, is to force Third World nations to open up their economies to Western investors who then seize the opportunity to plunder the resources of these nations under the codenames of "free trade, job creation, and transfer of technology." Indeed, privatization in Nigeria has caused more harm than good. The privatization scheme in Nigeria is the leading source of impoverishment and corruption in the country.

First, it undermined the 1972 Indigenization Degree that allowed certain strategic industries, such as Oil and Gas, Iron and Steel, Telecommunications, and Banks to be reserved for Nigerian citizens. Under the privatization program, vital Nigerian industries are once again under the control of foreign investors, whose objectives are clear: the exploitation of the wealth and riches of the country for their own benefits. These foreign investors are only interested in taking what they can get from the country without reinvesting some of the profits they earned in the local population, as a way of empowering these local communities economically as well as enhancing their socioeconomic well-being.

Rather than giving back to these local communities from where their wealth and profits are generated, most foreign corporations, especially those in the oil and gas sector of the economy, leave these communities ruined by polluting their environment and leaving them to their own fate. In part, these foreign corporations should not share all the blame.

The Nigerian authorities should be the one to demand that these corporations, both foreign and domestic, reinvest in the communities from where they earned their profit.

The Nigerian authorities should have been the ones demanding for the clean-up of the polluted areas of the country from those directly responsible for such environmental degradation and disaster. Nigerians know vividly well why the Nigerian authorities have failed to demand for such reciprocity; it is because their consciences have been bought over by the bribe they received from these foreign investors, especially those in the oil and gas sector.

Second, the implementation of SAP in Nigeria has escalated corruption in the country. Nigerians have seen the unprecedented amount of corruption SAP brought to bear since it went into effect in the 1980s. Today, Nigerians are witnessing how foreign companies (Halliburton, a US company; Siemens, a German company; Safran, a French company; and other unrevealed foreign companies) have been bribing the Nigerian government officials simply to gain access to the country's strategic natural resources. This kind of behavior cannot be tolerated in the home countries' of these foreign companies, as demonstrated above in the cases of CNOOC-UNOCAL and the Dubai Ports World.

Nigerians have witnessed the massive corruption plaguing the oil industry where phony companies, not registered with the Corporate Affairs Commission (CAC) or with the Petroleum Products Pricing and Regulatory Agency (PPPRA), were paid billions of Naira for services they did not render. Under the oil subsidy probe, Nigerians have also learned that those indicted over the mismanagement of the fuel subsidy regime are sons and relatives of top government officials and politicians (the untouchables or the sacred cows).

According to Daniel (2012), the government has adopted a subtle method to stop further disclosure of the identities of the owners of the indicted companies by the House of Representatives Ad-hoc Committee on Fuel Subsidy regime.

Daniel also noted that the files of 87 out of 143 companies indicted by the Lawan Farouk-led committee had been removed from the CAC's shelf and put away with a notice saying that the files were not available for public scrutiny.

Nnochiri (2012), in his own article, quoted Oby Ezekwesili, the former Vice-President of the World Bank for Africa, as saying that Nigeria has lost more than $400 billion to oil thieves since the country gained her political independence in 1960. Nigerians are also aware of how the so-called "new generation banks" floated around the country during the 1980s and 1990s, due to the privatization scheme, looted depositors' lifetime savings and went into liquidation, thereby, leaving depositors to their own fate. Nigerians are equally aware of the many billions of Naira siphoned from the Federal Pension Scheme by the very people who were to oversee the Fund's activities.

Third, the ruling elite in the country has used the privatization scheme to amass personal wealth for themselves. They bought government properties at below market value; they also used this means to patronize party members, friends, and relatives, as some party members were awarded oil block wells, others were allocated government lands and the list goes on, while a vast majority of Nigerians were left with nothing. A case in point, is the Ajaokuta Steel Complex, one of the country's prime state enterprises, costing the Federal Government over $4.7 billion to build, but was later sold at $300 million. The sale of this vital resource for less than its value prompted the former Speaker of the House of Representatives, Dimeji Bankole, to make the following statements: "the sale of government asset (the Steel Complex) for less than its value was a product of unjust law and an example of how things were not properly done in the country" (Aderinokun, 2008).

The sale of the Steel Complex was instituted by the Obasanjo administration, another champion of privatization, who helped in dismounting and frustrating government's activities in the country. When President Obasanjo ran for his second term in office, he promised Nigerians that his administration would raise the profile of the country's electricity and power to a height never seen before. After his successful election in 2003, $16 billion was appropriated to get the job done, but to the dismay of many Nigerians, the electricity power problem became worse than ever. In his own words, the former House Speaker, Bankole, lamented that "despite the huge amount of money sunk into the power project, the nation now generates less than the megawatts of electricity generated ten years ago." This sentiment led to a House of Representatives investigation, where it was discovered that the Obasanjo administration only released $13.5 billion out of the $16 billion appropriated "with no identifiable projects and results."

It is absurd that up till today, no one, not even the former president himself, can give an account of where the money went. If the appropriated amount meant to revamp the country's power supply was utilized as it should, surely significant improvements and changes in that sector would have been recorded.

This is a typical example of how leaders responsible for government operations, those who are supposed to make government work and become efficient, end up looting its funds and turn round to blame the very institution for being too bureaucratic, incompetent, corrupt, inefficient and wasteful. These are the adjectives the governing class uses to discredit the important roles government plays in any given society.

The recent sale of Power Holding Company of Nigeria's (PHCN) plants to private companies in Nigeria with their foreign subsidiaries is another clear indication of how government parastatals are sold for less than market value. It was said that the six companies (Transnational Corporation of Nigeria Plc., Amperion Consortium, CMEC/Eurafric Energy JV Consortium, JBN-NESTOIL Power Services Limited, Mainstream Energy Solutions Limited, and North-South Power Company Limited) that emerged, as bid winners of the sale of PHCN, offered a total sum of N107 billion for the five electricity generating plants sold in auction (Amaefule, 2012). The amount of proceeds realized from the sale of these five generating plants was far less than the amount the Federal Government of Nigeria invested in these plants over the years. The beneficiaries of this deal are friends and associates of the country's ruling elite who favored the privatization of the country's precious assets.

The Transcorp/Woodrock/Sumbion/Media/PSL/Thomassen was said to have bought part of the Ughelli Power Plc for $300 million; Amperion Consortium bought the Geregu Power Plc for $132 million and bought the other part of Ughelli Power Plc for $252 million; The Mainstream Energy Solution Limited bought the Kainji Hydro power Plc for over $50.760 million in annual fee and a commencement fee of $257 million; The CMEC/Eurafric Energy JV Consortium bought part of the Sapele Power Plc for $201 million, while the JBN-NESTOIL Power Services Limited bought the other part of Sapele Power Plc for $106.5 million. The leading architect of the Nigerian privatization scheme, General Babangida, and his associates benefited from the sale as well. The North-South Power Company Limited, Babangida's company, bought the Shiroro Hydro Power Plc for over $23.602 million in fixed annual fee and a commencement fee of over $111.664 million (Anumihe, 2012; Usigbe, 2012).

Another ten Distribution Power Companies of the PHCN were also sold for N197.25 billion to six Nigerian companies and their foreign subsidiaries. It was reported that the former Military Head of State, Gen. Abdulsalami Abubakar's company, the Integrated Energy Distribution and Marketing Limited, won four of the ten electricity distribution firms. These distribution firms, according to Subair (2012), were Ibadan, Eko, Ikeja, and Yola. The Emeka Offor Company, the Interstate Electrics, won the Abuja and Enugu distribution companies. The Gbolade Osibodu Company, Vigeo Power Consortium, won the Benin distribution company. Other winning companies included: the Aura Energy Limited, which won the Jos distribution company; the Sahelian Power SPV won the Kano distribution company; and the Power Consortium won the Port Harcourt distribution company.

The bidding exercise did not go down well with some states' governors. For example, the governors of Edo, Delta, Ekiti and Ondo rejected the decision of the Bureau of Public Enterprises (BPE), which indicated that the Vigeo Power Consortium was the successful winner of the Benin Electric distribution firm. The governors called into question the bidding processes, which they claimed were fraudulent. They argued that the Vigeo Power Consortium did not meet the criteria, as established by the Technical Committee of the National Council on Privatization (NCP). The criteria stipulated that for a firm to win a bid, such a firm must demonstrate competency in the following areas: technical competency, state participation, on the ground knowledge, and financial competency. The governors were said to have made the following statements jointly, claiming that:

> States were allowed to participate in the privatization exercise after exhaustive deliberations and consequent recognition of the value that the states were uniquely positioned to add to the success of the post privatization of utilities mostly in the troubled areas particularly, the Niger Delta Region. Some of these include Right of Way, rural electrification, legislation against theft and vandalism, policing to improve collection.... Our states have invested heavily in power generations, transmission and distribution across the length and breadth of our respective states as we recognize the importance of power as the pre-condition for socioeconomic growth and industrialization of our states. We participated and came out as the most technically competent and have the consortium that is most suited to the peculiarities of our states (Amodu, 2012).

The four states were major investors in the Southern Electric Distribution Company that lost out in the bidding process. By the same token, the South East governors were shocked when the names of the bid winners were made public (Opara, 2012).

While wondering why their company, the Eastern Electric Nigeria Limited lost out in the bidding, they expressed disappointment with the process and questioned why the Integrated Energy Distribution and Marketing Limited got four electric distribution firms, claiming that, that was a clear violation of the rule. The laid down rule stated that no bidder should be given more than two power distribution firms.

Based on the pressures from these states, and given the fact that the rule was clear that no bidder should be allotted more than two slots, General Abubakar's company, the Integrated Energy Distribution and Marketing Limited, reconsidered its gains. Emejo (2012) noted in his article that out of the four power distribution firms that the company acquired initially, the company has indicated a preference of retaining the Ibadan and Yola power distribution firms, while opting to forgo the Ikeja and Eko distribution companies. When the final list was later released by the NCP on Monday, October 29, 2012, a different list of winners emerged. Here are the names of winners and the distribution companies they acquired in the process:

- Integrated Energy Distribution and Marketing Limited took over the Ibadan and Yola distributing companies;
- KANN Consortium Utility Company Limited got the Abuja distribution company;
- Vigeo Power Consortium got the Benin distribution company;
- West Power and Gas took over the Eko distribution company;
- Interstate Electrics won the Enugu distribution company;
- NEDC/KEPCO got the Ikeja distribution company;
- Aura Energy Limited took over the Jos distribution company; and
- Sahelian Power SPV Limited took over both the Kano and Port Harcourt distribution companies respectively (Usigbe, 2012).

Folks, how can Nigeria build and sustain a viable manufacturing or industrial base when steel and energy are being decimated? The above narratives explain how the country's vital resources are being dismounted by the anti-government elite, when Nigerian private corporations do not have the expertise to execute the tasks of generating a constant supply of electricity.

The first priority should have been to train more Nigerians to acquire the necessary and needed skills and technology in managing the energy sector before embarking on privatizing it. Who benefits from this exercise? Of course, it is the foreign corporations (subsidiaries). The Nigerian corporate elite have failed to learn from the debacle of the Indigenization Decree, where many newly acquired companies by Nigerians went into liquidation because owners of these newly acquired businesses did not have the necessary managerial skills to run such companies. Inadequate business practices and other environmental factors like lack of good access road, lack of frequent power supply, and lack of sound government regulatory policies contributed immensely in the liquidation of these companies.

Ironically, most supporters of privatization in Nigeria benefited from government programs, such as free education, free housing scheme, and tax breaks. These people who now resent government programs would not have gotten to where they are today if it were not for the government assistance they received during their early years in life. The fact is that, virtually every Nigerian came from a poor background before and after independence. Without government programs aimed at improving the living standard of the people, most members of this anti-government group may not have been in the position they find themselves today. They have forgotten where they came from and how they got to where they are today. This is the reality of life which is unfortunate.

Most rich Nigerians today are tax dodgers; they are not giving back to the country what they received from it. Beneficiaries of government programs are the ones who now hate government programs aimed at improving the quality of lives of ordinary Nigerians. For instance, most Nigerian military leaders who ruled the country are today turning their backs away from government and vilifying the very institution that benefited them the most. These individuals have forgotten that their military training home and abroad, the education they received, and their lavish lifestyles were all paid for by government funds. The social amenities they enjoyed in their barracks and the free meals they received in their officers' canteens or mess, the free housing units, and free medical care they received were also parts of government programs. The Nigerian government had always been there for the people, providing services that no other institution was willing to undertake, until this "poisonous pill" (privatization of government parastatals) was injected into the Nigerian economic psyche by the so-called American-trained business administrators who dominated the country's business elite class in the 1980s.

This anti-government school must understand that government has an important role to play in peoples' life, especially when it comes to raising the living standard of its citizens and providing for the common good of all people. Private corporations, the so-called highly efficient and effective organizations, would always run to the very institution (government) they resent so much for rescue, whenever they encounter financial difficulties. For example, it was the Nigerian government that came to the rescue of the eight so-called "mega banks" (Afribank, Bank PHB, FinBank, Intercontinental Bank, Oceanic Bank, Spring Bank, Union Bank, and Unity Bank) when these banks came close to collapse in 2005/2006—a financial difficulty they encountered due to corporate greed and mismanagement.

To save these banks, the Nigerian government injected the sum of N620 billion to keep them afloat. Yet, the anti-government clique still claim that government is the problem, irrelevant and should be done away with.

Rather than undermining the role of government by dismounting its activities, the anti-government movement in Nigeria should help in improving its efficiency and effectiveness. They should work harmoniously with the institution in order to use its enormous resources and leverage to build a formidable and independent entrepreneurial base in Nigeria just as major Western countries, Japan, and now China did in their early developmental histories.

The sale of government assets to a few selected individual companies in Nigeria is not the best option because these local companies do not have what it takes to compete globally. When Nigerian companies win local contracts, say in road construction or in oil well drilling, they usually look for foreign companies to do the job for them.

The reason is because these local companies lack the needed expertise to execute those tasks. Because Nigerian local companies do not have the necessary expertise, they are often cheated and treated as junior partners by their foreign partners and, the bulk of profits generated from these projects are usually transferred overseas.

Nigerians will benefit tremendously if they do things for themselves rather than depending on foreigners to do those things for them. This is what is done in most advanced countries and in the newly emerging economies of the world, except in Nigeria. This is what self-reliance means, solving your domestic problems by yourself. Self-reliance also entails sacrificing and living within one's limit.

The Nigerian government should and must empower its indigenous inventors and scientists like Dr. Ezekiel Izuogu and his kind to help build the industrial base the country desperately needs. If Izuogu's effort and the efforts of other indigenous inventors such as those scientists who built the Biafran homemade "weapons of mass destruction" (Ogbunigwe) were supported by government grants after the Nigerian Civil War, perhaps, today, the country would have gained some home-grown technological know-how in military weaponry and science. If the corporate elite in Nigeria expect foreign corporations to transfer these vital technological skills to the Nigerian workers, they better think again.

It is interesting to note that the very people who awarded oil contracts to Multinational Corporations (MNCs) are the same people complaining today that these oil companies are not showing any willingness to help the country in rebuilding and maintaining its oil refineries to boost oil refined products in the country. Why would they help the country boost its oil refineries, when doing so would adversely affect their economic interests and profit?

For Nigeria to break through this barrier, the attitudes of the Nigerian governing elite that strangulate Nigeria's government activities must change. They must allow the government to invest adequately in its people's socioeconomic well-being. They must encourage government to develop research and production centers; they must encourage government to give Universities and Colleges "land grant status," and to do exactly what Brazil, China, Iraq under Saddam Hussein, Iran, and the Asian Tigers (Taiwan, Malaysia, South Korea and Singapore) have done to become self-reliant nations. These nations relied heavily on the technical skills of their indigenous populations to build, extract, and process their strategic natural resources rather than utilizing foreign expertise to develop such strategic resources that are essential elements of the country's national security. To achieve this feat, these nations invested heavily in the education of their local population, especially in the areas of Science, Technology, Engineering, and Mathematics (STEM). This is exactly what the Nigerian government operatives should have done with the country's huge oil revenue instead of diverting such revenues to personal overseas' bank accounts.

The author of this book agrees with the statements attributed to the IMF Senior Resident Representative in Nigeria, Scott Rogers, who addressed the Nigerian Journalists in Abuja on November 2, 2012, on the topic of "World Economic Outlook" and its impact on Nigerian economy. The IMF boss was quoted as saying that:

> The funds spent on petroleum subsidy could be redeployed to other critical sectors. Wouldn't you like to have a better-funded educational sector? Wouldn't you like a better health sector? Better transport system? Nigerians have to make a choice. Nigerians have to decide for themselves...The nation's wealth is not as much as some people think. The resources from oil which are depleting assets must be deployed to the expansion of the nation's economic base (Gabriel and Ujah, 2012).

Conventional wisdom dictates that Nigeria will never become a vibrant state if it cannot save some of its national surpluses for a rainy day. It is not a sound public policy for the country to keep on spending recklessly its vital oil revenues at the rate it is going without facing grave consequences down the road. Nigerians cannot keep borrowing money from international financial institutions or from foreign governments just to feed their corrupt and embezzlement habits or culture.

Under normal circumstances, Nigeria does not need anyone to lecture her about the importance of saving for the future but, because the country has not been blessed lately with visionary leaders who can steer the country in the right direction, the warning coming from the IMF Senior Resident Representative in

Nigeria becomes very crucial. The present administration should heed his advice and stop spending what is meant to be saved, and to stop borrowing money from world financial institutions, at a time when the country is realizing huge revenues from the oil windfall.

For example, the billions of Naira voted by the federal government to send Nigerian students to foreign universities for graduate studies is an example of how the country is spending what is meant to be saved. On the one hand, such a program is a good idea if the country's institutions of higher learning cannot pull such programs through.

But, from all we know, some of the country's tertiary institutions are capable of producing high caliber students with quality credentials, who will not have problems competing both regionally and globally. The obvious problem is that Nigerian Universities and Colleges are lacking adequate funding, proper vision, and motivation from the ruling class, as Dr. Idowu Ola rightly articulated in his recent write-up, where he emphasizes that Nigeria has what it takes to develop its own home-grown technology, but these institutions are not encouraged and motivated by the Nigerian government to pursue this path. Individuals who want to study abroad can do so on their own personal accord or effort, while government concentrates on attracting brilliant minds from home and abroad to establish a permanent scientific and industrial base in conjunction with social engineering programs to beef up the country's development base.

Second, Nigeria has traveled this path before with little success. For example, in the 1970s, the Gowon administration introduced a Scholarship scheme known, at the time, as "Crash Program." It was a program designed to send many Nigerians to overseas' universities and colleges to study in various fields and disciplines. Since the inception of the Crash Program, similar programs have been instituted for the same objectives. The Education Trust Fund—an auxiliary program of the Petroleum Trust Fund and the Presidential Scholarship Scheme for Innovation and Development (PRESSID) are examples of such programs, where the Nigerian government voted huge sums of money to send Nigerian students to overseas' universities for studies. The Education Trust Fund provided funds for overseas training of brilliant minds from Nigerian universities. The PRESSID, which was recently instituted by the Jonathan administration, is designed to send at least 101 top (first class) graduates of Nigerian universities to the best twenty-five Universities in the world to pursue graduate degree programs in natural sciences, basic medical sciences, economics, engineering and technology, and medicine. The twenty-five Universities identified are located in three continents: Asia (Hong Kong and Japan); Europe (Switzerland and United Kingdom); and North America (Canada and United States of America).

As noted above, the ideology sounds great, but it is not what the country needs at this time. Why hasn't Nigerian leadership learned from history? Why does history keep repeating itself? Nigerian leadership has forgotten so soon that many recipients of the Gowon's Scholar Scheme in the 1970s, who went for overseas' studies, never came back to the country after the completion of their courses. Many of these individuals took up the citizenship of these countries and stayed behind to enjoy the comfort, personal growth, and safety that these societies could afford them.

Nigeria's losses became those countries' gains. These types of programs have immensely contributed to the brain drain syndrome the country is witnessing today because of the ugly conditions the average Nigerian is subjected to in the country, such as inadequate electricity and security, lack of good and well-paying jobs, lack of good schools and quality health care, inadequate transportation system, and the list goes on.

Nigerian leadership must understand that it was the human hand that built-up these overseas' Ivy League institutions that the government is sending young Nigerians to. It was the same human hand that built-up the prestige, reputation, and the high standard of education these overseas' institutions are enjoying today. These things could be done in Nigeria with the right cadre of leadership coupled with right attitudes and patriotism.

Now is the time for Nigerians to learn how to do things for themselves. Now is the time for Nigerians to start believing in themselves. Nigerians are smart people, but they lack good initiatives. They should stop being copycats and unpatriotic people. Why can't Nigerians solve their internal problems by themselves without seeking help from the outside world?

Nigeria cannot take its rightful place in the world community if her leaders do not change their attitudes and their way of life, and if the country does not stop depending on other countries for virtually everything. There are several distinguished Nigerians residing abroad who have made names for themselves in their respective professions. The Nigerian government must find ways of bringing some of these people back to the country to help in the development effort of the country. What Nigeria desperately needs now is the development of its own home-grown technology and entrepreneurial base. These distinguished Nigerians abroad could play a pivotal role in this regard. And, if funds meant for these overseas' programs are reinvested into Nigerian universities' research and development programs, such investments will definitely go a long way to boost Nigeria's technological know-how.

Money Laundering: A Weapon of Impoverishing Poor Nations

Although money laundering, illicit capital flight and tax evasion are a world-wide phenomenon, it is another significant element of corruption in Nigeria. Money laundering has been identified as one of the major transnational crimes that produces serious consequences to nation-states' economies. It is a means or vehicle that most looters of public funds have been using to hide or shield their loots from being detected by law enforcement authorities.

It is also another means businesses use in hiding their profits from being taxed. Historically, money laundering began as a business practice, which most Western banks put in place to attract huge deposits from clients all over the globe, not minding how the money was generated. The loopholes that manifested from this secret banking program in some Western countries encouraged some Western business moguls or leaders to hide their money in what is being referred to as "offshore tax havens" to evade taxation.

Drawing from many sources, Christensen (2007), noted in his work that money laundering is a means used to transfer the proceeds of crime, drug trafficking, and terrorist activities by criminal syndicates. The proceeds from these illegal activities are lodged in the same financial networks put in place decades ago by Western banks and law firms to facilitate illicit capital flight and tax evasion (p. 42). Christensen, a Jersey native, who worked in Southeast Asia and North Africa in the 1980s, as economic development analyst (professional economist) and later worked in Walbrook Trustee (Jersey) Limited, a subsidiary of Deloitte Touché, which is a global accounting firm, had this to say about what money laundering and secret banking do to countries whose revenues are looted and siphoned into these offshore banks:

> The capital market and trade liberalization programs promoted by IMF and World Bank were making it far easier for wealthy people and corporations to evade taxes. Tax havens were playing a pivotal, but hidden, role in transferring money illicitly into secret bank accounts and offshore trusts—not just benefiting the world's wealthiest and most powerful individuals and companies but also sapping the prospects for economic development in the world's poorest nations. With their wealth disappearing offshore in vast amounts, developing countries take on debt to compensate for falling tax yields. This causes a vicious cycle: slower growth rates increase both economic uncertainty and social inequality,

further increasing political risks and encouraging more capital flight. Slower growth makes it more difficult for these countries to service their external debts while maintaining public services and infrastructural investments programs. In short, offshore tax havens undermine economic growth and cause poverty (Christensen, 2007, pp.43-44).

As noted earlier, money laundering was put in place by Western banks and their allies in government to recycle the petrodollar money flowing around in the Third World, especially from the Organization of Petroleum Exporting Countries (OPEC), which Nigeria happens to be a member. This secret banking practice encouraged government officials from these countries to embezzle public funds and transfer such funds into their offshore bank accounts, where their personal identities would be hidden forever and, also to avoid paying taxes on such loots.

Money Laundering is beneficial to Western economies and bad for the economies of poor countries whose funds are looted and transferred to Western banks. It boosts Western economies and impoverishes the economies of poor countries whose funds are laundered by their local officials. Money laundering generates huge deposits to Western banks that are involved in this illegal practice. With these huge deposits, the banks are able to give out massive loans to individuals and businesses in their areas of operation and the huge interests generated from these loans amount to super profit for the lending banks.

This is how most of these Western banks make their profits. Once again, poor nations' losses due to capital flight become gains to the receiving countries' economies. Through this practice, the looted funds from the Third World nations are used to subsidize Western economy at the expense of the Third World economy. These dynamics also explain the recent massive migrations from the Third World to the First World. Because of the abject poverty being experienced in the developing nations, which resulted from massive looting of these countries' revenues, the Western world, where most of these looted funds end-up, is now experiencing unprecedented legal and illegal migrants coming mainly from the developing nations.

Western banks that profited from the looted funds from Third World nations, according to Christensen, included the following banks: Citigroup, HSBC, BNP Paribas, Credit Suisse, Standard Chartered, Deutsche Morgan Grenfell, Commerzbank, and Bank of India. These institutions were said to have benefited from Gen. Sani Abacha's laundering of Nigeria's money. Drawing from many sources, Christensen (2007) claimed that Abacha's estimated fortune was between $3 billion and $5 billion, and they were sheltered and managed by the above-named financial institutions. Christensen further proclaimed that,

About $300 million of Abacha's ill-gotten loot ended up in Jersey-based banks, which would undoubtedly have known the origin of this money and charged top dollar for managing funds for such a politically exposed person (PEP). Needless to say, when international pressure finally forced the repatriation of this looted money to Nigeria after Abacha's downfall, not a cent of the banks' fees was repaid, and not a single white –collar criminal was indicted—let alone punished in any way—for having aided and abetted one of the most flagrant crimes in Africa's recent history. Instead, the Jersey authorities trumpeted loudly how virtuous they had been in repatriating the money (p. 45).

He also pointed out that corruption on this scale taking place in the Global South (Third World countries) cannot survive without the complicity of wealthy countries' financial institutions, which have been accused by their critics "for harboring, encouraging and enticing robbers of public treasuries around the world to bring their loot for safe keeping in their dirty vaults."

The locations of some of these offshore banks can be found in places like Switzerland, Monaco, the Cayman Islands, Bermuda, and Jersey. For those of you who may not know the geographic location of Jersey—Jersey is an Island off the coast of London "just about forty five minutes flight from London." There are other offshore trusts and companies (tax havens) locations found in places like Hong Kong, London, Singapore, and New York (p. 42).

What make these offshore banking operations unique in places where they exist are the banking secrecy laws governments of those countries enacted to protect the identity of the offshore banking trusts and their clients. This massive wall of secrecy is designed to make it difficult for the investigating authorities to learn about the identities of the people behind this obscured enterprise. It is also said that the number of these offshore tax havens has increased from twenty-five in the early 1970s to seventy-two by the end of 2005, this increase was recorded as a result of the huge expansion of the financial services industry found in the Western world between the 1980s and 1990s (Christensen, 2007, p. 55).

Ironically, money laundering was not a problem for Western governments until groups from outside their reach began to manipulate the loopholes put in place to make money laundering difficult to detect. Before now, money laundering was considered within the Western banking circles as a "normal business practice," because such an exercise was generating a lot of money for those banks that used the practice to increase their profit base.

In general, money laundering was a good business until outside groups like the Bank of Credit and Commerce International (BCCI) joined the club to cut their own deals and slices. Ironically, at this time, money laundering became a criminal act—one that can no longer be tolerated in the Western world.

To deny these outside groups the opportunity of using the banking secrecy laws to advance their own interests globally, Western governments began enacting laws to frustrate the enterprise. They used their leverage at the United Nations (UN) to adopt a series of Resolutions that would limit the successes of these outside groups in what had been considered within the Western business circles as "normal business practices." The said UN Resolutions included the UN Convention against Illicit Trafficking in Narcotic Drugs and Psychotropic Substances (1988), and the Basle Statement of Principles on the Prevention of Criminal Use of the Banking System for the purpose of Money Laundering (1988). Albanese (2011) indicated in his work that,

> These [UN] agreements outlined new banking principles to be applied internationally, requiring customer identification, cooperation with police authorities, limits on bank secrecy, and the confiscation of criminal assets. The United Nations has established a Global Programme against Money Laundering, which provides technical assistance to developing countries regarding implementation of proper banking procedures, training workshops, and research and analysis. The UN also coordinates the International Money Laundering Information Network on behalf of the Financial Action Task Force, Interpol, and the World Customs Organization. The international consensus needed to agree on these principles was an important first step, which then required an enforcement mechanism (p.111).

In tracing the history of money laundering, Albanese noted that the term "money laundering" was first used in 1973 during the Watergate scandal and first appeared in a court decision in 1982. The Watergate scandal exposed President Nixon's abuse of power—it was a scandal that forced him to resign from his presidency before the expiration of his term in office.

Activities that would be considered as money laundering included the following: the use of anonymous bank accounts in permissive jurisdictions; the use of legal businesses as a front to launder illegal cash; and moving money overseas outside the banking system (p. 108). To aggressively fight the concealment of funds in order to evade taxes, the US government, according to Albanese (2011), enacted the Bank Secrecy Act of 1970, which outlined the following provisions:

- The Act required that banks must file a Currency Transaction Report (CTR) for every deposit, withdrawal, or exchange of funds more than $10,000 ;

- A Currency or Money Instrument Report (CMIR) must be filed with the US Customs Service if more than $10,000 in cash or other monetary instrument (personal or cashier's check) leaves or enters the United States, and

- A citizen holding bank accounts in foreign countries must declare them on his or her federal tax return (p. 109).

Violators of these provisions were subjected to a fine of $500,000 and/or a civil penalty. The 1970 Act gave the enforcement rights to the US Treasury Department, but mandated that such an enforcement must be assisted by the following federal agencies: Internal Revenue Service; Customs Service; Comptroller of the Currency; Federal Reserve System; Federal Deposit Insurance Corporation; Federal Home and Loan Bank Board; National Credit Union Administration; and the Securities and Exchange Commission (Albanese, 2011, p.109).

Because the 1970 Act was not aggressively enforced, as it should have, another law was passed in 1986, known as the Money Laundering Control Act—the first money laundering law ever passed in the United States. The Act labeled money laundering as a criminal act and sought the prosecution and punishment of anyone who conducts a monetary transaction knowing that the funds were derived from unlawful activity. The passage of the Act was made when the Bank of New York informed the Federal Bureau of Investigation (FBI) of a series of suspicious transfers made through the bank by a company known as Benex Worldwide, run by Semion Mogilevitch, an alleged Russian organized crime figure.

After the investigation, the agency found that more than $10 billion had been transferred by the said company through the Bank. From the same investigation, the agency also discovered that the company had skimmed billions of dollars loaned to the Russian Federation by the IMF (Albanese, 2011, p.111).

Albanese also noted that the Bank of America and other involved parties were charged and prosecuted for failing to take adequate steps to verify the accuracy of information provided by their depositors in order to ensure that the money was not a product of criminal activity. The USA Patriot Act of 2001, enacted after the terrorist attacks on US soil on September 11, 2001, was also put in place to broaden the reach of money laundering laws. The USA Patriotic Act was specifically designed to go after the Middle East terrorist groups' major sources of funding. Some of these terror groups (al-Qaeda and Osama bin Laden) were created by the US government including its Western (Great Britain) and Gulf States' allies in the 1970s, to fight their dirty war in Afghanistan against the Soviet troops whom they accused of invading and occupying the country illegally (Reeve, 1999, p. 2).

The provisions of the US Patriot Act also affected nonbanking institutions like check-cashing companies, money transmitters (Western Union and Money-Gram), jewelers, pawnbrokers, casinos, credit card companies, and issuers of traveler's checks and money orders. The Act authorized the US Treasury to boycott financial institutions in countries that were uncooperative with the control of money laundering. The law also gave the enforcement agency the power to seize the assets of foreign banks operating in the US that violate the provisions of the 2001 Act. This mandate "makes it possible to bring a money laundering case in the US, when a foreign bank or government is not cooperative" (Albanese, 2011, p.111).

After the terrorist attacks, several steps were taken by the US authorities to avoid the repeat of such attacks in the future. In military terms, the actions taken to address the 9-11 incident are known as counterterrorist measures, which entail going after the terror groups' source of funding and using military campaigns against the perpetrators of the 9-11 attacks and their supporters. The military aspect of the counterterrorist measures adopted by the US and members of its North Atlantic Treaty Organization (NATO) allies included the invasions of Afghanistan and Iraq, and covert activities the US is undertaking in Pakistan, Yemen, and Somalia.

In response to the terrorist attacks on America, President Bush made two significant speeches before the US Congress and to the nation: the first speech was delivered immediately after the attacks on 9-11; and the second speech was delivered on September 20, 2001. In his second address, President Bush was quoted as saying that:

> Our war on terror begins with al Qaeda, but it does not end there. It will not end until every terrorist group of global reach has been found, stopped and defeated. This war will not be like the war against Iraq a decade ago, with a decisive liberation of territory and a swift conclusion. It will not look like the air war above Kosovo two years ago, where no ground troops were used and not a single American was lost in combat. Our response involves far more than instant retaliation and isolated strikes. Americans should not expect one battle, but a lengthy campaign, unlike any other we have ever seen....And we will pursue nations that provide aid or safe haven to terrorism. Every nation, in every region, now has a decision to make. Either

you are with us, or you are with the terrorists. From this day forward, any nation that continues to harbor or support terrorism will be regarded by the United States as a hostile regime (Tuman, 2003, pp. 97-98).

As noted in his speech to the US Congress, President Bush identified al-Qaeda and Osama bin Laden as the Middle East terrorist group that attacked the United States of America and he labeled the group as the enemy of the United States that would be destroyed. Consequently, the USA Patriot Act became one of the weapons the administration put in place to disrupt the group's terrorist activities; it went after the group's major sources of funding.

Unfortunately, the American people were not told in that speech that it was their government, the government of United Kingdom, and their Gulf States' allies in the Middle East that created al-Qaeda and taught the group how to move money around the globe without being detected, and that it was a Muslim bank, once supported by US government and influential Americans, that helped to facilitate the Jihad against America. The one singular vehicle the US government and its allies used in accomplishing this onerous task was, according to Komisar (2007), the BCCI—a Moslem banking institution that had a global reach. The bank was owned by "a Pakistani banker, Agha Hasan Abedi, with the support of Sheikh Zayed bin Sultan al-Nahyan, ruler of the oil-rich state of Abu Dhabi and head of the United Arab Emirates" (p. 69).

The bank also had "powerful men" in government in three regions of the world: the United States of America, the United Kingdom, and the Gulf States that helped broaden its operations. For example, the Bank of America was said to be an affiliate of BCCI until the bank's illegality was publicly exposed. BCCI was later accused of doing many bad things, which ranged from gunrunning, financing Islamic jihadists to laundering money. These illegalities, according to Komisar, prompted Robert Gates, who served in the administration of George H. W. Bush as the CIA Director and later served in the administrations of George W. Bush and Barack Obama as Defense Secretary, to describe BCCI as the "Bank of Crooks and Criminals International."

The bank had wide global reach. In 1977, BCCI was said to have 146 branches in forty-three countries. Its assets, according to Komisar, rose from $200 million to $2.2 billion. By 1983, the bank had 360 offices in sixty-eight countries: 91 in Europe; 52 in the Americas; 47 in the Far East, South Asia, and Southeast Asia; 90 in the Middle East; and 80 in Africa. By the mid-1980s, the bank had more offices in seventy-three countries and had assets worth $22 billion. Komisar's analysis also revealed that BCCI used several means to lure customers to its operation. These included: the bribing of central bankers and finance ministry officials. This was done to attract foreign central banks' deposits into its vault; it sought the rights to handle a country's use of US commodity credit or special treatment on processing money transiting a country with monetary control; and it sought the rights to establish banks in countries, where foreigners were not allowed to do so. Through these methods, the BCCI was said to have corrupted many officials in several countries, such as Argentina; Bangladesh; Botswana; Brazil; Cameroon; China; Colombia; the Congo; Ghana; Guatemala; India; Ivory Coast; Jamaica; Kuwait; Lebanon; Mauritius; Morocco; Nigeria; Pakistan; Panama; Peru; Saudi Arabia; Senegal; Sri Lanka; Sudan; Suriname; Tunisia; the United Arab Emirates; the United States; Zambia; and Zimbabwe (Komisar, 2007, p.74).

Drawing from many sources, Komisar described the deep relationship between the BCCI and CIA, how the CIA used the bank to launder money from Latin America to the Middle East, the role of CIA in supporting and sustaining al-Qaeda and Osama bin Laden, and the lessons Osama bin Laden and his group learned from their relationship with the CIA. Given these obvious facts, Komisar (2007) noted in her work that,

> BCCI had in fact become one of the agency's secret bankers, handling money for covert ops all over the world. CIA Director William Casey met with Agha Hasan Abedi several times in Washington at the Madison Hotel, across the street from the Washington Post. The CIA used BCCI branches in Islamabad and elsewhere in Pakistan to funnel some of the $2 billion that Washington sent to Osama bin Laden's mujahedeen to help fight the Soviets in Afghanistan. BCCI handled the cash that Pakistani military and government officials skimmed from US aid sent to the mujahedeen. It also moved money for the Saudi intelligence services. BCCI was more than a banker for the mujahedeen. It spread cash around to assure the passage of their weapons through Karachi's port and customs. It even organized mule convoys to transport the arms into Afghanistan (p.70).

She also noted that the BCCI operations gave Osama bin Laden an education in offshore black finance that he used when he organized the jihad against America; and that the CIA was well aware of its student's capabilities. After 9-11, the US agents headed straight for al-Taqwa's operations in Switzerland, Liechtenstein, and Nassau and shut down those tax haven trusts.

Komisar described BCCI as the central banker for everyone involved in the regional black ops (meaning illegal activities); the bank was said to be running accounts for the arms and drug traffickers, the mujahedeen, the Pakistanis, and the CIA. She maintained that "the CIA money passed from the US to the al-Taqwa Bank in Nassau to Barbados to Karachi to BCCI in Islamabad." She claimed that "the al-Taqwa was not a real bank with bricks and mortar, depositors and services," but "a shell bank set up to finance the jihad and was simply a correspondent account in the Banca del Gottardo, the former Swiss subsidiary of Banco Ambrosiano (the Vatican bank), which collapsed in 1982 after looting customers' accounts of more than $1 billion" (p.71).

The CIA used BCCI to launder money in Latin America as well. For example, Reagan's National Security Council (NSC) staffer, Oliver North, was said to have set up Panamanian shell companies and secret BCCI accounts to handle payments of $20 million for arms to the Nicaraguan Contras and to Iran between 1985 and 1986. Komisar (2007) also notes that,

> As part of its illegal operation, BCCI provided more than $11million in financing for 1,250 US TOW antitank missiles sold to Iran's Revolutionary Guards in a deal to buy the release of American hostages in Lebanon. Checks signed by North were drawn on BCCI's Parish branch, which—not surprisingly—had no records of the account when US law enforcement agents later sought them. BCCI also handled Reagan-Bush administration payoffs to Panama strongman, Manuel Noriega, who became a BCCI client at the CIA suggestion. Syrian drug dealer, terrorist, and arms trafficker, Monzer al-Kassar, made a deal to sell $42 million worth of arms to Iran as part of North's plan, using BCCI's offshore Cayman Islands branch to run the cash (p. 72).

To be seen as responding to both the US laws and UN's Resolutions on money laundering, the Nigerian government enacted its own laws: the Foreign Exchange (Monitoring and Miscellaneous Provisions) Act (2004) and the Money Laundering Act (2011). Because of the secret nature and the caliber of people involved in this criminal enterprise, the arrest, prosecution, and the imprisonment of culprits have been very difficult to execute.

The enactment of these laws is designed to deceive ordinary people. It is to make them believe that their governments are doing something concrete to checkmate the problems caused by money laundering. Since the passage of the laws in Nigeria, how many government officials in high places have been arrested and convicted for money laundering? Nigerians are aware that the major perpetrators of this crime are those in high places (the sacred cows), but none of them have been apprehended and prosecuted. Generally, money launderers use middlemen (couriers) that include some banks in the country to execute their transactions; this makes it difficult for ordinary people to know the identities of these individuals, unless their middlemen are willing to disclose such information to the public, which is highly impossible because of the handsome rewards they received as payoffs. Making such a disclosure to the public means risking their lives. In most instances, couriers are forced to swear oaths of allegiance before they are sent away. Breaking such an oath means a death sentence, which most couriers are not willing to risk.

The only individual in Nigeria, whose money laundering activity was exposed, was Gen Sani Abacha. The reason is because he is no longer alive. Had he lived, his money laundering scheme would never have been exposed. He was not the only Nigerian Head of State or Nigerian public official who embezzled government funds and stashed such funds away into his offshore bank accounts, as Christensen noted in his work. Others like him have not been exposed because they are still alive and, are well connected within the Web of global control; meaning that they are still protected by the banking secrecy law, even though such a law had been abolished by some Western countries, given the international pressure brought to bear on these banks.

The international pressure on money laundering seems to have yielded some dividends, as the recent statement made in Abuja by the Swiss Ambassador to Nigeria, Hans-Rudolf Hodel, indicated. In his address, the Swiss Ambassador warned Nigerian politicians and government officials to refrain henceforth from using his country, as a safe haven, to launder Nigerian money. The seasoned Ambassador was quoted as saying the following:

> Politicians and government officials who steal from Nigerian till with the intention of salting the loot away in Swiss banks may soon have difficult times, as the Swiss government has vowed to expose public officers who stashed away looted funds in the country's banks, following the country's new laws which frown on anonymous bank accounts.... Swiss banking secrecy protects the privacy of bank clients, but it is not unlimited. If there are suspicions of criminal activities such as terrorism, organized crime, money laundering or tax fraud, it is lifted and the authorities are given access to banking information. No anonymous accounts exist in Switzerland. Money laundering was recognized as an offense in the Swiss Criminal Code since 1990. On February 1, 2009 various improvements in Switzerland's anti-money laundering arsenal came into force, enabling Switzerland to stay abreast of the more sophisticated international standards   (Okeke, 2012).

The Swiss Ambassador revealed how the funds ($700 million) looted by Abacha and deposited in Swiss banks was returned to Nigeria as well as how the World Bank participated in the review of the use of the returned looted funds. The Ambassador noted that Abba Abacha, the son of the late Head of State, had a case to answer in Geneva for supporting a criminal organization, which the Ambassador did not name. The Ambassador also informed his Nigerian audience that the funds ($700 million) recovered from Abacha's loots in his country has been reinvested in several development projects, which included: rural electrification; economic development; roads; primary health care and vaccination programs; and basic and secondary education as well as provision of potable water and rural irrigation (Okeke, 2012).

Given the enormity of money laundering in the country, given the desperation of public fund looters, and given the adverse effects money laundering has inflicted on the country's moral and social psyche, including the negative images it is creating abroad, the Central Bank of Nigeria (CBN) launched a new offensive attack on the scourge of money laundering in the country. In its recent circular to all Nigerian commercial banks, the Apex bank reminded the other banks in the country of the consequences of allowing criminals to use their financial institutions "to dry-clean their dirty laundry in bribery, extortion, embezzlement, theft, drug trafficking and terrorism" (Oke, 2012).

Money laundering, according to the Apex bank, has the capacity to seriously distort the financial market by skewing the allocation of resources in a way that may give rise to shocks and imbalances in the operation of the market. The corrosive effects of money laundering may be felt throughout the financial system, thereby undermining confidence in large measure.

The Apex bank reiterated the aggressive enforcement of the existing relevant bank laws in its circle, particularly section (48) of the Bank and Other Financial Institutions Act (BOFIA) of 2004. This section of the Act makes it clear that "any person whose appointment with a bank has been terminated or who has been dismissed for reasons of fraud, dishonesty, or conviction for an offense involving dishonesty or fraud shall not be employed by any bank in Nigeria."

The Apex bank also encouraged banks in the country to use all measures out there, particularly the Nigerian Financial Intelligence Unit (NFIU) to protect themselves from the syndicates of money laundering.

The CBN reminder came as a result of the recent increase in the activities of money launderers, which are reported daily in the nation's Newspapers. As recently as September 27, 2012, for example, many Nigerians learned how their country's money is being laundered overseas, when security operatives at the Murtala Mohammed International Airport, Lagos State, intercepted Abubakar Sheriff Tijjani, who claimed to be a courier (middle man) for twenty individuals who hired him to smuggle over $7 million in cash to Dubai, the United Arab Emirates (Adewole, 2012). There were two other arrests made after the incident of September 27, 2012. One of the arrests involved an agent of the Federal Airport Authority of

Nigeria (FAAN), Akinyele Adetuba, who claimed to have worked for the agency for five years. Serving as a courier, the accused had in his possession a sum of $1.4 million.

He claimed during interrogation that he was asked by one Ifeanyi Urama, a bureau de change operator, to assist him in moving the bag full of hard cash through the security outpost, but with the watchful eyes of the security operatives at the airport, Adetuba was apprehended and turned over to the EFCC officials for prosecution (Akinkuota, 2012). The other arrest was made on October 17, 2012, at the Aminu Kano International Airport, Kano State, where two individuals serving as couriers were arrested for trying to smuggle $107,000 out of the country. The arrested individuals were Idris Hamza and Umar Kibiya. During the arrests, Hamza had in his possession $27,000, while Kibiya had $80,000 (Adewole, 2012).

Within the same month of October, the EFCC, through its spokesperson, Wilson Uwujaren, informed the nation that the anti-graft agency had frozen a Bermuda account in the sum of over N16 million traced to an undisclosed retired Nigerian public officer, who is now standing trial in the Abuja High Court. The Island of Bermuda is an overseas' colony of the United Kingdom, located in the North Atlantic Ocean, off the East Coast of the United States of America (Musari, 2012). Two more arrests were made in the month of November 2012. In one of the arrests, two persons were said to have been arrested at the Nnamdi Azikiwe International Airport in Abuja, the Federal Capital Territory.

These individuals, Abdulrasheed Ibrahim and Hyginus Ezedimbu, were accused by the EFCC authorities for attempting to smuggle out of the country over $238, 858. Before the apprehension of Ibrahim, he was to board an Ethiopian Airline plane bound for Dubai, the United Arab Emirates with a total amount of $188, 858, but he declared only $45,000. A further search revealed that he had $143,858, which he failed to disclose. Other items found on Ibrahim, according to the EFCC's spokesperson, Wilson Uwujaren, included forty British pounds Sterling and 5753 grams of solid gold said to worth N34, 518,000. On the other hand, Ezedimbu was to travel on an Ethiopian Airline plane to China before his arrest. He was accused of having $50,000 in his possession but declared only $49,971 (Olokor, 2012).

The other arrest was made at the Murtala Muhammed International Airport, where Chukwuonu Nnameka John was apprehended for attempting to smuggle out of the country the sum of $137,435 in cash. His destination was China. The money was hidden in textbooks published in Nigeria, but Customs Area Comptroller at the Customs Command Office at the cargo wing of the airport, Eporwei Charles Edike, claimed that "the suspect was exporting the books to

China with the purpose of re-importing them" back to the country—an act, which violates a copyright law. What led to Customs' Service suspicion of the accused was when the accused did not declare the total sum of money that was in his possession; he declared only $70,000, while leaving $67,437 undeclared. The Customs Area Comptroller also informed Journalists during his address to them that "on September 27, 2012, Hassan Ganiyat Oloruntoyin and Oteh Prince Eminike were refused boarding at the currency declaration desk when they were unable to produce evidence of purchase of $270,000 and $1,040,000, respectfully" (Usim, 2012).

On November 19, 2012, another arrest on money laundering was made at the Murtala Muhammed International Airport by the Nigerian Customs officials. This time, a passenger identified as Onwuekwe Anthony Chidi was arrested when he could not give an account of how he earned the said amount of US dollars he declared at the airport, nor did he show adequate proof of his business to the Customs officer (Mikairu and Eteghe, 2012). The said passenger was to travel on a Qatar Airways flight going to Doha, in the Gulf region, with the sum of $320,000 before he was arrested and turned over to the EFCC for further investigations.

In the same month of November 2012, two more suspects were arrested at the Murtala Muhammed International Airport by the newly constituted Airport Committee Special Task Force, for trying to smuggle out of the country the following amounts of foreign currencies: 2,073,160 United States Dollars (USD) and 20,300 Saudi Arabian Riyal (SAR) .The newly constituted Task Force included the EFCC, the State Security Service (SSS), the National Drug Law Enforcement Agency (NDLEA), and the Nigerian Immigration Services (NIS). The arrested individuals were identified as Talal Hammoud and Hassan Rmaiti, who were purported to be staff members of the FAAN. The two suspects failed to declare the money to the officers on duty at the airport. The suspects and the said three bags of money found on them were handed over to the EFCC for further investigation and necessary action against the suspects (Eteghe, 2012).

On December 19, 2012, another money laundering arrest was made by the EFCC operatives at the Aminu Kano International Airport in Kano State. Bashir Abdu was arrested for failing to declare the $130,000 he was carrying with him. According to the EFCC spokesperson, Uwujaren, the arrestee only declared the gold bars with him and 30,000 Saudi Riyals he had in his possession. Abdu was said to be heading to Dubai before his arrest.

A week earlier being December 12, 2012, at the same airport (the Aminu Kano International Airport), Aminu Lamido, the eldest son of the Jigawa State Governor, Sule Lamido, was arrested for not declaring the total amount of foreign currency he had under his possession. At the time of his arrest, Lamido was carrying with him a total sum of $50,000, but he declared only $10,000 to the security authorities. Lamido was said to be heading to Cairo, Egypt before he was nabbed (Adewole, 2012).

These cases are indications of what has been happening on a daily basis at Nigeria's borders, major airports and seaports. Tijjani, Adetuba, Hamza, Kibiya, Chukwuonu, Eminike, Oloruntoyin, Ibrahim, Ezedimbu, Onwuekwe, Hammoud, Rmaiti, Abdu, and Lamido are not the only couriers out there. This is just the tip of the iceberg; there are many others who have been traveling with foreign currencies without being caught. Like the US laws on concealment of funds, which fell within the parameters of the US Bank Secrecy Law of 1970, and the US Money Laundering Control Act of 1986, the Nigerian laws (Foreign Exchange Act of 2004 and Money Laundering Act of 2011) have similar provisions, which require that persons carrying foreign currencies of more than $10,000 must report that to the Nigerian authorities at the ports of departure from the country. Abdu and others, who failed to declare their excessive amounts of foreign currencies, as required by law, violated the spirit of the law and, as such they are subjected to prosecution.

The most shocking aspect of the entire money laundering saga was the recent Newspaper report that indicated that the United States government had frozen the accounts of the Nigerian embassy in Washington D.C. and its consulate in New York "on suspicion of money laundering after traffic on the accounts raised a red flag." The American banks said to be involved in the saga included, the Bank of America, M&T Bank, and Wells Fargo. What triggered the suspicion, according to the source, was the quick withdrawal of $3.6 million which was said to have been deposited into the accounts. Within one month of deposition, the entire amount was withdrawn. Another suspicion arose when $50,000 was withdrawn in hard cash by a top embassy official. Unknown to the Nigerian officials, several US federal law enforcement agencies, including the Federal Bureau of Investigation (FBI), and the Department of Treasury, had for several months, monitored the transactions taking place in all the accounts operated by the embassy (Oladipo, 2012)

A few days after the embassy's accounts were reported frozen several Nigerian daily Newspapers reported that Nigerian diplomatic corps in Europe and North America were stranded because the Federal Government of Nigeria could not pay the salaries and allowances of its diplomatic corps, when their salaries and allowances were due. Further investigations, according to Adisa (2012), revealed that the lapses were due to the failure of the Nigerian Ministry of Foreign Affairs to remit the salaries and allowances of the foreign services staff to the respective embassies and high commissions on time. Since the Nigerian government is neither confirming nor denying the alleged frozen accounts by the US authorities and since the Nigerian diplomatic corps in Europe and North America have not been paid for two consecutive months, one is left with no other option than to conclude that the frozen account story may have been the reason why these diplomatic personnel have not been paid. This event goes to show how corruption in Nigeria has adversely damaged Nigeria's reputation abroad.

If the US government's allegation is true that Nigerian Embassies accounts in overseas' banks are used as conduits for money laundering, this means that looters in Nigeria are becoming more desperate and sophisticated. Folks, imagine what these laundered funds could positively do to the Nigerian economy if they are reinvested wisely at home? Public service, as we know it today, is being used as a code word to speed up the accumulation of personal wealth. We must not forget that these looted funds are boosting the economies of those countries where such funds are deposited at the expense of Nigeria's economy. In other words, when we send the monies we stole from our government coffer to our Switzerland, United States, United Kingdom, Canadian, or Cayman Island's bank accounts, we are simply enriching these countries' economies and impoverishing ours. It is simple logic that does not need a rocket scientist to explain.

In supporting the above assertions, the Governor of Central Bank of Nigeria, Sanusi Lamido Sanusi, while addressing an event organized by the Bank Directors Association of Nigeria in Lagos, told his audience that, in this year only (2012), about $11 billion (N1.73 trillion) had been taken out of the country through the country's airports. He queried why many Nigerians preferred carrying out transactions with the United States dollars at the expense of the local currency, the Naira? In describing how common and frequent the US dollars are being used as the country's second currency, the Governor of the Apex bank was quoted as saying the following:

> The dollar has become a second national currency. Barely two month ago in Zambia, the nation passed a law stating that anyone who refuses to accept its local currency and who charges for a transaction in a foreign currency goes to jail for ten years. But you come to Nigeria and you see people paying their children's school fees in dollars. We laugh about this but it is an important issue. Can you go to America and buy something using pound sterling? Or you go to Tokyo and use dollars and see if the hotel will accept the currency? Before they will transact with you, you must change it into their local currency. So, this is a problem, and it is a part of the fact that we are in a country where monetary and economic policies have been subjects to popular vote. In fact, it is not an election. If I want popular vote, I will go and contest for the Chairman of a local government. Everybody is an economist, a central bank governor and many more (Nnodim, 2012).

The CBN governor must be reminded (if he does not know it already) that Nigerians are people who are not proud of themselves, who lack national identify, and who glorify at what others have achieved at the expense of their own accomplishments. They patronize foreign made products and vilify theirs. They always like to identify with winners, but they don't play to win. As the governor rightly pointed out, an inferiority complex is a common thing among Nigerians and, indeed, among Africans, who are unable to determine their own destiny and who they are.

In another twist, money launderers in Nigeria are becoming more sophisticated and adapting, as the current EFCC boss, Ibrahim Lamorde, acknowledged. He noted in one of his numerous public statements that "the fight against corruption at all levels of government may not be yielding positive results as politicians are increasingly using property acquisition and investment in the hospitality business to launder the money they stole."

This is an obvious fact, but the author of this discourse contends that in as much as that is true, it is the mechanisms put in place to checkmate money laundering in Nigeria and around the globe that are responsible for this change in strategy; this means that these measures are now gradually paying off. At least, they are forcing looters of public funds to change their method of operation. With these measures in place, moving money overseas is becoming too difficult for these looters.

Critics have identified Lagos, Abuja, Port Harcourt, and Kano as major cities in Nigeria, where laundered monies are used in property acquisitions. Drawing from many sources, the *Punch Nigeria Newspaper* reporter, Ademola Alawiye (2014), made the following observations to demonstrate why looters embrace this strategy:

> Buying properties is the best form of tying money down now. The demand is always there for properties and it does not involve the risk of travelling with cash to another country. For instance, a lot of politicians will put up their houses for sale this year so as to be relevant in their parties ahead of the 2015 elections.... Unscrupulous persons involved in money laundering preferred to pay for property acquisition with cash rather than purchase them with bank instruments. The property market may collapse but it cannot be like shares; your investment in property cannot be reduced to zero whereas your investment can be reduced to zero in shares.

Therefore, investing in real estate, hotels, tourism, and in other leisure industries has become a new strategy looters of public funds in Nigeria have embraced to hide their ill-gotten fortunes. To shield their identity from law enforcement agencies, looters (politicians) are acquiring "properties in the names of their family members, protégés, loyalists, and shadow business outfits" (Alawiyo, 2014).

In the recent Federal High Court decision, rendered by Justice Adeniyi Ademola, the Court empowered the EFCC to confiscate Brifina Hotel, which was traceable to Dr. Sani Teidi, the former Director of Pension Accounts in the Office of the Head Service. This event is an attestation that public officials are hiding their loots in real estate and the hospitality industry, as the EFCC boss had alluded. EFCC's Head of Media and Publicity, Wilson Uwujaren, told reporters that the former Chief of Pension Accounts was being prosecuted for allegedly looting about N18.3 billion from the Pension funds, and the Commission investigations revealed that Teidi bought the hotel, located at 1106 Cadastral Zone, B02 Durumi District, Abuja through his company, Badawulu Ventures, for N339 million. The reason the said property was forfeited to the Federal Government of Nigeria, according to Uwujaren, was because there was evidence that the proceeds of crime were used to acquire the property (Soriwei, 2014).

Coming back to the question raised by the CBN governor in which he asked why many Nigerians preferred carrying out transactions with the United States dollars at the expense of the local currency, the Naira? The answer to the question is simple. Nigerians are lovers of Western cultures and values and haters of their own being and existence. Recently, the Nigerian government had spent millions of Naira in advertisement, trying to change these negative images and mindsets that Nigerians have of themselves and their country. Indeed, the rebranding program was an effort to get Nigerians to think positively about themselves and their country. However, for this program to gain esteem or become fruitful, the author of this discourse contends that the rebranding of Nigeria must start from the top. The leadership of the country must always learn to lead by good example and must be bold to accept guilt whenever government policies or decisions are found faulty. The country's leadership must engage in self-criticisms, which most Nigerians do not practice. They must nurture and promote good cultural values that are indigenous to Nigerians—values that have made Nigeria and Africa unique in the world. For example, our concepts of communalism, or collectivism, and the notion of extended family, with slogans, such as "it takes a whole village to raise a child," and "being your brothers' keeper," must be constantly nurtured and upheld.

One of Africa's most cherished values is the value of *Ubuntu or botho* (humanity). The word Ubuntu is said to have its origins in the Bantu languages. According to Archbishop Desmond Tutu (1994) of South Africa, who popularized the concept through his numerous writings, the word Ubuntu simply means to be truly human.

> [Ubuntu or botho] refers to gentleness, to compassion, to hospitality, to openness to others, to vulnerability, to be available for others and to know that you are bound up with them in the bundle of life, for a person is only a person through other persons. And so we search for this ultimate attribute and reject ethnicity and other such qualities as irrelevancies. A person is a person because he recognizes others as persons (p.125).

The respect for humanity is the most sacred value that has guided and shaped Africa's ethos, philosophy, and morality. The concept of humanity is so central to Africa's way of thinking, and how Africans relate and react to each other. Tutu also went further to simplify the above phrases by noting the following: "a person with Ubuntu is open and available to others, affirming of others, does not feel threatened that others are able and good, based from a proper self-assurance that comes from knowing that he or she belongs in a greater whole and is diminished when others are humiliated or diminished, when others are tortured or oppressed."

Nelson Mandela of blessed memory, an icon of the African Liberation Movement, also saw *Ubuntu* as a moral persuasion that saw him through during his years in Robben Island prison. For him, *Ubuntu* (brotherhood) epitomizes a need for understanding but not for vengeance, a need for reparation but not for retaliation, and a need for brotherhood but not victmisation. *Ubuntu,* according to Mandela, is rooted under the belief that "people are human beings, produced by the society in which they live. You encourage people by seeing good in them." Ubuntu also calls for forgiveness of one another. It promotes the spirit of self-discipline and tolerance, and human relationships—meaning "a person is a person because of other people" (Sampson, 1999).

Unfortunately, these virtues have been thrown overboard by some privileged Africans who are occupying some strategic positions within their respective societies and, who have embraced Western values that induce the quest for material wealth acquisition and accumulation—a recipe for greedy attitude, corruption, war and conquest, unhealthy competitions, individualism, and selfishness. These groups of Africans are today living under a false mentality that produces slogans, such as "I am for myself and God for us all." They are also motivated by the doctrine of Social Darwinism—that called for "the survival of the fittest" Most of our African leaders and, especially most Nigerian leaders, have deviated from the true meaning of the concept of humanity, which is also reflected in the Biblical teaching that encourages Christians and Non-Christians alike to, "love your neighbor as thyself," or to "do unto others as you would have them do unto you." The "new generation" of leaders in Nigeria who see no wrong in how they govern the country have ignored these important virtues of humanity in their relationships with those whom they rule.

It is regrettable that while patriotic Nigerians abroad are remitting huge sums of money home to help fuel the economy, many Nigerian governing elite and their cohorts are busy salting away government funds into their overseas' offshore bank accounts. A World Bank report, published by the *Nigerian Tribune* article of April 7, 2008, revealed that Nigerians abroad remitted in 2007, a sum of $3.3 billion, an equivalent of about N400 billion to the country, the highest remittance in sub-Saharan Africa. This amount of remittance has doubled since the World Bank report was made public. Recently, a CBN statistics shows that Nigerians in the Diaspora have been remitting $10 billion (N1.6 trillion) annually into the country to improve the economy and encourage development (Daka, 2012).

Chapter 4

THE NATURE AND SCOPE OF CORRUPTION IN NIGERIA

Corruption is a crime against humanity. It robs a country of its vital resources needed to enhance the socioeconomic well-being of the country's poor and the powerless. Corruption in Nigeria has been widely acknowledged by Nigerians from all walks of life.

This cancerous tumor has eaten deep into the country's social and moral fabric and has spread its tenacious tentacles to all sectors, both public and private. Corruption in Nigeria has bled the country dry by depleting its limited resources, which are desperately needed in refurbishing and rehabilitating the country's dilapidated infrastructures.

Generally speaking, corruption is viewed as the country's worst nightmare and the most dreadful challenge confronting the nation today. It has, indeed, overheated the country's polity.

Corruption in the Nigerian Public Sector

The Nigerian endemic corruption raised its ugly head, when the country experienced an oil boom in the early 1970s, immediately after the Nigerian Civil War. Since then, many Nigerians have come to view public service as a viable career choice because it affords criminally minded individuals in the country the opportunity to loot public funds, generated mainly from the petro-dollar. The former Chief of the Economic and Financial Crimes Commission (EFCC), Farida Waziri, concurred with the above assertions by noting the following in her analysis:

> The reason many seek political office today is everything other than service. Politics appears [to be] the biggest industry for illicit wealth acquisition. The foundation for bad government is therefore laid in the nature of our politics. The only language in our politics is money. Integrity and competence hardly play any role. It is therefore not a coincidence that the root of our corruption is largely connected with public officers otherwise regarded as Politically Exposed Persons. This is not to say there are no good public office holders. They have simply been overwhelmed by the bad ones (Waziri, 2011).

This explains why many Nigerian elected officials, public civil servants and their cronies, whether at federal, state, or local governments, have been implicated in one form of corruption or the other. Some of those in the leadership of the country's military and police are also implicated in these corrupt practices. Many Nigerians, for example, know too well of Nigerian Heads of state (whether military or civilian), Presidents of the Senate, Speakers of the House of Representatives, State Governors, who were implicated in embezzling public funds, receiving bribes to perform their normal duties, or bribing others to obtain favors. Nigerians are also extremely cognizant of members of State Assemblies, Local Government Chairmen, Election Tribunal Judges, Heads of Ministries (Defense; Petroleum; Finance; Education, Health, Transportation, Federal Pension Scheme, Works, etc.) Central Bank Governors, and Inspectors General of Police, who were also implicated in embezzling public funds, receiving bribes to perform their normal duties, or bribing others to obtain favors.

It is sad to note that the institutions created to tackle corruption like the EFCC and the Independent Corrupt Practices and other Related Offenses Commission (ICPC), are extremely ineffective in executing their constitutional assigned duties. The reasons for this are due to the following facts: these institutions lack adequate resources and authorities to carry out their assigned duties and; more so, some of the leaders who would have made these institutions more   efficient and effective are themselves corrupt. Because of their corrupt nature, leaders in Nigeria cannot summon the courage to fight corruption aggressively the way they should. In every period of electioneering campaign, Nigerians were told by those seeking the highest office in the land that their top priority of things to achieve if elected, would be the eradication of corruption and that there would be no "sacred cow" during their time in government. Despite these promises, nothing has changed thus far. Corruption continues to increase instead.

Many Nigerians of goodwill and conscience are now questioning the inaction of the Nigerian government to confront corruption head-on. The false promises to fight corruption in Nigeria prompted the former Senator from the Orlu Senatorial Zone in Imo State, Arthur Nzeribe, to forward the names of 500 Nigerians who stole government funds to President Olusegun Obasanjo. The maverick Senator told a reporter, Ikenna Emewu, in a press interview he had with him in Abuja on October 28, 2011, that his reason for taking such action was to test the genuineness of Obasanjo administration's resolve in fighting corruption. Senator Nzeribe claimed that he was disappointed because no action was taken by the Obasanjo administration to investigate the matter after he submitted the names. Fighting corruption was one of President Obasanjo's campaign themes during his 1999 presidential campaign, where he pledged that there would be no "sacred cow" under his watch should he become the president of the country.

The flamboyant Senator reminded Nigerians that the country has had leaders who always paid lip-service to the war against corruption and, at the end of the day, nothing happens. The Senator also said that he was not surprised when he read a report attributed to the former EFCC Chairman, Mallam Nuhu Ribadu, where Ribadu allegedly described corruption under President Obasanjo as worse than it was under the late Gen. Sani Abacha. The Oguta-born Senator concluded that the report clearly supported what many Nigerians had already known, that corruption was well and alive in the country.

Nigerians have recently been bombarded with the Civil Service Pension scandal, where Pension Funds meant for retired public servants in Nigeria were looted and lodged in private bank accounts owned by those who manage the Funds. The Senate Committee on Federal Character and Intergovernmental Agencies claimed that Nigeria was losing about N3 trillion annually to corrupt practices through ghost workers' syndrome, falsification and inflation of contracts, as well as other 'sharp practices' in the Civil Service. By the same token, the Senate Joint Committee on Establishment and Public Service and States and Local Government, investigating the Pension Funds scandal also claimed to have uncovered 73,000 'ghost' pensioners. They learned in the process, how some of the employees of the Pension Accounts Office were used as conduits in siphoning pension funds.

A clerk in the Pension office told the investigating Senators that, for four years, his bank account was used in looting N30 billion out of the pension fund. In the investigation, the EFCC—the very body that was created to monitor, investigate, and prosecute corrupt Nigerians was also implicated in the scandal for its role in the illegal withdrawal and transfer of the pension funds. The Chairman of the Pension Reform Task Team (PRT) was equally accused of operating seventy-two illegal bank accounts. The accusation of the EFCC and the Chairman of the PRT, Alhaji AbdulRasheed Maina, was made by both former Director of the Pension Accounts Office, Dr. Sani Teidi Shuaibu and Assistant Director from the same office, Toyin Ishola (Folasade-Koyi and Omolehin, 2012). Another investigation by the Senate Joint Committee on Establishment and Public Service and States and Local Government revealed that N26 billion belonging to the Police Pension Funds were recovered in five commercial banks in the country. The investigation, according to Umoru and Shaibu (2012), revealed that N10 billion was deposited in First Bank, N8 billion in Fidelity Bank, N3 billion in UBA, N3 billion in Ecobank, and N3 billion in GTB. Umoru and Shaibu noted in their article that these amounts of money were part of the N31 billion the Minister of Finance, Dr. Ngozi Okonjo-Iweala, froze following the allegation of fraud at the Police Pension Office.

Further investigations by the EFCC implicated two more banks and seven Bureau de-change operators in helping the looters steal N80 million and N38 billion respectively from the Pension Funds. The N80 million was lodged into sixteen fake accounts in the two banks. The banks included Afribank, where twelve fake accounts were opened and Union Bank, where the four remaining fake accounts were opened. The anti-graft agency also told the Federal High Court in Abuja how five civil servants in the Office of the Head of Civil Service of the Federation (OHCSF), including its former Director of the Pensions Department, Dr. Sani Teidi Shuaibu, used seven Bureau de-change operators to steal over N38 billion (Oyesina, 2012; and Nnochiri, 2012). The seven operators, according to Nnochiri of the *Vanguard Newspaper Online Edition*, included Aliyu Abubakar Kiruwa, Musa Mohammed, Bello Alhaji, Minister Hussaini Muhammad, El-Mustafa Yahya, Alaneme Chukwuemeka Sylvester, and Sidi Gambo Umar.

The PRT, which was set up by President Jonathan's administration to investigate the scandal also reported that, it recovered additional N182 billion after its earlier recovery of N151 billion from the administrators of the Pension Scheme. The Task Force report also revealed that a sum of N74 billion from the earlier recovery (N151 billion) was channeled into the 2012 federal budget (Lawal and Musari, 2012). The Senate Joint Committee investigation revealed that the looted monies deposited into the five commercial banks mentioned earlier were made without the authorization of the Accountant General of the Federation (AGF). It is not surprising news that some bank officials in Nigeria will connive with looters to defraud the government or any other entity for that matter; they do not mind doing so, as long as huge sums of money are in play.

The second EFCC Chief since the creation of the agency, Farida Waziri, had strong words for the bank executives who encouraged the deposit of such looted pension funds into their banks. She accused them of colluding with corrupt pension officials to swindle the country of billions of Naira. She also confirmed the allegation that the banks used some EFCC operatives' accounts to launder money. The seasoned Chief Law Enforcer was quoted as saying:

> The fraud [the Pension Scandal] that was discovered was monumental and I was shocked because I never would have believed that civil servants could do this to each other because one day, they are going to be also pensioners and these are their brothers and kins and the money meant for them, they carted them away....The recoveries were monumental. Every day we recovered monies, in some of the accounts, they put money there and forgot and fraud went on for long time in the pension office. These banks are not helping this country, they want funds at all cost, whether they are from dead bodies, they do not care as long as the monies is in their accounts. Without the banks' collusion, they couldn't have stolen these billions; it is the banks and they know it (Folasade-Koyi and Omolehin, 2012).

Why would these bank officials bother when they knew that nothing would happen to them as a result? It is a known fact that corrupt officials always get away with their ill-gotten wealth and no harm befalls them once they remain in the country. The recent saga of the former Delta State Governor, James Ibori, proves the point. If Ibori had not fled Nigeria, a safe haven for looters and where the rule of law means absolutely nothing, he would have been walking around a free man, but he fled to countries where the rule of law means exactly what it says. Ibori will now be languishing in a British prison for thirteen years for the crime he committed when he lived and worked in the United Kingdom during the 1980s and 1990s, and for looting Delta State's treasury when he was governor. We hope that Ibori's conviction in UK's court sends a strong message to other looters in Nigeria that "you can run, but you cannot hide from the law."

Corruption in Nigeria has gone on for too long without the culprits being prosecuted. Unfortunately, these "ill-gotten moneys" stashed away in many foreign and off-shore bank accounts have strangulated the Nigerian economy while boosting the economies of those foreign countries, where these ill-gotten monies are deposited. The only reason the government of Nigeria went aggressively after General Abacha's ill-gotten wealth was because he was dead. If he was still alive like other living corrupt Nigerian Heads of State, no one would publicly accuse him of any embezzlement not to talk of freezing his overseas' accounts or assets. Many of the government officials arrested by the EFCC for looting public funds have not gone on trial; only a few of them have been tried and convicted, while many others were released on bail. Once bail is granted that will be the last time Nigerians will ever hear about the cases again. This indefinite silence does not mean that these public officials (state governors in particular) were innocent of the charges brought against them. The silence persists because there is no "political will" in the country to prosecute corrupt officials.

The country lacks the political will to prosecute corrupt officials because those responsible for prosecuting cases of this nature or enforcing the law of the land are themselves corrupt and, in most cases, the alleged suspects have connections with those at the upper echelon of the country's leadership (the rich and powerful). Because the hands of these leaders are dirty, they have no moral courage to order the prosecution of their corrupt friends and relatives. By doing so, they frustrate the prosecutorial process thinking that with time the average Nigerian will forget what has transpired. This kind of attitude makes it impossible to put corrupt officials behind bars. In Nigeria, release on bail has always come to mean not guilty of the crime charged. It simply means that once bail is granted, the case is over.

The first Chairman of the EFCC and former Presidential candidate of Action Congress of Nigeria (ACN) during the 2011 general elections, Mallam Nuhu Ribadu, indicted the Nigerian judiciary for aiding many corrupt Nigerians to get away with corruption. In an interview he granted to *Zero Tolerance Magazine,* which is published by the EFCC, the former Chief Law Enforcer was quoted as making the following statements:

> A judge even said one man should not even be taken to court. So, there are many Nigerians getting away with the help of the judiciary. The judiciary is also part of the challenge. There are judges that got a lot of them convicted. Even in the case of James Ibori, a Federal High Court Judge sent him to prison and kept him there for two and half months. He was a judge that exhibited unbelievable honesty, integrity, competence and knowledge of the law. He is also a Nigerian, let's celebrate him and forget the other judge that gave our country a bad name....There were worse people than James Ibori in Nigeria. I think probably Ibori was not the smartest one among them. There are some crooks worse than Ibori; and I

still see them. Some of them are even being celebrated right now in our country. Some of them are trying to rewrite history. Ibori didn't handle his own criminal affairs smartly, and he ended up paying dearly for it. There are smarter crooks than Ibori, who did more damage to the EFCC; but God will judge them (Ogundele, 2013).

Ribadu also claimed that the reason he prosecuted his former boss, Inspector-General of Police (IGP), Tafa Balogun, was because he crossed the line. For him, Justice is blind and, whosoever crosses the line must be punished in accordance with the letters and spirits of the law; "whether a constable or an Inspector-General of Police, it's the same thing." Ribadu noted that Balogun did things that were wrong, which were brought to the attention of the EFCC, and the law took its course.

On the other hand, a retiring judge of the Federal High Court, Justice Adamu Bello, gave reasons for the high level of corruption in the judiciary. During the valedictory session held in his honor for bowing out of active judicial service, at age 70 the mandatory retirement age, the distinguished Justice pointed to "poverty and lack of welfare package for judges as key factors behind the spate of judicial impunities, currently ravaging the country." In his humble critique of the judiciary, Justice Bello was quoted as saying:

> I will not end my speech without making few comments on the state of the Nigerian judiciary. I am one of those who believe that the Nigerian judiciary is among the best in the world. We may have our ups and downs and even harbour some bad eggs, but that does not give anyone the licence to lampoon the whole institution of the judiciary like it is being done in this country. Our critics should tread softly and avoid undermining the whole institution of the judiciary while exercising their rights to criticize for good reason. The judiciary can and has always tried to sanitise itself through the instrumentality of the National Judicial Council (NJC), under the able-leadership of the honourable, the Chief Justice of Nigeria, Justice Mariam Aloma Muhktar (Nnochiri, 2014).

The retired Justice reminded Nigerians that "other organs of government in Nigeria do not have such internal disciplinary control mechanism to deal with their erring officials. The judiciary therefore deserves commendation rather than condemnation." He also reminded the judiciary that "while it is right and proper for NJC to discipline erring judges, it should also intensify efforts to secure the welfare of judges and protect their tenure."

Another retiring Judge, this time from the Nigerian Supreme Court, Justice Stanley Shenko Alagoa, was said to admit that, "some judges collect bribe from politicians and traditional rulers to pervert the course of justice." In his analysis of corruption within the judiciary, Justice Alagoa was quoted as having made the following revelations:

> I will be failing in my duty, especially at this time, if I do not say a word or two about allegations of corruption in the judiciary. There was a time when this canker worn was confined to the Magistracy and Customary or Native Courts. With time it is said to have spread and has now gained ground in the High and some say appellate Courts. This trend must be worrisome to any discerning person as some highly placed persons including distinguished and respected retired Justices of the Supreme Court and other legal luminaries have expressed grave concern over this ugly trend. The greatest challenges to the judiciary are politicians followed by businessmen. Traditional rulers must also share in the blame. It is this class of persons that bribe, intimidate, harass or influence judges to depart from their sacred oath of office and the path of honour and rectitude....A judge who hobnobs with this group may well be unwittingly allowing his position to be compromised and possibly jeopardized. A judge must hold fast to his faith in God and be bold. This done, these class of persons, like bees can only buzz around but must certainly lack the power and ability to sting (Nnochiri, 2013).

Justice Alagoa also went on to suggest that "only men and women of proven integrity and courage should be picked to sit on the bench." It is obviously true what Justice Alagoa had said that powerful persons in the Nigerian society use their wealth and positions to corrupt government officials in an attempt to buy their way through or to control the system. We must be mindful of the fact that this behavior is not peculiar to Nigeria, but a worldwide phenomenon.

Another way to frustrate the prosecutorial process of corruption is by denying prosecutors the relevant information needed to proceed with the case. This is done by destroying the evidence.

Desperate looters will go to any length to cover their acts; even to the extent of setting buildings, where pieces of evidence are kept, on fire. Ayittey (1992), in his analysis, eloquently described how these dastardly acts are executed in Nigeria:

Theft of public resources was not only rampant but destructive. Mysterious fires razed buildings housing important government agencies that had become enmeshed in scandal, including the Ministry of External Affairs and the Development Authority in Abuja. In 1983, fire broke out at the 37-story headquarters of the Nigerian External Telecommunications, a state agency in Lagos. The building was the pride of Nigerian architecture, and the fire, described by the government-owned New Nigeria as a calculated act, planned and executed to cover up corruption and embezzlement in the company, visibly quickened the pace of political decay. To both ordinary Nigerians and the country's intelligentsia—students, intellectuals, professionals, and military officers—it symbolized the rapaciousness of the ruling elite (pp. 250-251).

This method was commonly used in Nigeria during the 1980s and its devastating impacts on the country's image and economy quickly forced the students to take to the streets of Lagos and several state capitals to call for the return of the military. Their plea was obliged when Maj. Gen. Muhammadu Buhari booted out the Shagari's government in a December 31, 1983 coup (Ayittey, 1992: 251).

In furtherance of her analysis on corruption in Nigeria, Waziri (2011), alleged in her address delivered at the 8th National Seminar on Economic Crime held at the Commission's Training and Research Institute in Karu, Abuja, that the reason the nation was not winning the war on corruption was because of the interference of influential Nigerians whose unpatriotic activities were hampering the work of the Commission and worsening corruption cases in the country. She eloquently articulated the devastating consequences of corruption in Nigeria, which she claimed have taken heavy tolls on the country. According to her,

The Seminar is coming at a time of great national economic and security challenges. These challenges are man-made and are largely traceable to corruption. A few individuals are bleeding the nation and causing great pain to the larger society. The corruption of a few has caused and is causing crushing and debilitating poverty and unemployment. This poverty has led to despair and anger which in many cases have ignited violent unrest with attendant unpleasant consequences, including loss of innocent lives and poverty. Entrenched corruption is responsible for the state of our poor infrastructure including power and roads. Our aspiration as a great country stands threatened by corruption. In spite of the above state of affairs, a few are still working daily to make the situation even worse. A corruption free and transparent Nigeria will put them out of business and they are determined to maintain the status quo.

She indicted Nigerians for being too complacent and for tolerating corruption for too long. She argued that to combat corruption, the country must abandon its traditional method of dealing with the menace and embrace unorthodox approaches. She was of the opinion that the traditional method was no longer working; that such a method was inefficient and ineffective. The former anti-graft Chief also indicted some human rights activists in the country whom she accused were quick to defend the human rights of the suspects of corruption who tried to frustrate the legal process of their trials, but refused to acknowledge the human rights of millions of victims of corruption in the country.

In concurring with Farida Waziri's assertions on corruption and the complacencies of Nigerians over the issue, the second democratically elected President of South African, Nelson Mandela's successor, Thabo Mbeki, was quoted as saying:

> In Nigeria, it appears nothing can provoke the people into demanding accountability from political office holders. Things that would jolt a government in any other clime go unnoticed in the country. For instance, how does one explain the continued deterioration in the quality of infrastructure amidst an endless flow of money from the sale of crude oil? How can the decline in the quality of education and health care delivery be explained in view of the amount that accrues to the country from the crude oil sale? It is in this same country that a government came to office when the price of oil was $18 per barrel was able to pay off the country's debt of over $30 billion and saved over $50 billion in foreign reserves and more than $20 billion in Excess Crude Account. But the country is now accumulating debts, even when the price of oil in the international market has remained largely above $100 per barrel in the past six years. Yet, Nigerians are not asking questions and are so enfeebled that their views, when expressed, don't count (*Nigerian Punch Newspaper editorial*, November 24, 2013).

Nigerians are yet to realize that it is their sole responsibility to demand for good governance; that without such an effort, the status-quo will not change. For this change to occur, all hands must be on deck. No outside force will institute this change but Nigerians themselves.

Nigerians have also seen situations where awards of government contracts are used to favor individuals or groups who donated substantially to the political campaigns of the winning parties. This is not a problem because such practices are common in other countries as well, but what makes it a problem in Nigeria is that once contracts are issued, the contracting officials will not bother to check whether or not the contracted projects are successfully completed. There are facts on the ground that show that most contracted projects in Nigeria go uncompleted and funds meant for them are never accounted for. This is where the problem lies, and it is another way of spending public money without checking whether or not the appropriated funds are used for their intended purposes.

Indeed, Prof. Achebe (1983) puts this issue in its proper perspective when he describes how the Patron-Client relationship manifests itself in the Nigerian context:

> Public funds are now routinely doled out to political allies and personal friends in the guise of contract to execute public works of one kind or another, or licences to import restricted commodities. Generally, a political contractor will have no expertise whatsoever or even the intention to perform. He will simply sell the contract to a third party and pocket the commission running into hundreds of thousands of naira or even millions for acting as a conduit of executive fiat....Alternatively he can raise cash not by selling the contract but by collecting a mobilization fee from the Treasury, putting aside the contract for the time being or forever, buying himself a Mercedes Benz car and seeking elective office through open and massive bribery....If in spite of all his exertions he still fails to win nomination or is defeated at the polls, he may be rewarded with a ministerial appointment. Should he as minister find himself engulfed in serious financial scandal, the President will promptly re-assign him to another ministry (p.54).

The difference between Nigeria and other countries, especially the advanced countries, is that in Nigeria political corruption is a way of life and is commonly accepted and tolerated while such practices are not tolerated in many advanced countries. There are no "sacred cows" in these countries when it comes to corruption. Once public officials are caught for corruption either by receiving or giving bribes for favor or for other illegal activities, such officials would be prosecuted to the fullest extent of the law regardless of their positions in office.

Generally speaking, political office seekers in Nigeria and elsewhere in the world have always viewed politics as a lucrative occupation where personal wealth can be accumulated much quicker and easier. This assumption is due to the structural loopholes found in politics. Office seekers whether in Nigeria or elsewhere always claim that their primary motive for entering politics is to serve the people, but in reality they are into politics for personal gains and ambitions; they are into politics for self-advancement, and for securing a comfortable lifestyle for themselves, relatives, and friends (Harris, 2003).

By its very nature, politics breed corruption. For instance, every political structure creates various offices and assigns certain responsibilities and powers to those offices. It is easy, therefore, for office holders to use these powers and influences attached to their offices to their own advantage if there are no adequate oversights in place to hold office seekers accountable for their actions. We have seen politicians using their influence to patronize their supporters and using the same means to widen their support base. This is done through what political scientists referred to as Patron-Client relationship.

Within the Nigerian political circle, the Patron-Client relationship is known as "Political Godfatherism." This concept is chiefly responsible for most of the corrupt practices that overheated the Nigerian polity. Nigerians are too familiar with the Uba-Ngige saga of 2003.

Chris Uba (the purported godfather of the Anambra State politics) and Chris Ngige (a former Governor of Anambra State) engaged in a power tussle, where Uba tried to remove Ngige from office for refusing to mortgage the state treasury to him. Uba felt betrayed after his client, Ngige, refused to honor his promise of siphoning the state's money into his coffer. This incident dominated most of Anambra's State politics until Governor Ngige was removed from office on March 15, 2006 by an election tribunal. Social analysts in Nigeria were of the opinion that this singular act brought to the fore a new dimension to the practice of godfatherism in Nigeria. "This was in contrast to the roles played by godfathers in Nigeria's democratic practice between 1958 and 1983" (Adeoye, 2009).

The Uba-Ngige case is not the only example of the Patron-Client relationship in the country. Governor Chinwoke Mbadinuju, Ngige's predecessor, for example, claimed that he was forced to pay a godfather N10 million monthly when he served as Anambra State governor. In the interview he had with a *Nigerian Punch Newspaper* reporter, John Alechenu (2013), the former governor of Anambra State stated that President Obasanjo had asked him to pay this sum of money to "one of his boys" in the state whom Obasanjo wanted to be the governor of the State. According to Mbadinuju, godfatherism in Anambra State started with "the former President Obasanjo because he wanted his boys to be governor....He wanted his boy Andy Uba (a brother to Chris Uba) to rule Anambra and, indeed, his nominee became governor for a few weeks." The only reason these events are cited here is because they made national and international news commentary and were widely publicized compared to other similar practices that were always conducted behind closed doors.

Corruption in the Nigerian Private Sector

Corruption runs deep in Nigeria's private sector. The most notables are the country's banking and petroleum industries, the two most vital industries that have, over the years, sustained the country's economic growth. These institutions are the mainstay of the nation's economy, but their future growth and enhancement have been seriously damaged by widespread corruption that confronts them today. A detailed explanation of corruption in these industries and their impact on the Nigerian economy will be presented separately.

The Banking Industry

Nigerians are extremely familiar with the massive corruption that engulfed the Nigerian banking sector, where some Managing Directors (MDs) and their Executive Directors (EDs) helped themselves, relatives and friends to depositors' money under the guise of loans, but with no intention of repaying them. These loans were given out without adequate documentations, and such transactions were never disclosed to the appropriate owners, who mainly, were the shareholders of those banks. Within the Nigerian banking circle, this type of loan is often referred to as "toxic" or "non-performing" loan.

These are bad loans that cannot be easily recovered. The fraudulent behavior of certain bank executives created immeasurable distress within their banks, and its ensuing disastrous impact, was adversely felt at the Nigerian Stock Exchange (NSE). The shockwaves resulting from the mismanagement of these banks coupled with the global economic meltdown of 2008-2009, triggered the collapse of the Nigerian stock market. The near-collapse of some of these banks forced the Central Bank of Nigeria (CBN) to intervene by rejecting the sum of N620 billion into these institutions, thus rescuing what critics termed as "too big to fail banks."

To stabilize the Nigerian banking industry and return confidence to the market, the country's Apex Bank dismissed the MDs and EDs of eight distressed banks that facilitated the collapse of the stock market and took over their management. The affected banks included Afribank, Bank PHB, FinBank, Intercontinental Bank, Oceanic Bank, Spring Bank, Union Bank, and Unity Bank. The CBN governor, Sanusi Lamido Sanusi, defended the action of the Apex Bank in a speech he delivered at the Bayero University, Kano during the University's annual Convocation Ceremony, held on Friday, February 26, 2010. In his speech, Sanusi noted that the CBN could no longer sit idly by and watch commercial banks in the country continue to violate their corporate governance with impunity without the Apex bank putting a stop to such flagrant abuses.

The CBN Governor painfully described how the Chief Executive Officers (CEOs) and the management team of the eight rescued banks overstepped their boundaries and compromised the ethical standard of their profession. An Excerpt from the Governor's speech revealed that,

> The CEOs set up Special Purpose Vehicles to lend money to themselves for stock price manipulation or the purchase of estates all over the world. One bank borrowed money and purchased private jets which we later discovered were registered in the name of the CEO's son. In another bank the management set up 100 fake companies for the purpose of perpetrating fraud. A lot of the capital supposedly raised by these so-called "mega banks" was fake capital financed from depositors' funds. 30% of the share capital of Intercontinental bank was purchased with customer deposits. Afribank used depositors' fund to purchase 80% of its IPO. It paid N25 per share when the shares were trading at N11 on the NSE and these shares later collapsed to under N3. The CEO of Oceanic bank controlled over 35% of the bank through SPVs borrowing customer deposits. The collapse of the capital market wiped out these customer deposits amounting to hundreds of billions of naira. The Central Bank had a process of capital verification at the beginning of consolidation to avoid bubble capital. For some unexplained reason, this process was stopped. As a result, we have now discovered that in many cases consolidation was a sham and the banks never raised the capital they claimed they did.

The seasoned banker went on to say that corporate governance in many of these banks was not enforced. The CBN Governor claimed that some members of the executive management of these banks lacked moral conscience to enforce their banks' rules and regulations, because they also participated in obtaining un-secured loans without authorization. The CBN governor blamed the audit system at all banks for not recognizing "the rapid deterioration of the economy and for not taking adequate measures to guide against risk assets."

Corporate indiscipline (insider abuse) was not the only reason that precipitated the failure of banks in Nigeria. Other factors, according to banking experts, included: boardroom squabbling and quarreling arising from ownership structure; frauds and forgeries; inadequate disclosure and transparency about financial position of banks; non-performing assets; lack of investor and consumer sophistication; lack of adherence to CBN Prudential Guidelines; Poor and Weak management; Macroeconomic instability; and Political factors (Adeyemi, 2011;

Cowry Research Desk, 2009; and Sanusi, 2010). Even in the face of these factors, the most significant culprit of bank failures in the country is greed, a vice, which Plato once referred to as the "insatiable appetite." Human greed and lack of enforcement of the banking laws by the country's Apex bank were what drove the looters of the failed banks in Nigeria to circumvent the instrumentalities put in place to safeguard the banks from undergoing such an expensive and unethical experience.

The CBN Governor, in his address at the Bayero University in Kano, cautioned Nigerians about the misuse of terms like "failed banks." He argued that banks did not fail by themselves. They failed because the individuals responsible for steering the operation of the banks in the right direction turned round and looted the funds, leaving depositors in an awkward and hopeless situation. He noted that losing one's life-time savings meant so many things to those affected. It meant losing their children's school fees, losing their savings for retirement, and not being able to pay their medical bills.

In bringing these sad situations to the understanding of an average Nigerian, Sanusi (2010) raised the following questions: How many of these depositors have died of heart attacks because they lost their life savings? How many honest businessmen have been rendered bankrupt because their hard earned savings were looted? How many people have committed suicide because of losing their savings to looters? How many people have died because they were unable to pay medical bills because their money was trapped in these institutions? How many children have dropped out of school because their parents' life savings mysteriously disappeared?

The answers to these provocative questions represent the extent of the grave consequences the looted banks in Nigeria brought to bear on poor Nigerians (depositors) who adequately performed their civic responsibility by patronizing their nation's banks. Instead of being rewarded for their patriotism, the corrupt owners and management teams of the failed banks took undue advantage of the very people, the depositors, they were to protect. And rather than putting the looters behind prison bars, they were handsomely rewarded, as the CBN governor, Mallam Sanusi Lamido Sanusi, alluded in his discourse:

> What we do know is that we have today, among those parading themselves as role models in society, people who profited from failed banks. Owners and managers, who go on to become governors and senators, and bad debtors who are multi-billionaires by taking money belonging to those poor dead souls and not paid back. So here is the reality. The owners and managers of banks, the rich borrowers and their clients in the political establishment are one and the same class of people protecting their

interest, and trampling underneath their feet the interest of the poor with impunity...So this time we turned the tables and said "enough is enough." The banks did not fail. They were destroyed and brought to their knees by acts committed by identifiable people. We named human beings-the management that stole money in the name of borrowing, the gamblers that took depositors funds to speculate on the stock market and manipulate share prices, the billionaires and captains of industry whose wealth actually was money belonging to the poor which they borrowed and refused to pay back (*An Excerpt from the CBN Governor's address at the Bayero University in Kano,* 2010).

Some social analysts in the country also took issue with the CEOs of the liquidated banks for threatening to drag the CBN to court for revoking their licenses. Abdullahi (n.d.), in his article, indicted the CBN for not introducing the recapitalization policy much earlier than it did, noting that such a policy would have saved the depositors' savings from the looters.

Abdullahi then advised the CBN to speed up the recapitalization process in the interest of the depositors whose lives hinge on those savings. He was not happy that the CEOs of the liquidated banks were allowed to get away with the fraud at the expense of the taxpayers after mismanaging their banks. His expressed disgust was as follows:

> The banks earmarked for liquidation were being run like private business enterprises by their CEOs and the regulatory authority was fully aware of this. Why should it be surprised now if these CEOs drag it to court to either protect what remains of their investments or their necks from the noose of EFCC? There is no doubt the regulatory authority created the enabling environment for the CEOs of these banks to wreak this havoc by parading personal business enterprises that were no better than Bureau de change outfits as banks and have the guts to challenge their liquidation in court.

To buttress his point, Abdullahi quoted a paper written by Prof. Chukwuma Soludo (the CBN Governor at the time) that the latter had presented at the breakfast meeting organized by the United Bank for Africa (UBA) Plc in Abuja for the Nigeria-South Africa Chamber of Commerce (NSACC). Prof. Chukwuma Soludo, the governor of the country's Apex bank argued that, "the former Chief executives of the liquidated banks knew they would be jailed if they were in a civilized society for the havoc they wreaked on their banks and depositors. Instead they are now finding ways of escape by going to court."

The looters knew that by going to court the recapitalization process could be delayed indefinitely and they knew that with their looted money, justice could be bought at court with the assistance of corrupt judges parading all over the country's courts. Here are the names of Nigerian banks that went under, as a result of the reasons mentioned above. Frauds and forgeries played a pivotal role in the liquidation of these banks. The licenses of these liquidated banks were revoked by the CBN, while other distressed banks were absorbed by the so-called "mega banks" during the country's consolidation exercise that went into effect in January of 2006.

List of Failed Banks in Nigeria

NAME OF BANK UNDER LIQUIDATION	DATE OF CLOSURE
Abacus Merchant Bank Ltd.	January 16, 1998
ABC Merchant Bank Ltd.	January 16, 1998
African Express Bank Ltd.	January 16, 2006
Allied Bank of Nigeria Plc	January 16, 1998
Allstates Trust Bank Plc	January 16, 1998
Alpha Merchant Bank Plc	September 8, 1994
Amicable Bank of Nigeria Plc	January 16, 1998
Assurance Bank of Nigeria Plc	January 16, 2006
Century Merchant Bank Ltd.	January 16, 1998
City Express Bank Plc	January 16, 2006
Commerce Bank Plc	January 16, 1998
Commercial Trust Bank Ltd.	January 16, 1998
Continental Merchant Bank Plc	January 16, 1998
Coop. & Commerce Bank Plc	January 16, 1998
Credite Bank Nigeria Ltd.	January 16, 1998
Crown Merchant Bank Ltd.	January 16, 1998
Eagle Bank Plc	January 16, 2006
Financial Merchant Bank Ltd.	January 21, 1994
Great Merchant Bank Ltd.	January 16, 1998
Group Merchant Bank Ltd.	January 16, 1998
Gulf Bank Ltd.	January 16, 2006
Hallmark Bank Plc	January 16, 2006
Highland Bank of Nigeria Plc	January 16, 1998

ICON Ltd. (Merchant Bankers)	January 16, 1998
Ivory Merchant Bank Ltd.	December 22, 2000
Liberty Bank Plc.	January 16, 2006
Kapital Merchant Bank Ltd.	January 21, 1994
Leed Bank Plc	January 16, 2006
Lobi Bank of Nigeria Ltd.	January 16, 1998
Mercantile Bank of Nigeria Plc	January 16, 1998
Merchant Bank of Africa Ltd.	January 16, 1998
Metropolitan Bank Ltd.	January 16, 2006
Nigeria Merchant Bank Ltd	January 16, 1998
North-South Bank Nigeria Plc	January 16, 1998
Pan African Bank Ltd.	January 16, 1998
Pinacle Commercial Bank Ltd.	January 16, 1998
Premier Commercial Bank Ltd.	December 22, 2000
Progress Bank Ltd.	January 16, 1998
Republic Bank Ltd.	June 29, 1995
Rims Merchant Bank Ltd.	December 22, 2000
Royal Merchant Bank Ltd.	January 16, 1998
Trade Bank Plc	January 16, 2006
United Commercial Bank Ltd.	September 8, 1994
Victory Merchant Bank Ltd.	January 16, 1998

(Source: Cowry Research Desk: Nigerian Banking Report, June 30, 2009).

List of Merged Banks in Nigeria to Avoid Further Banks' Liquidation

Below are the "mega banks' with their merger banks after the consolidation exercise, including their post- recapitalization capital base amounts:

Mega Bank	Constituents	Capital base (N billion)
First Bank Group:	MBC International	44.62
	FBN Merchant Bankers Ltd.	
Diamond Bank Group:	Diamond Bank	33.25
	Lion Bank	
Oceanic Bank Group:	Oceanic International	33.10
	International Trust Bank	

Mega Bank	Constituents	Capital base (N billion)
Intercontinental Bank Group:	Intercontinental Bank	51.70
	Global Bank	
	Gateway Bank	
	Equity Bank	
Fidelity Bank Group:	Fidelity Bank	29.00
	FSB International Bank	
	Manny Bank	
UBA Group:	UBA	50.00
	Standard Trust Bank	
FCMB	FCMB	30.00
	Coop Dev. Bank Nig.	
	American Bank Ltd.	
Spring Bank Group*	Citizen Bank International	25.00
	ACB International	
	Guardian Express Bank	
	Oceanic Bank	
	Tran-International Bank	
	Fountain Trust Bank	
Access Bank Group:	Access Bank	28.50
	Marina International Bank	
	Capital Bank International	
Unity Bank Group:	Intercity Bank	30.00
	First Interstate Bank	
	Tropical Commercial Bank	
	Centre Point Bank	
	Bank of the North	
	Societe Bancaire	
	Pacific Bank	
	NNB	

Mega Bank	Constituents	Capital base (N billion)
Equatorial Trust Bank Group:		
	Equatorial Trust Bank	26.50
	Devcom Bank	
Union Bank Group:	Union Bank of Nigeria	58.00
	Union Merchant Bank	
	Broad Bank	
	Universal Trust Bank	
First Inland Bank Group:	First Atlantic Bank	28.00
	Inland Bank	
	IMB	
	NUB	
Afribank Group:	Afribank International (Mer. Bank)	29.00
	Afribank of Nigeria	
	Trade Bank	
IBTC Chartered Group*	IBTC	35.00
	Chartered Bank	
	Regent Bank	
Skye Bank Group:	Prudent Bank	37.00
	EIB	
	Bond Bank	
	Reliance Bank	
	Cooperative Bank	
Wema Bank Group:	Wema Bank	26.20
	Lead Bank	
	National Bank of Nigeria	

Mega Bank	Constituents	Capital base (N billion)
Sterling Bank Group:	Trust Bank NBM Bank Magnum Bank NAL Bank Indo Nigeria Bank	25.00
Platinum Habib Bank*	Habib Bank Platinum Bank	26.00
Zenith Bank	Alone	38.00
Nigerian International Bank:	Alone	25.00
Ecobank	Alone	25.00
Standard Chartered	Alone	26.00
Guaranty Trust Bank	Alone	34.00
Stanbic Bank*	Alone	25.00

*IBTC Chartered bank recently merged with Stanbic Bank.
*Platinum Habib Bank has also been acquired with Spring Bank.
(Source: Cowry Research Desk: Nigerian Banking Report, June 30, 2009).

The Petroleum Industry

Corruption flourished with impunity in the Nigerian petroleum industry. As the chief source of the country's revenue, one expects that this sector of the economy will be effectively and efficiently managed, but the reverse is the case. On a daily basis through the print media (newspapers and magazines), Nigerians are learning about the scandals plaguing Nigeria's petroleum industry. The scandals include:

1) the bribing of Nigerian Heads of state and other government officials by foreign Multinational Corporations (MNCs) in their attempts to secure oil and gas contracts; 2) the illegal sale of Nigerian oil by unauthorized person or persons through what is known in the Nigerian oil circle as bunkering; 3) inflating oil prices and issuing of licenses to undeserving marketers under the oil subsidy regime; 4) the allocations and misuse of oil well blocks; and 5) lack of accountability of the oil windfalls resulting from the unexpected high oil prices due to the uncertainties resulting from global crises, especially the crisis in the Middle East region.

Kellogg Brown and Root (KBR), a former subsidiary of Halliburton, an American oil and gas exploration giant, went into a joint venture with French firm Technip SA, Dutch and Italian firm Snamprogetti Netherlands BV and a Japanese firm, JGC Corporation, to build a liquefied natural gas facility on Bonny Island in Bayelsa State. This project has been identified as the first of its kind on the Continent of Africa. A few years later, an indictment from the US Department of Justice revealed that the joint venture (TSKJ, KBR's business partners) had paid $180 million in bribes to several Nigerian government officials, including former Nigerian Heads of State whose names appeared on the purported indicted list. The investigation source revealed that the bribery scheme was executed between 1995 and 2004, an act orchestrated to obtain contracts worth more than $6 billion (Gilbert, 2012; Uwechue, 2010; Vanguardngr.com, 2012).

Since the revelation, none of the Nigerian officials implicated in the scheme has ever been indicted or prosecuted. Nigerians were told in 2010 that six Nigerians would be tried for their role in the scheme, but nothing has happened since then. It is, indeed, a mockery for the Nigerian government to indict the former US Vice President and the former Chairman of Halliburton, Dick Cheney, for the bribery scheme in Nigeria, when none of the Nigerian officials who received the bribe money has been indicted or imprisoned by the Nigerian government for abuse of office. To avoid further embarrassment from the US government, the Nigerian government dropped the charges it claimed it had against Dick Cheney.

While Nigerians are still waiting to know the truth of what transpired in the contract deal from their government, foreigners who were directly involved in the bribery scheme are now serving prison sentences in the United States for violating that country's Foreign Corrupt Practices Act (FCPA) and other mail and wire fraud laws. For example, the former chief executive officer of the KBR, Albert Stanley, was convicted in a Houston federal court in the United States after he pleaded guilty for his role in bribing the Nigerian officials to obtain contracts for his company. A US federal court judge sentenced Stanley to two and half years (30 months) imprisonment for bribing Nigerian officials. Stanley was also ordered by the court to pay his former company, KBR, the sum of $10.8 million in restitution, and KBR's parent company at the time, Halliburton, was fined $579 million for its role in the bribery in Nigeria.

The other foreign participants in the bribery saga were adequately punished as well. According to the Houston court decision, the two British men involved in the scandal, attorney Jeffrey Tesler and businessman Wojciech Chodan were both convicted by the Houston judge for their role in the Nigerian bribery case. Tesler was sentenced to one year and ten months (21 months) while Chodan was sentenced to one year probation. The "Japanese trading house Marubeni, which the joint venture, TSKJ, hired to help get the engineering contracts, agreed to pay a $54.6 million fine to the United States." It was also said that in 2010, Technip and Snamprogetti, each agreed to pay $240 million in fines while JGC settled for nearly $219 million. Again, Nigerians are still waiting to know the truth of what happened and why these individuals were indicted by the United States Department of Justice (US DOJ).

The Halliburton case was not the only known case in Nigeria, where MNCs (foreign companies) bribed Nigerian officials to obtain contracts. Another case in point was the Siemens' bribery scam, where a German telecommunications firm paid 17.5 million Euros to some Nigerian government officials and government officials in Libya and Russia to secure telecommunications contracts in those countries.

The Nigerian government officials implicated in the bribery scandal, according to sources, included four former ministers of telecommunications, a former Executive Director of the Power Holding Company of Nigeria (PHCN), a former Permanent Secretary of the Ministry of Power and Steel, a former General Manager of Finance of Nigerian Telecommunications Limited (NITEL), a former Managing Director of Mobile Communications (MTEL), and a member of the upper house of the Nigerian National Assembly (Alaneme, 2010; Abby, 2007; and Ilallah 2008).

Like the Halliburton case, the German court had prosecuted, convicted, and sentenced top German executives who were involved in the bribing of the Nigerian officials, while those Nigerians indicted by the same German court for receiving the bribery money were left untouched in spite of the order the former President, Umaru Musa Yar'Adua, issued to the EFCC to investigate and prosecute those involved.

Instead of going after the indicted Nigerians, the Nigerian government threatened to bring a law suit against the German firm and, in a plea bargaining arrangement entered by the two countries, the German telecommunications giant agreed to pay the sum of N7 billion to the Nigerian government in an attempt to redeem its corporate image and to continue its business in Nigeria. Upon announcing the agreement to members of the Nigerian Press and public, the Attorney General of the Federation (AGF) and Minister of Justice, Mohammed Adoke, a Senior Advocate of Nigeria (SAN), was quoted as saying:

> In consideration of the company's sober expression of regret and solemn undertakings, agreement to pay a penal fine of N7 billion, representing three times the amount of bribes given by the company and undertaking to put in place a monitoring committee, comprising of two nominees of the Federal Government, the government has agreed to discontinue the criminal prosecution it instituted against Siemens....The heavy fine imposed on Siemens, apart from the deterrence effect, will go a long away in financing infrastructural delivery in the country. Furthermore, the practice of insisting on the disgorgement of such bribes and other proceeds of corruption is to show that corruption no longer pays in Nigeria and that any person engaging in such corrupt practices stands the risk of not only going to jail, but also paying back whatever sums that can be traced to him or her (Oyesina, 2010).

This is a sad day for the country, when Nigerians who conspired with foreign entities to defraud the country of its resources escape justice while foreign perpetrators are punished, as the AGF's statements indicated above. Foreign corporations would not have succeeded in bribing Nigerian officials if those officials were not willing to accept such bribes. It is unfair, therefore, to punish one party when there are two parties involved in the crime.

The *Punch editorial* of November 2, 2012 eloquently summarizes the lackadaisical attitude of the Nigerian authorities when it comes to corruption:

> Corruption is a deeply corrosive issue that, left unchecked, will rapidly eat away at the government's legitimacy. Corruption robs Nigeria of billions of dollars each year that should be used to reverse poverty, provide infrastructure, create jobs and fund social programmes. While the United States, France, Italy, Switzerland and Germany punished companies and individuals involved in handing bribes to Nigerians in the Halliburton, Wilbros, Siemens, AG Daimler and Panalpina scandals, the Nigerian bribe takers are walking free, mingling in the highest political circles, including Aso Rock Presidential Villa.

Criminologists argue that more criminality occurs when criminal behaviors go unpunished. One of the basic tenets of the Classical School of Criminology, as Cole and Smith (2010) pointed out in their work, stipulates that "crimes may result from the rational choice of people who have weighed the benefits to be gained from the crime against the costs of being caught and punished. People may choose to commit a crime after weighing the costs and benefits of their action. Fear of punishment is what keeps most people in check."

Thus, if people realize that they will not be punished for their criminality, the tendency is that they will continue to do the same thing all over again. Crimes committed by foreign entities in Nigeria should be blamed on the lapses of the Nigerian government for not keeping its house in order.

The damage done to the country by the Halliburton, Siemens, Julius Berger, Safran, and AG Daimler and Panalpina bribery cases is enormous. Excluding the indicted Nigerian officials from prosecution and punishment has emboldened more Nigerian officials to engage in corrupt practices because they know that such criminal behavior is beneficial and that their illegal activities will go unpunished.

In January of 2012, Nigerians were shocked to learn that Jonathan's administration had removed the oil subsidy which the administration claimed had become too exorbitant for the government to bear. By the administration's action, it meant that the Nigerian government was spending exorbitant sums of money to keep the local oil price down, lower than the international market price. In justifying his decision to eliminate the oil subsidy regime, President Jonathan argued that the huge amount of money spent annually in sustaining the regime was hampering the implementation of other social programs he had promised the Nigerian people, when he ran for the presidency. President Jonathan, however, did not tell Nigerians that it was the misguided oil policies of previous administrations that were directly responsible for the massive corruption that plagued the oil industry.

To understand the context of the recent corruption in the oil industry and how the country got itself enmeshed in the oil subsidy, a brief history of oil exploration in the country is provided. The history of oil exploration in Nigeria was said to have begun in 1956, when petroleum crude oil was discovered in commercial quantities in Oloibiri, and the first known oil refinery in the country was built by a joint effort of Shell and British Petroleum. The said refinery was cited in Alesa-Eleme, near Port Harcourt.

In 1960, both companies (Shell and BP) created a joint company known as the Nigerian Petroleum Refining Company (NPRC) to refine local crude oil for both domestic and foreign consumptions. The construction of the refinery began in 1963 and its production went into effect in 1965.

The increase in demand for locally refined oil in Nigeria and the oil embargo of the 1970s precipitated the Nigerian government's action to acquire an equity share of 60 percent in all private foreign companies working in the Upstream and Downstream sectors of the petroleum industry in the country. Alex Ogedengbe noted in his writing that:

> The acute and prolong nationwide shortage of refinery products, especially petrol, started between 1973 and 1974. These shortages resulted from several factors but were generally due to the sudden sharp increases in demand. The main reasons for the high demand were attributed to a considerable increase in the economic activities following the end of the Nigerian Civil War. This also coincided with the beginning of the so called oil boom in Nigeria which started in the mid 1970s. Nigeria suddenly began to earn unprecedented amounts of revenue from oil. International oil prices had risen sharply following the oil embargo of 1973 by Arab countries as a result of the invasion of Egypt by Israel. These earnings were mainly from Royalties and the Petroleum Profit from Tax (PPT) paid by the oil companies (Ogedengbe, 2009).

However, the so-called oil boom of the 1970s was not sustained for too long, as world demand for oil fell drastically and prices dropped until OPEC intervened to stabilize prices. The accrued revenue generated from the oil embargo was adequately put to proper use by the military regimes headed by Gen. Yakubu Gowon and Generals. Mohammed/Obasanjo, despite the massive corruption recorded during Gowon's era. The oil revenue was used for infrastructural development of the country, such as the construction of Iron and Steel Industries in Oshogbo and Ajaokuta, the construction of major highways and bridges, and the construction of two local oil refineries.

The implementation of the Nigerian Enterprises Promotion Decree (NEPD) Number 4, 1972 was one of the significant achievements General Gowon made while he was in power. This promulgation was popularly known within the Nigerian circles as the "Indigenization Decree," which went into effect in April of 1974. The intent of the Decree was to empower Nigerians economically by excluding foreign companies from owning certain strategic businesses in the country. "Twenty two of such business activities were exclusively reserved for Nigerians and international commercial banks were asked to reserve at least 40 percent of all loans and advances to Nigerian business" (Omoigui, 2007). The 1972 Indigenization Degree was also expanded in 1977 to increase the stake of Nigerians in foreign businesses operating in the country. Another accomplishment of Gowon's regime was the introduction of the local currency in the country. Before the introduction of the Naira in 1973, as the country's local currency, Nigeria was using the British pounds sterling as its medium of exchange.

Uche (2011) noted that the conceived idea of the Indigenization Decree stemmed from two major events: the first was the creation of the Nigerian Local Development Board (NLDB) in 1946 by the British colonial government. The purpose of this Board was to grant loans to Nigerian owned enterprises. The second event was the formation of a National Committee on the Nationalization of Business Enterprise in Nigeria (NCNBE) in 1956.

The intent of this Committee was to study the possibility of nationalizing foreign businesses operating in the country. In its report, according to Uche, the Committee recommended barring foreign companies from distributive trade in the country. Uche also claimed that "although the Committee's recommendation was generally accepted by a majority of Nigerians, it was never implemented because the Balewa's administration was sympathetic towards western interests"—a source of conflict between nationalist and non-nationalist politicians in the country at the time.

From all indications, the NEPD had never been without controversy. Omoigui (2007) noted in his article that although the Decree was conceived by patriotic motives, it "was plagued by allegations of ethnic and insider favoritism and corruption and may even have been premature given the underdevelopment of appropriate business ethic among indigenous entrepreneurs." He claimed that, "many shares were acquired for little or no value, feeding into the consumptive (rather than productive) mentality of many Nigerians." Omoigui concluded that, "because of the alleged ethnic distribution of those who were said to have benefited the most, there is—to this day—a residual bitterness in certain parts of the polity about the Indigenization Decree." He reminded critics that "at the time the decree was conceptualized, foreigners owned about 70 percent of commercial firms in Nigeria"—an important factor for Nigerian nationalists who wanted to take the country back from colonial imperialists.

The adherent critics of the Indigenization Decree were the Igbos who stated that the timing of the implementation of the Decree was bad. They claimed that the decree was implemented, at a time, when the country was just recovering from a three-year Civil War and, at a time, when no Igbo person had the adequate capital (money) needed to buy shares from the newly acquired foreign investments. The exercise was viewed among the Igbos as a ploy to further marginalize them socially, politically, and economically. Indeed, this was a legitimate concern for Ndigbo, but no one listened; their concern and yearning fell on deaf ears; and the attitude explains why some ethnic groups, especially Ndigbo were angry and bitter over the implementation of the Decree. The Igbo nation was not given the opportunity to compete with other major ethnic groups in the country, such as the Yorubas and the Hausa-Fulani, in the Indigenization Decree exercise—an exercise that should have been expanded to all Nigerians of all persuasions.

Back to the oil refinery issue: in addition to building the Iron and Steel Industries, the construction of major highways and bridges, and the building of two local oil refineries, much of the huge oil revenue generated from the "windfall" of the 1973 oil boom also went into the pockets of Nigerian workers through the Udoji's Awards for Salary Increases and Arrears Program. According to Alex Ogedengbe, the Awards benefited those employed in public and private sectors. He went on to say that,

> [The Udoji Awards] gave a huge step increase in purchasing power of a large number of Nigerians. This temporarily created a middle class in the country. Purchase of all types of vehicles, especially tokunbo cars, electrical and electronic household goods sky-rocketed. The domestic demand for petrol more than doubled. Electrical power consumption also sharply increased nationwide (Ogedengbe, 2009).

The sudden emergence of a middle class in Nigeria, as a result of the oil boom, exacerbated the demand for refined petroleum products in the country. To address this problem, three additional petroleum refineries were built, bringing the total number of refineries in the country to four.

These four refineries were as follows: 1) the old refinery built in 1963 in Alesa-Eleme, near Port Harcourt by the joint venture of Shell and BP, known at the time, as the NPRC, which now became the Nigerian National Petroleum Corporation (NNPC) refinery. The change of name from NPRC to NNPC was a result of the Nigerian government's acquisition of the remaining 40 percent equity of NPRC in 1978; 2) the Warri refinery whose construction was awarded in 1975 and was completed in 1978; 3) the Kaduna refinery whose construction was awarded in 1976 and was completed in 1979; and the second Port Harcourt refinery whose construction was awarded in 1985 and was completed in 1989 (Ogedengbe, 2009).

Even with this number of refineries, the consumption for refined oil products intensified, as more vehicles from Asia, Europe, and North America made their way into the country. During the late 1990s and up to the present day, successive governments in Nigeria did not pay proper attention to the oil refineries. There were reports that the refineries were producing below their normal capacities;

they were breaking down without adequate maintenance and that there was a scarcity of spare parts to fix the problems. The Nigerian government is known for building gigantic infrastructures, but lacks the culture of maintenance.

For example, the country's highways and bridges, railway lines, iron and steel industries, electric power, public institutions like schools and hospitals, and other government facilities were left to deteriorate. Instead of fixing the problems that were associated with the oil refineries, the Nigerian government, both military and civilian, turned to private oil refineries (private oil marketers) to supply the country with the needed refined oil products. Consequently, Nigerian petroleum oil refineries became a casualty of the privatization scheme introduced into the country by Babangida's regime.

The Recent Challenge to Oil Corruption

Prior to the 2011 elections, none of these leaders who had plunged the country into its present massive corrupt practices—one that leads to personal wealth acquisition—had ever come out publicly to admit their role, especially in the oil sector, or to explain to Nigerians why the paradox of poverty amid plenty existed in the country. Since none of these individuals were brave enough to admit their guilt, the former Army General and Presidential candidate of the Congress for Progressive Change (CPC) in the 2011 general elections and now President under the banner of the All Progressives Congress (APC), Gen. Muhammadu Buhari, took "the bull by the horn," and lay the blame squarely where it belongs. The former military Head of State could no longer conceal the facts of how Nigeria got itself into this mess, and wasting no time, General Buhari publicly accused the administrations of Babangida, Obasanjo, and Jonathan of being responsible for the spiraling wave of corruption in the Nigerian oil industry and in the country as a whole.

In an usual manner, the former Army General told Nigerians that corruption came into the petroleum sector during the eras of Ibrahim Babangida, Olusegun Obasanjo, and Goodluck Jonathan, because they were men who had the mind of cheating the masses. In his write-up, Luka Binniyat quoted Buhari as making the following statements:

> [The] inability of these industries to work has brought mistrust and corruption to Nigeria. Therefore, our leaders have to be sincere and lead with the fear of God and carry all along for Nigeria to be a better place....All leaders should stand up and keep promises to the people. We cannot move

forward if things that are supposed to be put in place are not done. The money which was siphoned in the recent pension scam and the petroleum industry scam must all be brought back into the government's coffer for good leadership.   All those that want the masses to vote and be voted for should go to the masses and get their mandate. The era of using money to bribe the masses or use it to get political office is gone (Binniyat, 2012).

Buhari told Nigerians that for the country to "move forward and realize its quest for development, its people must come out with trusted leaders to steer the affairs of the nation. There is no country in the world, where impunity strives like Nigeria. A leader that wants to be a good leader must look at the needs of the people, the suffering, and the humiliation and proffer solution to those problems and together we shall achieve greatness." These are characters and leadership qualities that most Nigerian leaders do not have.

In concurrence with Buhari's accusation of those administrations that succeeded his, Professor Tam David-West, a former Minister of Petroleum Resources, who served under the Buhari administration (1984-1985) and a former Minister of Mines, Power, and Steel under the Babangida administration (1986), unequivocally stated in a press interview he had with the *Daily Sun* Newspaper reporter, Akeeb Alarape, on September 23, 2012, that "the Babangida government ruined the oil industry." David-West claimed that there were strict conditions (rules or policies) put in place to avoid the massive corruption that overtook the oil industry in recent years.

He claimed that these conditions guided Buhari's performance when he served as the country's Oil Minister and, claimed also that he was guided by the same rules, when he became Buhari's Oil Minister. In the press interview, David-West maintained that the Buhari administration jealously guarded the oil revenue generated at the time, knowing full well that "oil makes 90 percent of all the money Nigeria has outside (foreign reserve), and that oil makes up about 80 percent of the country's annual budget."

The renowned Professor of Virology and a social critic was vividly quoted as saying that the established conditions for lifting Nigerian oil during the Buhari era reflected the following criteria:

> To lift Nigerian oil, you must be an end user. By end user, it means we don't give oil to people who will resell at Rotterdam. You must get a refinery. If you don't have a refinery, which you must or should, you should show a contract [evidence] that you have a long time contract with a

refinery at least 10 years. Then, you must deposit with the Nigerian National Petroleum Corporation three consecutive annual audit reports of your company before you could be allowed to sign the contract to lift oil. This is to show that such a company is healthy. Then, you must be prepared to pay a non-refundable fee of $1 million to NNPC as proof of good faith....You must not sell to South Africa because of apartheid. Your company must show a staff strength of at least 20 people. All oil revenue must be paid into the Federation Account. These are the conditions you must fulfill before you can lift Nigerian oil (Alarape, 2012).

In the interview, David-West emphatically stated that the Babangida administration broke all the rules under the funny name of liberalization (privatization). "When he broke the rules, he made it easy for a lot of people to jump into lifting of Nigerian oil and, this was done to the detriment of the country. This was the beginning of the disaster in the oil industry as we know it today."

David-West was also quoted as saying that Babangida failed to deposit the extra $1.2 billion oil windfall that was generated during the 1990-1991 Gulf War into the Federation Account, as the rule stipulated. Instead Babangida established a parallel account that was called "Dedicated Account," which only himself and the then Governor of the Central Bank, the late Alhaji Uba Ahmed ran and controlled. No Nigerian knew how this money was spent or the whereabouts of the said oil windfall revenue because Babangida had refused to account for it whenever critics raised the issue. Congratulations to General Buhari and Prof. David-West for their painstaking revelations. Today, Nigerians are becoming aware of who the true enemies of the State are.

Unfortunately, a court action instituted to compel the former Army General, Ibrahim Badamasi Babangida, to account for how his regime spent the $12.5 billion oil windfall between 1988 and 1994 was dismissed by a Federal High Court sitting in Abuja, the Federal Capital Territory. The High Court judge, Justice Gabriel Kolawole, who heard the petition, dismissed the case filed by a group of six Civil Society organizations on technical grounds and not on the merit of the case. The presiding judge noted in his ruling that the plaintiffs, who included the following groups: 1) the Socio-Economic Rights and Accountability Project; 2) the Women Advocates and Documentation Centre; 3) the Committee for Defense of Human Rights; 4) Access to Justice; 5) Human and Environmental Development Agenda; and 6) Partnership for Justice, "lacked the legal right to institute the action as they failed to adduce any cogent reason that confers them the right to sustain the action." The presiding judge noted that the suit was barred by statutory limitation, "because it was not filed within the statutory twelve months period after the Okigbo panel report was produced and submitted" (Soniyi, 2012). The judge also maintained that the plaintiffs did not tender the Okigbo panel report as an exhibit, but only relied on uncertified photocopies of the News magazine's report on the contents of the Okigbo report, which the judge dismissed as having no value to the court.

On the other hand, the embattled report of the Ribadu's Petroleum Revenue Special Task Force and the House of Representatives Ad-hoc Committee Report (Resolution:HR.1/2012) have vindicated General Buhari's accusation and Prof. David-West's testimony of facts, as both reports revealed what really went wrong in the nation's oil industry after some aspects of the oil industry were privatized. For the sake of proper auditing and accountability, the time frame for the HR Ad-hoc Committee's inquiry was three years (2009-2011) while that of Ribadu's Special Task Force was ten years (2002-2012).

At the wake of the widespread protest against the removal of the oil subsidy, in which some lives were lost, the House of Representative, under Resolution HR.1/2012, instituted its own investigation to verify what went wrong in the oil subsidy regime. The Ad-hoc Committee, in its Executive Summary report, reechoed the arguments advanced by both the Jonathan's administration and the general public. It reads as follows:

> The Federal Government had informed the nation of its inability to continue to pump endless amounts of money into the seemingly bottomless pit that was referred to as petroleum products subsidy. It explained that the annual subsidy payment was huge, endless and unsustainable. Nigerians were led to believe that the colossal payments made were solely on PMS and HHK actually consumed by Nigerians. Government ascribed the quoted figures to upsurge in international crude price, high exchange rate, smuggling, increase in population and vehicles etc. However, a large section of the population faulted the premise of the Government subsidy figures, maintaining that unbridled corruption and an inefficient and wasteful process accounted for a large part of the payments. To avert a clear and present danger of descent into lawlessness, the leadership of the House of Representatives took the bold and decisive action of convening the first ever Emergency Session on a Sunday (8th January 2012), and set up the Ad-hoc Committee to verify the actual subsidy requirements of the country (HR Ad-hoc Committee Report, 2012).

The Ribadu's Petroleum Revenue Special Task Force was instituted by Jonathan's administration as a reaction to the general public's demand for explanations, as to why the Nigerian government should be importing oil from Benin Republic and from other places, while Nigerian oil refineries were allowed to rust. The establishment of Ribadu's Task Force was also a reaction to the House of Representatives Ad-hoc Committee's inquiry that brought many indictments against some "sacred cows" and "political untouchables" in the country.

The real mandate of the Task Force was to recover oil and gas revenues owed to the Federal Government of Nigeria by major Multinational Oil Corporations and to establish a governance structure to guide operations in the sector, which had been crippled by corruption and brazen theft of public funds (Soriwei, Okpi, and Baiyewu, 2012). After lengthy and painstaking investigations, the two reports came out with mind-boggling revelations of massive corruption in the country's oil sector. Both reports shed even more light on the nation's moral decadence. The reports found many irregularities and lack of transparency and accountability within the oil industry. They contended that the loss of revenue to the country, as a result of rots in the oil and gas sector, was huge. Ribadu's report, for example, claimed that Nigeria lost over N16 trillion from oil and gas because of these irregularities and lack of transparency and accountability. These irresponsible actions metamorphosed into fraud and scam schemes. Both reports concluded that these irregularities and practices had deprived the nation of vital revenue from its resources desperately needed for the country's development.

This obvious fact was highlighted in a brief speech that the Chairman of the Petroleum Revenue Special Task Force gave while officially handing over his Committee's report to President Jonathan. In that speech, Mallam Nuhu Ribadu, was quoted as rendering the following emotional statements:

> The companies that are operating in Nigeria are making huge money from our country. Many of them are going out and investing in other parts of the world. We have found out that so many of them, even simple things such as royalties they don't pay. We need the money. We need them here. We need them to continue to do business but let them also look at us and give us what is certainly our own entitlement.... Mr. President, you are doing well in fighting corruption but you still have to do more. With corruption you cannot get anything done. Corruption means taking the money to wrong direction. If it continues, it is likely that we are going to get to a standstill. Mr. President, you are carrying out reforms, we are pleased with that. From my own personal experience which I want to share with you, carrying out reforms requires integrity otherwise it will come to nothing (Adetayo, 2012).

Below are the outcomes of the irregularities and practices the embattled report highlighted, as they affect the oil sector and, thereby, putting the country's primary revenue generating industry in an awkward situation—one that creates despair, hopelessness, and disappointment to many Nigerian people.

As a result of these irregularities and lack of transparency and accountability, the Task Force came up with the following discoveries:

- The international oil traders sometimes buy crude oil without any formal contracts;

- The NNPC, the state oil firm, sold its crude to traders, including some with no expertise, noting that Nigeria was the world's only major oil producer that sells 100 percent of its crude to private commodities traders, rather than directly to refineries;

- The industrial scale of oil theft is up to 250,000 barrels per day, or 10 percent of the total production, which is worth $6.3 billion a year and may be reaching "emergency levels;"

- The existing laws and agreements with oil companies were outdated, do not reflect current economic or legal realities or they include ambiguous clauses;

- The missing revenue from signature bonuses and unpaid debts of oil companies also ran into billions of US dollars;

- The gas revenue losses accrued in the dealings between Nigeria LNG (NLNG), a company owned by NNPC, and three Multinational Oil Corporations: Shell, Eni, and Total amounts to approximately $29 billion over the last ten years (2002-2012);

- The price at which feedstock gas was sold to the NLNG seems too generous, compared to prices obtainable on the international market;

- The NNPC made N86.6 billion over the 10-year period by using overly generous exchange rates in its declarations to the government, and there was no sign of the money;

- The Discretionary decision-making in awarding oil blocs—a key way of rewarding political patronage in the country—was also causing big revenue losses;

- The Petroleum Ministers between 2008-2011 handed out seven discretionary licenses but there is $183 million in signature bonuses missing from the deals;

- Three of these oil licenses were awarded since Mrs. Alison-Madueke took up her position in 2010;

- Nigeria imports most of its fuel needs because its refineries are too small and poorly maintained (Ribadu Panel Report, 2012).

The report noted that "Nigeria's long history of corruption in the oil sector has enriched its elite class and provided the major oil companies with hefty profits while two thirds of the people live in abject poverty." The Task Force recommended that the NNPC be reorganized or scrapped. It also recommended that an independent review board for the use of traders be set up and, that a transparency law be passed, requiring oil companies to disclose all payments made to the country. The House of Representatives Ad-hoc Committee has also made several useful recommendations, which the Jonathan administration is yet to act upon.

The Jonathan administration should be applauded for summoning the courage to call for the removal of the oil subsidy and instituting a probe of this kind to investigate the rots in the oil sector. The Nigerian masses should also be congratulated for demanding answers from the ruling class as to why they should pay high petroleum prices when Nigeria is blessed with abundant oil. Nigerians should be appreciative of the fact that without these investigative efforts, the masses would not have known the magnitude of inefficiencies, the graft and criminality that were perpetrated in the petroleum industry. It is unusual and unheard of for a country that is known as the eighth largest oil producer in the world, exporting over two million barrels of oil a day and the ninth biggest gas reserves in the world to institute an oil subsidy regime for its domestic consumption. Nigeria does not need such subsidy. You don't subsidize what you have in abundance. You only subsidize what you don't have.

It is ironic that those leaders who instituted the subsidy regime in the oil sector were the very leaders who removed subsidies in crucial areas that positively affected the society; such areas include education and health care. These are areas where government subsidies are desperately needed. Before these leaders took over the administration of the country, Nigeria had free quality education, and free access to quality health care; all were provided for by the government.

Many Nigerian youths from poor backgrounds were given the opportunity to obtain free primary and secondary education, even free education up to College and University levels. The same thing could be said about the country's health care program. During those good days, many Nigerians were proud of the things the Nigerian government provided for them, because at that time, life was more bountiful than it is now.

To make a case for privatization scheme, those leaders, who oversaw the governance of the country then and now, purposefully ran the oil refinery industry as well as other government parastatals to the ground by looting funds meant to sustain this vital and strategic industry and other government businesses. They intentionally refused to maintain the existing oil refineries and the country's electric generating plants whenever they broke down.

They consistently refused to expand the existing capacities of those refineries, blaming such situations on government lack of funds, inefficiency and bureaucracy. The blame games are efforts made to frustrate and discredit government programs that benefit the poor. All that was needed in the oil refinery case was for government operatives to constantly maintain and expand the capacities of the four existing refineries and not the importation of refined petroleum products from neighboring countries into the country. The amount of money spent to sustain the oil subsidy regime would have been enough to put the refineries back to work to make refined petroleum products much cheaper for Nigerians, thereby, eradicating fuel scarcity and high costs of transportation and food items, which many Nigerians are experiencing today because of the high prices of petroleum products.

Chapter 5

HOW CORRUPTION CONTRIBUTES TO UNDERDEVELOPMENT IN NIGERIA

Consequences of Corruption in Nigeria

As the saying goes, every action has a reaction or consequence. The same analogy goes for corruption. Corruption in Nigeria has both domestic and foreign implications. As noted previously in several sections of this discourse, corruption is said to have absolutely weakened the country's economic, social, and political structures, as Akin Oyebode lamented in his recent article. In that article, Professor Oyebode asserts that "there is hardly any issue that has dominated national discourse in recent times more than that of corruption."

Driving his point home, the Professor of International Law, and Chair of International Relations, Partnership and Prospects, at the University of Lagos, stated eloquently how corruption had eaten deep into the country's social, economic, and political fabrics:

Corruption has become so pervasive that no sector or institution is immune, not churches, mosques, public sector or the private sector, schools, colleges or universities. The pervasiveness of the odium is such that many discerning minds have opined that if Nigeria did not stop corruption, corruption is most likely to stop Nigeria. Nigeria's notoriety in terms of corrupt practices is such that the notion of the ugly Nigerian looms very large in the international landscape as the country continues to draw a large profile in the Transparency International's corruption perception index (Oyebode, 2012).

It is said that Nigeria loses about N240 trillion annually to corruption. This revelation came from the Attorney General of the Federation and Minister of Justice, Mohammed Bello Adoke (SAN). The Minister of Justice was quoted as saying that half of this amount was looted from the country's treasury, while the other half originated from the bribing of public officials by foreign governments and corporations (Oyesina, 2011). This is how serious corruption has become in Nigeria.

Corruption in Nigeria has negatively impacted the economic growth of the country, as funds that should have been used in developing the country's infrastructures, enhancing the social well-being of the Nigerian people, and empowering them economically, continue to be looted and siphoned overseas. Consequently, adequate public services, social amenities in areas such as medicine and health care for the sick and elderly, education for children, nourishment and housing for the poor and working class, and the building and maintaining of economic infrastructures in the country have been grossly neglected.

Corruption has, indeed, hindered sustainable development, eroded confidence in democratic institutions, and facilitated transnational crimes like money laundering and human and drug trafficking. Today, Nigeria lacks a manufacturing base (industries and factories) and confronts endemic poverty. These problems are due to misguided national policies of the past and present administrations.

Impact of Corruption on Nigeria's Electric Energy Sector

Energy is an essential element of economic development and growth. No country develops its economy without having a sustainable energy sector for its manufacturing base. This important aspect of the Nigeria economy has long been neglected, as funds appropriated for this sector were often misused or looted, thereby, rendering the sector nonfunctional. The lack of constant supply of electricity has made matters worse. Because of the electricity problem, Nigerians are witnessing the massive exodus of some foreign companies operating in the country to other African countries, such as South

Africa, where there are constant power supplies. This movement has led to many job losses in the country. As noted previously in one of the sections of this work, the $16 billion which was appropriated during Obasanjo's second term in office to revamp the country's ailing electricity supplies did not produce the intended results. To the dismay of many Nigerians this huge sum of money allegedly claimed to have been invested in the power sector, could not be accounted for until today. What a shame!

Instead of tackling the electricity problem head-on, the Federal government privatized the energy sector, thinking it was the right and noble thing to do. Instead of fixing the problem confronting the government agency that oversees the electrification scheme of the country, the PHCN was sold to private companies as highlighted above in the section dealing with privatization.

Instead of fixing the problem of electricity in the country, the government is now spending billions of Naira running generators as an alternative to investing in electricity generating companies' thereby making Nigeria a "generator nation," where government offices, industries, and the general public rely on generators for energy. It is absolutely absurd to hear about the amount of money the federal government is spending annually to operate generators in its various Ministries, Departments, and Agencies, including the Presidential Villa in Aso Rock, when such funds could have been wisely invested in getting the country's electric energy sector up and running.

For example, Amaefule, Soriwei, and Alechenu (2012) noted in their article that the Office of the President had proposed N654.02 million in the 2013 budget for the operation of generators in the Villa (the president's residence) and other offices under the presidency.

The proposed sum of money was to cover the cost of maintaining generators as well as the cost of fueling them. The said amount would also cover the replacement of some generators in the government institutions under the presidency. Amaefule, Soriwei, and Alechenu also claimed that the total costs of fueling generators for the entire federal government agencies and departments were not released by the time their article went into circulation.

However, the punch reporters claimed that in the 2012 budget, the Federal Government proposed to spend more than N1.31 billion in fueling generators of the entire federal government Ministries, Departments, and Agencies, plus the president's residence and other offices under the presidency.

In the 2013 budget, the Jonathan administration was said to have budgeted N200 million for the maintenance and fueling of generators in Nigerian Embassies in foreign countries, including Europe and North America. Some members of the Senate Committee on Appropriation have questioned the rationale behind such a proposal, noting that spending such an amount in places like the United States, the United Kingdom, Germany and Belgium, where power stability is not taken for granted, is unconscionable (Josiah, 2012).

The saddest thing about this situation is that investments in generators are not only slowing down the country's economic growth, but also creating more health hazards, resulting from the pollution of air, which people breathe, and the loud noises the generators make.

Impact of Corruption on Nigeria's Infrastructure (Roads, Bridges and Other Communication Systems)

Roads and bridges, railways, shipping, and aviation are other essential elements of economic growth that must be jealously guarded but, in the Nigerian context, these essential elements have been neglected over the years. The neglect of these vital elements of economic growth has taken a heavy toll on the economic development of the country. If, for example, these infrastructures were adequately put to use, the country's economy would have grown tremendously and would have been much better than what it is today. Their adequate use means substantial revenues and employment opportunities for the able-bodied young men and women, who are currently unemployed.

It is a shame that a country like Nigeria has no national air carrier today because of poor management and privatization. Nigerian private airlines are ill-equipped and ill-managed to compete with foreign airlines that dominate the Nigerian aviation industry and its airspace. Today, air transport has become a lucrative business and money-making venture. The number of Nigerians traveling to other parts of the globe is huge. It is sad to note that the country's leadership has not taken full advantage of this huge and lucrative market to boost the country's economy. Rather, it is the European, North American, and the Middle East airlines that are taking full advantage of the market. The Ethiopian Airline is said to be the best managed national air carrier in Africa, offering frequent flights into many cities across the world, including its new route to China. The Ethiopian Airline has direct international flights from Addis Ababa, the Ethiopian capital, to Enugu since the Enugu Airport has been elevated to an international status. Today, the Ethiopian Airline has become the country's economic mainstay, generating huge revenue for the country and, at the same time, creating job opportunities for many Ethiopians. This is what the defunct Nigerian Airways could not do because of mismanagement and corruption in the aviation sector.

The recent pronouncement coming from the Director of Operations of the FAAN, Henry Omeogu, indicating that Jonathan's administration has agreed to float a new national air carrier with at least thirty brand new aircrafts by 2014, is a welcome development—one that is long overdue. The Director of Operation was also quoted as saying that the new effort would be private sector-driven and one of President Jonathan's transformation agenda for the aviation sector (Akasike, 2012). The notion that the new national air carrier would be private sector-driven does not make sense at all. Why are the Nigerian governing elite so distrustful of government when, in actual sense, governments are merely institutions run and controlled by the very elite?

If governments are corrupt or inefficient, as critics often claim, who is to blame, the institutions themselves or those individuals who are directly in-charge of their affairs? If the newly proposed national carrier cannot be operated directly by a government entity, the administration should forget the whole exercise. We would not like to see this very project go down the same path as the Iron and Steel industry, the Aviation industry, the PHCN, the Nigerian Ports Authority (NPA), and other privatized government parastatals that have not yielded any positive results since they had been sold, nor changed the lives of average Nigerians.

One cannot invest a huge sum of public money into government parastatals for the sole purpose of providing essential services to the people and, turn round to sell such ventures to private companies for less value—companies that are driven by profit motives. This is exploitation at its best. The Privatization Scheme, which is currently dominating the Nigerian economic psyche is, indeed, a neo-imperialist philosophy—one that exploits Nigeria's resources for the benefit of the owners of private corporations. Nigerians would like to know how the existing private airlines in the country are doing first, before the auctioning of any national carriers to private corporations. This is what we know of capitalism: it encourages market competitions and discourages monopoly. With privatization, the Nigerian governing elite have been promoting monopoly and not a free market economy, which creates alternatives and serves customers better because there are choices to make, when there is competition in the market. Private individuals can set up their businesses to compete with government run-businesses (Mixed Economy) without shutting government businesses down to feed corporate greed.

On the other hand, the Nigerian leadership has forgotten the usefulness of good access roads in building economic growth. Without good access roads, commerce and trade will not flourish. This is taking the Nigerian government operatives decades to realize. If commodities cannot be easily and freely transported from one region of the country to another, such lapses frustrates production and when production of goods and services ceases to be an ongoing thing, such trends will affect the entire economy adversely and, if care is not taken, inflation and starvation will overwhelm the society. This is economics 101. You don't have to be a rocket scientist to realize this obvious fact.

The people of South-East and South-South political zones have, for years, been clamoring for a Second Niger Bridge to be built to ease the traffic bottleneck that frustrates commerce and trade and free movement of people in that part of the country. No one is listening nor responding to this clarion call. What the people of the zones have been getting most of the time is, empty promises from the Nigerian government authorities in Abuja. No concrete action has been taken to actualize a project which many Nigerians consider, a vital national security interest. The federal government authorities seem to think that by building the Second Niger Bridge, it will be doing a big favor to the people of the South East and South-South zones. It is a project that benefits everyone—one that will also boost the national economy. It is a must-do project, given the strategic nature of the bridge and the regions involved.

Going down memory lane, Luke Onyekakeyah, in his article of December 2013, reminded Nigerians of the promises made by several Nigerian administrations to ease decades of agonizing experiences and sufferings that thousands of travelers who travel through the over five-decade old (1965-2016) bridge encounter, especially during Easter and Christmas holidays. The prolific columnist claimed that the need to build a Second Niger Bridge has been on the drawing board for a long time, but the administrations involved, have failed to live up to their promises:

> It was during the regime of General Ibrahim Babangida in the 1980s that it first came into public domain but nothing was done in practical terms. During the General Abacha regime, the Federal Government tried to present a weak explanation as to why work could not commence on the bridge. That followed the charge by the former Lagos State Governor, Alhaji Lateef Jakande, the then Minister of Works, that Nigerian engineers could not produce a design for the bridge project. After Abacha's regime ended in 1998, nothing was heard about the bridge again until the Olusegun Obasanjo administration took over in May 1999. Obasanjo was in power for eight years. But rather than taking concrete action towards commencing work on the second bridge, he instead awarded billions of naira worth of contracts for the re-furbishing of the old bridge. The bridge was virtually left unmaintained over the decades. Government argued that it wanted to secure the old bridge before building a new one. It was Obasanjo's Minister of Works, Chief Cornelius Adebayo, who in 2006 announced that the Federal Government had approved the construction of the Second Niger Bridge. But work did not commence as expected. On May 24, 2007, just five days to his exit from office, President Obasanjo, in a show of sarcasm, went to Anambra State to lay the foundation stone for the Second Niger Bridge. It was obvious from the timing that the event was sheer mockery. The reported N60 billion contracts for the bridge under a Private Partnership Programme (PPP) between the Federal, Anambra, and Delta State governments never saw the light of the day. Nothing came out of that presidential fanfare (Onyekakeyah, 2013).

What the Federal government officials failed to realize is that, it is their sole responsibility to ensure that there is a free movement of goods and services and free movement of people throughout the entire country, and that the Second Niger Bridge is one of the ways to accomplish this noble responsibility and task. It has always been a gruesome experience and sometimes a nightmare for travelers traveling from Lagos to Enugu, Owerri, Aba, Uyo, Port Harcourt, and vice versa. Sometimes, a journey of eight hours may end up taking a day and half to complete due to heavy traffic bottlenecks on the over five-decade old bridge and other factors resulting from lack of adequate road maintenance, reckless drivers, and several breakdowns of unmaintained vehicles on highways. Because of these deteriorations and total neglect, many precious lives have been lost on this major highway linking different ethnicities in the country.

Reacting to this ugly situation in the region, the governors of South East Zone (Rochas Okorocha of Imo, Peter Obi of Anambra, Martin Elechi of Ebonyi, and Theodore Orji of Abia), went to Abuja to meet with the Federal government authorities over the deplorable federal road conditions in the zone. In meeting with federal authorities, the governors demanded that actions should be taken to address the Enugu-Port Harcourt Expressway, Enugu-Onitsha Expressway, and the Second Niger Bridge issue.

In response, the Federal Minister of Works, Mike Onolememen, assured the governors that final arrangements concerning the Second Niger Bridge have been concluded and that work would commence on the said bridge by the end of the first quarter of 2013. The Minister also made it clear to his guests that the project would be executed under the principle of the Public Private Partnership (PPP) initiative, where "the Federal Government would take up 30 percent equity in the stake, while the successful concessionaire would be required to provide the balance of 70 percent counterpart funding" (Taiwo-Obalonye, 2012). Onyekakeyah (2013), also recalled that a similar pronouncement was made by the Works Minister at a stakeholders' meeting, which was conducted at the palace of the Obi of Onitsha, Igwe Alfred Achebe, where the Works Minister, Mike Onolememen, told his audience that the time has come for action on the bridge, and that the project design to cover Asaba, Ozubulu and Oghara areas would be completed before the expiration of President Goodluck Jonathan's administration in 2015.

With all these promises, no construction work has commenced on the said Second Niger Bridge, but on March 10, 2014, President Jonathan was slated to inaugurate the take-off of the project, which is said to cost N117.8 billion. In his inaugural speech, President Jonathan said that, "it is my resolve and that of my administration to ensure the unity bridge is built to connect Asaba and Onitsha. We have every reason to deliver the Second Niger Bridge."

He also commended the people of South-East and South-South zones for their patience over delays in the construction of the Second Niger Bridge, noting that with the groundbreaking of the project, his sincere promise during the electioneering campaign is now a reality (Eze et al, 2014). The inauguration ceremony was conducted at Krisoral ground in Atani, in Ogbaru Local Government Area of Anambra State.

It is said that the project was awarded to a German Construction Firm, Messrs Julius Berger, and that "the Federal Government had committed 25 per cent of the total cost of the bridge, which is N40 billion, adding that other funding for the project would come in due course." All eyes will be watching to see whether, this time, the construction of the Second Niger Bridge will come to fruition, or whether Jonathan's administration, like its predecessors, is playing politics with Ndigbo, as All Progressive Congress (APC) spokesperson in the South-East Zone, Osita Okechukwu, alluded to, when he accused President Jonathan of toying with issues and projects that concerned the Igbo people of the South-East (Ubabukoh, 2014).

The need assessment from members of the Works Committee of the Federal House of Representatives, who undertook an eight-day tour to the South East of the country to inspect federal road projects in that geo-political zone, supported what many Nigerians had known already. The Works Committee visits to the region shed more light on how deteriorated and deplorable roads in that zone were and still are. Members of the Works Committee were not satisfied with what they saw on the ground. They found that nothing serious was being done to combat the menace. They described the conditions of most roads in the zone as intolerable, a rolling calamity, and heart wrenching. They vented their anger and frustrations on foreign construction companies that had received substantial sums of money for their projects, but failed to accomplish much in return.

In describing the lackadaisical attitude of some of these foreign companies (the leader of the Works Committee to the zone, Hon. Toby Okechukwu and his team), were quoted as issuing the following warnings to unproductive construction companies:

> There are fundamental engineering standards that should be met in executing projects of this nature. Engineering ethics suggest that jobs paid for must be done well. The House of Representatives will not give its support to the idea of paying for substandard jobs. The House will see to it that whatever action is required to ensure that maximum quality is recorded is taken....Tell us what you have been doing with all the money you have been collecting, nothing here justifies the money and it is wicked, it is a shame. This is a clear case of non-seriousness; I don't know why it is only in the South East that we see all this type of nonsense (Nwosu, 2012).

The warning came as a result of the gross negligence that the lawmakers observed while inspecting the Enugu-Abakaliki Road. Along this strategic road is a bridge at Emene, linking Ebonyi and Enugu States. The bridge was said to be in a deteriorative and life threatening stage, but the foreign company, SETRACO, handling the rehabilitation of the road was not doing much to ensure that the bridge was fixed. Because of this situation, residents in the area were subjected to horrible experiences. The poor state of the bridge was said to be seriously hampering commerce and trade and the free movement of people in the area.

After inspecting the thirty-seven ongoing federal road projects in the five states of the South-East in eight days, members of the Works Committee articulated their experiences in a few phrases. Honorable Daramola, for example, was quoted as saying, "the experience is better imagined. I can say that the only good road in the South East

Zone is the Onitsha-Owerri Expressway. It is a pity that government would allow the situation to get to what it is today. For me, the firms that are handling road projects in the zone have no business being there because most of them don't have the capacity to handle the projects" (Nwosu, 2012).

By the same token, another member, Honorable Ayuba, was also quoted as saying: "it is wrong to leave things the way they are in the zone right now. For a long time what I saw will linger in my mind. If the roads are left the way they are, it is as good as telling people from the zone and other Nigerians who visit there on a daily basis that government has approved that they should go and die. Roads that animals like goats and cows cannot cross tell you how bad they are" (Nwosu, 2012).

The Committee also indicted the Federal Ministry of Works for failing to carry out soil tests before awarding road contracts in the South East zone—a major problem which is hindering the completion of most road constructions in the area. The Committee noted that late payments to companies for work done are another major problem hindering the completion of work in the zone. The ongoing prosecution of the former Federal Minister of Works, Hassan Lawal, by the EFCC, at the Federal High Court in Abuja supports the merit of the above claim. The former Minister was accused of diverting over N75 billion meant for the construction of a bridge across the Benue River. The charges brought against the former Minister and four others ranged from conspiracy, and money laundering to breach of public trust (Nnochiri, 2012).

The five connivers (Hassan Lawal, Adeogba Godwin Ademola, Dave Enejoh, Okala Philip Yakubu, and Thahal Paul) were said to have used "five separate companies to sequentially siphon the funds raised for the project"—a project built under the concept of the so-called PPP initiative--an initiative introduced by Obasanjo's administration (1999-2007). It was said that both men pleaded not guilty as charged and the case was adjourned until February of 2013.

Most road constructions in Nigeria are never completed because funds meant for such constructions are diverted by looters, which also exacerbate the problem. In most cases, they are abandoned and, where they are completed, the quality of the work is often substandard in nature, because a huge portion of the fund designated for such a construction is made away with, leaving the construction companies with little money to finish the project.

The story of deplorable road conditions is the same everywhere you go in Nigeria, especially in big cities. For example, Akoni and Olowoopejo (2012) reported the ordeal citizens of Lagos State had to endure on a daily basis, which they described as enormous and terrifying. In their article, they described how a journey that should have lasted between thirty minutes and one hour was taking up to five to ten hours to complete.

According to them, it was not the time wasted in the journey that was the biggest problem motorists and passengers encountered in the gridlock, but the toxic gases they inhaled from the crawling vehicles, the fatigue they experienced for sitting in a spot for several hours and, most painfully, many of the motorists and travelers were often robbed by bandits at various bad spots on the roads. Government critics have always reiterated what is an obvious fact: those bad roads cripple business activities in communities or societies where they exist. However, the governor of Lagos State, Babatunde Fashola, must be commended and congratulated for his administration's efforts to rehabilitate most of the roads in the State, given the enormous odds facing the State, which include the overcrowding of people and too many vehicles plying the streets of Lagos.

In most parts, these factors have contributed immensely to the massive traffic congestion experienced throughout the State. The administration should, however, continue to make strides in rehabilitating all the roads in the State, realizing the importance of good access roads to the economic growth of the State and beyond.

Impact of Corruption on Nigeria's Public Education

On the social front, corruption has also reared its ugly head. It has taken a heavy toll on education and health care to the point, where these vital social programs have been relegated to the backburner. By enforcing the IMF conditionalities, which forbids governments from subsidizing programs that are so vital to the poor, Nigerian government operatives have allowed public education and public health to lose their steam, fervor, and their true meaning. Years before privatization scheme came to Nigeria, public education and public health care centers were well funded and maintained. Those programs were admired and cherished for the benefits they provided to the Nigerian people, at the time.

The reverse is the case today. Because of privatization, the governing elite have allowed these vital institutions to decay from the inside out. When one travels around the states, especially to my state of origin, Imo, what one sees are dilapidated public school buildings that look much like abandoned property. The schools have no adequate facilities, equipment, or school supplies. The architectural designs of most of these schools were designs that prevailed in the early 1930s and 1940s. The surrounding environment of these schools is nothing to brag about and, they are not conducive for educational learning.

Funds meant for education in most states of the federation have always ended up in the private pockets of State and Local Government officials and their cronies, to say the least. Most of these officials do not care about good and quality education in their respective jurisdictions because they send their children away to Ivy League Institutions in North America and Europe, where their ill-gotten wealth is lavishly wasted on the education of their wards. In a *Punch editorial* of December 11, 2012, Dr. Wale Babalakin, Chairman of the Committee of Pro-chancellors, indicated that the cost of educating Nigerians abroad is huge.

In his analysis on how much Nigerian parents are spending annually in educating their children in Ghana, Dr. Babalakin reported that a high cash flight of about N160 billion was leaving Nigeria annually to Ghana, being the cost of university education of about 75,000 Nigerian students studying in Ghana (Nwogu, 2012). By the same token, the *Punch editorial* commentary also pegged the cost of educating Nigerians abroad, especially in European and North American universities, at $500,000 annually. Both sources claimed that the amounts spent in educating Nigerians abroad were far greater than the amounts the Federal Government of Nigeria spent annually in educating Nigerians at home.

The reasons most well-to-do parents in Nigeria are sending their children to foreign universities stem, in part, from the troubles with Nigerian universities, as revealed by Prof. Mahmood Yakubu-led Committee on Needs Assessment of public universities in Nigeria. The committee report outlined the challenges plaguing Nigerian public universities. Some aspects of the report blamed greed and instability of the governing councils, as reasons the principal officers of many of these universities were not getting their priorities in order. In a brief summary, here are some of the Committee's findings, as reported by *This Day Newspaper*:

> These challenges which have remained over the years include overcrowding in hostels and lecture rooms; inadequate and dilapidated infrastructure; outdated and broken down equipment; lack of basic amenities; inadequate, under-trained, and overworked teaching staff; and collapse of academic culture and archaic libraries...The councils of some of the schools are more interested in awarding new contracts instead of completing abandoned projects or standardizing existing facilities, and prefer to expend hundreds of millions in mundane administration cost. The report acknowledged the well-known challenge of limited resources for the universities, but added that the quality of leadership and governance and the prioritization of resources allocation are more real problems. The report accused some of the universities of not getting their priorities straight by spending millions to erect super-gates when their libraries are still at foundation level, spending millions to purchase exotic vehicles for university officers even though they lack basic classroom furnishings and spending hundreds of millions in wall-fencing and in-fencing when students accommodation is inadequate and in tatters (Oyedele, 2012).

Another problem with Nigerian education is the way in which governments treat teachers in general. In the Nigerian context, teachers are not valued as important stakeholders in the society. They are not viewed as a group of people who play a pivotal role in nation building. To make matters worse, teachers and other public servants in most states of the federation would continue working for months without pay. On the job, they are never provided with the adequate tools and facilities that are central to executing their jobs efficiently and effectively.

These kinds of situations discourage teachers from taking their jobs seriously. When teachers are not performing at their best, such an attitude affects nation building and national development adversely. Prof. Chike Anibeze, Deputy Provost of Abia State University College of Medicine, Uturu was right when he was quoted as saying that "the future of the Nigerian child and the society at large can only be secured if the welfare of teachers is given top priority by government and other concerned authorities" (Abayomi and Asomba, 2012). The Deputy Provost was also credited with the following thought provoking message to the nation:

> Teachers play an extraordinary role in the lives of children, especially in their formative years. The importance of teachers in the development of society cannot be understated as their influence can and will stretch on long after the final bell rings beyond the walls of the school. The role of the teachers is complex, far beyond what people can assume as just someone who teaches what has been programmed in the curriculum (Abayomi and Asomba, 2012).

If the standard of Nigeria's education is to be improved, Prof. Anibeze affirmed that "issues bordering on teachers' welfare and professional development, incentives for teachers, retirement age, improved teaching facilities, regular promotion of qualified teachers, and strengthened monitoring system and pragmatic teachers unions must be revisited." (Abayomi and Asomba, 2012). Because the significance of being a teacher has been swept under the rug, many teachers rarely go to school to teach.

When teachers are not paid for months, they will find ways to survive. As a result, most of them will spend their quality time in their farms or in their private businesses in order to fulfill their financial obligations to their families. Many of these teachers have families to cater for and; therefore, they must find a legitimate means of sustaining their families if state governments cannot pay them their earned salaries at the end of every month. Unfortunately, it is the school children who are the casualty of this misguided policy. Often times, they are the ones who are exploited either by their teachers who use them as farmers or by the system that does not care about their social wellbeing. How can children of these circumstances learn in an environment of this kind? This is the chief source of the problem that has led to the poor standard and poor performance we see today in most of Nigerian educational institutions, whether at the primary, secondary, or tertiary level.

When children do not have the proper educational foundation at the primary and secondary levels, many of them will not succeed when they move upward. The inability to perform or succeed at the top of the educational ladder frustrates many young people.

This explains why many young Nigerians, especially those from the South East Zone, are no longer seeing education as the sole legitimate means of uplifting themselves to an envious position in the society. Many of these young people have concluded that the only way for them to climb out of poverty and reach for the stars is by owning and managing their own businesses. This obvious fact explains the reason behind the large number of small businesses found around the country today, especially in big cities like Lagos, Kano, and Onitsha.

Many of these young people also know that other young men and women with secondary and university education have no means of livelihood because, there are no jobs available for these people after they graduate from universities and colleges. Some of these young graduates are also unemployable due to the substandard education they have received.

Studies have shown that a majority of Nigerian graduates from secondary and university levels are ill-prepared to face the challenges of the outside world after graduation. This scenario is not only unique to the South-East Zone; it is an ugly picture seen throughout the country. Because education is not worth its value anymore and because there are insufficient jobs to go around, many young men have today chosen to become commercial motorcyclists (Okada) and, thereby, making Okada their profession or stock of trade.

Many young Nigerians view commercial motorcycling as a legitimate means of survival and, as the only way they can support their families financially. Unfortunately, many State governments have banned Okada as a means of commercial transportation in the country, while others are in the process of doing the same. The ban of Okada in some states of the federation has generated a lot of controversies between states' authorities and Okada operatives. As it is generally known, the use of Okada as a viable means of commercial transportation has its own problems: Okada's visibility on the streets has added more to the existing traffic bottlenecks that commuters experience on a daily basis, especially in major cities like Lagos, Owerri, Uyo, and Umuahia to mention just a few.

Critics charge that the use of Okada has intensified the commission of crime occurring in most of these cities. On the other side of the coin, there are some advantages to be derived from the use of Okada, especially at a time, when millions of young Nigerians are unemployed and, when there are no government safety nets for the unemployed people in the country.

State authorities should, therefore, weigh the various options available to them first, before imposing a ban on cyclists. Okada operatives are self-employed people and if the government takes this singular means of livelihood away from them, such an action will drive many of these motorcyclists into crime, as they have no other legitimate means of making a living or surviving. Already, there are too many criminals and discontented people in the country already. It would be a bad policy to create more criminals when the polity is already overheated.

Implications of University Strikes on Nigeria's University Education

Every industrial action, whether instituted by public or private sector employees, produces consequences, which will affect workers, employers and, particularly, the nation's economy either positively or negatively. As the civilized world knows it, a strike is a weapon or an instrument workers use in getting the attention of their employers when they fail to reach an agreement with them. Chijioke Uwasomba of the Department of English, Obafemi Awolowo University (OAU), describes this phenomenon as

> An organized action involving work stoppage by a body of workers to enforce compliance with demands made on an employer or a group of employers. It is usually a form of protest to force recalcitrant employers to respect the value of labour and accord the latter its rightful place taking into consideration the historical exploitative relationship between labour and capital. In organizations or countries where the principle of collective bargaining is not respected by the employers of labour, the tendency for workers to employ the strike option is very rife. Workers with deep class consciousness and a strong capacity to understand the intriguing manipulations of their employers always exercise their democratic rights to fight industrial injustice and dictatorship (Uwasomba, 2013).

Nigeria public education, including university education, has never been a stranger to this phenomenon, meaning that the Academic staff in Nigeria have never stopped going on strike when the policies of the governing elite undermine public education and/or the welfare of the teachers. Critics of university industrial actions in Nigeria have attributed such actions as the leading cause of deterioration of standards and rating of the country's tertiary institutions.

In his own analysis, as to why Nigerian universities are ranked low globally, Prof. Bamitale Omole, the Vice-Chancellor of OAU, blamed the Academic Staff Union of Universities (ASUU) and student strikes as the chief source of the problem. He made this remark at the fiftieth-year celebration of the institution. The eminent scholar claimed that those events had taken heavy toll on the ranking of Nigerian universities. He further argued that the low ranking of Nigerian universities would not improve if incessant closures of universities continued, as a result of these strikes.

He queried how Nigerian universities could be among the best ten in Africa when our universities are locked up for two, three months (Odesola, 2012)? Professor Omole pointed out that the cognizance of the smooth running of the system was one of the basic criteria for ranking universities' performance, but in Nigeria, the smooth running of the system had always been hampered by industrial and student strikes that lasted for too long before they were resolved.

The Executive Secretary of the National Universities Commission (NUC), Prof. Julius Okojie, has joined ranks with critics of ASUU over its frequent strikes, arguing that the instability of Nigeria's universities' calendar, caused by incessant strikes, had affected Nigeria's universities taking "the pride of place" in Africa in terms of research and manpower development. He decried the recent five month strike (July 1, 2013--December 17, 2013) organized by members of ASUU, claiming that such a strike was unfortunate and that it came when proposals for the African Centres of Excellence (ACE) projects were being reviewed. The eminent scholar was quoted in an article published in the *Punch Newspaper* on September 3, 2013, which states the following:

> I must say that it is so unfortunate that this is happening at a time doors of the universities are shut and our colleagues who know what the benefits are have not been responsive. Money is involved, $8 million (grant provided by the World Bank for the ACE projects); if we are able to get those centres, they will help us, just like the Step-B project. The Federal University of Technology, Akure, got a project of $7 million; for an institution, this is a big leverage. There is money out there begging for people to apply, yet we keep saying there is no funding for universities. I hope that the African Union will take a cue from this and initiate a programme to support some of these projects when the fund from the World Bank is finally over (Okojie, 2013).

The Executive Secretary of the NUC reminded his Nigerian audience that the reason Nigerians are rushing to study in Ghanaian's universities is simply because of the stability in that country's education system, a phenomenon or circumstance that is lacking in Nigeria.

The analyses of the two eminent and distinguished scholars (Professors Omole and Okojie) are true statements of fact, but what was seriously lacking in their criticisms of the striking staff of the Nigerian Universities was their failure to inform the Nigerian people as to why such frequent and sustainable industrial strikes were occurring. To fill this void, Uwasomba (2013) came up with cogent reasons behind such University strikes in Nigeria. In his recent article titled, "Why Does ASUU Always Go on Strike," the English Professor concluded that industrial strikes by Nigerian Universities could not be avoided, because members of the Academic Staff Union are dealing with government functionaries who do not respect the principle of collective bargaining and who do not fulfill the promises they make. Secondly, that the Nigerian government officials have repeatedly failed to recognize the obvious fact that they are dealing with a Union of workers, like members of ASUU, who have deep class consciousness and a strong capacity to understand the intriguing manipulations of their employers. Thirdly, that the Nigerian governing elites have repeatedly ignored the fact that members of ASUU, like other aggrieved workers in other sectors of the country's economy, would always exercise their democratic rights to fight against industrial injustice and dictatorship, whenever their socio-economic wellbeing and the wellbeing of their institutions are threatened or not met.

Uwasomba informed those Nigerians who did not know, about the rationale behind ASUU's creation in 1978, which he summarized as follows: 1) to protect and enhance the wellbeing of its members; 2) to uphold and nurture the academic integrity of Nigerian universities; and 3) to checkmate government's heavy handedness in undermining these noble objectives. Uwasomba reminded critics of ASUU's recent strike action that the Academic Staff Union is doing exactly what it was created to do. In justifying ASUU's 2013 industrial action, which has been described as the longest strike ever organized since its creation, the English Professor gave a lengthy history and instances where ASUU had used strikes to address issues the Union believed were injustices perpetrated against its members and associates by several Nigerian administrations that included civilian administrations as well as military:

> ASUU fought Shagari's government following Justice Balonwu's Visitation Panel Report which had directed the Council of the University of Lagos to remove six senior members of the academic staff from their jobs. Given the nature of its mandate, ASUU fought the Federal Government under Alhaji Shehu Shagari in 1980 and 1981 on issues bordering on funding, salaries, autonomy, and academic freedom, brain-drain, the survival of the university system in particular and the direction of the country in general.... Throughout the military era, ASUU waged a lot of struggles revolving around conditions of service; funding; university autonomy/academic freedom; the defense of the right to education; broad national issues such as the anti-military struggles; actions against privatization, SAP and other neo-liberal policies of the government including the World Bank's attempts to take over the Nigerian University system through its $120 million loan under the regime of Babangida (Uwasomba, 2013).

Uwasomba also pointed out other good causes ASUU were involved with. Such struggles included ASUU's effort in battling the Buhari/Idiagbon military regime policy of retrenchment of workers and freezing of wages. The Academic Union supported the Nigerian Medical Association (NMA) and the National Association of Resident Doctors (NARD) when they went on their patriotic strike to rescue the deteriorating health services in Nigeria in 1984. It also assisted the Nigeria Labor Congress and the National Association of Nigerian Students to protest the brutal murder of the Ahmadu Bello University (ABU) students by Mobile Policemen in 1986. The Academic Staff Union also fought the illegal dismissal of its president, Dr. Festus Iyayi and others in 1987. It participated fully in the 1988 general strikes occasioned by the effects of the IMF Structural Adjustment Programme, which the Babangida military regime had imposed on the country.

Although ASUU's strikes may have been painful and sometimes destructive, strikes of this nature have equally produced some positive results. To revive or revamp the Nigerian educational sector, a body like ASUU is desperately needed to keep government functionaries on their toes. Critics must be reminded that the 2013 ASUU strike would not have commenced or occurred if the Federal Government of Nigeria had fulfilled the agreements it reached with the Academic Staff Union in 2009. Below are the nine-point programs the Federal Government of Nigeria struck with the Academic Staff Union in 2009, but refused to implement them in full:

- Funding requirements for Revitalization of the Nigerian Universities;
- Federal Government Assistance to State Universities;
- Establishment of NUPEMCO;
- Progressive increase in Annual Budgetary Allocation to Education to 26% between 2009 and 2020;
- Earned Allowance;
- Amendment of the Pension/Retirement Age of Academics on the Professorial cadre from 65 to 70 years;
- Reinstatement of prematurely dissolved Governing Councils;
- Transfer of Federal Government Landed Property to Universities; and
- Setting up of Research Development Council and Provision of Research Equipment to laboratories and classrooms in our universities (Osun Defender, 2013).

Lack of government implementation of these vital programs precipitated ASUU's 2011 strike--a strike which was halted when the government promised to look into the matter, but later failed to do so. In its 2013 industrial action, ASUU vowed not to call off the strike until the Federal Government of Nigeria implemented in full the 2009 agreement it had reached with the Academic Staff Union. A credible government always keeps to the agreements it reaches with other entities within its society; that is how such a government earns its legitimacy and respect.

The Chairman of ASUU at the Abubakar Tafawa Balewa University in Bauchi State, Dr. Lawn Abubakar, reechoed the above sentiment by accusing the Federal Government and the National Assembly of gambling and playing politics with the future of students in the Nigerian universities by refusing to implement an agreement it consciously entered into with the Union four years prior. The eminent scholar was quoted as saying:

> I can recall vividly that in December of 2011, ASUU went on strike over this same non-implementation of the 2009 agreement. In January of 2012, we sat down again with the government and drafted a Memorandum of Understanding (MOU), on how the 2009 agreement would be implemented. In the MOU, all the nine demands of ASUU were given deadlines for their implementation. If the government had sincerely followed the MOU, implementation would have been completed within June of last year [2012], but the government kept dragging the issue, without any positive headway (Edeh, 2013).

From this backdrop, many groups, including students' leaders, have called on the Federal Government to honor the agreement it entered with ASUU to save the country's educational sector from total collapse. In his own contribution to the ongoing ASUU strike, the Chairman of the Past Rivers State Students' Leaders' Forum (PARSLEAF), Amakiri Amakuro, noted that the disagreement between ASUU and the Federal Government would have been resolved if government had acted swiftly on the warning notice from the Union. He, therefore, pleaded to both parties to return to the negotiating table in the interest of the country. PARSLEAF's Chairman was quoted as making the following statements:

> We appreciate the Federal Government's appeals for understanding and commitment to meeting ASUU's demand. We, however, call on the Federal Government to make further commitment to honouring the agreement entered into with ASUU in order to save the educational system from total collapse. We also call on the leadership of ASUU to explore other means of engaging with government in drawing their attention as the option of strike is no longer fashionable and acceptable. If a strike must be used, it should not last for more than a few hours as is the practice in developed countries. We passionately appeal to the Federal Government, ASUU, and other stakeholders in the educational sector to sheath their swords (Akasike, 2013).

No matter what critics say about ASUU's unyielding attitude on the strike, the Union must be congratulated for its resolve in rescuing Nigeria's education from the Bretton Woods jugular grip. By embarking on the strike, ASUU forced the Nigerian government to place Nigeria's educational system on sound footing, which it has done for now. For this purpose, the government released N200 billion for infrastructural development in public universities as well as an additional release of N40 billion for payment of Academic Earned Allowance (AEA) to the lecturers. In coordinating this effort, the Federal Government of Nigeria created a twelve-man Implementation Monitoring Committee (IMC) whose duty is to monitor the implementation of the recommendations of the Committee on Needs Assessment of Nigerian Universities, as part of the agreement reached between the government and ASUU. The IMC is headed by Barrister Nyesom Wike, the Supervising Minister of Education (Idoko, 2014).

Why did it take this long to resolve an issue of national significance; one that borders on the security interest of the country? What boggles the mind of many Nigerians is that when it comes to raising the socio-economic wellbeing of ordinary Nigerians and, in the process, raise the profile of the country, the governing elite always claim that the country does not have the necessary financial resources to fulfill the obligation the government owes to the Nigerian people, but government functionaries always find money to address the needs of the elite class. Why would this be the case?

How can members of the National Assembly, for instance, come up with the money to pay themselves the jumbo salaries and allowances that have been disclosed to the public, when the same government entity cannot find the money to fund Nigerian Universities and pay decent wages to the Nigerian Universities' workforce? The CBN governor, Mallam Sanusi Lamido Sanusi (2009-2014), was the first Nigerian to disclose the large salaries and allowances paid to the 469-members of the National Assembly. At the time, some members of the National Assembly denied knowledge of lawmakers ever making such huge amounts that the CBN Governor alleged. To lower the tempo of public outrage and anger that such a revelation generated, the leadership of both the House of Representatives and the Senate promised to make the lawmakers' salaries and allowances public, which they have not done.

Oby Ezekwesili, an Accountant by profession, a co-founder of Transparency International--a global anti-corruption body based in Berlin, Germany, a former Vice President of the World Bank's Africa Division, a former Minister of Solid Minerals, and a former Minister of Education, has become another forceful voice against the "Jumbo Salary" appropriated to the nation's lawmakers.

Drawing from many sources, the seasoned public servant claimed that the country's Apex Legislative body had spent about N1 trillion in the last eight years (2005-2013) on its salaries and allowances. The data from which the former Minister of Education based her claims came mainly from the Federal Ministry of Finance, and the data revealed the amounts of funds appropriated to the National Assembly during those years in question to include the following: 2005, N54.79 billion; 2006, N54.79 billion; 2007, N66.4 billion; 2008, N114.39 billion; 2009, N158.92 billion; 2010, N150 billion; 2011, N150 billion; 2012, N150 billion; and 2013, N150 billion.

In addition to the above revelation, the former Vice President of the World Bank's African Division was quoted as having made the following remarks:

I also provided information available in recent global comparison of legislators' remuneration across the world recently published by the United Kingdom based *The Economist Magazine*. I stated that the report alleged that Nigerian federal legislators with a basic salary of $189,500 per annum (N30.6 million) were the highest paid lawmakers in the world. In reaction to various versions of news media report of my speech a number of members of the House of Representatives and Senators speaking as spokesmen of the National Assembly (NASS) and perhaps without the benefit of my full speech, strangely chose to haul verbal assaults and threats at me. The NASS in its prestige as the most important symbol of our democracy has a duty to promote at all times the democratic culture of tolerance for dissension. Would it therefore not have been more dignifying of our democracy if the spokesmen had used the opportunity of their reaction to offer their own data to contradict or clarify anything conveyed in my speech after reading it? Shouldn't the issue of management of our public finance be the core of good governance and too important, rather than [our lawmakers] be personal in their reaction? .... I wish to state with absolute respect for our lawmakers and our institution that it will be more valuable and enriching for our democracy instead of the abusive language of their recent reaction. The NASS should have immediately offered me and the rest of the Nigerian public, the opportunity of a Public Hearing on their Budgetary Allocations and the very relevant issue of their remuneration (Ujah, 2013).

Like the CBN governor, Ezekwesili had challenged the lawmakers to a public debate to which they have not followed through. She did not only reveal the annual remunerations of members of the National Assembly, but also informed the Nigerian public in one of her numerous public presentations or appearances that N9.08 billion is spent annually in maintaining a presidential fleet. A *Vanguard Nigerian* Newspaper article written by Johnbosco Agbakwuru and others (2013) reported that Ezekwesili had decried the country's budgetary allocation system, which she describes as giving more impetus to recurrent expenditure than capital projects.

Interestingly, after the lawmakers had repeatedly denied being paid the alleged huge sum of money and after they could no longer hide the truth from the Nigerian masses, they quickly shifted the blame to the Revenue Mobilisation Allocation and Fiscal Commission (RMAFC), claiming that the RMAFC is the body that fixes the salaries and allowances of the nation's lawmakers, and that they (the lawmakers) knew nothing about how their salaries and allowances were determined. The Deputy House Majority Leader, Leo Ogor, speaking on behalf of the embattled members of the National Assembly over the controversial huge pay, was quoted as making the following statements:

Federal legislators were always amazed whenever critics attacked lawmakers over the pay package as if they fix their own wage. We are tired of responding to the same issue every time; our explanations seem to be falling on deaf ears. We did not fix our salaries and allowances; that is the role of RMAFC. If you think that our salaries and allowances are too much, ask the agency to slash what they recommended (Ameh, 2013).

By the same token, the Senate has recently come to terms with the National Assembly annual budget of N150 billion and justified it by claiming that such an amount represents only three percent of the nation's annual budget of N4.8 trillion. The Senate also noted that the said sum of money for the nation's Apex Legislative body was not out of place.

Speaking on behalf of the Senate, Sen. Victor Ndoma-Egba, denied the claim that the nation's federal legislature had become expensive; he asserts that the National Assembly's annual budget of N150 billion cannot be held responsible for the wastage

Nigerians are experiencing in the governance of the country. According to him, "the N150 billion, which represents three percent of the annual national budget, was infinitesimal to the remaining 97 percent of the total budget of the country." The Senate leader was quoted as saying that "the N150 billion was not meant for the salary and allowances of the legislators alone but included salaries and allowances of other institutions within the National Assembly." The other institutions, according to Senator Ndoma-Egba, included the staff of the National Assembly Service Commission; the staff and management of the National Institute for Legislative Studies (NILS) and legislative aides of the lawmakers as well as the medical staff attached to the National Assembly (Agbakwuru and Erunke, 2013).

While the officials of the Federal Government of Nigeria are telling Nigerians that the government does not have the financial resources to fulfill the contractual obligation it had with the striking Universities' Academic Staff Union, an agency of the federal government, the Nigerian Civil Aviation Authority (NCAA) had the money to purchase two bullet-proof cars for the Aviation Minister, Stella Oduah--cars that were worth N255 million. Although the Aviation Minister denied during the House of Representatives Committee on Aviation hearing that the two alleged armored BMW cars were bought for her personal use and that they were registered in her name and claimed they were registered in her agency's name, the NCAA did not convince Nigerians as to whom the cars were meant for and why their price tags were bloated.

The main culprits involved in the bullet-proof car scandal (the NCAA and importer of the said cars, Coscharis Motors Nigeria Limited) told the House Committee on Aviation that the Lagos State government had requested the two BMW bullet-proof cars as part of the 300 vehicles the state used during its 18th National Sports Festival, held in 2012, in which Coscharis Motors Nigeria Limited became the official Automobile Partner to the said Festival (*Vanguard Nigeria News*, 2013).

The same actors in this case also told the House Committee on Aviation during the hearing on the bullet-proof cars scandal that they got a waiver from the Federal Government of Nigeria, which exempted them from paying importation fees and other value added taxes on the vehicles in question. The Lagos State government and the Federal Ministry of Finance quickly reacted to the allegation by denying any knowledge of the two BMW armored cars in question.

The Lagos State government, for example, denied ever requesting for any bullet-proof BMW vehicle or any other bullet-proof vehicle for use during its National Sports Festival, held between November 27 and December 9, 2012. Rather it recalled making a request to the federal government for a waiver of destination inspection charges and duty exemption on 300 vehicles, which were to be used for the festival and, such a waiver, was duly granted by the President's Office. According to the *Vanguard Nigeria Newspaper* article of November 1, 2013, the vehicles requested from Coscharis Motors Nigeria Limited, the auto dealer the article identified as the sponsor of the festival, were limited to saloon cars, four wheel drive vehicles and buses to convey the 14, 000 athletes and 10, 000 officials who attended the festival across the country.

By the same token, the Coordinating Minister for the Economy and Minister of Finance, Dr. Ngozi Okonjo-Iweala, denied granting a waiver for the clearing of the controversial armored cars. Speaking on her behalf, Paul Nwabuikwu, the Senior Special Assistant to the renowned Economist and a two-time Minister of Finance said that his boss only granted a waiver for the clearing of cars to be used for 2012 National Sports Festival, known as "EKO 2012," an event hosted by the Lagos State Government. The Finance Minister was vividly quoted in a *Vanguard Nigerian Newspaper* article of November 1, 2013, as saying that,

Recent media reports which claim that the Federal Ministry of Finance granted a waiver to Coscharis Motors Nigeria Limited for the purchase of armoured cars are totally false and without foundation. Rather, on June 23, 2012, the Lagos State Government applied for Waiver of Destination Inspection Charges and Duty Exemption for Coscharis Motors Nigeria Limited, the official Automobile Partner for the National Sports Festival (EKO 2012), to purchase 300 vehicles on its behalf for the event. Since the Lagos State Government met the laid-down criteria, the waiver was granted. It is also important to clarify that the waiver granted to the Lagos State Government for the event did not include the purchase of armoured vehicles (Okonjo-Iweala, 2013).

From the above scandal and the controversies surrounding it, it seems that there is something absolutely wrong with Nigeria if there is such money out there to buy a Minister, two expensive bullet-proof cars, at a time, when there are too many starving Nigerians who cannot afford three square meals a day. It is also unfortunate and heartbreaking that this is happening, at a time, when Nigerian Universities are poorly funded and the EFCC, the anti-corruption agency, is said to be broke due to government underfunding.

A report from *Punch editorial* of October 29, 2013 revealed that the EFCC was so broke that it could not pay for the services of the lawyers it hired to prosecute corruption and money laundering cases in court. The report went on to say that the lack of adequate funding of the agency "has affected the Commission's public enlightenment programmes through the mass media, making the agency a toothless bulldog that can only bark and not bite. The Editorial report stated also that "with corruption becoming more virulent than ever before, the Goodluck Jonathan Administration should live up to the billing by turning things around for the EFCC." It noted that "for a nation listed in the 139th position out of 176 countries ranked by Transparency International on its Corruption Perception Index in 2012, the deliberate denial of funding to the EFCC is the wrong way to go."

The *Nigeria Punch Newspaper* article of October 23, 2013, indicated that the Nigerian Presidential fleet has become larger than three domestic airlines combined. The article went on to list the brand of those planes that make up the presidential fleet. Among them are two Falcon 7X Jets, two Falcon 900 Jets, one Gulfstream 550, one Boeing 737 BBJ, one Gulfstream IVSP, one Gulfstream V, one Cessna Citation 2 Aircraft, and Hawker Siddley 125-800 Jet (Abioye, 2013).

The *Punch* article pegged the price tag of these aircrafts at an estimated price of $390.5 million (N60.53 billion). In comparing Nigeria with major countries in Europe and Asia, the article claimed that most countries in those continents have two aircrafts in their presidential fleet. This information is alarming and troublesome. How could Nigeria reconcile this anomaly, when it spends more money where it is not needed and ignores the need to spend more money where it is desperately required, like in public education and public health; and addressing the issues of unemployment, poverty and underdevelopment?

On January 8, 2014, another *Nigeria Punch Newspaper* article claimed that Jonathan's administration was planning to acquire one additional presidential jet for Nigeria, bringing the total number of planes in the Presidential Air Fleet (PAF) to eleven (11). The Newspaper noted that the administration has budgeted N1.52 billion for the maintenance of the ten (10) aircraft currently in the PAF in 2014; that the administration has also earmarked N458.5 million for international training of the fleet's personnel. The Newspaper also revealed that another chunk of the budget for the fleet is the N675.9 million budgeted for rehabilitation/renovation/repairs of the PAF Barracks, including a whopping sum of N405.5 million being proposed for the completion of a hangar project under the PAF budget for the year, while N106 million is earmarked for tyre bay tools and equipment. The PAF's security vote, including operations, is said to be N259.55 million; insurance premium N445.7 million; as well as N58 million for cleaning and fumigation services (Ojo, 2014).

The *Punch Newspaper* article of January 8, 2014, revealed that N71.74 million was budgeted for 797 units of LG2HP air- conditioners for PAF Barracks; N40.5 million was earmarked for three units of Toyota Coaster buses and N26.4 million for four units of Toyota Hilux Motor, vehicle fuel would gulp N29.6 million, other transport equipment fuel would cost N26. 5 million; plant/generator fuel cost would be N14.5 million while the cooking gas/fuel would cost N2 million.

"The N67 million devoted to miscellaneous included: meals, N28.9 million; postage and courier services, N15 million; medical expenses, N12 million; corps members kitting, transport and feeding allowances, N3.7 million; and honorarium and sitting allowance, N3.6 million" (Ojo, 2014).

Given this reckless spending by the Federal Government of Nigeria, Jide Ojo, in his own opts, concludes that,

I must hasten to say that the request for an additional presidential jet is not the only absurd thing in the 2014 appropriation bill. Several others including the sum earmarked for travels, acquisition of animals for the presidential zoo, maintenance of presidential guest houses and the likes should be deleted from this year's budget. State governments that are buying jets for their governors' use and ordering a fleet of bulletproof cars for their comfort at the expense of the suffering masses are doing a lot of disservice to their people. It is quite ironic that these frivolous requests are being made in the budgets of different levels of government even in the face of dwindling income and when much of the budget is being financed with local and international debts (Ojo, 2014).

In drawing some inference from *The Nation's* editorial of January 3, 2014, the Punch reporter reminded the Nigerian governing elite that, as leaders, they should learn to cut their coats according to their country's purse. It is not only the citizens who should make sacrifices in times of economic adversities.

With these lavish expenses, Nigerians are not convinced one bit, as the Nigerian ruling class would want them to believe that the country lacks adequate financial resources to improve and raise the academic profile of Nigerian Universities. As we observed from the analyses above, the country's governing elite have a misplaced priority, which is specifically aimed at enhancing the wellbeing of the elite class at the expense of the general masses.

For example, if the children of the governing elite were enrolled in Nigerian Universities, they would not allow the five-month old strike to go on for this length of time. Because most of their children are studying abroad, the elitist class does not care about what becomes of University education in Nigeria.

Impact of Governments' Lack of Funding and Commitment to Nigeria's Public Education

The deterioration of educational performance and standards in Nigeria has recently caught the attention of President Goodluck Jonathan, who decried the poor ratings of Nigerian universities—a remark made on his behalf by his former Minister of Education, Prof. Ruqqayatu Rufai, at the 41st Convocation Ceremony of the University of Nigeria Nsukka (UNN). Reflecting on the poor ranking of Nigerian universities, the president was quoted as saying:

It was unacceptable that no Nigerian university is among the top ten providers of tertiary institutions in Africa, not to mention globally. Nigeria cannot be a great nation on the back of poorly trained youth. It is for this reason that the transformation of our nation must start in the classrooms....There is no doubt that the University has been a transformational force in the evolution of our country. The founding fathers' vision was for a united, strong and prosperous Nigeria. These values underline our present transformation initiatives. The University of Nigeria should lead because of its age, quality of staff and students and its achievements in research and community service. Transformation is not just another slogan. We cannot tolerate the attitude of business as usual. Let me assure you that our decision to support the education sector is resolute. We will continue to work until our universities become centres of excellence (Edike, 2012).

While lamenting on inadequate skills among Nigerian graduates, President Jonathan through the Supervising Minister of Education, Nyesom Wike, who represented him at the 29th Convocation Ceremony of the University of Ilorin, told the graduating class of that institution that the country would not tolerate a situation where a large number of graduates produced by universities lack relevant skills due to poor training. The President blamed the poor training on University lecturers whom he said must re-orient themselves and avoid distractions at work occasioned by unnecessary strikes which remain the bane of the country's educational system with its attendant consequences.

The President's spokesman at the University of Ilorin Convocation also noted that with 129 universities and several other higher institutions, the country has no reason to lag behind in the quest for technological development. In exonerating Jonathan's administration from the steady decline and deterioration of University education in Nigeria caused by decades of government underfunding and its lack of commitment to education, the President's spokesman told participants and the 2013 graduating class that the administration was leaving no stone unturned in its quest to transform Nigerian Universities in making them globally competitive.

In keeping to the administration's pledge of transforming university education in Nigeria, Wike stated that President Jonathan had increased the budget for education progressively from N234.8 billion in 2010 to N426.5 billion in 2013, with N55.4 billion allocated to the university subsector alone. The Supervising Minister of Education also lamented in his speech that "barely a month ago, the federal government released the sum of N130 billion to universities for infrastructure development and payment of earned allowances to staff" (Vanguard Nigeria, 2013; Ameh and Josiah, 2012), a statement to which ASUU's leadership publicly denied as untrue and misleading.

The purported release of N130 billion to Nigerian universities by Jonathan's administration was quickly denied by the Chairman of the Federal University of Agriculture Makurdi branch of ASUU, Dr. Celestine Aguoru, who spoke after leading members of his branch on a peaceful march around Makurdi town in protest of the lingering Federal Government/ASUU face-off. In a *Vanguard Nigeria Newspaper* article reprinted in *allAfrica.com* on November 1, 2013, Dr. Aguoru was quoted, as making the following remarks:

> As we are talking today, government has not released one kobo out of the N100 billion they claimed they have given the universities; this goes to show the level of insincerity of the government. The truth is that government is paying lip service to the development of education in this country and has therefore resorted to playing politics with the education sector and the future of our children. It is rather unfortunate that majority of those who are leading us today went to school in their time on scholarships, but today they do not want our children to benefit from that same gesture, all because of greed. Today we are faced with a situation where the amount Nigerians spend yearly to educate their children in Ghana is far more than the yearly budgetary allocation to the education sector. Our leaders are not being fair to our country; government should as a matter of priority implement its agreements with ASSU, Nigerians are tired of this deceit, they should remember that if they continue to negate their responsibilities to the people, one day they will certainly give account to God (Duru and Amamdi, 2013).

Dr. Lawn Abubakar, Chairman of ASUU at the Abubakar Tafawa Balewa University in Bauchi State, was another voice, who refuted the claim dominating the Nigerian air waves, as was claimed by the President's spokesman at the 29th Convocation of the University of Ilorin, who indicated that the Federal Government had released the sum of N100 billion to universities, being part of the N400 billion meant for the Infrastructural Intervention Fund to the fifty-nine benefiting universities in the country that was already due.

He noted that the additional sum of N30 billion released by the Federal Government for earned allowances of Federal Universities was unacceptable to ASUU because, by the Union's calculations in 2012, the cost implication of the arrears was N87 billion and not N30 billion. Dr. Abubakar told his Chapter members that Governor Gabriel Suswan, the Chairman of the Implementation Committee on the Needs Assessment of Universities, was the chief source of the claim, but refused to disclose when the government would release the remaining amount of the N400 billion intervention funds to tertiary institutions. In another twist, Abubakar informed Nigerians that none of the tertiary institutions in the country had received its 2013 allocations from the government.

The transformational measures President Jonathan has for Nigerian University education and his effort to increase the revenue for education in his 2013 budget are noble and must be applauded. It is the right thing to do because education is an important cornerstone in any nation building effort, especially for a nascent democratic society such as Nigeria. Nigerian democracy cannot grow and blossom if our educational sector is weak and underperforming, as it is today.

Government functionaries in Nigeria must acknowledge the obvious fact that for many decades Nigerian public education has been left to rot. It was a shocking moment for many Nigerians to hear President Jonathan lament on the inadequate skills among Nigerian University graduates, as if he was unaware of this steady decline and deterioration of University education in the country. How could Nigerian university students perform at their best, when their university environments are not conducive to learning?

Most Nigerian universities' infrastructures are dilapidated; their libraries do not have modern textbooks on their shelves, nor modern equipment, not even well-equipped computer labs and other experimental laboratories on their various campuses.

It is natural to blame the victims rather than blaming those who created the problems and failed to take responsibility for their actions. Nigeria Universities cannot develop the caliber of students and skills that President Jonathan alluded to at the 29th Convocation Ceremony of the University of Ilorin without adequate commitment and funding of these institutions by governments in Nigeria. Education in Nigeria cannot be properly funded when the Nigerian governing elite recklessly spend public funds and, thereby, create waste in government.

Another eminent scholar, who provided a meaningful assessment and analysis as to why Nigerian Universities, especially State Universities, were performing below their counterparts in the world, was Prof. Julius Okojie, the Executive Secretary of the NUC. In his remarks, he blamed the state governors for lack of adequate funding and the appalling state of the learning environment in some state universities. His assessment of the situation indicated that the standard of learning environment and infrastructure in many universities across the country needed to be upgraded. When the observation was reported to the National Economic Council (NEC) by the Committee on Needs Assessment of Public Universities in the country, Professor Okojie expressed shock upon learning about the nature of some of the curricula and programs students were studying in some of these universities.

The following statements were attributed to Professor Okojie, as he blames state governments and universities' administrations for their contribution in lowering the educational standards in many Nigerian universities and the poor performance of students in these institutions. His criticisms of the state governments and universities' authorities, according to Success Nwogu, were as follows:

State governments do not fund universities. There is a good turnover of governors. When a governor comes, he wants to move the university to his place of origin, or the vice-chancellor cannot disclose how many students he has and the governor will say, I cannot fund the university if I do not know the number of students you have. There is lack of integrity in the system. Another issue is part-time programmes (Nwogu, 2012).

Another major problem Professor Okojie foresaw in his assessment was the friction between universities and their host communities, which he claimed had impeded educational development and national growth. To buttress his claim, he cited the ugly incidents that took place at the University of Port Harcourt, where four students were murdered by villagers outside the university campus, and in Mubi, Adamawa and Maiduguri, where students living off campus were also massacred.

He pointed out that the NUC had recommended for a full residential policy where all students would reside on campus instead of staying in towns, as a way of addressing the issue of friction between universities and their host communities. It was "the opinion of the NUC that such a policy will enhance the students' safety and education." Additionally, the eminent scholar called on Nigerian universities to engage in more research to address the nation's problems, as the *Guardian editorial* of December 6, 2012, agrees:

> The quality of postgraduate training and research has plummeted and can hardly drive the process of national development. Research output and outlets for dissemination of results are no longer in first-rated journals. Nigerian universities hardly attract international students, as was the case in the good old days. Even at home, reputable employers now raise critical eyebrows when dealing with Nigerian graduates. The roots of these problems may not be as obvious as the report [Committee on Needs and Assessment of Public Universities] reveals, but they show irresistibly that all is not well with the system, by bringing to the front burner, the deepening crisis of public universities, like other public institutions in Nigeria…. From the report, the main problem is linked to corruption in all phases of university governance, including a dearth of qualified teachers, over-bloated bureaucratization where non-teaching staff almost doubled teaching staff; and the heavy reliance on adjunct lecturers, among others. These negative factors are the sad realities of the country's public universities.

What State Governments Are Doing to Revitalize Public Education in their Respective States?

The above observations relate to what is wrong with Nigeria's public education, including university education since governments (federal, state and local governments) have taken their eyes off the ball. There is, indeed, a renewed hope on the horizon, since some state government officials are fighting back seriously to right the wrong done to education in Nigeria, especially to make education easily accessible and affordable to all citizens of their states, regardless of their citizens' socio-economic status, and regardless of the IMF policy on public education, which forbids governments from subsidizing education in the country. One such governor who is changing the dynamics of education in the country today is the Imo State governor, Owelle Rochas Anayochukwu Okorocha, who was overwhelmingly elected in 2011 by the Imo electorate and re-elected in 2015 because of his track record on education in the State.

Coming from a poor and humble background, Governor Okorocha worked his way to the top. Given his life experiences, he knew what it meant to be poor. He was not born with a golden spoon in his mouth, as his life experiences indicate—experiences he openly revealed to the public during his fiftieth birthday anniversary, which was celebrated on October 8, 2012. In a press interview he granted to the *Daily Sun Newspaper* reporter, Chidi Obineche, the flamboyant governor told his audience how his life journey began. He told them that he became a petty trader at a tender age of twelve; that he sold oranges, okrika (used clothes), used cars, and cement; and from there, he made his mark and rose to national prominence. He said that he was married at the age of twenty four, and at the age of twenty-nine, he became a member of the National Constitutional Conference; that he was a former member of the Federal Character Commission; that he had once contested for the governorship of the state and lost; that he ran twice for the country's presidency and lost; and that he was once a presidential advisor (Obineche, 2012).

These were the experiences he acquired over the years that gave him the wisdom and virtue to understand the plight of the poor. They were experiences that motivated him to reach out to the poor after realizing his life ambition. Before he became the Imo State governor in 2011, Gov. Rochas Okorocha had built several primary and secondary schools in the state and in other parts of the federation, where the children of the poor were given an opportunity to live out their dreams. Students in Governor Okorocha's private schools were given free education, including free textbooks, free meals, school uniforms, and other school supplies. All these, the governor paid for with his own personal money.

When he became the governor of the state, free education at all levels became the cornerstone of his administration—something that had never been done before in the history of the state and in the former Eastern Region, which today comprises two political zones, the South-East and some parts of the South-South Zones of the federation. This is a feat most political icons in the region were unable to achieve before the ascendency of Gov. Rochas Okorocha to the governor's mansion. Some of these political icons include: Dr. Nnamdi Azikiwe of blessed memory, when he was the Premier of Eastern Region; Michael Opara, who took over from Dr. Azikiwe, as the Premier of Eastern Region; Gov. Sam. Mbakwe, as the first democratically elected governor of Imo State--the most productive governor the state has ever produced, and other governors both military and civilian, who came before Rochas.

Governor Okorocha's critics had wondered how he could pay for the program, but he surprised them when he took out N4 billion from his Security Vote to pay for it. This is the same amount of money that other elected governors before him were receiving from federal accounts, but they were unable to use this instrument or medium to raise the profile of education in the state. During these governors' tenures in office, many children in Imo State stopped going to school because their parents could not afford the school tuition and could not buy the necessary school supplies. The coming of Governor Okorocha has reversed these anomalies.

Today, many young people of school age are back in the classroom. This is a remarkable achievement for the Okorocha administration. Indeed, the people of Imo State are very grateful to the governor for this singular accomplishment. The free education program has brought huge financial relief for many parents in the state and has made education accessible to poor children who would not have gotten the opportunity to obtain a university education if this program had not been instituted.

The governor of Akwa Ibom State, Chief Godswill Akpabio, is hailed as another productive governor in the federation. This assessment came as a result of the good work Akpabio has done as governor of his state in spite of the difficulties he underwent. Based on this fact, his Eminence, Dr. Sunday Ola Makindle, the Primate of the Methodist Church of Nigeria, described the governor as a disciple of Awo and Zik.

By borrowing from Dr. Nnamdi Azikiwe's good leadership qualities, vision, and initiatives, the governor, according to the Primate, transformed his state to an envious position, thereby, making his state to look like a "little London," and borrowing from Chief Obafemi Awolowo's noble services to his region and to the nation, the governor has made education and health care free for all (Samuel, 2012). Those who could not afford these vital services are now having free access to them. There are other State governors who have done so much in their states to undo the damage done to Nigerian public education by IMF's Privatization Scheme.

Chief Obafemi Awolowo would not be forgotten when it came to the issue of "free education" in Nigeria. Having served in many capacities in Nigeria, the first Premier of Western Region, former leader of the defunct Action Group (AG), former

Finance Minister of the Federation and member of the Supreme Military Council (SMC) under Gen. Yakubu Gowon's administration, and the former leader of the defunct Unity Party of Nigeria (UPN), Chief Awolowo was and is still regarded as the "father" of free education and free health care in Nigeria.

Coming from a poor and humble background and being a self-made man—one who worked his way up to the top, Chief Awolowo understood what it meant to be poor during his days. While his contemporaries in other regions of the federation refused to offer free education and free health care to their citizens, Chief Awolowo invested much of his regional resources on his people's education and health.

During his tenure as the Premier of Western Region, he made primary and secondary education compulsory and free for all. Every child of school going age who resided in the region had the opportunity of being educated free of charge regardless of where that child's parents came from and regardless of that child's parent's socioeconomic status. Chief Awolowo's free education and free health care policies eased the financial burden of many poor parents and guardians, and his educational and health care policies attracted many Nigerians from all walks of life both from far and near, including Lagos, to several parts of the Western Region. Being a self-educated man, Awo, as he was popularly known among his admirers and supporters, knew the importance of education and health to nation-building. Throughout his political career and activism, Awo did not rest until free education in Nigeria became a national policy. While serving as a Finance Minister in General Gowon's administration, he persuaded the regime to embark on a compulsory Universal Primary Education (UPE) and free education to all levels, which the regime adopted at the time. This singular national policy gave hope to millions of Nigerian young men and women, who otherwise would not have had the opportunity to be educated.

Though Chief Awolowo was a controversial political figure in Nigerian body polity, as Chinua Achebe's latest book, titled *There was a Country* indicated, most of the ideas he advanced were to the benefit of humanity. He gave hope to those who had none and, became a voice to the voiceless. Although some Nigerians did not approve of his method of political activism and approach, he was a man of many good ideas. He was well ahead of his contemporaries when it came to public administration and good governance. He would have changed Nigeria for better had he had the opportunity to rule the country. This conclusion is drawn from Awolowo's performance in the Western Region, where he set the region on the path of success by creating industrial estates and several boards to handle various projects that projected the region to prosperity. For this singular reason and in spite of their differences, Awo was described by late Gen. Chukwuemeka Odumegwu Ojukwu as, "the best president Nigeria never had."

Today, members of the Nigerian intelligentsia are said to come mainly from the old Western region. This is because of the energy and resources Awo and his group invested in the education of their people. His efforts to educate his people have paid off in the long-run and, have made life much easier for those who utilized the opportunity.

Chief Edwin Clark, the famous Ijaw leader, politician, and former Minister of Information rightly pointed out in an article published by the *Nigerian Tribune Newspaper* on November 7, 2013, that "Chief Obafemi Awolowo was instrumental to the rapid development of the Western states and the Yoruba nation as a whole."

In making the case for a national conference in Abuja in November of 2013 before the Southern Nigeria Peoples Assembly (SNPA), a group whose members were drawn from the South-East, South-West, and South-South political zones, Chief Clark reminded those who attended the Abuja SNPA's meeting that

> The demand for national conference did not start during the Jonathan government; it is an age-long demand particularly by Western Nigeria. But no government had the courage to listen to Nigerians particularly when they heard sovereign, they thought it was a move to overthrow their government. We should commend the then three regional leaders, who fought for the nation's independence, particularly Awolowo who brought great development to the western region that is why they are the most educated and enlightened ….Nigeria belongs to all of us. This country was made one by our colonial masters and they didn't say either north or south should be superior or inferior to the other. There is no country in the world where some people are second class and others are first class citizens so we must sit down and discuss the basis of our unity in this country (Oyesina, 2013).

In acknowledging what Chief Awolowo meant to his people, region, and country, Chief Olumuyiwa Akinboro, the former member of the House of Representatives in Nigeria's Second Republic, described Awo as the greatest leader the country ever produced and remained the only Nigerian leader who selflessly worked for the best interest of all Nigerians.

This legal practitioner also points out that "Awo succeeded in maximally utilizing the meager resources at his disposal to advance education, agriculture and other sectors in the country." He concludes that, "nobody has ever been able to beat his enviable record. Any administration that endeavors to follow his footsteps will always be acceptable to the people and become the best political bride among the compatriots." In addition to his analysis on Awolowo's accomplishments, the ex-lawmaker was quoted as making the following remarks:

> Corruption is the cradle and genesis of all our seemingly insurmountable and intractable social, moral and economic tribulations, abject poverty, bad roads, decayed infrastructure, declining education standards, Boko Haram,

and all other maladies manifesting steadily in our nation. Unless there is a better management and a more equitable distribution of our national resources, there will be neither peace nor appreciable progress in Nigeria (Olukoya, 2013).

Many state governors from the old Western region both past and present have continued Awo's legacy by making education and primary health care accessible and affordable to their down-trodden population. These are programs the Central government operatives must revisit, given the economic hardship that millions of Nigerian parents are facing today in educating their children.

The recent policy proposal made by Northern States' Governors to abolish Secondary School fees paid in their region is, indeed, a welcoming development. The group's agreement to harmonize fees paid in their tertiary institutions, its effort to re-introduce the Grade II teacher training program abolished across the country several years ago, its resolve to establish schools of preliminary studies, and its proposed education summit must be applauded. The reasons for this sudden change of heart include:

1) To improve the standard of teaching in northern region's schools;
2) To close the educational gap between male and female students in the region;
3) To prepare students for admission into tertiary institutions within and outside the region; and
4) To address all the problems associated with the growth and development of education in the region, especially the problem of almajiri and failing standard of education.

The Chairman of the Northern States' Governors Forum and Governor of Niger State, Babangida Aliyu, in an address delivered on his behalf by Muhammed Nuhu, during the National Association of Niger State Students Award Ceremony, described "education as the bedrock of any development," adding that his administration has established schools of preliminary studies in three different locations within the State. These locations are Agaie, Ibeto, and Tegina. The Governor also said that his administration "had computerized the payment of scholarships to students in tertiary institutions and introduced the scratch card to all beneficiaries as a way of blocking areas of wastage, saying so far, that the administration had paid about N1.8 billion in scholarship and other allowances" (Opara, 2014).

Impact of Corruption on Nigeria's Public Health Industry

Another public sector that is so vital to Nigerians is the health care industry. Like other sectors, public health in Nigeria has been grossly neglected or mismanaged by the country's governing elite. The little funds appropriated for public health both at the federal and state government levels are usually looted by those who are entrusted to steer the affairs of the country's health programs.

The privatization scheme in the country, which emanated from IMF directives, has made matters even worse for public health. Because of such IMF directives and because of the massive corruption, which engulfed the Nigerian public health sector, government operatives have once again taken their eyes off the ball; they are no longer subsidizing the health care sector the way they did so many years ago, especially during the 1960s and 1970s.

Because of this singular fact, Nigerians are dying by the thousands annually, as a result of inadequate health care programs, and lack of facilities and equipment. Several reports reveal that Nigerians are today dying from both treatable diseases (high blood pressure and diabetes) and those that are chronic in nature. What this means is that the country lacks adequate health education and preventive care mechanisms to tackle the endemic health problems facing the nation.

To bring this obvious fact home, some medical experts in the country; for example: Consultant Neurosurgeon at the Cedacrest Hospital in Abuja, Dr. Abiodun Ogungbo; the Chief Medical Director of Dayspring Hospital, Agah, Lagos, Dr. Samuel Adebayo; and the Managing Director of Pathcare Nigeria, Dr. Pamela Ajayi have raised the alarm that young Nigerians in their twenties and thirties are dying of hypertension, a disease often described as a silent killer worldwide (Adebayo, 2013).

According to these experts, about 250,000 lives could be saved yearly with early detection of hypertension, if there is an increased awareness of the prevention and early detection of the disease. In their analyses, these experts attributed terminal diseases such as, heart failure, cardiac arrest, kidney and liver failure to high blood pressure. In describing the complexities of hypertension, Dr. Ogungbo was quoted as saying that,

> One in every four adults in Nigeria has hypertension and this is a very high percentage. More young persons are also dying of the complications of hypertension. Sadly, many people who have it do not know. Millions of people are literally walking time bombs because of their high blood pressure because when it remains untreated, it causes heart attack, stroke or kidney disease.... Hypertension is not caused by stress, lack of sleep or depression. It is also not caused by the old women in the village or by an evil arrow sent by a colleague at work or your next door neighbour. It is not that problem at the home front. In about 90 percent of all cases, the cause of hypertension still remains unknown (Adebayo, 2013).

In his own analysis, Dr. Adebayo observed that many years ago, hypertension was not a common phenomenon with young Nigerians; but today, young people between the ages of twenty and thirty are diagnosed with hypertension every day. He attributed the high number of young Nigerians with high blood pressure to their lifestyle. Though hypertension could be hereditary, Dr. Adebayo noted that the disease is linked to increased intake of salt and fatty foods, obesity, lack of exercise and inadequate intake of vegetables and fruits. He also added alcohol and cigarettes to the list of things that trigger high blood pressure. Dr. Ajayi also gave the Nigerian youth the obvious fact of the disease. She describes it as a disease of the African race—meaning that Africans are more genetically predisposed to developing high blood pressure than any other racial group in the world.

The Nigerian governing elite are aware of these facts, but refused to tackle the health problems facing the country with uttermost sincerity and urgency. There is no reason on earth why diabetes, hypertension, arthritis, malaria associated diseases, and water-borne diseases should not be eradicated in the country, in this day and age, given the country's enormous wealth and resources. The Nigerian health sector has been totally abandoned due to inadequate funding coupled with the misappropriation of the little funds allotted to the sector.

Because of this abandonment, the governing elite with their family members, their associates, and other well-to-do Nigerians have been traveling to several foreign countries in search of adequate medical treatments. Their famous foreign destinations are the United States of America, Great Britain, Germany, India, and Saudi Arabia, to mention just a few.

Nigerians would be amazed if they knew how much money Nigerians spent on foreign medical treatments. For example, the Honorable Minister of Finance, Dr. Ngozi Okonjo-Iweala was quoted as saying that "if Nigerians, who travel abroad for medical services can attend to their health in the country, a whopping of N30 billion will be saved annually" (Onuba, 2011). In her paper, titled "Creating Jobs: A Short to Medium-Term Agenda"—a paper she unveiled in Abuja in 2011. In that paper, the Finance Minister, lay out the importance of healthcare in nation building efforts. The seasoned economist and a long serving official of the IMF lamented that "good health contributes to economic growth and poor health reduces workforce efficiency and output." She noted that Nigeria could save $200 million (about N30 billion) from medical services abroad; and that the health sector had potential for job creation, adding that healthcare was ranked number ten out of the twenty fastest growing occupations in the United States. Her areas of focus included: maternal and child services; core circuit training for pregnant women; and school feeding programs.

By the same token, the spokesperson of New Horizon Healthcare Limited, Lagos, Henry Mojekwu, was also quoted as saying that "Nigerians spend over N2.5 billion every year on trips to India in search of medical treatment" (Adebayo, 2011). Mojekwu noted in his analysis that many Nigerians are attracted to India because it has one of the best medical practices in the world. They even go for things as little as a medical check-up because it is affordable which cannot be said of our health system in Nigeria. But, we are losing a lot of resources to their economy."

He called on the government of Nigeria to consider a long term solution to the dilapidated state of health facilities in the country's hospitals, noting that Nigerians could not rely solely on foreign medical treatment at the expense of theirs at home; and that, the time has come for Nigeria to upgrade its hospitals to an international standard (Adebayo, 2012).

In response to the surge in cost of foreign medical treatment, President Jonathan told his audience at the fiftieth year anniversary of the Nigerian Medical Association (NMA), that the Federal Government would no longer be interested in funding medical trips abroad for its officials. From his observation, the funds used for such medical trips had led to tremendous loss of the nation's scarce foreign exchange, the direct result of unbearably rampant trips abroad by officials seeking medical care. He noted that such money would be channeled into developing tertiary hospitals of international standards (Onuba, 2011).

In corroborating with what most Nigerians know already, Pres. Goodluck Jonathan, while commissioning the Nigerian-Turkish Nizamiye Hospital in Abuja, noted that private sector initiatives such as this will help government's effort to halt the enormous capital flight arising from increased medical tourism and the avoidable stress experienced by Nigerians on such missions.

In describing the measures taken by the Jonathan administration to curb medical tourism, the Minister of Health, Prof. Chukwu Onyebuchi, reiterated how Nigerian politicians and individuals are rushing to foreign countries for medical attention, which he claimed, is depleting the country's foreign reserve. While in Benin City, the Edo State capital, attending the burial ceremony of the father of the President of the Nigerian Medical Association, Dr. Osahon Enabulele, the Health Minister was quoted as making the following statements regarding the ordeal some Nigerians experienced while seeking medical treatment abroad:

> There are some Nigerians detained in other countries because they could not settle their medical bills. Some of them, their communities have written me letters for financial assistance as they cannot come back to Nigeria because they are owing. It is a big problem. There are things we have achieved in the last one year. For more than 10 years, we couldn't do an open heart surgery in Nigeria, now two hospitals are doing it in Enugu and Ibadan...We have people who go abroad and they are in two classes, one are people, who are spending their private money, whether well-earned or not too well-earned. There are others, who are sponsored by other persons including religious bodies. The others are those sponsored by government whether at local, state or federal levels, but it is government sponsorship (Enogholase, 2014).

The Health Minister claimed, as other analysts on the subject-matter have done, that the country is losing over N78 billion annually, because individual Nigerians and public officials were seeking medical treatment abroad. To curb these huge expenses, Professor Onyebuchi said that the federal government will not allow public servants whose medical cases are not approved by his office to seek treatment abroad. This directive means that foreign medical treatment is no longer free and accessible to all public servants, including the political class, as was the practice. This is a step in the right direction, but legislation is needed to enforce the ban.

The *Daily Sun Newspaper,* in its March 4, 2014 *editorial commentary*, joined the public debate on medical tourism undertaken by Nigerian political class. In reemphasizing some of the sentiments expressed above, the paper noted the following:

> Although there is no agreement on the actual amount of money Nigerians spend on medical tourism annually, it has been acknowledged that the nation loses billions of naira annually to avoidable medical trips. Some of our governors and other political elites have been hospitalized in one foreign hospital or the other due to accidents or other ailments at a huge expense. It is public knowledge, also, that many Nigerians troop to Asian countries, especially India, and Europe to treat kidney and cancer-related ailment, citing the poor health services in the country.

The paper went on to say that "the Federal Government's determination to halt medical tourism in the country is a commendable move that should be embraced by all Nigerians." It further noted that "for this to work, our leaders will need to lead by example, which is better than precept. The discipline required to ensure that medical tourism is curbed in the country must flow from the top to the bottom. Anything short of this will amount to hypocrisy and double standards." The *editorial* called for adequate funding and equipment of local hospitals both public and private so that the number of Nigerians seeking foreign medical treatment can be minimized if not eliminated. It also called for adequate remuneration and motivation of local medical practitioners, such as doctors, nurses, pharmacists and others so that brain drain in the sector can be curbed.

The Federal government and other state governments should take a cue from the Kaduna State government whose State House of Assembly had proposed a bill banning state governors and deputy governors from using state resources to fund their medical bills abroad after leaving office (Bello, 2013). Although this is a symbolic gesture (one that is not inclusive but weak) it is an idea whose time has come. The bill should have banned all current serving government officials, including political elites in the state from using state resources to fund their medical bills abroad. Such a policy will force politicians to do something concrete to upgrade Nigeria's hospitals as is done in those foreign countries where they seek medical attention.

The House of Representatives was said to have questioned the rationale behind encouraging affluent Nigerians to seek medical services overseas. The House concluded that such a "trend was not only detrimental to the improvement of healthcare services locally, but a drain on the nation's scarce resources." Additionally, Nigerians are yet to see the fulfillment of President Jonathan's promises. Nigerian government officials always talk big but do so little.

Nigerians are not only witnessing the deterioration of the country's public health sector, but also the brain drain of medical professionals, such as doctors and nurses, who are leaving the country in a large number to several foreign countries, where life is bountiful. Indeed, talk is cheap. What Nigerians want to see is action not mere promises. As a saying goes, "action speaks louder than words." Nigerian leaders know exactly what to do in this regard, but have failed to do the right thing simply because medical tourism is another means of siphoning the country's meager funds into their overseas' bank accounts.

A lot needs to be done to repair the damage done to Nigeria's public education and public healthcare sectors. A drastic and meaningful change is needed if the country is to become vibrant, take its rightful place in the comity of nations, and fulfill its obligations to the Nigerian people. The country needs healthy citizenry in order to develop its potential, as a nation.

It is absurd that Nigerians allow this ugly practice to continue, when hospitals of international standards could have been built to provide adequate and quality health care for all. Nigerians must not be short-sighted in knowing that highly educated and healthy citizenry are an integral part of what scholars of international relations and diplomacy refer to as "national security." This is why advanced countries take these issues very seriously; they spend enormous resources to educate their citizens and provide them with quality health care. This is not the case in Nigeria, but Nigerians want to compete globally and join the G-20 member-states, which comprise industrialized and developing economies. How can Nigeria compete globally when these vital elements of nation-building (education and health) are absolutely neglected by the country's governing elite?

How Corruption Contributes to Massive Poverty and Crime in Nigeria

Corruption has been identified by many Nigerians and foreign entities, as the leading factor of the country's massive poverty and crime. Poverty and crime are chiefly responsible for the decline in the country's moral fabric. Nigerians are witnessing today the increasing wave of violent crimes, which include: extra-judicial killings, including political assassinations and mass killings; rape; mistreatment of detainees (torture); kidnapping; armed robbery; human trafficking; drug trafficking; fraud; and money laundering, etc. These crimes have enormous consequences on the people and on the nation's economy, as Senator Gaya rightly pointed out in his critique of the country's insecurity. Many Nigerians are victimized daily by both criminals and the very criminal justice professionals (police officers), who swore an oath to protect the innocent from being abused.

Violent crime has now become the order of the day in Nigeria. No one in the country is spared by these gangs of criminals, not even government officials and their relatives. Nigerians hear daily through the country's mass media, including electronic and print media, about the kidnapping of some family members of highly placed Nigerians, such as the kidnapping of President Jonathan's adopted father and Dr. Ngozi Okonjo-Iweala's mother. Other Nigerians who have suffered similar fate in the hands of kidnappers include a vast segment of university lecturers, traditional rulers, businessmen and women, and the clergy.

Individuals who involve themselves in this criminal enterprise do so because of the huge sum of money they collect as ransom. Because of this high incidence of kidnapping in the country, many business executives are now acquiring insurance coverage to protect themselves from the risk of being kidnapped. The Managing Director of Equity Assurance, Ekpe Ukpabio, and the Group Managing Director of Continental Reinsurance, Femi Oyetunji, confirmed that this sort of policy protection against the risk of being kidnapped is being made available to those who want it. In explaining what the new policy entails, Ukpabio was quoted as saying: "we are having cases of kidnapping for ransom request and we have actually done some policies already. We have renewed our partnership with some foreign reinsurers and brokers that are providing it; we have been able to give cover for this class of business" (Popoola, 2014). This is what Nigeria has become; a situation or phenomenon never heard of before now.

Poverty has always been blamed as the chief source of violence and petty crime found in most societies. A famous Greek Philosopher, Aristotle, described poverty as "the mother of revolution and crime." Many critics agreed with this great philosopher's proposition that, indeed, poverty is the underlying cause of revolutions. But while they lean toward Aristotle's assertion, some of them disagreed, stating that increase in crime rates in countries has nothing to do with poverty.

By stretching Aristotle's proposition further, an *Ultimate GP Blogger*, named Murphy, demonstrated in his article how poverty led to many world revolutions, but disagreed that poverty causes high crime rates in countries. In his conceptualization of poverty, Murphy noted that "poverty is being without things, having little money, not many material possessions and, in need, of essential goods." He further went on to describe poverty as,

> Being poor means that the people have nothing, and they have to struggle
> to even survive every day. After physically and mentally tortured for a long
> period of time due to poverty, evil thoughts of getting out of the vicious

cycle through illegal ways or new ideals that they think will improve their lives will gradually start to form in the poor people's minds. These thoughts and ideas cause them to forsake their values and they may eventually change their attitude and behaviour towards issues that are happening around them as long as they can stop being poor (*Golden-Panther.Blogspot.Com, 2007*

As he agrees with Aristotle that poverty leads to revolution, Murphy also cites the Bolsheviks revolution in the former Soviet Union (1917), the French revolution (1789-1799), and the Iranian revolution (1979), as revolutions caused by poverty. Blogger Murphy concludes that apart from these revolutions, there were other revolutions that emerged as a result of "poverty of people." He cites the Arab Spring or Arab Awakening of 2011 as an example of such a revolution led by poverty.

While some Nigerians see Boko Haram's violence and mayhem in the North-East part of Northern Nigeria as a religious issue, others attribute such violence to poverty. Whatever the case may be, one thing is certain and that is, a majority of Boko Haram's members come from poor families. When people do not have any meaningful means of livelihood, the tendency for them to engage in criminal activities is always high. Another typical example of this scenario was a crime story that the *Nigerian Punch Newspaper* published on March 18, 2013. The criminal event occurred in Lagos, Nigeria, where a security guard with Honda Place Company proudly justified his action in conniving with thieves to steal goods worth over N28 million from the company he worked for. When he was arrested by the Lagos State Police Command, the confessed conspirator or accessory to the crime was quoted as saying that,

> The police should stop going after petty thieves like himself; that they should focus their attention on politicians, especially Senators and House members, who are the real thieves. There are many thieves in Nigeria and most of us are jobless youths, we have nothing. I earn N12, 000 a month which is too small. We are all criminals in Nigeria and we have criminal blood in our body so nobody should pretend (Akinkuotu, 2013).

Although this is an unfortunate story that must be condemned outright, it is a story that resonates with many Nigerians given the massive looting of public funds that is taking place in the country. The culprits move around freely and enjoy the best comfort money can afford. Looting public funds has become a cultural norm in today's Nigeria—one that has replaced our once cherished cultural values of personal integrity and self-worth, honesty, decency, protection and guarding jealously one's family name and reputation.

All these important features have been thrown out of the window, as Professor Akinyemi eloquently acknowledged in his Akure Lecture of 2013, which was dedicated to the second term inauguration of Governor Olusegun Mimiko. The seasoned professor was further quoted as saying: "Today, nobody asks anymore how people become suddenly wealthy. Nigerian leaders are no longer leading by good examples and they are no longer seen as good role models for the younger generation. You send a wrong message when you give national awards to criminals or grant them pardon or clemency and allow them to contest political office" (Aborisade, 2013). Professor Akinyemi describes the ugly situation in the country succinctly, when he noted that "no one in the country believes anymore in the concept of society: it is everyman for himself and God for us all."

The eminent scholar and Nobel laureate, Prof. Wole Soyinka, in his disapproval of how the country is governed, rejected the acceptance of the Centenary Award, on the ground that he could not share the nation's "Roll of Honour" with the late military Head of State, Gen. Sanni Abacha, whom he described as "a murderer and thief of no redeeming quality." In his article titled "the Canonisation of Terror," Professor Soyinka, eloquently and brilliantly articulated the atrocities General Abacha committed that disqualified him from receiving the Centenary Award. The Nobel laureate described Abacha as:

A vicious usurper under whose authority the lives of an elected president and his wife were snuffed out. Assassinations-including through bombs cynically ascribed to the opposition-became routine. Under that ruler, torture and other forms of barbarism were enthroned as the norm of governance. To round up, nine Nigerian citizens, including the writer and environmentalist Ken Saro-wiwa, were hanged after a trial that was stomach churning even by the most primitive standards of judicial trial, and in defiance of the intervention of world leadership. We are speaking here of a man who placed this nation under siege during an unrelenting reign of terror that is barely different from the current rampage of Boko Haram. It is very unfortunate that Abacha was recently canonized by the government of Goodluck Jonathan in commemoration of one hundred years of Nigerian trauma....When you proudly display certificates of a nation's paragons of human perfection. What the government of Goodluck Jonathan has done is to scoop up a century's accumulated degeneracy in one preeminent symbol, then place it on a podium for the nation to admire, emulate and even- worship. Such abandonment of moral rigour comes full circle sooner or later. The survivors of a plague known as Boko Haram, students in a place of enlightenment and moral instruction, are taken to a place of healing dedicated to an individual contagion- a murderer and thief of no redeeming quality known as Sanni Abacha, one whose plunder is still being pursued all over the world and recovered piecemeal by international consortiums- at the behest of this same government which sees fit to place him on the nation's Roll of Honour (Soyinka, 2014).

The above-stated assertions explain exactly what the social structural theorists had in mind, as the Nigerian society of today is suffering from social disorganization, status frustration, and social mobility. If there are many Nigerians like the Achebes and Soyinkas, positive changes will surely come; positive changes will not come to a country where its leaders turn blind eyes to injustice and abuse of power. Nigeria is far from achieving positive changes because the country has fewer men and women of honor and patriotism. It will take many generations to produce a cadre of decent, trustworthy, and patriotic Nigerians before such positive changes will come.

The Global Competitive Index (GCI) has, according to a *Vanguard Nigeria Newspaper* article of September 6, 2013, ranked Nigeria among the world's poorest competitive countries. By using its twelve pillars of competitiveness as a measuring yardstick, the GCI ranked Nigeria 120th of the 148 countries studied. This ranking places Nigeria in the poorest pool of economic development possible, the Newspaper article noted. The GCI's pillars of competitiveness are said to include the following:

- Institution;
- Infrastructure;
- Macroeconomic Environment;
- Health and Primary Education;
- Higher Education and Training;
- Good Market Efficiency;
- Labor Market Efficiency;
- Financial Market Development;
- Technological Readiness;
- Market Size;
- Business Sophistication; and
- Innovation.

The GCI's report, according to the *Nigerian Vanguard Newspaper* article, identified "weak institutions, engrained corruption, undue influence, weakly protected property rights, insecurity, poor infrastructure, and poor primary education as reasons for the country's abysmal rating." The report also points to the over reliance on oil and the poor penetration of Information and Communication Technologies (ICT) as other reasons for the country's poor showing.

Massive unemployment is another huge contributing factor to the country's poverty, as Omoh Gabriel's (2012) assessment revealed. He claimed that the country's unemployment ratio of 23.9 percent of the total population would mean that 38 million Nigerians are unemployed. He argued that if the nation's resources are put into proper use, the country will not face the high level of youth unemployment that confronts it today. If more manufacturing bases are built around the country, such industries and factories would create more employment opportunities to millions of Nigerians, who are jobless today.

The death of twenty-one job seekers that took place on March 15, 2014, is an attestation that there are millions of unemployed Nigerian youths in the country. These young people lost their lives trying to gain employment with the Nigerian Immigration Service (NIS). The agency was said to have 4,556 vacant positions, but over 526,650 people applied for these positions, and each of the applicants was made to pay a sum of N1, 000 non-refundable fee. The incident of March 15, 2014 was not the first time Nigerian youths lost their precious lives during a NIS recruitment exercise. Given such an ugly experience, the former Comptroller-General, Rose Uzoma, during her tenure in office, chose a different method to recruit people, but her detractors mounted a vicious campaign against her, accusing her of using the method to favor people from her own ethnic group. As a result of this unfounded allegation, the recruitment exercise she initiated was halted and she was sent on a compulsory retirement leave by President Jonathan.

The recent deadly tragedy of applicants seeking employment with the NIS has vindicated Uzoma's professional judgment and moral consciousness, while her detractors are being quizzed for the loss of lives that occurred at the NIS recruitment centers across the country. Some human rights groups in the country, such as the Citizen Advocacy for Social and Economic Rights (CASER) have called for the immediate suspension and prosecution of the Minister of Interior, Abba Moro, and the Comptroller General of the NIS, David Parradang for their gross negligence in the recruitment exercise. Additionally, the President of the NLC, Abdulwaheed Omar, blamed the NIS for the tragedy, arguing that "the agency should have employed a more rational recruitment process that would have reduced the number of applicants drastically, but failed to do this because of the intention to make huge profits from jobless young Nigerians." He also noted that "the whole process was a scam to defraud the jobless people without any hope of getting the job. This follows a condemnable pattern, which has now become common, even in the private sector, where thousands of applicants are invited in droves to compete for extremely limited opportunities" (Usigbe, et al., 2014).

During a Senate Committee hearing, held on March 27, 2014, over the tragic deaths of young Nigerians who lost their lives at the NIS recruitment centers, the Interior Minister, Abba Moro, took full responsibility for the tragedy and asked for forgiveness. The following statements were attributed to the Interior Minister during the hearing:

> We sincerely made appropriate and adequate preparations for a hitch-free exercise, but as most things in administrative and human conditions; the yield curve of expected outcome is mostly undefined. My heart goes out to the families of those who have lost their loved ones. I sincerely sympathize with those injured. I share in their grief. I share in their pains. May I at this juncture, assure you Distinguished Senators and Nigerians of my respect of

the sanctity of human life? The loss of these young Nigerians, who are needed as a critical human resources factor for nation-building is most regrettable. As the Minister of Interior, under whose purview this unfortunate exercise took place, I cannot abdicate my responsibility. The buck stops at my table...when we were planning this exercise, we didn't know the devil had its own plans. In 2008, there was only one centre but we created 37 centres. Even after creating 37 centres, the albatross has refused to go. If this is a recurring problem for this country, how can we find a solution so that another person's child will not die (Folasade-Koyi, 2014)?

Although an apology may not be sufficient for most critics who want the Interior Minister to resign from his position, they must also understand that it is rare in the country to see an official coming out openly to accept responsibility for the "public wrongs" committed by his/her agency. Abba Moro should be applauded for summoning the courage to acknowledge his poor decision that led to the tragedy. Indeed, this is a rare moment never seen before within the Nigerian government circle. Most of his kind will shift the blame to someone else and will ignore the clarion call for their resignations until they are forced to resign. We hope that other errant Ministers will tow similar lines and save the country from being ridiculed.

The human tragedy that occurred at the NIS recruitment centers across the country has also forced some high profile Nigerians to come up with ways to solve youth unemployment, which is plaguing the country. In response to the calamity, the Finance Minister, Ngozi Okonjo-Iweala, quickly suggested that the best way to remember Nigerian youths who lost their lives at the NIS recent recruitment exercise is to create more jobs for the unemployed. In recalling the job opportunities the Jonathan administration has created, the Finance Minister, stated the following:

> We created 1.6 million jobs as confirmed by the National Bureau of Statistics (NBS), but these are not enough. Every year 1.8 million new entrants come into the job market. This is in addition to 5.3 million that have accumulated over time. So we need to work harder and faster to create more jobs for our youths. We are focusing on housing because this sector can significantly increase the number of jobs in addition to growing the economy. This sector will create jobs for builders, carpenters, plumbers, managers, interior decorators and so many jobs. This event is not for long grammar. It is about action; it is about numbers; it is about meeting targets and deadlines so that the jobs will be created and the houses built (Ujah, et al., 2014).

It is absolutely absurd that it will take a tragedy of this magnitude to get the country's governing class attention to do the right thing. The Finance Minister proposal should have been implemented a long time ago to reduce the number of youth seeking employment in the country. The governing elite should have known that the only way government creates jobs is through constant maintenance of dilapidated infrastructures, such as highways and bridges, seaports and airports, public housing, school and hospital buildings, army barracks, police college buildings and police barracks. Other sources of job creation by government include expanding the existing infrastructures and developing new ones. The reason adequate maintenance of most public infrastructures is lacking in the country is because the funds earmarked for their repairs always end up in the private bank accounts of some government officials. If there is no money to pay for the repairs, it then means that no job offers can be made to those jobless youths who are willing to do the repairs.

On the other hand, Ngozi Okonjo-Iweala has joined the public debate on the debilitating consequences of poverty in Nigeria. Speaking at a breakfast dialogue organized in Lagos by the Nigerian Economic Summit Group (NESG), held in December of 2013, the Finance Minister was quoted by the *Daily Sun Newspaper Editorial* published on December 20, 2013, as making the following statements or commentaries:

> While the overall economy was on a clear path of growth, this does not appear to be reflecting on the lot of the critical mass of the populace. Despite encouraging economic indices such as stable exchange rate, manageable inflation rate and increasing contributions from non-oil revenue sources, widespread poverty persists and continues to grow at an alarming rate. Two main challenges responsible for this are inadequate job creation and rising inequality between the haves and the have-nots. The sectors that seem to record the biggest growths are those that are not high employers of labour. Consequently, only about 10 percent of the population appears to be enjoying the benefit of this economic growth. While this 10 percent at the top of the commanding heights of the economy continues to capture all the growth, the remaining 80 or so percent stuck at the bottom rungs of the economic ladder continues to wallow in poverty....Nigeria is, indeed, creating wealth, but not creating jobs.

The *Daily Sun* editorial applauded the Finance Minister for her honest observations, which the *editorial* described as refreshing, giving the fact that such observations were "coming from the government that had, before now, buried its head in the sand like the proverbial ostrich, believing only in figures generated by its own agencies and departments."

The Newspaper concludes that "these are figures that tend to give the erroneous impression that all is well. It is good to know that government has finally realised that there is a world of difference between theories based on figures generated from computers inside posh, air-conditioned offices and the reality in the streets."

The *editorial* reminded the Nigerian political class that "the duty of governments, anywhere in the world, is to confront challenges and fix problems. These are reasons they were elected in the first place. Government must, therefore, go beyond rhetoric and stop telling us the problems we already know. What we want is action. Let out leaders move from talking the talk to working the work." The *editorial* also concludes its commentary on the subject-matter (poverty in the midst of growth) by issuing the following words of caution:

> Until we do something serious and sustainable, the country may well be sitting on a keg of gunpowder with the growing army of jobless, angry and frustrated citizens. Already, it has been established that there is a direct linkage between joblessness, crime and insurgency. This then means that Boko Haram insurgency, which has far proved intractable, could become a mere child's play by the time the army of employable but unemployed Nigerians decides to take their destinies into their own hands. It would be portend grave danger, not only for the poor who are getting poorer, but also for the rich who are getting richer. It is not just enough for the economy to grow, government must also concern itself with the pattern of that growth. An economic growth that is restricted to a small group of the elite, without carrying the mass of the population along, is trouble-big trouble-waiting to happen.

Given the massive poverty plaguing the country, it is unconscionable for the country's ruling class to appropriate N3.19 billion in its 2012 budget for pension fund and allowances of former Presidents, Military Heads of State, their deputies, former leaders of the National Assembly, and their families, when many Nigerians barely eat one meal a day. In the 2011 budget, the amount spent on these retirees was N1.2 billion. The 2012 budget saw an increase of more than N2 billion, which triggered quick reactions from some members of the Senate Committee on Appropriation who wanted answers, as to why the amount of pensions and allowances meant for former Presidents, Military Heads of State, their deputies, former leaders of the National Assembly, and their families, rose from N1.2 billion in 2011 to N3.19 billion in 2012.

As a result of this misguided policy, social critics in the country had demanded to know why such a huge amount of money should be budgeted for leaders who have plunged the country into its present disaster, hopelessness, and despair. These critics vehemently argued that the increase is coming at a time when millions of Nigerians cannot afford three square meals a day, and at a time when unemployment and poverty are deeply widening. One such critic was the National Publicity Secretary of the All Nigerian Peoples Party (ANPP), Emma Eneukwu, who was quoted as making the following statements:

> We keep on saying it that this government [the PDP government] has no human face and that it does not care what happens to the people. It was telling Nigerians that it was going to cut expenses, yet, it went ahead to increase the budgetary provision for these leaders. This same government told us that the economy would collapse without the removal of petroleum

subsidy. It did not tell us that the economy of individual would collapse. This government is proving it day-by-day that it is a government that lacks vision and cannot be trusted. Nigerians cannot be deceived forever. One day is for the thief, the rest are for the owners (Fabiyi and Josiah, 2012).

The other critic, who also reacted angrily to the increase, was the President of Campaign for Democracy, Joe-Okei Odumakin. She claimed that such an increase was a smack of insensitivity. She further noted in her argument that "voting more money for the care of former leaders suggested that the poor would remain poorer while those who misruled the country would continue to grow richer."

Consequences of Poverty and Crime on the Nation's Psyche

The current insecurity in the country, resulting from poverty and crime, has forced many Nigerians from all walks of life (skilled and unskilled) to flee the country to foreign countries, where comfort and decent living are obtainable. There are several reports showing the number of Nigerians leaving the country to various destinations. For example, a recent *Guardian Nigeria Newspaper* article published on September 5, 2013 claimed that 3,936 Nigerian medical doctors are practicing in the United Kingdom, placing Nigerians and other nationals at the top of the list of foreign doctors practicing in Great Britain. According to the British National Health Service (BNHS), India tops the list with 25,336 doctors; Pakistan, 8,998; South Africa, 5,695; Ireland, 4,010; Nigeria, 3,936; Germany, 3,291; Egypt, 3,141; Greece, 2,711; Italy, 2,499; Sri-Lanka, 2,335. Others include: Sudan with 1,418; Libya, 727; Burma, 691; Syria, 671; Cayman Islands, 28; Kazakhstan, 26; Liberia, 9; Burundi, 8; and Haiti, 4 (Muanya, 2013).

The Guardian Nigeria Newspaper article also quoted the President of Nigerian Medical Association (NMA), Dr. Osahon Enabulele, as saying that "the country has currently about 71,740 medical and dental practitioners listed on the register of the Medical and Dental Council of Nigeria (MDCN), while about 27,000 are currently practicing in Nigeria. This indicates a doctor ratio of 1:6,187 assuming the population of Nigeria to be 167,000,000." In explaining why these brilliant minds are leaving the country for countries such as, the United Kingdom, United States, Canada, Australia, Saudi Arabia, South Africa, Botswana, Ghana, among others, the NMA President blamed the situation on poor conditions of service for medical doctors and other health workers. He was further quoted as saying that the exodus of Nigerian medical practitioners from the country is an indication that,

Government needs to create good conditions for developing medical practice. In most hospitals, doctors work under terrible conditions. That is the reason people are traveling abroad. Nigeria is producing medical doctors for other countries. Definitely the pull factor is going to continue to lure doctors outside our shores. It is time for Nigeria to open its eyes and move to retain the brains that are being exploited by other countries. The situation is an indication that a lot needs to be done. There is the need to encourage the doctors here. Doctors are highly skilled but the conditions under which they work here are not conducive. I was in London recently and there is the National Association of Nigerian Doctors in UK. I interacted with them and I could see the pain in their hearts. Each time I ask them to come back they remind me of the poor electricity supply, the bad roads, the insecurity, among other societal ills that have befallen the nation. There is need for the government to encourage those of us that are here to prevent and reduce the migration of Nigerian doctors (Muanya, 2013).

There was another article from *Nigeria Vanguard Newspaper*, indicating that there are about 25,000 Nigerian medical consultants currently practicing in the United States, a figure to which President Jonathan said came from the US President, Barack Obama. This revelation was made when the NMA president, Dr. Enabulele, led a special delegation to President Jonathan in Abuja, who pledged that his administration "will fully explore the option of creating a special intervention fund that will facilitate rapid establishment of more centres of medical excellence across the country." President Jonathan was further quoted as saying that:

My administration is committed to working with professionals and the private sector to establish better medical facilities in the country and reduce the number of Nigerians who have to go abroad annually for medical reasons....I believe that we must manage both sectors in such a way that people will not think of going on strike again. We will continue to proactively evolve measures that will help us to permanently overcome the problems that lead to strikes by health and education professionals (Agande, 2013).

His New Year's speech, titled "What Obama told me About Nigeria," was delivered on January 1, 2014, at Our Lady Queen of Nigeria Pro-Cathedral, Catholic Church in Area 3, Abuja. In that New Year's speech, President Jonathan reechoed the sentiment attributed to him above; he informed his audience at the Church Service that the US President, Barack Obama, told him in one of their encounters that over 25,000 Nigerian medical consultants work in the United States, the number which the US president said, was crucial to the American economy.

In the New Year message, President Jonathan concurred with world leaders, including President Obama, that Nigeria has great potentials to lead Africa and he was convinced that the year 2014 would be far better than 2013. President Jonathan was further quoted as making the following statements:

> All what we need to do is to make sure that we continue to do things rightly. That is why I always plead with my fellow politicians that yes, we must play the politics, but let us take the interest of the country more than our own individual interest. And as we continue to play the politics in that direction, leaders will come and go, but the country will stay. Luckily, we have a Constitution that says that nobody will be a governor or president forever. It is only in the parliament that you can be there till you die. As long as we consider the interest of our country, children, grandchildren and we begin to plan for the next generation instead of wasting all our energies to think about ourselves, before we get to the 100 years, the country will be better. Nigeria can even change in the next few years and things will be better for everybody (Taiwo-Obalonye, 2014).

The governing elite in Nigeria should not forget that there are other Nigerian professionals, who have been driven out of the country because of its misguided policies and these Nigerians are making meaningful contributions in their host countries. Unfortunately, not all Nigerians who fled the country in search of "Golden Fleece," have been so lucky to realize their dreams or ambitions. Some of these unlucky Nigerians have ended up in the criminal justice system of their host countries. There are several reports out there showing that many Nigerians are languishing in foreign countries' jails and prisons for committing various crimes in those countries, which range from the violation of the host countries' immigration laws, the selling of illegal drugs, the commission of cybercrimes, to human trafficking, medical fraud, auto theft and insurance fraud, to name just a few.

For example, there was a *Nigerian Daily Sun Newspaper* article published on December 11, 2013, but cited in the *Nigeriaworld.com,* which indicated that over 8,000 Nigerians are incarcerated for various jail terms, including life sentences in foreign prisons. Such foreign prisons, according to the Newspaper's article, included prisons in South Africa, Brazil, China, India, and European countries. The Chairman of the Federal House Committee on Diaspora, Hon. Abike Dabiri-Erewa, who represents the Ikorodu Federal Constituency in the House of Representatives, made this revelation during the Nigerian Leadership Summit, held in December of 2013, at the Oriental Hotel in Victoria Island, Lagos State.

While giving details of the prisoners, the lawmaker was quoted as saying that "409 Nigerians are serving prison terms in South Africa, while over 600 Nigerians, including women are serving prison terms in Brazil" (Otti, 2013). She also noted that "some of these convicts were graduates of Nigerian universities, who left the country in high hopes for greener pasture abroad but ended up behind bars in the prime of their age."

It was also reported in the *Nigerian Vanguard Newspaper* article of November 25, 2013 that 562 Nigerians were arrested by the Saudi Arabian authorities for illegally entering the country after the three months of amnesty given to undocumented immigrants in the country to regularize their stay ended. The *Nigerian Punch Newspaper* article of December 31, 2013 reported that 131 Nigerians, the last batch of the 518 Nigerians deportees from Saudi Arabia, have arrived home.

The Director, Consular and Immigration Service in the Ministry of Foreign Affairs, Abdulazeez Dan-Kano, was quoted as saying that "all the 518 deportees arrived in the country in six batches between December 25 and December 31, 2013." He appealed to other Nigerians still hiding in the slums of Saudi Arabia to embrace the benevolence of the Federal Government and return home to avoid the wrath of the Saudi authorities, noting that the Saudi Government had started the deportation of more than 951 Nigerians in its custody.

Other incidents, where Nigerians were either thrown into foreign prisons or deported, appeared on the pages of several Nigerian Newspapers. For example, the *Nigerian Punch Newspaper* had an article written on September 11, 2013, indicating that 90 Nigerians, including 14 children were deported from Tunisia, while the *Nigerian Daily Sun Newspaper* article of September 19, 2013 revealed that the Senate President, David Mark, pleaded with the Chinese government to release the 490 Nigerians locked up in Chinese prisons. It was said that out of the 490 Nigerians that were held behind bars, 366 of them were serving various prison terms; four were sentenced to death, while 120 were awaiting trial (Folasade-Koyi, 2013).

The *Nigerian Guardian Newspaper* article of September 7, 2013, also reported that the NIS had expressed worry over the deportation of 361 Nigerians within two months. The Comptroller General of the Nigerian Immigration Service, David Parradang, was quoted as saying that "at least twenty three airlines both foreign and local owe the Service $548,000 a fine of $2,000 each, for inadmissible passengers they brought into country" (Shadare, 2013). The said deportees were mostly from Europe, Asia, United States, South Africa and other African nations.

A *Vanguard Newspaper* article of January 12, 2014, also reported that no fewer than 100 Nigerians were languishing in Moroccan prisons. The Nigerian Ambassador to Morocco, Abdallah Wali, told Newsmen in Sokoto that most of these men were being held for offenses relating to illegal migration, drugs and petty crimes. The Ambassador also acknowledged that there was a couple of thousands of Nigerians illegally residing in Morocco; he gave reasons why these Nigerians and others from countries, south of the Sahara, frequently come to Morocco.

He says "the whole idea of visiting Morocco illegally is because of its proximity to Europe. It takes only 15 kilometres to cross the Mediterranean Sea into Spain." The

Ambassador stated that his Mission in Morocco had done a lot to discourage Nigerians from coming to Morocco. He claimed that his Mission was partnering with the Ministry of Foreign Affairs in Abuja to stem the tide of illegal migration of Nigerians to Morocco; and that his Mission had conducted a series of workshops to sensitize Nigerians against illegal migration through the Moroccan route, because of the risk involved in travelling, staying as illegal residents in Morocco, and the risk involved in crossing over to Europe.

Another *Nigerian Vanguard Newspaper* article of November 21, 2013 revealed that about 200 Nigerian girls are trafficked to Russia monthly for prostitution. The Nigerian Ambassador to Russia, Asam Asam, made this revelation while speaking to journalists in Berlin, Germany, on challenges facing the Nigerian Diplomatic Corp in Eastern Europe. The seasoned Ambassador was then quoted by the *Vanguard Newspaper*, as making the following remarks:

> The major consular challenge we face in Moscow is the influx of trafficked persons from Nigeria, not less than 200 girls are trafficked every month, and we have so many of them exposed to danger. Some are thrown out of the window and treated harshly, there must be a way of stopping these racketeering, these girls are not tourists, students or government officials yet they are given visas from the Russian Embassy in Abuja. So far we have deported over 240 girls since 2012, you will be shocked, at the extent of resistance from the girls, we tell them Russia is not a destination for prostitutes yet they still come...the strategy is to stop them from Nigeria, and fish out those involved in the trade. I spoke to the mother of one of the girls and she said her daughter should remain in Moscow and try to survive the ordeal; this is very sad indeed coming from one's parent (*Vanguardngr.com*, 2013).

In a recent conference organized in Makurdi by both the United Nations Office on Drugs and Crimes (UNODC) and the country's National Agency for Prohibition of Trafficking in Persons and other related matters (NAPTIP), Nigerians were thoroughly educated on various facets of human trafficking, including: the nature and scope of the problem; the root causes and consequences of human trafficking in Nigeria and elsewhere in the world, and what the Nigerian government has done to curb this menace.

In analyzing the nature and scope of human trafficking world-wide, Arinze Orakuwe, who heads NAPTIP's Media and Communication Department, describes human trafficking as:

> A modern form of slavery and has been in existence dating back to centuries with its abolition over 200 years ago. The crime, though abolished, still strives all over the world where human beings are purchased like common commodities with a more disturbing trend in the sale of human parts and women embryo. It involves the recruitment, transportation, transfer, harbouring or receipt of persons, by means of threat or use of force or other forms of coercion, of abduction, of fraud, of deception, of the abuse of power or of a

position of vulnerability or of the giving or receiving of payments or benefits to achieve the consent of a person having control over another person, for the purpose of exploitation. Every day, you read in the pages of newspapers about rape of a minor, two, three, four and five year-olds. And you ask yourself, where are we going to? You also want to ask: how does it connect to human trafficking? But these are the makers and the source and they are symptomatic of a society that is going down. Trafficking is just an adjunct of it (Balogun, 2014).

Orakuwe also noted that trafficking in persons (TIP) is prevalent within the under aged and young women, as they remain the most vulnerable, deceived, recruited, transported and transferred to a recipient, solely for exploitation. He further claimed that the victims, in most cases, are coerced through deception with unfulfilled promises, while some are forced against their will for the benefit of the traffickers.

In tracing the underlying causes of trafficking in persons, Orakuwe was quoted as saying:

There are various causes of TIP emanating from different economic, political, social and cultural factors. Some of the most common are poverty, lack of human rights, greed, civil unrest, natural disasters, lack of social or economic opportunities, dangers emanating from conflicts or militarism, unemployment, corruption, and bad governance. However, in Nigeria, the root causes are mainly poverty and greed, as people are driven by the get rich quick syndrome, not minding the risk involved. In some other communities, the patriarchal system of rule, where power is controlled only the men, devalues the women and girls, and making them vulnerable to trafficking. In addition to these are issues of porous borders, the involvement of organized criminal groups or networks, weak enforcement of migration laws and the lack of adequate laws to enforce legislation on TIP. In Nigeria, reports have it that children, teenagers and females are most vulnerable to TIP. They are exploited as domestic servants, street hawkers, beggars, prostitutes and other forms of domestic servitude. Nigeria is rated as a source, transit and destination country for TIP (Balogun, 2014).

In response to this menace, the Nigeria government created the NAPTIP in 2003 to tackle the issues of human trafficking in Nigeria. The agency was authorized to coordinate all laws on TIP and related offenses, which include prevention of all forms of human degradation and exploitation, eliminating the scourge of trafficking in persons and child labor, as well as giving assistance to victims of human trafficking through rehabilitation and programs aimed at improving the lives of TIP victims.

The NAPTIP policies have empowered the agency to adopt a strategic tool, which Orakuwe referred to as the Four Ps--Prevention, Prosecution, Protection, and Partnership. So far, the Nigerian government has collaborated with countries, such as Italy, the

Netherlands, the United States of America, Finland, Norway, Britain, and organizations like UNODC, the International Organization for Migration (IOM), UNICEF, and Women Trafficking and Child Labor Eradication Foundation (WOCLEF) in combating the menaces of human trafficking (Balogun, 2014). WOCLEF is said to be a Non-Governmental Organization initiated and founded in 1999 by Amina Titi Atiku Abubakar, wife of the former Vice-President of the Federal Republic of Nigeria,

James Ayodele, an Outreach and Communication Officer of the UNODC, was another individual who made a meaningful contribution to the Makurdi Conference on human trafficking, according to the *Daily Sun Newspaper* reporter, Balogun. Ayodele's topic demonstrates how human trafficking facilitates the spread of HIV/AIDS. In explaining the vulnerability of victims of TIP to HIV/AIDS infection, the Outreach and Communication Officer of the UNODC noted the following: "Trafficking increases a person's vulnerability to HIV infection; 40-90% of trafficked persons are infected with HIV, according to findings by the UNODC. Children who have lost at least one parent to HIV/AIDS are more susceptible to traffickers' manipulations. The highest rates of HIV infection in the world exist in centres of sex tourism--Ukraine, Russia, Belarus, South Africa and Botswana, among others." He also explained how a trafficked person is prone to HIV/AIDS infection. These, according to Ayodele, include unsafe sex practices (homosexual or heterosexual), noting that about 89% of HIV infections are sexually transmitted; injecting drugs and sharing of piercing instruments and the clandestine and illegal status of trafficked victims makes them invisible and reduces their access to health services, particularly those that focus on HIV/AIDS (Balogun, 2014).

Because of the massive poverty plaguing the country, many young Nigerian mothers have become baby-making factories, who are handsomely paid by organized syndicates, who arrange to put the children up for adoption. Many of these factories have been identified in different locations throughout the country, prompting the Executive Secretary of NAPTIP, Beatrice Jedy-Agba to speak out against this inhumane practice. She criticized the anti- trafficking laws as they are currently enforced in the country, declaring that the sale of babies is currently enjoying a boom. She claimed that the perpetrators of this vicious crime were abusing the country's adoption processes, thereby, inflicting misery on their unfortunate victims by conscripting them into prostitution and other forms of forced labor, a clear case of manipulating the law to oppress the socially vulnerable and powerless.

The *Tribune Newspaper editorial* of January 2014 noted that the NAPTIP boss had stressed the need to strengthen the relevant laws by providing stiffer penalties, but the *editorial* noted emphatically that "the Jedy-Agba submissions are hardly surprising given the proclivity for mindless manipulation of the nation's laws, particularly by the heavily money and richly connected elite." It also concluded that "those who even go through the supposedly normal adoption process are abusing the privilege is an indication that those saddled with monitoring the process have become captured regulators, overcome by the widespread corruption in the country."

In occurrence with the NAPTIP boss, the *Tribune editorial* agrees that "the agency should be further empowered given the modest gains it has recorded so far, including, in 2013 alone, 46 convictions in the law courts." Consequently, it urged "the National Assembly to expeditiously work on the agency's 2013 proposal for an amendment to the NAPTIP enabling Act to block observed leakages, bringing the nation's anti-trafficking legislation in conformity with the trafficking in persons protocol, including clearer definition of the offences, removing the option of fine and increasing penalty for traffickers."

Another consequence resulting from the massive poverty and crime engulfing the country is the absence of foreign investors and tourists from the country, as foreign countries, especially the Western countries have warned their citizens not to travel to Nigeria for the fear of being kidnapped by armed gangs for ransom. This sort of warning has ripple effects on the economy; it discourages tourists and investors from coming to invest and to spend their money.

As this trend is becoming obvious, unemployment in the country is deepening. Criminologists, especially the social structural theorists have eloquently argued that what causes delinquent behaviors in societies are the social and cultural environment in which adolescents grow up or the sub-cultural groups in which they choose to become involved. To buttress their argument, they claim that forces such as cultural deviance, social disorganization, status frustration, and social mobility are so powerful that they induce lower-class youths to become involved in delinquent behavior (Bartollas, 1997, p. 130).

This conclusion goes to support the notion that poverty is "the mother of revolution and crime," as advanced by Aristotle. As indicated above, poverty, crime, and insecurity have created a huge brain drain in Nigeria, which has seriously affected the development of the country and, such episode will continue for a long time to come unless the government tackles the underlying causes of the problem.

How Corruption Contributes to Nigerian Criminal Justice Agencies' Poor Performance

Apart from the horrifying scenes caused by poverty and crime, the country's criminal justice system is seriously weakened and has become ineffective in handling the increasing wave of violent crimes engulfing the country. In spite of the fact that insecurity exists today because of poverty, the country's security apparatus is ill-equipped to deal with the contending threats facing the country. Criminals are roaming the streets with impunity and with little or no countermeasures coming from the law enforcement community to deal with these criminals. Most times, criminals are assisted in their criminality by the very agencies that were designated by law to apprehend, prosecute, convict, and punish those individuals who violate the country's laws.

Like in other sectors in Nigeria, corruption has decimated the Nigerian criminal justice agencies, which include the police, courts, and corrections (prisons). For example, some high ranking police officials in the country have been relieved of their duties because they embezzled and/or misappropriated funds meant for the enhancement of police performance in the country, as the rot at the Nigerian Police College (Police Academy), Ikeja, Lagos demonstrated. It was discovered that funds meant for the Police College welfare scheme were not utilized for its intended purposes. The non-utilization of these funds has made it impossible for the management of the Police Academy to procure the necessary instructional materials and equipment the College desperately needs to enhance the training of the country's police personnel. The embezzlement of the police funds has also prevented the management of the Academy from rehabilitating the dilapidated infrastructure of the institution, which tarnishes the image and the national pride of the country, if there is anything of such anymore in Nigeria. A deterioration of this kind speaks volumes as to the level of infrastructural decay in the country.

President Jonathan was said to be unhappy with the prevailing condition of things at the institution, responsible for the training of the country's law enforcers, when he paid a surprise visit to the College. It was his unannounced visit to the Police College campus that "raised the dust" or "set the wheel of justice into motion" (Adepegba, 2013; Ogbodo, 2013). Given what transpired at the Ikeja Police College in Lagos, an eight-man Committee was formed to investigate what really happened to the funds appropriated for the Police College welfare scheme. The Committee was also given the task to determine whether other Police Colleges across the country were affected by the scandal or that the Ikeja episode was an isolated case.

The rot at the country's Police Colleges is not the only depressing story uncovered at the institutions designated to boost the morale and performance of the Nigerian criminal justice agencies. The ugly stories told about the deplorable nature of the Nigerian Police Barracks in Lagos and, possibly elsewhere in the country, have led observers to describe the barracks as refugee camps. The *Nigerian Punch Newspaper* reporter, Temitayo Famutimi (2013), who visited some of these barracks, described them as refugee camps, which he concluded were an eyesore to the nation.

In describing what he saw in those barracks, Famutimi noted in his article that "from Obalende, Surulere, Iponri, Bar Beach to Women's barracks, all in Lagos the story is that of a sad tale of utter neglect. But the picture is similar in other states of the federation. While the sewage pipes in many of the barracks visited are damaged, their rooftops bristling with satellite dishes were adorned with large broken, sagging roof sheets--many of which have indeed fallen off." The *Nigerian Punch* reporter recalled that in the Surulere barrack, it was observed that rodents and reptiles moved freely into the kitchens, toilets and bathrooms as the windows and doors have broken off and they are yet to be fixed. He also reported that the cement castings covering the decking on some of the storey buildings are already giving way.

The irony of this saga is that the Federal Government appropriates funds for the rehabilitation of police barracks on a yearly basis, as it does to the Police College welfare scheme, but these funds are not used for the purposes for which they are appropriated. Famutimi (2013) noted in his article that "the National Assembly allocated the sum of N425, 060, 826 for the rehabilitation and repairs of police stations and barracks across the country, yet the state of many of these structures remain abysmal across the country."

The Police have also allowed themselves to be used in aiding electoral malpractices in the country. In using what transpired in the Esan North East Local Government election in the state as a framework for his analysis, the Edo State Governor, Comrade Adams Oshiomhole, indicted the Nigerian police for assisting in electoral malfeasance. During the said election, the former NLC president, now turned politician, accused the police of involving themselves in ballot box snatching, supervising electoral fraud, and intimidating voters. Consequently, the flamboyant Governor had this to say:

> What I heard yesterday and I am still investigating; if the reports are correct, then Nigeria should be put on notice that the police may well have chosen to become the INEC or EDSIEC officials and have chosen to overthrow those who are authorized by law to conduct elections....As a Nigerian, I am embarrassed that the police are involved in carrying electoral materials, arresting EDSIEC returning officers and coercing them into a police station and converting it into a collation centre supervised by policemen imported from Abuja and Lagos to subvert the will of the people of Esan North- East (Ebegbulem, 2013).

The Governor claimed that the law that established the electoral commission was clear. Nowhere did it state that the police post should be used as an electoral office. He went on to condemn the behavior of the governing elite who use the police to rig themselves into political offices.

The Governor eloquently and brilliantly described how the elite classes in his State and in the nation are misusing their discretionary powers. In referring to what took place in his State, Comrade Oshiomhole summarizes the unpatriotic attitude of this elite class in the following manners: "the Minister of Works and other federal functionaries, including Assemblymen, used their exalted positions, taking unfair advantage of the police assigned to protect them and deployed them for election purpose, detaining returning officers and treating them as if they were prisoners of war and compelling them to sign fake results" (Ebegbulem, 2013).

Back to the deplorable living conditions found in most police barracks across the country. Experts have also taken a look into this issue. For example, a clinical psychologist at the Lagos State University Teaching Hospital, Ikeja, Leonard Okonkwo, had studied the situation and came up with the notion that there was a correlation between shelter and performance.

In quoting Abraham Maslow's Hierarchy of Needs, Okonkwo noted that "shelter is one of the basic physiological needs of humans which should not be toiled with." Stretching this point further, the renowned psychologist was quoted as saying:

> When a policeman is made to live under shabby conditions you cannot get the best from him or her...toiling with the adequate shelter of those saddled with the responsibility of internal security of the country will only breed a police force populated with disorganized and disorderly thinking officers and men. If a man is not well sheltered he is not well motivated as shelter is a symbol of safety. When a policeman goes out to work, he should come back to the safety and comfort of his house. But in a situation where the barracks is not in a good shape, the policeman's performance is affected. The policeman is always thinking about his or her welfare. If you are not well sheltered in a tidy and decent environment, the level of disorganized thinking is promoted and concentration on the job is affected. It is worthy of note that where you live boost your confidence and in view of this, taking proper care of barracks improves the ego of the policemen as they are proud of their job, thereby ultimately boosting their performance (Famutimi, 2013).

The clinic psychologist further cautioned that

> Until our policemen and women are well taken care of in terms of the provision of descent shelter, Nigerians are not likely to get the best from them; therefore, their welfare should be a top priority...since they are saddled with the responsibility of maintaining law and order and in the course of doing that their lives are at stake, the authorities concerned should know that our policemen will be more courageous to do their job when they know that their welfare is taken seriously" (Famutimi, 2013).

A Sociologist from the Obafemi Awolowo University, Dr. Oludele Ajani, has done a study examining the effects on children raised in such deplorable environments and dilapidated structures. His analysis reveals that "while the morale of an average policeman and woman who lives in a slum-like barracks is dampened, experience has shown that their offspring tend to exhibit deviant behaviours." In the furtherance of his analysis, Dr. Ajani concludes that "the environment where one lives dictates and influences one's behaviour, conduct and attitude to life." Thus, in summarizing his thought-provoking discourse, the social scientist was quoted as saying the following:

> The effect of the dilapidating state of our barracks is one of the issues we as academics have raised over the years. And that is why when you interact with our law enforcement officers, they are always on the edge, you begin to wonder who annoyed them. Poor environment and housing units affects their output and interaction. But more worrisome is the fact that children raised in such environment are generally deviant and become social misfits as they tend to take after the behaviour of their parents. And that is why people tag children raised in the barracks as barrack kids--to depict those traits they exhibit which are against social norms. We are products of the environment...Allowing policemen and women as well as their children to stay in overcrowded housing units, which lack drainages and basic amenities, is not in the best interest of this all important institution. The children may not see beyond their immediate environment and this may affect their goals (Famutimi, 2013).

These are important facts that the Nigerian ruling class does not always take into consideration, when making policies that affect the average Nigerian either directly or indirectly. The above stated analyses explain why a low ranking police officer will take a bribe from motorists or from other members of the public, or demand that a bribe be paid in US dollars, as the officer caught on video camera on February 3, 2014, in Lagos revealed. On the video, the officer demanded dollar bribe from a Nigerian-American and two other Nigerians for an alleged traffic violation in Lagos (Adepegba, 2014). It also explains why low ranking police officers will join ranks with criminals to engage in crimes of various sorts. Similar conditions are found in the Nigerian Prisons and in the Judiciary, where prison facilities and court houses are in a dilapidated state, especially at the state and local government levels.

PART THREE

INSECURITY AND PUBLIC SAFETY IN NIGERIA

Chapter 6

GROUP VIOLENCE AND INSECRUITY IN NIGERIA

Failures of Nigeria's Founding Fathers to Unify the Country

Group violence leading to the insecurity of a country is a dire consequence of the failure of that country's leaders to provide adequately for the social and economic well-being of its people. The history of group violence and insecurity in Nigeria could be traced from the way the country's boundaries were drawn by the British colonial government. The country was designed to fail from the onset, when different ethnic nationalities were arbitrarily brought together under one political umbrella, without taking into consideration the cultural and religious differences that existed among these various ethnicities. The political arrangements in Nigeria were strictly designed to benefit the British colonial authorities and not the indigenous people. As noted previously in this discourse, Nigerian leaders who emerged after independence did not help issues either.

Although they favored the decolonization of the country that began in 1929 and ended in 1960, they differed strongly on the method and time frame of achieving true independence. This meant that they neither agreed on a particular time frame when colonial rule in the country would be brought to an end, nor did they agree on a political framework that would truly unite the country and promote a genuine national identity. These divergent opinions and differences stemmed from the distrust those Nigerian leaders who emerged after Independence had of each other; and this distrust made them to be each other's worst enemy.

Leaders from both the Northern and Southern Nigeria had different time frames for ending foreign domination in the country. For example, while Southern leaders were aggressively demanding "independence now," their Northern counterparts showed no readiness or willingness to support Southern leaders in their agitation for "independence now," a popular slogan that dominated the event of the day in Southern Nigeria during that historical period. Northern leaders, at the time, claimed that the North was not ready and prepared for self-governance, noting that the North needed more time to prepare itself for such an undertaking. As a result, both Western and Eastern Regions opted for self-government in 1957, and two years later, the Northern Region embarked on self-governance in 1959 (Falola and Heaton, 2010:154).

The reasons the North gave for not joining the bandwagon in seeking self-governance when the South did, were based on a number of factors, which included the following: 1) Northerners feared that the incorporation of the country into a unitary Nigerian state would mean that they would ultimately become politically and culturally dominated by the South.

This sentiment or fear stemmed from the fact that the Northern Region lacked a large European-educated population and did not have enough qualified people to take up positions in a European-style legislature. It was said that the North did not have enough Western educated manpower to represent the region in the country's Civil Service Administration, both at the national and regional levels. It was also said that the Colonial Civil Service in the North was dominated by "transplanted Southerners" for most of the colonial era and, Northern leaders did not want to see a repeat of such a situation in post-independent Nigeria; and 2) conservative elements in the North feared that a Southern-dominated central legislature would force a secular state on the North, preventing Northerners from governing themselves through the Islamic law or Sharia (Falola and Heaton, 2010:150).

The cord of disunity and mistrust in Nigeria manifested itself in the general elections of 1954, 1956, and 1959. This cord subsequently introduced tribal and regional politics into the Nigerian political consciousness as the Action Group (AG), the National Council of Nigerian Citizens (NCNC), and the Northern People's Congress (NPC) dominated their respective regions in both regional and central legislatures (Falola and Heaton, 2010:154). From these periods onward, regionalism and ethnic loyalty became the order of the day and left Nigeria a fragmented and fragile state. Tribal politics prevented the country from developing a true national unity and identity. Apart from these three main regions (North, West, and East) dominated by Hausa-Fulani, Yoruba, and Igbo ethnic groups, there were hundreds of small ethnic groups within these regions that equally expressed fear of domination themselves.

The Nigerian working class and peasants were also uncomfortable with the post-independent leaders whom they viewed as the country's new "bourgeoisie class." The working class and the peasants did not trust this class of elite because they did not represent nor share the values or views the working class and the peasants had on the future prosperity of the country. As a result of these cadres of leaders, the country's unity, national consciousness and identity were sacrificed and undermined. Many of the post-independent leaders were not interested in unifying the country to overcome the legacies of British colonialism. Rather, they were interested in promoting regional and tribal politics, a cultural value which still dominates the Nigerian political culture and psyche today. Tribal politics, for example, has been identified as a major source of instability in Nigeria, one which foreign powers have always exploited to their own advantage.

Another affront to the Nigerian unity and national consciousness was the inability of those leaders who emerged after independence to restructure and transform colonial institutions left behind by the British colonial government in ways that would fit into the Nigerian political environment or context. Rather than transforming the Nigerian contemporary society to suit the reality in Nigeria, the newly emerged leaders were only interested in perpetuating Western culture at the expense of African civilization and identity. By retaining colonial institutions without modifications, the leaders' inaction simply demonstrated that they were ashamed of who they were. By embracing Western values without modifications, the newly emerged leaders viewed themselves and their country men and women as inferior to European civilization. This mentality or mindset explains why these leaders had always sought and continued to seek approval from Western governments before they embarked on any project of national significance. The newly emerged leaders in post-independent Nigeria collaborated in tying the country's political economy to Western economy. This phenomenon explains why Nigeria depends heavily on European knowledge, connections, technologies, and market conditions (Falola and Heaton, 2010:157).

The major reason Nigeria and other African countries are lagging behind today is because they did not isolate themselves from the world stage at the time they gained their political independence from European powers. African leaders stretched their countries' meager resources very thin by establishing foreign diplomatic missions virtually in every country of the world, when they knew that their national economies could not sustain such missions. One of the things they did, for example, was to join the United Nations and its specialized agencies. Consequently, they became token members of the UN and other international organizations because they had no leverage or power to dictate the agenda of these organizations. The African countries, including Nigeria made an absolute mistake by joining the UN at the time they did, when they were neither a party to the UN formation nor drafting members of its founding documents. One may conclude that the reason behind African leaders' early participation in some of these international organizations, at the time, was to identify with the "big boys' league," when they knew they did not have what it takes to be viable members of the league. By being members of these international organizations, the African leaders, including the Nigerian leaders, squandered their countries' limited resources which they would have used in building up their countries' economic base, as their American counterparts did when they obtained their independence from Great Britain on July 4th 1776.

Comparison between Nigeria's Founding Fathers and their US Counterparts in Nation Building after Independence

The Nigerian Founding Fathers did not borrow a single leaf from their American counterparts who took a different approach in tackling the problems of their new nation. For instance, the moment the United States of America became an independent nation, President George Washington, the country's first president, and his cabinet went straight into nation building efforts, realizing the enormous tasks ahead of them.

The American Founding Fathers did several things to reposition America to take its rightful place on the world stage, and by doing so they rekindled the American spirit of patriotism and exceptionalism, which were lacking in the Nigerian context. One of the things the American Founding Fathers did to strengthen the Union was to replace the *Article of Confederation* with what has become known within the American political class as the *US Constitution*, which is often described by American political pundits as, "the longest human serving document ever written in history." The US Constitution created a federal structure with a strong national government that called for a collective action against foreign attacks on either one or more of the states that made up the United States of America. Should such an attack occurs, it would generally be viewed as an attack on all states of the Union.

The American Founding Fathers also isolated the country from what was happening in the European theater and elsewhere in the world. In his Farwell Address, President Washington warned Americans not to have a political connection with Europe. He reminded the new generation of American leaders that they should stay home and build America's unity and strength and to steer clear of permanent alliances. Combs (1986) noted in his work that although many Republicans, at the time, were not convinced of the wisdom of Washington's advice, the President's address quickly entered the realm of American gospel. Americans printed it in children's schoolbooks, engraved it on watches, and wove it into tapestries. Indeed, the Farewell Address was very significant in the struggle between neutrality and foreign alliances (p.34). This isolationist policy enabled the country to stay home and build up its economic base and other institutions that have withstood the test of time.

Once the country had unified itself, built up its national consciousness and identity, built up its economic base and military arsenal, it began flexing its muscle outside its borders. Caribbean, Latin, and South America became the first military laboratories or battle grounds, where the US government tested its military readiness and preparedness (Grandin, 2006).

These regions were and still are referred to as the Western Hemisphere, or the American southern neighbors, or the US sphere of influence. The US government wanted to keep these regions to itself without sharing them with any foreign powers, not even with the regions' former European colonial powers, such as Spain, Great Britain, and France. The Monroe Doctrine of 1823 was instrumental in opening up these new frontiers to the United States.

The Monroe Doctrine, which was built on three philosophical principles, gave the Americans the edge to dominate the entire affairs of its southern neighbors. The doctrine gave Americans the edge to exploit these regions' natural resources to their own benefit; and gave them the edge to subjugate these regions to US military interventions and occupations.

According to Combs (1986), the three underlying principles of the Monroe doctrine stipulated the following:

> The first of these principles declared that while the United States would not interfere with European colonies already existing in the Western Hemisphere, the hemisphere was no longer open to European colonization. Second, our policy in regard to Europe, which was adopted at an early stage of the wars which so long agitated that quarter of the Globe,...is, not to interfere in the internal concerns of any of its powers. Third, Europe must keep its hands off the independent nations of the Western Hemisphere. The Doctrine also went further to say any attempt to extend the European system into the Americas would be regarded as "dangerous to our peace and safety (pp. 71-72).

With these principles, the United States was able to expand its territorial ambition and interests beyond Louisiana territories, which Thomas Jefferson's administration bought for $15 million in 1803 from Napoleon Bonaparte of France. The Monroe Doctrine enabled the US to acquire a transcontinental domain from Florida to Oregon. It enabled the US to proclaim unilaterally its interests in the independence of Latin America and left open the possibility of the US acquiring Cuba and Texas; and the doctrine gave the US the cover it needed to back away from committing itself fully to Latin American independence (Combs, 1986: 72-73).

The United States government has, over the years, exported its military experiences acquired from its numerous interventions in the Caribbean, Latin, and South America to other regions of the world, where its military had been and are still actively engaged in military combats or in covert or clandestine operations. For example, the current war doctrines Americans are using in executing their war efforts in Iraq, Afghanistan, Yemen, and Pakistan, and Somali, wars known to the US leadership as "war against terrorism" or "counterterrorist insurgency," are the same scripts they used in bringing the Caribbean, Latin, and South American countries to the United States' military and economic orbit and control. With the exception of the newly invented armed drones, which are the latest weapons in the US military arsenals, other military logistics used in these war theaters are old playbooks that emanated from the Latin American experiences or experiments.

Without a doubt, the isolationist policy made enormous positive impacts on US development efforts. The period of isolationism (1776-1945) gave the American governing class the opportunity to consolidate its various divergent forces in the country to rally around the flag; it gave the American governing class the opportunity to sow the seeds of national consciousness in the minds of ordinary Americans. This period of isolationism gave the American governing class ample opportunity to offer formal education and other social programs to its population, and to build a sound and efficient national economy and a formidable military capability. In summation, the United States of America, a one-time colony with an agrarian economy, would not have been able to accomplish these uphill feats or tasks without a policy of this kind. Generally speaking, this period gave the country ample opportunity to put its house in order; this is what the African nations failed to do when they gained their political independence.

Indeed, President Washington, his administration, as well as the American people, should be applauded for their virtue and wisdom in keeping themselves out of European turmoil for that period of time, in spite of many attempts made by the European warring factions to drag the Americans into their regional conflicts. The American leadership and people were not fooled into giving up their isolationist aspiration. In spite of their reluctance and resistance to join World War I (1914-1918), Americans eventually succumbed for three major reasons, which they could not overlook or ignore. One of the events that changed the Americans' stance on the war was Germany's aggression against civilian vessels, including US Vessels plying on international waters around the British Isles. The other event was what historians tagged as the "Zimmermann telegram."

Woodrow Wilson's administration was very reluctant to join the war though many American lives were lost in the vessels that were sunk by the German Submarines and U-boats. Some of the vessels sunk by the German navy with American passengers in them included the following: 1) British steamer, *Falaba*; 2) American ship, *Gullflight*; 3) British giant passenger liner *Lusitania*, said to be carrying over 1,900 people from New York to England was attacked on May 15, 1915. The ship was sunk off the coast of Ireland, and out of the 1,200 passengers that drowned, 124 were Americans; and 4)

British passenger liner, *Arabic* was also sunk and two Americans died in the attack (Combs, 1986: 213-214). In each of these incidents, President Wilson protested vehemently against the German aggressions and did all he could to keep the Americans out of the war.

The Wilson administration could no longer keep the Americans out of the conflict when, a telegram to Mexico from the German foreign secretary, Arthur Zimmermann, was intercepted by the British government and was handed over to US officials for verification. The contents of the telegram revealed that the German government had proposed an alliance between Germany, Mexico, and Japan against the United States, if America joined the war. The telegram assured the Mexican authorities that Germany would help Mexico regain the territory it had lost in the American-Mexican War of 1846-1848. The Zimmermann telegram, as it was known by historians, was "the straw that broke the camel's back." It convinced the Wilson administration that Germany preferred war to the abandonment of its submarine campaign on international waters. On reaching this conclusion, the Wilson administration then asked the US Congress for a formal declaration of war against Germany, which the administration got without much hindrance or objection.

The third reason, if you will, why Wilson had asked for war against Germany was to strengthen America's negotiating power during peace talks once the war was over. One of Wilson's reasoning was that if the United States was an active and powerful participant in the war, America would have great influence over the peace settlement. His other rationale was that by joining the war, America would have the opportunity to create a just peace that would promote democratic government and eliminate the causes of war that had plagued the old World for so long (Combs, 1986: 218).

Because of the country's isolationist stance, Americans refused to join the League of Nations, an organization that came into existence in 1918-1919, and whose chief architect was President Wilson. The lack of US participation in the League of Nations brought the League to an abrupt end. During and after World War II (1939-1945), Americans abandoned their isolationist policy and became internationalists. For example, during World War II, reluctant Americans were once again dragged into the war in 1941, when the Japanese air force attacked America's naval base at Pearl Harbor, off the coast of Hawaii. After the war, Americans vowed never to stay home again, and given the country's strong economy, national resilience, and their spirit of adventurism, Americans became major players on the world stage and have remained relevant since then.

The US became one of the two superpowers that emerged from the war; the other superpower was the former Union of Soviet Socialist Republics (USSR), or for short, the Soviet Union. Europe, once an epicenter of global power, had lost its global preeminence and was replaced by these two emerging superpowers. After World War II, the US became instrumental in the creation of the United Nations with the help of Britain, USSR, and to a certain extent, the Chinese, just as it was instrumental in the establishment of the League of Nations after World War I. The difference this time was that the American people threw their support behind the new world body, while the League of Nations never received such support from the American people. As it was intended, the new world body became a major tool the UN Founding Fathers used and continue to use in advancing their national interests at the expense of those "token" member-states' interests, like the African countries and other Third World countries.

In their competition to dominate the global system and attract allies to themselves, the superpowers became bitter rivals and; consequently, plunged the global system into two opposing ideological camps (the Capitalist camp versus Communist camp or the West versus East). The US also facilitated the creation of NATO, as a military alliance to protect itself and its Western allies from the Soviet Union and its Warsaw Pact allies' attacks. The articulation and implementation of these ideological camps culminated into what became known as the Cold War (1945-1990), which led to an unprecedented arms race. The Cold War was a war that was never fought physically by those nations (United States and Soviet Union) that declared it, but became a physical and real war, whose battle fields loomed all over the Third World from Asia, Africa, Caribbean, Latin, and South America, to the Middle East region.

In its attempt to halt the spread of Communism around the world, the US government, under the Truman Doctrine, engaged in acts that were contrary to the letter and spirit of its Declaration of American Independence and Clause III of the Atlantic Charter of 1941, which guarantee's all nations the right to choose their form of government. To gain access to the natural resources of the Third World nations, and to dictate and control events in these regions of the world, the superpowers, especially, the US government and its Western allies, armed and funded disgruntled groups to disrupt the social order in their respective countries.

Through military coups, direct military interventions, and proxy wars, the superpowers overthrew governments (both democratically elected and nondemocratic ones) that did not subscribe to their ideology. Most Civil Wars or proxy wars waged throughout the Third World during that period were instigated and fueled by foreign intruders or what became known as "the invisible hand." The containment policy, which was instituted by the US government, became a destabilizing force in the Third World, and it became a major source of violence and instability in those regions. The numerous military coups in Nigeria, including the bloody Civil War the country underwent in 1967-1970, had foreign involvements in them. The consequences of these destabilizing forces are still felt today in Nigeria and the hatred they generated are still fresh in the minds of those victimized by such violent acts.

As noted previously, the United States would not have accomplished these things if it hadn't been for its isolationist policy, which strengthened and gave the country ample time to restructure its society and prevent it from over spending its meager resources. We should remember that after independence, the United States was not an industrialized country like Great Britain, or Germany; it was an agrarian nation that played for catch up. The isolationist era allowed the country to transform itself from an agrarian society to an industrialized nation and into the present day information age where the US is the leader. America, however, is paying dearly for over stretching itself so thin and for over spending its resources because of its internationalist stance, which has forced the country to take "more than it can chew." After World War II, the country arrogated itself to a position of becoming "the world policeman," thereby, interfering in the internal affairs of most nation-states. By doing so, it gained few friends and created many enemies; hence becoming the target of terror.

With the demise of the Soviet Union in 1991, the US saw itself as the sole surviving superpower around, a superpower that could virtually do no wrong, or could do anything it wanted without being held accountable for its actions. However, the leadership of the country is beginning to realize that there is an ultimate price to pay for assuming such enormous world responsibilities.

It has come to realize that regime change, inventing enemies, invading countries, and waging wars around the world are not the best options in building world peace, and promoting democracy and human rights around the world. Rather, such an aggressive foreign policy has its own "blowback" effect, as the US government has come to realize, given the 9-11 attacks on its soil.

In assuming and sustaining these world responsibilities, the US has squandered its huge accumulated revenue reserves it had after World War II. As one could see, these revenues were used in building up US military arsenals, including its foreign military bases and funding of armed insurgencies in the Third World.

Ironically, the US government failed to learn from its European allies' mistakes that acquiring and maintaining colonies in foreign lands are costly in terms of fiscal and human resources, that the subjugation of people to a foreign rule creates resentments and hatred against foreign invading and occupying armies. Secondly, the US also failed to learn from the Soviet Union's sad experience. The Soviet Union became a failed state in 1991, when the Union broke apart to become what is today known as the Commonwealth of Independent States (CIS).

This huge Empire broke apart because it over spent its revenue reserves during the Cold War for several reasons, which include the following:

1) Keeping up with the emerging military technologies and military build-ups;
2) Funding liberation movements around the world; and
3) Sustaining its poor Eastern European allies both economically and militarily.

Incurring these huge expenditures by overstretching itself globally, the Soviet Union was unable to enhance the quality of life of its people. Consequently, the people became agitated, disillusioned, and began to demand for reforms. Mikhail Gorbachev, the last Communist Party's Secretary to rule the Soviet Union, embarked on a number of reforms to resuscitate the country's sluggish economy but, unfortunately, those reforms came too late and the country could not be salvaged. Since the demise of the Soviet Union, the Russian Federation, which assumed much of the old empire's responsibilities, retreated and isolated itself from world events, until its recent involvement in Syria, where it is fully backing the administration of Bashar al-Assad in the ongoing Civil War in that country.

The collapse of the Soviet Union and the self-imposed isolation undertaken by the Russian Federation has forced it to abandon most of the former Soviet bloc's commitments, such as maintaining and funding the Warsaw Pact military alliance, supporting former Soviet allies such as Cuba, Yugoslavia, and other allies in Asia and Africa. Russia's recent military interventions in Georgia and Ukraine (former Soviet Union Republics) would not have been easy had the Russian Federation not used the isolation period to restructure its society, build-up its economy and modernize its military.

As we know it today, the Warsaw Pact had been dismounted, while its NATO counterpart is still waxing stronger and has expanded beyond its original membership, to include members of the former Soviet Republics, especially the three Baltic states of Estonia, Latvia, and Lithuania. Other former Soviet Union blocs that joined NATO after its collapse are, Poland, Hungary, Czech Republic, Slovenia, Bulgaria, and Romania (Boese, 2004). The NATO troops are used today to fight the war against terrorism, like the wars in Iraq and Afghanistan. NATO's troops were also used by the West to invade Yugoslavia in 1999 over the Kosovo crisis and in Libya in 2011 to overthrow Muammar Gadhafi. NATO's involvements in Yugoslavia and Libya flagrantly violated Article five of its (Charter) founding document, because these nations did not militarily attack any NATO member-state.

Nations must understand that there is a huge price to pay for overstretching their resource capabilities. By overspending its revenue reserves, the US has become the biggest debtor nation in the world. Today, it borrows money from some of its allies and friends to execute some of its governmental obligations. For example, it borrows money to execute its war efforts against terrorism in Iraq and Afghanistan. Corporate greed has also contributed enormously in putting the US economy in distress and on a shaky ground.

By sending many American jobs away, especially the manufacturing ones to other countries, to such places as China and India; and by hiding corporate profits in corporations' offshore accounts to avoid paying taxes, the US corporations have not been creating the jobs many Americans had anticipated. The outcome of this is the millions of Americans who are now out of work and who have lost their homes, as a result. The sustenance of corporate America has resulted in huge investment in military build-up, the massive maintenance of oversea military bases, and the privatization of government businesses. Middle class America and the poor are the people who are negatively affected the most by this consistent decline in the country's economy. The outcome of this decline has created disillusionment and frustration among the American working class and the poor.

Homelessness, poverty, drug and gun violence, illegal immigration, and the war against terrorism have been identified as major social problems facing the United States, but the aggressive prosecution of these crimes by the country's criminal justice agencies has given the country a "black eye," thereby, making it the only country within the industrialized democracies that send more of its people to prison, especially its minority groups, who are disproportionally incarcerated (Alexander, 2012). In combating these problems, different proposals are articulated by the two major political parties that dominated the country's polity for centuries. Unfortunately, these proposals seem irreconcilable because these parties are firmly holding on to their parties' ideologies, with no compromise in sight. If this trend continues unabated and if no concrete solutions are reached, the crises that brought the Soviet Union to its knees may rear their ugly heads here in America.

How a Defective Political Institution Contributes to Group Violence and Insecurity in Nigeria

Whenever an organization has an inadequate organizational structure, such an organization is bound to fail. This same analogy applies to countries as well. Any country without adequate political institutions is doomed to fail, because political structures are set up to ensure that government functions are executed in ways that will accomplish the intended goals and to ensure that harmony and good governance are enhanced and nurtured. Defective institutional structures have always led to group violence and insecurity, where such institutional imperfection exists.

In the case of Nigeria, the biggest mistake ever made by the country's Founding Fathers during post-independence was their inability to modify the federal structure created by the Lyttleton Constitution of 1954, which did not conclusively address the issue of creating a strong national government while granting greater autonomy to the regions, as suggested by some Nigerian political actors, at the time. For example, the NCNC led by Azikiwe advocated for a strong national government with less regional autonomy for the country, while the NPC led by Ahmadu Bello advocated for a strong regional autonomy, with a weak center.

At the end of the day, those who had sought for a strong regional autonomy prevailed. This meant that the NPC had gotten its way because of "the fear of domination by one region against another" expressed vehemently by both the North and South at the time. The strengthening of regional powers while weakening the powers of the central government became the best alternative available to all parties concerned because of the overwhelming suspicion and mistrust that existed among regional leaders in the country.

Many political scientists would agree that the ideal political structure for a country like Nigeria with huge multi-ethnic nationalities and with multi-religious groups would be a federal structure with a strong national government and, a high degree of decentralization of powers between the national and state governments. A true federalism shares powers between national and state entities and, thereby, creates what is known, as inter-state relations or inter-governmental relations that encourages all states on the one hand to work together on issues that affect their states. On the other hand, inter-governmental relations encourage state and national governments to work together on issues that affect the country as a whole.

The political institution that prevailed in Nigeria between 1960 and 1966 was not a true federalism but a confederation, where regional governments were more powerful than the center. True federalism is instituted in countries with a huge population and diverse ethnic nationalities, as seen in the US, Canada, and India. The purposes of instituting a true federal system in such heterogeneous societies are to promote national cohesiveness and unity, and to encourage mass political participation at the grass root level. Falola and Heaton (2010), in their work, gave a good description of the Nigerian brand of federalism and how it operated:

> The federal system that had solidified regional divisions in the 1950s devolved into utter dysfunction in the period from 1960 to 1966, as the main political parties in each region fought bitterly and without scruples to gain or maintain control of both the federal and regional assembles, which controlled the bulk of Nigerian resources, with the result that control at the regional and federal level was the key to power over how Nigeria's resources would be distributed. Those parties that had control over the assemblies were able to distribute government resources among themselves and their supporters and, equally, were able to deny these resources to their opponents (p. 165).

In describing how these phenomena played out in Nigeria, Falola and Heaton noted that regional governments collected import and export taxes, and controlled the produce marketing boards, which consistently underpaid producers for their goods and, by doing so, were able to maintain huge annual surpluses. Revenues from these sources were then used to fund development projects.

In addition, they noted that the parties that controlled the regional and federal assemblies were therefore able to determine when these projects would be undertaken, which ones would be prioritized, who would get the contracts to complete the projects, and so on. "Under these conditions, it became imperative for parties once in power to stay in power and for those out of power either to ally with the majority party, or to wrest control of the government away from the party in the next election, as opposition parties faced the prospect of perennial marginalization" (Falola and Heaton, 2010: 165). What this phenomenon translates to, is that, whatever region of the country that controls the central government of Nigeria controls the country's resources. This obvious fact explains why elections in Nigeria are rigged, especially national elections, and why tribal politics still prevail. It also explains why political parties in Nigeria were and are still formed along regional lines or along tribal identity.

During Nigeria's First Republic (1960-1966), Northern leaders were very comfortable with regional structure, because it fitted into their political mode or agenda. Before this period, the North had always gotten its way because it was perceived by the British colonial authorities to have enormous political clout in the country, given its numerical strength.

The British colonial authorities had always respected and tolerated the traditional institutions that existed in the North. For example, in executing its "indirect rule" policy, the British colonial government in Nigeria used Northern Emirs to rule the North, but this was not the case in other parts of Nigeria, especially in Eastern Nigeria, where the colonial government handpicked people, some of whom were of questionable character, to rule. This was one of the reasons for the Aba Riots or the Women's War of 1929.

Another reason why the North was favored by the British colonial administration was because the administration viewed Northern leaders to be more conservative and more polite than their Southern counterparts whom the administration viewed as radicals and arrogant. The British hatred for Southern leaders is understandable: these were the folks who ignited the forces that dislodged colonial rule in Nigeria. The above-stated facts explain why in 1956, the North was given ninety-two seats out of the 184 seats in the central government legislature.

The North had enjoyed this notoriety until Nigerian Fourth Republic (1999 to present) when it became crystal clear to Northern leaders that the political power in Nigeria was drifting away from their corridor of power to another. This change in power equation is not sitting well with most of these Northern leaders who have always favored the status-quo and who have come to believe that the governance of Nigeria is the Northerners' divine inheritance.

The imperfection of the Nigerian political institutions was unmasked on January 15, 1966, when five Southern military officers, four of whom were of Igbo extraction, executed the first military coup ever recorded in the annals of Nigerian military history. The reasons given by these officers for their conduct were to unite the country and rid the country of tribal politics and corruption. These social vices (bribery, nepotism, and patronage), which threw the country into social turmoil and disaster, made Western Nigeria ungovernable.

These five Army Majors thought that the only way to rescue the country from this turmoil and the carnage that ensued thereafter was through military intervention. The execution of the coup was problematic, because its method of execution was faulty and questionable. Unfortunately, the outcome of the coup did not match with the rhetoric of the coup plotters, which was the eradication of tribalism and corruption from the Nigerian political discourse. The outcome of the coup left many doubts in the minds of many Nigerians, especially those from Northern Nigeria.

Although the coup was heavily supported in most of Southern Nigeria at the time, it did not achieve its intended goal; rather, it deepened the division of the country. In the execution of the coup, prominent leaders from Northern and Western regions were murdered. For example, the country's first Prime Minister, Alhaji Tafawa Balewa, who hailed from the North; Premier, Ahmadu Bello, who also came from the North; and Premier, S.L. Akintola, who came from the West, were all assassinated in the coup. According to Falola and Heaton (2010), the coup plotters saw these men as those who were directly responsible for the chaos of 1964 and 1965 that brought instability to the country (p. 172).

Others killed in the coup were senior military officers from the North, including: 1) Brig. Zakariya Maimalari; 2) Col. Kur Mohammed; 3) Lt. Col. James Pam; and 4) Lt. Col. Abogo Largema, and the country's first Finance Minister, Festus Okotie-Eboh (Siollun, n.d.). The execution of the coup shocked the conscience of many Nigerians and questions were raised as to why no political leaders or senior military officers of Igbo extraction suffered similar fate, and why the Igbo Premiers of the Mid-Western Region, Chief Dennis Osadebey, and Eastern Region, Dr. Michael Okpara were released after being arrested by the coup plotters. The only Igbo senior military officer killed in the January 15, 1966 coup by the coup plotters was Lt. Col. Arthur Unegbe who, at the time, was the Quartermaster-General of the Nigerian Army.

The ascendancy of Major General Johnson Thomas Umunnakwe Aguiyi-Ironsi to the throne did not help issues. From the moment he took over the helm of affairs from the January 15, 1966, coup plotters, Northern leaders viewed him as part of the Igbo military officers' strategy of using the Nigerian military to impose a new era of Igbo domination in the country. In the eyes of Northern leaders, General Aguiyi-Ironsi, was part of the Igbo conspiracy, installed to fulfill the wishes of the January 15, 1966, coup plotters. For this sake, General Ironsi was accused of many things by Northern leaders, which included the following:

1) Surrounding himself with Igbo advisers throughout his time in power;
2) Allowing the coup plotters to remain in detention, rather than bringing them to trial for the crime they committed; and
3) Accelerating the promotion of Igbo officers in the military, counter to the dictates of the quota system in place at the time.

In giving account as to why Northern junior army officers embarked on a counter-coup on July 29, 1966, Lt. Gen. Jeremiah Useni (rtd.) claimed that they acted because the Igbo military officers who were behind the killing of Northern leaders, which included civilians and military officers, were not arrested. General Useni also claimed that although the Igbo officers (the January 15, 1966 coup plotters) were later arrested and taken to jail, the information reaching the counter-coup plotters was that the Igbo officers were just enjoying themselves there; their ranks were returned to them and they were wearing their uniforms inside the jail.

In General Useni's interview titled "Why We Killed Ironsi and Installed Gowon," an interview conducted on September 27, 2013, in Hausa by the *Hausa Language Newspaper, Rariya* and translated into English by the *Premium Times* reporter, Sani Tukur, the former Minister of the Federal Capital Territory, Abuja under the regime of Gen. Sani Abacha, articulated the following events as reasons for the counter-coup:

> While we continued to meet in secret and strategising on how to take revenge, words started going round about what the Igbo officers were saying: that they had killed the snake, but had failed to cut off the head. Which meant those of us left might make them suffer later, that there was therefore the need to finish us off. Instead of them to show remorse and apologise, they were planning another sinister attacks. We were together with Col. Remawa at the time, he was serving in Abeokuta, and we heard of a grand plot to kill our emirs. A meeting of all emirs was called in Ibadan; all our emirs gathered in Ibadan, that the head of state, Ironsi, would address them. So we said, are we going to let him come address them and leave? Or should we just kill him or what? Our fear was that he was in the company of our emirs, and you know bullets do not select whom to hit. What do we do? We don't want even a single emir to die. We also considered arresting him at his lodge before he goes to meet with them. Col. Adekunle Fajuyi was the governor of South West at the time, and the head of state, Ironsi, was staying in his house in Ibadan. So we don't want a situation where they would say he conspired with us. So we decided the best thing to do was to open fire there even if Governor Fajuyi was also caught, so that they would just be buried together, and that was what happened (Tukur, 2013).

"Jerry Boy," as General Useni was often referred to during his military days, narrated how the January 15 coup plotters plotted to annihilate the remaining Northern soldiers in the 4th Battalion, Ibadan. In the interview, General Useni stated that before General Ironsi and his host Col. Adekunle Fajuyi were assassinated by Northern soldiers in a counter-coup, a party was organized for officers of the 4th Battalion in Ibadan. At that party, General Useni described the sort of drinks offered to soldiers of the Battalion; saying that since he joined the Nigerian Army, he has never seen as many assorted drinks as the ones offered to them on that day. The plan, according to Useni, was to get the soldiers all drunk, so that they would just come and open fire on them and kill them all. "That was what they planned for us at the 4th Battalion, Ibadan because we were the most feared, because we were the ones who lost a Brigade Commander, Largema. When Murtala returned from Lagos empty handed, everyone was just crying because Largema was a very nice man" (Tukur, 2013). General Useni rhetorically claimed that after the counter-coup, Gowon was made the Head of state.

The most damning evidence against General Aguiyi-Ironsi in the eyes of Northerners, according to Falola and Heaton (2010), was Decree #34 of May 24, 1966, which officially abolished the federal system and replaced it with a unitary system (p. 173). The Decree was intended to restructure the political institution that encouraged tribal politics and promoted instability in the country. The Decree was also intended to grant autonomies to oppressed ethnic groups within the regions. As a result, the regional structure, which barred the development of national unity and identity, ceased to exist and was replaced by "groups of provinces." Both the military and civil service, which were previously administered regionally, were integrated and administered from the center.

In the minds of Northern leaders, this meant giving too much power to the central government. With the implementation of the Decree, Northern leaders then concluded that their fear that the South would dominate the North had manifested and had come full circle. In the minds of Northerners, the implementation of the Decree meant that the gains the North had anticipated to achieve under regional arrangement would now vanish, and Northerners would not be actively involved in the governance of the country to an extent commensurate with their population. To Northern leaders, the Decree meant that the North faced the prospect of being occupied by Southern military officers, and being administered by Southern civil servants—a situation Northern leaders were not willing to accept or tolerate.

To maintain the status–quo and to prevent Northerners' perceived gains from slipping any further, the country, once again, descended into anarchy and violence, when a group of Northern Non-Commissioned Officers (NCOs) and junior military officers carried out a counter-coup on July 29, 1966. This was a devastating coup, in terms of its tenacity, ferociousness, and destruction. The counter-coup, which targeted the Igbos and other Easterners living in the North, was the bloodiest coup ever recorded in Nigerian military history. As noted by General Useni in his interview, Lt. Col. Yakubu Gowon, a Northerner, was chosen by the Northern military officers who executed the counter-coup to replace General Aguiyi-Ironsi, whose administration was toppled, following his assassination by the Northern military coup plotters.

The counter-coup took between 80,000 and 100,000 lives of Easterners living in the North. This mass killing of the Igbos in Northern Nigeria sparked retaliatory attacks in the Eastern Region against people of Northern extraction who were living there. Given the uncontrollable nature of events in the country, at the time, and given the fact that the lives of Igbos and other Easterners were no longer guaranteed anywhere outside Eastern Nigeria, especially in Northern Nigeria, Lieutenant Colonel Chukwuemeka Odumegwu Ojukwu and other Igbo leaders of thought questioned whether Igbos could ever live in harmony within a federated Nigeria. When the answer to this question was a resounding no, given the situation on the ground, the Igbo leaders of thought urged all Easterners outside the region to return home. They equally advised all northerners living in the East to do likewise. When many attempts to keep the Union together failed to yield positive results, the people of Eastern Nigeria had no other option available to them than to secede from the Nigerian Union. Consequently, the then military governor of Eastern Nigeria, Lt. Col. Emeka Odumegwu Ojukwu, acting on the advice of leaders from the region, declared that the region was no longer part of Nigeria, and on May 30, 1967, Eastern Nigeria became known as the Republic of Biafra. The secession of Eastern Nigeria from the Union led to a bloody Civil War that lasted over two and half years (May 30, 1967- January 13, 1970).

When Northern Nigeria assumed total control of the country's governance following its victory in the battle field, one expected Northern leaders to lead with good example by correcting those wrongs or ills they accused the Igbos, especially the Aguiyi-Ironsi administration of committing. That was not the case, rather, they did exactly what they accused Aguiyi-Ironsi of doing. One of the things Northern leaders did when they took over control of the Federal Government of Nigeria was to abandon the regional structure for which they had once advocated. They granted more powers and responsibilities to central government, thereby creating a strong national government, leaving the regions with little or no power.

What a contradiction! This was exactly the structure the NCNC and Decree #34, May 24, 1966 had called for. Remember that General Aguiyi-Ironsi's Decree called for the abolition of regions, to be replaced by groups of provinces and, that both the military and the civil service previously administered regionally, be integrated and administered from the center. This was what the North did when it took over the governance of the country.

The reason for replacing the four existing regions (Northern, Western, Eastern, and Mid-Western) in the country with groups of provinces, was to give each ethnic nationality in the country an opportunity to determine its own fate and destiny, and to encourage mass political participation or what political scientists refer to as "grass root politics." We should not forget that there were hundreds of small ethnic nationalities in each of these regions who were suppressed by dominant ethnic nationalities in those regions. The dominant ethnic nationalities in the country then and now include the Igbos found in Eastern Nigeria, the Yorubas found in Western Nigeria, and the Hausa-Fulanis, found in Northern Nigeria. The Mid-Western region was carved out of the old Western Region.

The marginalization and suppression of small ethnic nationalities in the country is still going on, especially in Northern Nigeria, where ethnic minority groups in the North West, North Central, and North East political zones are threatening to pull out of the Arewa Consultative Forum (ACF) because of what the ethnic minority leaders in the North described as endless repeated killing of minorities in the North. The *Nigerian Tribune Newspaper* article of April 22, 2014, reported that "the leaders of the minority groups had decided that they could not continue to sit on the same forum with ACF leaders who had refused to rein in the rampaging Fulani herdsmen whose activities had led to the death of no fewer than 3,000 persons from the North West, North Central, and North East in recent years" (Adisa, 2014).

Minority leaders, according to the *Newspaper,* came to this conclusion because leaders of the Hausa Fulani ethnic group in the North were notable patrons of the Miyetti Allah, and the Fulani herdsmen, whose clashes with farmers across the North had left huge casualties. The minority leaders in the three Northern zones have accused the ACF of failing:

> To prevent the incessant killings of members of minority groups across the North. The decimation of the minorities amounts to another genocide. We cannot continue to sit in a forum that cannot call its members to order, since it is confirmed that leaders of ACF are also patrons of the Miyetti Allah. The right to self-determination of the people of this world is well recognized by the United Nations as well as the African Charter on Human and People's Right. The ACF must call the Miyetti Allah to order. There are known patrons of the group that can be called to intervene. If the killings of our people do not end before June 30, 2014, we will pull out of ACF and chart a new course (Adisa, 2014).

This is the kind of situation General Ironsi's Decree #34, May 24, 1966, was designed to prevent. But the Decree's intent was misunderstood at the time and, unfortunately, the messenger of the Decree was made to pay the ultimate price.

Following the toppling of General Aguiyi-Ironsi's administration by Northern military officers, General Gowon, a Northerner, took over power in Nigeria, and what transpired after that, was interesting: one of General Gowon's public policy agendas was state creation. His administration created twelve states and, from that moment, state creation in Nigeria became more apparent and imperative. Do not forget that the idea of creating "groups of provinces"—a similar program as states, was rejected by Northern leaders and; consequently, such an idea led to the murdering of General Aguiyi-Ironsi and many other Igbos living in the North at the time. Today, the country has been partitioned into 36 states, 774 local governments, and 9,572 political wards, including the Federal Capital Territory (FCT) in Abuja. The creation of state and local governments, and political wards was executed under the leadership of Northern military heads of state. Under their leadership, the country's army and civil service (once regionally administered) became federalized and expanded. The country's security apparatus, including its criminal justice agencies, education, health, elections, and the country's economy were also federalized.

The National Youth Service Corps (NYSC) that was established in 1973 by General Gowon's administration to promote national unity, was an idea borrowed from General Aguiyi-Ironsi's Decree #34 that called for a unitary government. The intent of the NYSC

Program was to make young Nigerians active participants in the activities of government in order to increase their sense of patriotism for the country. The other intent of the Program was to bring young Nigerians together from across the country to work together towards common goals. According to Falola and Heaton (2010), the program was also intended to guarantee that young Nigerians would develop relationships with Nigerians of religious and ethnic backgrounds that were different from their own, by requiring that their service take place in a part of the country other than their own (p. 190).

During General Gowon's era, the Nigerian national currency note was introduced, Indigenization Decree Act enacted, and the huge oil reserve in Southeastern Nigeria, which was the main reason for the Civil War, became federalized. The execution of these programs called for more federal departments and ministries to be established. For example, The Joint Admission Matriculation Board (JAMB) was set up to oversee the entrance examinations of the country's tertiary institutions. The Nigerian National Oil Company (NNOC) was established in 1971 to supervise oil extraction and provide guidelines to the multinational corporations that extract the oil. It was also said that Nigeria, being the seventh oil producer in the world, at the time, became a member of OPEC. In 1976, NNOC merged with the Ministry of Mines and Power to form the Nigerian National Petroleum Corporation (NNPC). By instituting these programs at the central government level, Northern leaders granted enormous powers and responsibilities to the center.

Why did the Northern leaders raise the profile of the central government this time, when they rejected such an overture a decade ago? What had changed? What changed was that the North was in absolute control of the central government and they saw a lot of benefits derived from federalizing most of the programs. By creating and dominating this hegemony, as long as they did, Northern leaders were able to use such a platform or instrument of power to enrich themselves and patronize few of their cronies both inside and outside the region, at the expense of a majority of Nigerians.

As revealed by many sources, Northern leaders were said to have acquired more of the country's oil well block allocations than their Southern counterparts, when the country's huge oil reserves are located in Southeastern Nigeria. For example, the *Nigerian Tribune Newspaper* editor for the South-South/South-East political zones, Donald Ojogo (2012), noted in his report that unknown to many Nigerians, more than eighty-five percent of ownership of the nation's oil reserves is in the hands of some influential Northerners who acquired marginal fields, Oil Mining Licenses (OML) and Oil Prospecting Licenses (OPL).

The report also claimed that the executions of such allocations were instituted by different military regimes of Gen. Ibrahim Babangida, the late Gen. Sani Abacha, as well as Nigeria's last military head of state, Gen. Abdulsalami Abubakar. The editorial report revealed some names of the owners of the oil well blocks and the number of barrels of crude oil each of the wells produces daily. These are some of the gains Northern leaders derived from enhancing the powers and responsibilities of the central government and possessing them. With regional structure, no Northern leader would have gotten access to the Southeastern oil reserves; such reserves would be strictly reserved for those in the region.

Senator Ita Enang, representing Akwa Ibom North-East (Uyo) Senatorial District and Chairman of the Senate Committee on Business and Rules, concurred with the above-stated revelation. He was quoted as saying that, "eighty-three percent of all present oil blocks are held by northerners" (Josiah, 2013). He made this revelation on the floor of the Senate during one of the debates on the Petroleum Industry Bill (PIB), a contentious debate that divides senators along North-South lines, whenever the issue comes up for discussion. A provision of the bill requires oil corporations operating in the oil producing states, especially in the Niger Delta region, home to Nigeria's vast oil resource, to pay ten percent of their net profits to the account of these states for the development of their communities—a provision, which Northern leaders have strongly opposed. To buttress his argument, Senator Enang provided names of some of the major oil blocks and their owners.

General Gowon's reluctance to hand over power to a democratically elected government in 1974, and his failure to do so when the time came, was a plot to ensure that the North consolidated its gains at the center. The subsequent bloodless coups that ensued, with the exception of General Mohammed's, which took few Northern military officers' lives, was part of a Northern strategy to remain in power in perpetuity. Reasons they always gave for overthrowing one another were weak. Reasons given for overthrowing one another in what became known in Nigeria as "palace coups," were to rid the country of corruption, indiscipline, and misrule—same sentiments the January 15, 1966 coup plotters gave to justify their action, but Northern military officers rejected the group's justification. The irony to this saga was that whenever Northern military officers shot their way into the corridor of power with the rhetoric of fighting indiscipline and corruption, corruption in the country quadrupled. What really happened at the time was that military regimes in Nigeria became an effective vehicle to loot the country's treasury, because they were accountable to no one. However, it must be noted here that the administrations of Gen. Murtala Mohammed and Gen. Muhammadu Buhari were not as affected by corruption, unlike other military administrations headed by Northern military heads of state. Most of these military administrations became corrupted by the huge revenues the Nigerian oil reserves generated. These turned out to be more of a curse than a blessing, as oil reserves in Nigeria were and still are the major source of corruption and tension in the country's polity.

The list of former Northern Heads of State, including civilian and military, given below makes the argument that there was a Northern strategy after the Nigerian Civil War to dominate the country's governance. Since Nigeria gained her political independence in 1960, the North has had four democratically elected Heads of State and six military Heads of State, while its Southern counterpart has had two democratically elected Heads of State and two military Heads of State. Another important factor to conclude that the North had a designed plan to dominate the governance of the country was the annulment of the June 12, 1993 presidential election by General Babangida, who promised to return the country back to a civilian government. Babangida's Civilian Decree #19 of 1987 was a plot to make Nigerians believe that the North was ready to give up its domination of the country's leadership. When the time came for electoral politics, Babangida failed to uphold the promise he made to the country. He annulled the presidential election, which his administration put together, because the favored Northern candidate did not win. The favored Northern candidate was Bashir Tofa, a Kanuri businessman from Kano State, who ran under the ticket of the National Republican Convention (NRC).

Unexpectedly and surprisingly to Northern leaders, Chief M. K. O. Abiola became the winner of the election—an election described by most political observers, as the most free, most fair, and most peaceful ever held in Nigerian history to date. Chief Abiola, who hailed from Southwestern Nigeria, ran under the banner of the Social Democratic Party (SDP), and as a Muslim himself, one would think that he would be acceptable to a group of people who had always wanted to Islamize Nigeria. Hiding his real intention for annulling the best election ever conducted in the country, General Babangida came up with bogus excuses to justify his unpatriotic act, declaring that, "Abiola had won on a platform that sowed ethnic discord, that both parties had illegally used funds to buy votes, and that the national election machinery had not been secured enough to prevent electoral malpractices."

Northern leaders thought they could get away with this obvious injustice unshackled, but they were wrong; they never knew what was in store for them. The fatigue of Northern hegemony was becoming obvious and real to many Nigerians, especially those from the South, who were no longer willing to tolerate the hegemony. For example, people of Southwestern Nigeria publicly rejected the annulment of the presidential election and demanded that Abiola be installed as the country's president, as the 1989 constitution stipulated.

The refusal to install Abiola, as the country's elected president, brought unprecedented pressure on Babangida's administration. These pressures were instituted by many civil society organizations in the country, which included the Campaign for Democracy (CD), the Nigerian Labor Congress (NLC), the National Association of Nigerian Students (NANS), and the Movement for the Advancement of Democracy (MAD). The activities of these organizations forced Babangida to declare a state of emergency in many places. His machinery of state suppression was insufficient to curtail the violence and disturbances that were brought to bear against the regime by these pro-democracy groups. It was said, at the time, that some Yoruba activists were openly talking about the possibility of the Western Region seceding from the federation if the election results were not restored. "Rumblings of the possible resurgence of Biafra in the East could be heard, as Nigerians again contemplated the possibility that the federal system was simply unworkable" (Falola and Heaton, 2010: 227-228).

Based on the cancellation of the June 12, 1993 election and the crises it generated, the country seemed to be descending into another Civil War. Remembering what happened in 1967, the fear of another Civil War, resulting from the June 12th saga, triggered a huge mass migration, in which people uprooted their families from the places where they lived and worked and went back to their places of origin. By recognizing the fact that no country had survived two major Civil Wars, and by recognizing the fact that the violence and social unrests that engulfed the country would not be brought to a halt unless the results of the June 12 election were restored, General Babangida reached a compromise with political actors in the country by agreeing to hand over power to an Interim Governing Council (IGC), which he created. The IGC was headed by Ernest Shonekan, another Yoruba man; Shonekan's appointment to head the IGC was an appeasement plot to quell the Yoruba anger over the cancellation of the June 12 election, which was won by a Yoruba man of a Muslim sect.

Northern leaders could not tolerate the compromise, even though they knew they had no more cards left to play, because time had run out on them. Nigerians were fed up with the Northern military oligarchy and they wanted power to shift from the North to the South.

However, there were some diehard leaders in the North who did not want to see this power shift manifest and; consequently, Chief Shonekan was pushed aside by Gen. Sani Abacha, in a military-style coup. General Abacha's takeover of the country by force of arms became crystal clear to the people of the South that the Northern strategy to dominate the country's leadership was well and alive.

The people's pressure on Abacha's administration became more intense, as more organizations, including NADECO, led by many well-established politicians and scholars in the country joined forces together to demand that Abiola be crowned as the country's new president. While massive protests mobilized against Abacha's arbitrary takeover of the country were going on, Chief Abiola declared himself president of Nigeria and held a public inauguration ceremony in Lagos. Many Labor Unions in the country staged massive strikes in support of the movement against Abacha. The strikes were said to have brought much of Southern Nigeria, including parts of the petroleum sector, to a standstill in the months of June and July 1993 (Falola and Heaton, 2010: 230).

General Abacha could not withstand the popular oppositions mounted against his regime. Acting like other world dictators, Abacha did not allow the oppositions to continue their activities, concluding that by allowing such protests to continue unabated they would seriously undermine his legitimacy to rule the country—a situation that would endanger Northern hegemony.

In maintaining the status-quo of Northern dominance of the country, General Abacha used his administration's machinery to suppress groups and individuals who spoke up in favor of the June 12th election or who criticized his administration. To this end, the regime took enormous measures to stifle dissent in the country. The regime banned the existing political parties in the country and the activities of pro-democracy groups like NADECO. The regime began the arrests of prominent Nigerians from the South, especially from the Yoruba extraction, which included both civilian and military officers.

Chief Abiola, General Obasanjo, Gen. Oladipo Diya, and some Yoruba senior military officers were arrested and imprisoned under a bogus accusation that they were plotting a coup to overthrow the regime. Chief Abiola and General Shehu Musa Yar'Adua, one of the few Northern individuals who were implicated in the bogus plotted coup, died mysteriously in prison. Till today, no one knows how these men died or what caused their death. On the other hand, General Obasanjo who also was imprisoned along with Shehu Musa Yar'Adua, by Abacha, was one of the lucky ones to escape death while in prison. The lives of Gen. Oladipo Diya and other Yoruba senior military officers who were detained and waiting for a military tribunal trial for their alleged military coup against the Abacha regime, were spared because of the sudden death of Gen. Sani Abacha.

Because of the bad blood generated from the Northern leaders' intrigue over the June 12, 1993 presidential election, the Yoruba ethnic nationality, a one-time trusted ally of the North during and after the Nigerian Civil War, was no longer willing to accept its "junior partnership status" within the North-West alliance. Northern leaders understood this sentiment well.

When Abacha died suddenly in office, Northern leaders agreed that power had to change hands temporarily, fearing that the country may disintegrate if the North continued to dominate the governance of the country. Since the North was in control of the country's military, Northern leaders agreed that Gen. Abdulsalami Abubakar would be given the realm of power and that his major role would be to return the country to a democratically elected government within the shortest period of time. Within the Northern circles, General Obasanjo, one of the surviving prison inmates in the Abacha's prisoners' ordeal saga, was endorsed by Northern leaders to lead the country. To Northern leaders, the successful election of Gen. Olusegun Obasanjo to the nation's highest office in the land in 1999 was seen as a gesture extended to the Yoruba people in order to right the wrong done to Chief Abiola and his presidency.

General Babangida alluded to this fact in an interview he granted to Ikeddy Isiguzo, Chairman of *Nigerian Vanguard Editorial Board* on August 18, 2011. In that interview, the Minna-born Army General and former military president, noted that his decision to persuade General Obasanjo to join the presidential race in 1999, when he (Babangida) visited Obasanjo at his Otta farm after Obasanjo was released from prison, was a very sound decision. Babangida was then quoted, as saying that, "we were proved right in our choice of General Obasanjo.

We wanted someone who could keep the country one." But, a few years later, Babangida sounded a different tone, when he fell out with General Obasanjo after the latter had served two consecutive terms in office, as the country's executive president. In the altercation that ensued between the two former military Heads of state, General Babangida made it known to the Nigerian public that Obasanjo would not have become the president of the country in 1999, if it weren't for Babangida; and by the same token, he reminded Obasanjo that he should not bite the finger that fed him.

Today, Northern leaders are not happy about how things are turning out in the country or how things are manifesting themselves in the corridors of power within the Nigerian state since the emergence of the Fourth Republic (1999 to present). There are sentiments of "reverse discrimination" being expressed within certain Northern Nigerian quarters. Indeed, there are some Northern leaders who feel that the North has lost the grip of power in the country, especially after the demise of President Umaru Yar'Adua of blessed memory. These leaders feel that the North has lost the control of the Nigerian military, an instrument of power the North once dominated and used in controlling the country. They saw the retirement of some Northern senior military officers as a plot to weaken Northern resolve in staging coups, a practice Northern Nigeria does best and is well known to others.

It is a true statement that after the Nigerian Civil War, the Igbo ethnic nationality was marginalized in certain strategic federal government positions, until recently. Let it be known that since the demise of General Aguiyi-Ironsi in 1966, no Igbo military officer has ever headed the Nigerian Army until the presidency of Goodluck Jonathan, who in September of 2010, appointed an Igbo man, Lt. Gen. Azubuike Ihejirika to serve as the country's Chief of Army Staff (COAS). Since his appointment to this strategic position, General Ihejirika, the Chief of Army Staff, has been accused by those whom he described as "faceless groups;" individuals who feed on rumors and do not wish the country well, of making lopsided recruitment, promotion, retirement, and deployment exercises in the Nigerian Army in favor of Igbo officers.

Nigerians of good conscience and goodwill should not forget that this same allegation was made against General Aguiyi-Ironsi in 1966 by northern machination, which led to his assassination. General Ironsi was accused of promoting more Igbo military officers to high ranking positions than officers from other ethnic nationalities, when he became the country's first military Head of State—a position he occupied as a result of the January 15, 1966, failed coup. These rumor peddlers, according to the *Nigerian Vanguard Newspaper* article written by Omonobi on February 13, 2013, accused General Ihejirika of "deploying an Army General of Igbo extraction (whose name was not given) to commence operations in Maiduguri against Boko Haram terrorists to avenge the killing of Igbos during the Nigerian Civil War." In that *Newspaper* article, the Chief of Army Staff defended the recruitment, promotion, retirement, and deployment exercises executed under his Watch, noting that such exercises were done devoid of ethnic and religious colouration, and that the Army does not discriminate against any person on the basis of ethno-religious background."

For the sake of clarity, the retirement of military officers in Nigeria, like in other countries around the world, is usually based on established rules, regulations, and procedures that govern such retirement, promotion, recruitment, and deployment of military personnel. It was an understatement to suggest that the retirement of senior military officers in Nigeria, who met the retirement criteria, was a plot to rid the North of its senior military officers. It may seem so to laymen since most senior military officers in the Nigerian Armed Forces came from the North due to their longevity in the service and decades of Northern domination of the Nigerian military and other federal government agencies. Those making this allegation should not forget that there is a retirement system put in place to make way for more junior officers to rise to senior ranking positions.

In reacting to his critics, General Ihejirika reminded them that it was not himself only, who determines who is hired, promoted, retired, or deployed. He made his critics understand that, "it is the Army Council that approves the retirement of any officer of the army before such an officer can be asked to go." The composition of the Army Council, according to the Chief of Army Staff, includes: the country's President, who chairs the Council; the Minister of Defense, Permanent Secretary; Chief of Defense Staff; and the Chief of Army Staff. To debunk the myth that General Ihejirika was favoring people of his own ethnic nationality (Igbos), the seasoned soldier was quoted as saying:

> You might wish to know that in my deployments, I have General Gani Wahab in first division, Kaduna, I have Brigadier General M. Ibrahim in first Brigade, and Brigadier General Lliya Abbah in second Brigade. And I sit here very comfortable with that posting. Concerning General Olayinka Oshinowo (former GOC 92 division Enugu), who happened to have been mentioned in one of the write-ups as one of those short changed, it might interest the public to know that General Oshinowo had missed his promotion before I became the Chief of Army Staff and that he was promoted to the rank of Major General under my watch.... It is however surprising that some few media chose to celebrate this calculated attempt of some frivolous, unpatriotic and unscrupulous elements aimed at insinuating that the recruitment, promotion, retirement and recent deployment of senior officers in the Nigerian army were ethnically motivated. For the advancement of doubt, there is no ethnic or religious consideration in this routine exercises in the Nigerian Army (Omonobi, 2013).

From the list of high ranking army officers mentioned above, no such names resemble an Igbo name, meaning that General Ihejirika was not favoring Igbo officers, as alleged by his Northern critics. Most of these officers mentioned above are from Northern extraction, with the exception of one officer, who comes from Yoruba land in Western Nigeria.

It is, indeed, shocking to hear and learn from the very group of people, who dominated the country's military for generations, now suggesting that they are being marginalized. What irony! In giving account of his stewardship since he took over the leadership of the Army, General Ihejirika claimed that "it is on record that the number of Major Generals promoted since the coming of the present leadership increased from 2008 to date in line with Nigeria army order of battle. This was a view not only to enhance our force structure, fighting efficiency and cohesion, but also to boast the morale of personnel. While (8) eight and (12) twelve Brigadier Generals were promoted in 2008 and 2009 respectively, (26) twenty-six were promoted in 2010, (25) twenty-five in 2011, and (22) twenty-two in 2012."

I hereby present you with the evidence demonstrating that Northern Nigeria dominated the country's governance, including its military (Army, Air Force, and Navy), and the Police Force leadership hierarchy for years. Of the sixteen indigenous military officers who served as **Chiefs of Defense Staff** since this Office was created in 1979, nine of these officers were from Northern Nigeria, while seven of them came from Southern Nigeria. From the Nigerian military context, the Office of the Chief of Defense Staff is said to be the highest ranking military position within the country's Armed Forces. Constitutionally, the occupant of this prestigious Office is a senior commissioned officer who is appointed by the country's President, who also happens to be the Commander-in-Chief of the Nigerian Armed Forces. The Chief of Defense Staff reports directly to the President on matters of national security; additionally, he/she formulates and executes policies and programs towards the attainment of National Security and operational competence of the country's Armed Forces. In executing these responsibilities, the Chief of Defense Staff is assisted by the Chiefs of Army, Air Force, and Navy Staff.

Below are the nine names of Chiefs of Defense Staff from Northern Nigeria and the years they served:

- Lt. General Gibson Jalo   1981-1983;
- General Domkat Bail   1984-1990;
- General Sani Abacha   1990-1993;
- General Abdulsalami Abubakar   1993-1998;
- Air Marshal Allamin M. Daggash   1998-1999;
- Admiral Ibrahim Ogohi   1999-2003;
- General Martin Luther Agwai   2006-2007;
- Vice Admiral Ola Sa'ad Ibrahim   2012-2014;
- Air Chief Marshal Alex Sabundu Badeh   2014- 2015.

Below are the six names of Chiefs of Defense Staff from Southern Nigeria and the years they served:

- Lt. General Ipoola Alani Akinrinade   1980-1981;
- Lt. General Oladipo Diya   1993;
- General Alexander Ogomudia   2003-2006;
- General Owoye Andrew Azazi   2007-2008;
- Air Chief Marshal Paul Dike   2008-2010;
- Air Chief Marshal Oluseyi Petinrin   2012-2012.
- Gen. Abayomi Gabriel Olonisakim   2015-present*

Sources: (*Wikipedia, the free Encyclopedia*, 2014; *The Ambrose Ehirim Files, 2013*)
*He is a new appointment by President Buhari. This is an update to the source.

Of the twenty-five indigenous **Chiefs of Army Staff** since post-independence, eighteen of these officers came from Northern Nigeria, while seven of them came from Southern Nigeria. The Chiefs of Army Staff from Northern Nigeria and the periods they served are as follows:

- Lt. Col. Yakubu Gowon,   January 1966- July 1966;
- Lt. Col. Joseph Akanhan,   May 1967- May 1968;
- Maj. Gen. Hassan Katsina,   May 1968- January 1971;
- Lt. Col. Theophilus Danjuma,   July 1975- October 1979;
- Lt. Gen. Gibson Jallo,   April 1980- October 1981;
- Lt. Gen. Mohammed Inuwa Wushishi,   October 1981- October 1983;
- Maj. Gen. Ibrahim Babangida,   January 1984- August 1985;
- Lt. Gen. Sani Abacha,   August 1985- August 1990;
- Lt. Gen. Salihu Ibrahim,   August 1990- September 1993;
- Lt. Gen. Aliyu Gusau Mohammed,   September 1993- November 1993;
- Maj. Gen. Chris Alli,   November 1993- August 1994;
- Maj. Gen. Alwali Kazir,   August 1994- March 1996;
- Lt. Gen. Ishaya Bamaiyi,   March 1996- May 1999;
- Lt. Gen. Victor Malu,   May 1999- April 2001;
- Lt. Gen. Martin Luther Agwai,   June 2003- June 2006;
- Lt. Gen. Luka Yusuf,   June 2007- August 2008;
- Lt. Gen. Abdulrahman Bello Dambazau,   August 2008- September 2010
- Lt. Gen. Tukur Yusufu Buratai   July 2015- present.

Below are also names of the seven Chiefs of Army Staff from Southern Nigeria:

- Maj. Gen. Johnson Aguiyi-Ironsi,   1965-1966;
- Maj. Gen. David Ejoor,   January 1971-July 1975;
- Lt. Gen. Ipoola Alani Akinrinade,   October 1979-April 1980;
- Lt. Gen. Alexander Ogomudia,   April 2001-June 2003;
- Lt. Gen. Owoye Andrew Azazi,   June 2006- May 2007;
- Lt. Gen. Onyabor Azubuike Ihejirika,   September 2010 to January 2014,
- Maj. Gen. Kenneth Tobiah Jacob Minimah,   January 2014- July 2015

Source: *Nigerian Army Official Website* (http://army.mil.ng/Chronicle-of-Command.html).

Of the seventeen indigenous **Chiefs of Air Staff**, eleven of these officers were from Northern Nigeria, while the remaining six officers were from Southern Nigeria. Here are names of the eleven Chiefs of Air Staff from Northern Nigeria and the years they served:

- Colonel Shittu A. Alao   1967-1969;
- Brigadier Emmanuel E. Ikwue   1969-1975;
- Air Vice Marshal John Nmadu Yisa-Doko   1975-1980;
- Air Vice Marshal Abudullah Dominic Bello   1980-1983;
- Air Marshal Ibrahim M. Alfa   1984-1990;
- Air Vice Marshal Femi John Femi   1993-1996;

- Air Marshal Isaac M. Alfa   1999-2001;
- Air Marshal Jonah Domfa Wuyep   2001-2005;
- Air Marshal Mohammed Dikko Umar   2010-2012;
- Air Marshal Alex Sabundu Badeh   2012-2015
- Air Chief Marshal Sadique Baba Abubakar   2015-present.

Below are names of the six Chiefs of Air Staff from Southern Nigeria and the periods:

- Brigadier General George T. Kurubo   1966-1967;
- Air Marshal Nuraini Oladimeji Yussuff   1990-1992;
- Air Marshal Akin Dada   1992-1993;
- Air Marshal Nsikak E. Eduok   1996-1999;
- Air Chief Marshal Paul Dike   2005-2008;
- Air Marshal Oluseyi Olusegun Petinrin   2008-2010

Sources: *Nigerian Air Force Official Website:* (http://airforce.mil.ng/former_cas)

Of the nineteen indigenous **Chiefs of Navy Staff,** fourteen of these officers were from Southern Nigeria, while the remaining five officers came from Northern Nigeria. Below are the names of these Chiefs of Navy Staff from Southern Nigeria and the years they served:

- Vice Admiral Joseph Edet Akinwale-Wey   1964-1973;
- Vice Admiral Nelson Bossman Soroh   1973-1975;
- Vice Admiral Michael Ayinde Adelanwa   1975-1980;
- Vice Admiral A. Akin Aduwo   1980-1983
- Rear Admiral Augustus Akhabue Aikhomu   1984-1986;
- Rear Admiral Patrick Sebo Koshoni   1986-1990;
- Vice Admiral D.P.E. Omotsola   1992-1993;
- Rear Admiral Allison Amaechina Madueke   1993-1994;
- Rear Admiral Okhai Mike Akhigbe   1994-1998;
- Vice Admiral Jubril Ayinla   1998-1999;
- Vice Admiral Victor Kare Ombu   1999-2001;
- Vice Admiral G.T.A. Adekeye   2005-2008;
- Vice Admiral Dele Joseph Ezeoba   2012-2015
- Vice Admiral Ibok-Ete Ekwe Ibas   2015 to present.

Below are names of Chiefs of Navy Staff from Northern Nigerian and the years they served:

- Vice Admiral Murtala Nyako   1990-1992;
- Rear Admiral Suleiman Sa'idu   1993-1993;
- Vice Admiral Samuel Olajide Afolayan   2001-2005;
- Vice Admiral Ishayalko Ibrahim   2008-2010;
- Vice Admiral Ola Sa'ad Ibrahim   2010-2012.

Sources: *Nigerian Navy Official Website:* (http://www.navy.mil.ng/Chronicles-of-Command)

The Nigerian Navy is an aberration. Since independence, this is the only unit of the Nigerian Armed Forces, where more Southern officers were appointed to head the unit. But, in the leadership hierarchy of the Nigerian Police, the story of Northern domination of the country's security apparatus remained the same until recently following the appointment of a Southerner by the out-going President, Goodluck Jonathan, bringing the total number of indigenous Inspectors-General of Police to eighteen. Of the eighteen indigenous **Inspectors-General of the Nigerian Police**, nine of these officers were of Northern extraction, while nine officers came from Southern Nigeria.

The Inspectors-General of Police who came from Northern Nigeria were as follow:

- Kam Salem — 1966-1975;
- Muhammadu Dikko Yusufu — 1975-1979;
- Adamu Suleiman — 1979-1981;
- Muhammadu Gambo Jimeta — 1986-1990;
- Aliyu Atta — 1990-1993;
- Ibrahim Coomassie — 1993-1999;
- Hafiz Ringim — 2010-2012;
- Mohammed D. Abubakar — 2012-2014;
- Suleiman Abba — 2014- 2015.

Inspectors General of Police who came from Southern Nigeria were as follow:

- Louis Edet — 1964-1966;
- Sunday Adewusi — 1981-1983;
- Etim Inyang — 1985-1986;
- Musiliu Smith — 1999-2002;
- Mustafa Adebayo Balogun — 2002-2005;
- Sunday Ehindero — 2005-2007;
- Mike Mbama Okiro — 2007-2009;
- Ogbonna Okechukwu Onovo — 2009-2010;
- Solomon Ehigiator Arase — 2015 to present.

Source: *Nigerian Police Force Official Website* (http://npf.gov.ng/past-igs/).

The above lists are facts on the ground. To reopen the canker-worn of tribal sentiments in the country, the Northern Elders Forum (NEF) led by Prof Ango Abdullahi maliciously accused the Chief of Army Staff, Lt. Gen. Azubuike Ihejirika, who retired from his military position in January of 2014, of extra-judicial killing of innocent civilians of Northern extraction in Baga, Borno State and the group threatened to drag him and six others to the International Criminal Court (ICC) in The Hague. The incident at Baga occurred during a military engagement with Boko Haram insurgents who have always lived in the midst of civilians and have always used them as human shields during combat.

As noted previously, the retired Chief of Army Staff, Lt. Gen. Azubuike Ihejirika, is the second Igbo man to be promoted to that position after Maj. Gen. Johnson Aguiyi-Ironsi since Nigeria became independent in 1960, and the proposed plan by the NEF to drag the Army Chief and six others to the ICC has drawn sharp reactions and condemnations in Igbo land.

Many Igbo indigenes have condemned such an idea, claiming that such a sinister plan would unleash a national ill-wind that would do no one any good and would eventually open a Pandora box that the country would deeply regret. One of the NEF's critics is Sen. Uche Chukwumerije, a former Director of the Biafran Information Agency during the Nigerian Civil War. The Honorable Senator from Abia State had these words to say:

> The plan of Northern Elders Forum to drag the immediate past Chief of Army Staff, Lt. Gen. Azubuike Ihejirika and six others to the International Criminal Court in Hague is capable of unleashing a national ill-wind that will do no one (including Prof. Ango Abdullahi's group) any good in this federation. The approach of the group to a national problem is selective, patently biased apparently in search of preconceived culprits, pointedly indifferent to the demands of national unity, and highly provocative to the sensibilities of all who genuinely desire the unity and stability of this federation. As Ango Abdullahi's team opens the doors and walks into the hall of the world court, let them realize that they have at last opened the Pandora's Box.... The indigenes of Odi, Zaki-Biam and Katsina Ala will in quick succession file into the hall. At the same time, Ndigbo of South East and Anioma will dust their files and head for Hague. Let it be emphasized that senseless sacrifice of a human life is indefensible. Violations of human rights have remained the bane of Africa. A society that has no respect for human life is nearer the status of a community of animals (Agbakwuru and Erunke, 2014).

It was unfortunate that some innocent lives were lost in Baga during a military mop-up operation to dislodge remnants of Boko Haram militants who have been terrorizing the community and the entire state for months. The group that the NEF should blame for the deaths of those innocent civilians in Baga is Boko Haram, and not the Nigerian military. It is the Boko Haram that openly declared a war against the North East region of the country and the Federal Government of Nigeria. The threat from the NEF to drag the Chief of Army Staff and six others to the ICC in The Hague for defending the country from members of Boko Haram who have killed thousands of innocent Nigerians, both Christians and Muslims, is a mockery, absurd and, at best, begging the question.

Senator Chukwumerije was absolutely right in his description of Northern hatred against the Igbos. The seasoned Senator was right when he said that "every citizen (including Prof. Ango Abdullahi) knows that the anti-terrorism campaign in the North is a joint military operation under the command of the Chief of Defense Staff. In singling out Lt. General Ihejirika, the then Army boss, the likes of Prof. Ango Abdullahi are merely betraying old prejudices and embarking on a new hazardous search for bad names to hang hated dogs." The Senator was forced to pose the following rhetorical and provocative questions given Northern hatred for Ndigbo, which the NEF has, once again, exhibited: 1) Why the Northern Elders Forum would single out the Baga incident for Hague's adjudication? 2) Why Prof. Ango Abdullahi and his team kept silent on past cases of wholesale massacres which were more gruesome than the Baga case? Senator Chukwumerije went on to list those massacres, which included the Odi case, in which the whole community was decimated. He also made mention of the Katsina Ala case and demanded to know if the Odi case did not arouse the conscience of Ango Abdullahi because the people do not belong to his hallowed Northern enclave, not to mention Zaki-Biam and Katsina Ala (Agbakwuru and Erunke, 2014).

Another voice condemning the call for the prosecution of the former Army Chief in The Hague came from the Anglican Bishop of Enugu, the Rt. Rev. Emmanuel Chukwuma, who was unhappy with the threat issued by the NEF to drag the immediate past Chief of Army Staff, Lt. Gen. Azubuike Ihejirika to the ICC for alleged extra-judicial killings of some Northerners. Like Senator Chukwumerije, the Anglican cleric warned Northern Elders that the move could lead to a major crisis that would threaten the nation's corporate existence. Bishop Chukwuma was also quoted as saying that:

> Any attempt to sue him [General Ihejirika] or drag him before the ICC will be resisted by the Igbos. Let them know that we are ready to defend our brother because he has done nothing to warrant anybody taking him to The Hague. Northern elders should be warned or they will set up inter-tribal war in Nigeria. Is it because Ihejirika is an Igbo man (Edike, 2014)?

The suggestion that the people of Northern Nigeria are losing the grip of power in the country may have explained why the machination against Ndigbo in Nigeria went after the twelfth and (second female) Comptroller General of the Nigerian Immigration Service, Rose Chinyere Uzoma, who was also appointed by Jonathan's administration on July 30, 2010. In January of 2012, Uzoma was forced to retire from her post after being accused of using her position to favor people from her state of origin. In her defense before the National Assembly on the allegations of favoritism and ethnic bias in the recruitment exercise conducted by the NIS, and why the hiring of 4,560 NIS employees was not openly advertised, the Comptroller General gave two cogent reasons to support her agency's decision or rationale: 1) to avoid the recruitment of bad eggs into the service, at a time, when the country is confronted with serious internal security threats—security threats that are making part of the country ungovernable and, insecurity supported by both internal and external forces; and 2) to correct the existing anomaly in the service workforce in which twelve states were at disadvantaged positions, as they were disproportionally represented in the Immigration workforce.

Interestingly, an article on the NIS hiring saga written on January 17, 2013, by Soni Daniel, a *Vanguard Newspaper* regional editor of the North, indicated otherwise. The article revealed that out of the 23,316 employees of the Nigerian Immigration Service: the North-Central political zone tops the list with (5,144); followed by South-South political zone with (4,306); North-West political zone has (4,089); North-East political zone has (3,095); South-East political zone, the zone from which the embattled Comptroller General comes from, has (3,415); and South-West political zone, has (3,267). When one adds up the number of Immigration employees from the three Northern political zones, what one sees is that the North has more NIS employees (12,328) than its Southern counterparts (10,988) coming from the combined three political zones in the South. With these numbers, how could anyone accuse the Comptroller General of favoring her state of origin at the detriment of others?

No person of good conscience and goodwill will ever encourage job discrimination or support any form of discriminatory practices in the work place. Only people with sinister minds will do so. The author of this work sincerely condemns what transpired at the NIS hiring exercise, if the allegations made against the NIS boss are found to be true.

On the other hand, the author equally questions why issues surrounding decades of job discriminations in the federal civil service, Nigerian Customs Service, and the Nigerian military were not raised by these critics, or why such discriminatory practices were not made an issue when the North was in full control of the country's bureaucratic agencies, as the recent public hearing held by Senate Committees on Federal Character and Employment, Labor and Productivity revealed. The recent public outcry against job discrimination and favoritism at the federal government level has produced an indictment of thirteen Federal Ministries, Departments and Agencies (MDAs) by the Senate for such discriminatory practices (Folasade-koyi, 2013).

According to Folasade-koyi (2013), the thirteen federal MDAs indicted for colluding with outsiders to run illegal cash-for-job racketeering scheme included the following: the Ministry of Interior; Federal Airports Authority of Nigeria; Nigerian Airspace Management Agency; Independent National Electoral Commission; National Examination Council; Joint Admission and Matriculation Board; Nigerian Civil Aviation Authority; Nigerian Meteorological Institute; Nigerian Security and Civil Defense Corps; Federal Road Safety Corps; Nigerian Immigration Service; Nigerian Customs Service; and National Youth Service Corps.

The indictment against these MDAs came as a result of numerous complaints from victims who were refused employment after paying huge sums of money to job syndicates and schemers within those agencies. Given the enormity of the job scam, the Senate President, David Mark, laid the blame on the failed judgment of the heads of MDAs, the military and Para-military, labeling or categorizing them as the worst culprits in the cash-for-job scam.

In his criticisms, the Senate president described situations, where heads of MDAs employed their relatives and undermined the principle of federal character. The one-time Army Colonel, now turned politician was quoted as saying:

> We are generally concerned about the issues of job insecurity in the MDAs. Similarly, we are concerned that people who have found themselves in positions of authority think first about their immediate relations, other extended family members and not the best and the most competent....Most heads of federal establishments secure for their relations unwarranted advantaged favour which they are not ordinarily legally or morally entitled to. This is a manifestation of a corrupt society where there is no equity or fairness (Folasade-koyi, 2013).

If we recall, these were some of the issues (bribery, nepotism, and patronage) that prompted the five Southern Army Majors to strike on January 15, 1966, but their intention to eradicate these unjust practices and behavior within government circles was misunderstood because of the way the coup turned out in the end. The Northern military leaders who took over the governance of the country after their successful countercoup attempt and their victory in the Civil War that ensued did not help issues; they perpetuated the culture of corruption (bribery, nepotism, and patronage) instead, which today, has devastated the country's bureaucratic institutions or organizations.

The domination of the country's central government by Northerners has resulted in an over concentration of powers at the center which, in turn, has prevented state and local governments from benefiting from the dividends of a true federalism. Some of the problems Nigerians are encountering today stem from this imbalance. We know that too much concentration of power at the center is problematic for national unity, especially for a diverse country like Nigeria. It is so, because such a structure makes the center more enviable and attractive to overzealous and power hungry politicians who may do the unthinkable to dominate the center.

A structure of this nature causes monopoly of power and makes the governance of the central government highly competitive and difficult, especially for people who do not trust one another, as is the case in Nigeria. This scenario explains why most national elections in Nigeria are rigged, given the fact that whosoever controls the central government of Nigeria controls the country's resources. To minimize group violence and the instability of the country resulting from defective politico-religious institutions, Nigeria must reduce the powers of its central government and grant more of these powers to state and local governments, as is the case in the United States of America and in other countries, where true federalism is the norm.

Let it be known that the concept of a strong national government does not necessarily mean giving away too much of the country's political and fiscal powers to the central government, as is the case in Nigeria. It simply means giving the central government some inherent powers to intervene in state matters when it is deemed appropriate and necessary; for example, the Supremacy Clause, which enables federal laws to prevail when they are in conflict with state laws, and the equal protection clause, a clause that will enable the federal government to intervene on behalf of Nigerian citizens whose constitutional rights are not protected by their state governments. Other inherent powers of the central government are the power to defend the entire country from external enemies, the ability of the central government to coin money and to negotiate treaties with other countries. These are factors that strengthen central government positions. Therefore, the concept of a strong national government is not achieved when you give away the responsibilities of state and local governments to the central government.

In his recent interview with Gbenga Oke of the Vanguard Newspaper in March of 2013, Prof. Ben Nwabueze, the eminent Nigerian legal scholar, acknowledged some of the flaws of the 1999 Constitution and took some of the blame for being a member of the committee that drafted it. In digesting those constitutional flaws, Professor Nwabueze was quoted as saying:

> Quite frankly, there are many flaws and many errors in the content of the constitution. So many errors, and I as a person, was partly responsible because I was a member of the constitution drafting committee set up by the military government in 1978. I was not only a member but chairman of one of the sub-committees that produced Chapter 2, the fundamental objectives and one of the cardinal flaws in the constitution is the concentration of powers in the centre. That is why I accepted that I am partly responsible for that because at the time, late Chief Rotimi Williams, a close friend of mine and nearly everybody in the Constitution Drafting Committee were so overwhelmed with this feeling, this patriotic feeling that we needed unity and the most effective way to achieve unity of the country is by having a very strong central government. Most of us in the committee shared that idea at the time. Chief Williams shared it because of the patriotism in us and we wanted a united Nigeria, we feel we can achieve unity by having a strong central government. Then, what we do to achieve our misguided objective? We took away fifty-percent of the items on the concurrent list and gave to the centre. We feel by doing this, we are establishing unity. We did not stop at that. We looked at the residual matters, these are matters exclusive to the states, we took a large part of it, more thirty-percent and close to fifty-percent; we took it away from states and gave to the centre. And the result is the almighty Federal Government, but what we discover was that instead of producing unity, we produced disunity because of the intensity of the struggle to control the centre. The intensity is so much and it is not just in the political power that was concentrated at the centre, much of the money also went to the centre and so by that action, we destroyed what is called fiscal federalism. Too much money at the centre increased the struggle for the control of the centre and the control of money itself and that has remained the feature of the Constitution up till today (Oke, 2013)

The eminent legal luminary also went on to say that when people struggled and agitated for true federalism and fiscal federalism, they knew what they were talking about and they were right. He claimed that unless those constitutional flaws are changed, the country would not achieve true federalism because the basis in which the constitution was written had proven to be misguided, meaning that the unity the country sought would not be achieved because of the struggle for the control of the center.

Professor Nwabueze agreed with those groups in the country that called for a National Conference, noting that there is a great need for all the 300 or more ethnic nationalities in the country to come together and discuss these constitutional deficiencies. He claimed that there were many other things in the Constitution, which experience had proven could not work. He concluded, therefore, that those anomalies were matters the National Conference could address and not matters the National Assembly could address alone.

Contrast between United States' and Nigeria's Political Institutions

In this section, efforts are made to compare and contrast the two countries' political institutions, as both countries have similar political systems but differ greatly in many outlooks. As you will see in the analyses, the United States of America practices a true federal system that nurtures and encourages mass political participation, while Nigerian federalism does not. How political powers are shared amongst the three branches of government at the national, state, and local government levels in each of these countries forms the basis of our analyses. Here are some of the similarities and differences we found in both countries.

For example, the president of the United States of America is elected indirectly every four years by way of Electoral College votes, while the Nigerian president is elected directly every four years by a popular vote. Bicameralism dominates the American political institutions both at the national and state levels, except in the state of Nebraska, where the state has a unicameral legislature—a single legislative body. The US national government and the rest of the forty-nine state governments have bicameral legislatures (two chambers), meaning that the US Congress has two Houses: House of Representatives and House of Senate and the forty-nine state legislatures have two Houses as well: House of Representatives and House of Senate. Local governments in the United States of America have a unicameral legislative body called City Council or Township Trustees that enact laws for cities or townships.

Nigeria has a combination of bicameral and unicameral legislatures. There are two chambers in Nigeria's National Assembly: House of Representatives and House of 'Senate. The thirty-six State Assemblies in Nigeria have a unicameral legislature, known as a State Assembly. Local governments in Nigeria also have a unicameral legislative body called Local Government Council. They enact laws within their respective jurisdictional boundaries.

The criminal justice systems in the United States of America, which includes the police, courts, corrections, and the juvenile justice system, are highly decentralized. This means that each level of government (national, state, and local) has its own criminal justice system which includes the police, courts, and corrections. Each of these agencies or institutions whether at federal, state, or local levels has its own autonomy or jurisdiction. The Nigerian criminal justice systems, on the other hand, are highly centralized. No state and local governments' police and correctional agencies exist in Nigeria; however, Nigeria operates a dual court system just like the United States, but does not have a juvenile justice system for youth.

In these countries (United States of America and Nigeria), the duties of police, courts, and corrections are placed under the executive branch. The executive branch of government in each of these countries uses the criminal justice agencies to enforce laws passed by their respective legislative branches. In the United States, for example, the enforcement of laws falls under the leadership of the US president, state governors, and city mayors or county commissioners, and local sheriffs. While in Nigeria, the enforcement of laws falls mainly under the leadership of the Nigerian president; and to a lesser degree, to State governors, and Chairmen of local government. For example, The Nigerian criminal justice institutions, which include the Nigerian Police Force, Nigerian Prison Service, Nigerian Immigration Service (NIS), Nigerian Customs service (NCS), State Secret Service (SSS), Nigerian Security and Civil Defense Corps (NSCDC), National Emergency Management Agency (NEMA), National Drug Law Enforcement Agency (NDLEA), and Federal Road Safety Corps (FRSC) are directly administered from the Office of the Nigerian president.

State governors in Nigeria rely heavily on national police and prison services, when it comes to the enforcement of laws passed by their State Assemblies, as state and local governments are not authorized by the country's constitution to operate their own police and prison institutions, as is the case in the United States. This criterion forces state and local governments to rely solely on the central government for the enforcement of laws in their respective states and local districts. Recently, some Nigerians have called for the creation of state police in the country. This sentiment is sounding loud and clear, given the security threats the country is confronted with, but not too much attention is given to the issue by those in authority.

There are three layers of law enforcement in the United States. The federal law enforcement agencies in the United States of America operate directly from two main departments, which are administered by the Office of the US President. These two departments are the US Department of Justice (DOJ) and the US Department of Homeland Security (DHS). For example, the Federal Bureau of Investigation (FBI); US Marshals; Drug Enforcement Administration (DEA); and Bureau of Alcohol, Tobacco, Firearms, and Explosives are housed under the US Department of Justice. The Bureau of Customs and Border Protection (CBP); Bureau of Immigration and Customs Enforcement (ICE); Federal Emergency Management Agency (FEMA); Transportation Security Administration (TSA); the US Coast Guard; and the US Secret Service are housed under the US Department of Homeland Security (DHS). This new department was created as a result of September 11, 2001, terrorist attacks on the United States (Walker and Katz, 2011, pp. 74-78). Before the 9-11 attacks on America, federal law enforcement agencies were housed under various US Departments.

The state law enforcement agencies in the United States of America include: the State Police; State Highway Patrol; State Bureau of Criminal Identification and Investigation; or other agencies the State Constitution may grant the authority to arrest and investigate crimes within the state. State law enforcement agencies operate directly from State Governors' Offices. There are forty-nine state law enforcement agencies in the United States. The state of Hawaii is the only state in the country that does not have a state police of its own unlike the rest of the forty-nine states in the Union. Both federal and state constitutions have provisions for Special District Police Agencies, such as the federal and state parks police, Metropolitan Transit Police agencies, Public schools and College and University campus police departments.

The local law enforcement agencies in the United States include: Municipal, City, or County Police Departments, and County Sheriff Departments. With the exception of County Sheriffs, who are responsible for about seventy-six percent of the County or Parish Jails in the United States of America, the local law enforcement agencies operate directly from the offices of the City Mayors, County Commissioners, or Township Administrators. In America, most police departments are found mainly at the local government level (Walker and Katz, 2011, p. 61). Private Police or Private Security Industries are also authorized by law to provide protections to public and private housing complexes, gated communities, business parks, malls, office complexes, power plants, and airports.

The Judicial structure in the United States of America is highly decentralized. There is a dual court system in the United States of America, meaning that at both national and state government levels, there are two separate court systems, with federal courts having a three layer structures and state courts have four layer structures. At the federal courts, there are: 1) the Federal District Courts, known as the trial courts. There are ninety-four of these courts scattered throughout the country; 2) there are appellate courts, known as Circuit Courts of Appeal. There are twelve of these Circuit Courts also scattered all over the country; and 3) the US Supreme Court or Court of last resort. State courts in the United States have the following structures: 1) Courts of Limited Jurisdiction; 2) Courts of General Jurisdiction; 3) Intermediate Court of Appeal; and 4) State Supreme Court or appellant court of last resort. Every state in America has a State Supreme Court.

Courts of Limited Jurisdiction also known as Misdemeanor Courts include the following: 1) Justice of the Peace and police Magistrates Courts; 2) District Courts or County Courts, Municipal and Magistrate Courts; and 3) Traffic, Family, Juvenile, Gun, Drug, and Other Special Courts. Courts of General Jurisdiction have different names in different states. In some states, they are referred to as Superior Courts, Circuit Courts, Courts of Common Pleas, and in New York State, for example, the Court of General Jurisdiction is known as Supreme Court. Both Courts of limited Jurisdiction and Courts of General Jurisdiction are trial courts, one for misdemeanor crimes and the other for felony crimes (Schmalleger, 2014, p.206).

Although the judicial branch of government in Nigeria is decentralized, it has a distinctive variation from those found in the United States of America. For instance, there is only one Supreme Court in the Nigerian legal system, known as the Supreme Court of Nigeria (SCN), housed at the federal level. This means that there is no State Supreme Court in Nigeria, as we have in the United States. There are other federal courts besides the SCN, which include the following: 1) the Court of Appeal; 2) the Federal High Court, this particular court is found in every state of the federation; 3) the High Court of the Federal Capital Territory, sitting in Abuja. The Federal High Courts in the states including the one in the Federal Capital Territory are similar in nature to those of the US Federal District Courts, where violators of all federal laws are tried first before the appeal process can commence.

Another variation in the two countries' judicial structures is the Court of Appeal in Nigeria, which is made up of other Courts of Appeal, which include 1) the Sharia Court of Appeal of the Federal Capital Territory, Abuja; and 2) the Customary Court of Appeal of the Federal Capital Territory, also sitting in Abuja. The Court of Appeal in Nigeria is authorized by the Nigerian Constitution to hear and determine appeals from all Federal and State Courts, including decisions of all Election Tribunals, Code of Conduct Tribunal, Court Marshals or other tribunals as may be prescribed by the National Assembly. The Supreme Court of Nigeria has the exclusive jurisdiction to hear and determine appeals from the Court of Appeal, and it is the highest court of the land, having both original and appellate jurisdiction to settle any justifiable dispute existing between the Federal and a State or between States.

States in Nigeria have multiple layers of court structures, which include: 1) State High Court; 2) State Sharia Court of Appeal; 3) State Customary Court of Appeal; 4) Magistrate Court; 5) Sharia Court; 6) District Court; 7) Area Courts; and 8) Customary Courts. Each of these courts has its own autonomy or jurisdiction. Sharia Courts are found mainly in Northern Nigeria, where Islamic religion is predominant, while Customary Courts are found in Southern Nigeria. State High Courts "have unlimited jurisdiction in their respective states to hear and determine civil and criminal matters subject to the exclusive jurisdiction conferred on the Federal High Court in respect of specific matters. State High Courts are also empowered to exercise appellate or supervisory jurisdiction over lower courts in their respective States." State Sharia Courts of Appeal and State Customary Courts of Appeal are also authorized by their state laws to review appeals coming directly from their lower courts. While Magistrate Courts, Sharia Courts, District Courts, Area Courts, and Customary Courts have limited civil and criminal jurisdiction conferred on them by their respective enabling laws.

The method of selection of judges in both United States and Nigeria varies widely. In Nigeria, for example, all court judges whether federal or state have appointive status.

All federal judges, including the Grand Kadi of the Sharia Court of Appeal of the Federal Capital Territory, Abuja and the President of the Customary Court of Appeal of the Federal Capital Territory, Abuja are appointed by the Nigerian President on the advice of the National Judicial Council (NJC), and confirmed by the Nigerian Senate. All state judges, including the Grand Kadis of State Sharia Courts of Appeal and Presidents of State Customary Courts of Appeal are appointed by State Governors on the advice of the NJC and affirmed by members of State Assemblies. Judges in Nigeria have a limited term of office. Constitutionally, they are retired once they reach the age of seventy years. They can also be removed from their judgeship without reaching the age of seventy years on grounds of illegal misconduct or abuse of office. If a Federal Judge is found culpable for illegal misconduct or abuse of office, the NJC will recommend the removal of such an errand judge to the President of Nigeria for the termination of the judge in question. The President's removal of a court judge from his /her judgeship is certain once the NJC has made its recommendation. The same thing goes for state judges, who are removed from office for illegality by state governors upon the NJC's recommendation. Death is another factor that creates a vacancy in both federal and state judgeship in Nigeria.

In the United States, the selection of judges differs. For example, all federal court judges are nominated by the US President and confirmed by two-third majority votes of the US Senate. All federal judges are appointed for life, but they can be removed from office through impeachment, retirement, or death. The selection of state court judges varies from state to state. Most state judges in the United State are selected by the following methods: 1) partisan election; 2) nonpartisan election; 3) gubernatorial appointment; 4) legislative selection; and 5) merit selection (Cole, Smith, and Dejong, 2015, p.365).

Corrections are the third major agency within the criminal justice processes. Corrections (prisons) are places where convicted offenders are punished beyond one year for breaking the country's laws. Federal and state governments in the United States operate their own correctional institutions separately. The correctional system in the United States is highly decentralized, while Nigeria's prison is centralized. The corrections agency in the United States falls into two categories: Institutional Corrections, which consists of prisons and jails, and Non-institutional Corrections, otherwise known as community-based corrections. They have programs, such as probation, parole, and intermediate sanctions.

The federal prisons are administered by the Federal Bureau of Prisons (BOP) that operates from the Office of US President, through the DOJ. The BOP has two major structures: the Central Office in Washington, D.C. and the six regional offices, whose duties are to oversee the smooth running of all federal prisons scattered all over the country (Hanser, 2013, pp. 356-357). State prisons are administered by the State's Department of Corrections and Rehabilitation that operates from the Office of the State Governor of each of the fifty states. Like the Central Office and regional offices of the

BOP, States' Department of Corrections and Rehabilitation coordinate and direct the activities and operations of all states' prisons in any given state in the country. In addition to states' prisons, most states' laws require that each maintain a separate juvenile center, known in history as the New Reform Schools (Hanser, 2013, p. 330).

Jails in America are under local supervision. They are unique and serve four main purposes: 1) they house those individuals who are arrested but awaiting trial; 2) they house those individuals who are convicted of a crime but awaiting sentencing; 3) they house those individuals who are serving a jail term for not more than one year for violating city ordinances, state statutory laws, and sometimes they may house those individuals who violated federal laws like the immigration laws; and 4) jails house those who violated their probation and parole conditions but are awaiting for their preliminary and revocation hearings. Jails are locally administered by County or Parish Sheriffs. Sheriffs, in most American states, have no term limit; they may remain in office as long as they choose and, as long as they are reelected to the Office of the Sheriff every four years.

There is no such thing as a jail in Nigeria. Jail functions are literally performed by the Nigerian Police, in what is known as (Police detention cells) where those arrested by the Police for alleged wrong doing are kept for some days before they are transferred to the Prison Authorities. The Nigerian Prison Service operates under the Office of the Nigerian President through the Controller General of Prisons, who is appointed by the President of Nigeria. The alleged offenders are kept in Prison until their court trials, which may take months or years. Most court trials in Nigeria are indefinite; this means that an individual may be detained in prison for ten years or longer without a court trial to determine his/her guilt or innocence. State and local governments in Nigeria have no police powers, meaning that they are not constitutionally authorized to operate their own police, prisons, or jails. For example, all instructions on how to administer justice and ensure individual rights and public safety, including the maintenance of law and order, and crime prevention efforts are executed directly from Abuja, the administrative seat of the Nigerian central government.

How Religion Contributes to Group Violence and the Insecurity of Nigeria

Another imperfect and divisive institution that has fueled group violence leading to the insecurity and destabilization of Nigeria is religion. From the time Usman Dan Fodio brought Islamic religion into Nigeria, the intent of the Founding Fathers of this sect was the Islamization of the country. The Nigeria nation had always been a multi-religious society, with two main religious sects competing for both memberships and dominance during pre and post-independence. One of these sects is more aggressive and violent than the other. Unfortunately, both religions are alien to the indigenous African religion.

One of these religious sects came from the Arab world while the other came from the Western world (Islam vs. Christianity). Both religious sects are deeply embedded in the political life of the country; therefore, becoming aggressive lobbyists in the country's polity, where each is lobbying the government to address the needs of its constituency. It was said that the politicization of religion in Nigeria began in the early 1970s.

Falola and Heaton (2010) maintained in their work that in the 1970s the Islamic organizations, such as the Supreme Council for Islamic Affairs (SCIA) and the Jama'atu Nasril Islam (JNI);

> Had long been pushing for the Nigerian government to adhere more to Islamic norm of governance. These included among other things, changing weekly day of rest from Sunday to Friday, removing symbols of Judeo-Christian traditions from public space, and above all, allowing the spread of Sharia laws and courts. Islamic organizations were opposed at the political level from the late 1970s by Christian organizations, most notably the Christian Association of Nigeria (CAN), which pushed to prevent the Islamization of Nigeria while also lobbying the government for greater employment opportunities for Christians and a state-sponsored pilgrimage for Christians to compliment the state sponsorship of the Islam hajj, which had benefited many Muslims since 1975 (p. 222).

The injection of religion into Nigerian polity has exacerbated group violence in the country, as Nigerians witnessed how the Islamic religious sect claimed to be built on the foundation of peace, love, and tolerance which made the country ungovernable, through intimidation and violence; and how the country's overzealous and power hungry politicians have used religion to advance their group selfish interest.

Nigerians, especially the Christians were alarmed when they learned in 1986 that General Babangida, who at the time, was the country's military head of state had unilaterally and secretly enrolled Nigeria into the Organization of the Islamic Conference (OIC), as an official member of that organization without the consultation of the ruling body, nor the conduct of a plebiscite or referendum to determine the collective will of the Nigerian people before embarking on such a mission. The objectives of OIC were well known to many Nigerians.

As an International Organization, OIC was established to promote Islamic issues and the spread of Islamic norms of governance and social organization among its member-states. With this singular act, it dawned on Christians and other non-Muslims in the country that Usman Dan Fodio's ambition of spreading Islam from the Sahara Desert to the Atlantic Ocean, as a way of making Nigeria an Islamic nation, had come to fruition or full circle. General Babangida's action was an attestation that Usman Dan Fodio's pronouncement was not just mere rhetoric, but a statement of fact. This was what the country had been put through by those who thought that the country belonged to them alone.

The consequences of this singular action were enormous. The enrollment of Nigeria in the OIC generated bitter animosity between Christians and Muslims, which continues till this day. Christians in Nigeria did not allow this arrogance of power to go unchallenged. The group unleashed massive pressure on Babangida's administration, which forced the administration to shelve the idea. Nigerian Muslims, especially those in the North have not forgiven Christians for their opposition to the country's membership into OIC. This singular issue, according to sources, ignited riots and clashes between Christians and Muslims in many Northern cities. In 1986 alone, there were several riots reported in the following Northern cities: Ilorin; Kafanchan; Kaduna; Katsina; Funtua; and Kano. In 1987, a religious riot was reported in Zaria. In 1991, Bauchi had its own taste of the violence; and in 1992, there was another riot in Zaria. These riots led to the burning of Christian Churches. Most of these riots claimed the lives of many innocent people from both faiths. In the Bauchi riots alone, it was estimated that at least 1,000 people were killed and a similar number of deaths reported in the 1992 Zaria riot (Falola and Heaton, 2010: 222-223).

Prior to Babangida's years in office, it was reported that Northern Nigeria was inflicted with religious violence, one of which was unleashed by a radical Muslim sect, known as the Maitatsine Movement—a sect that emerged in 1980 and was led by Mohammed Marwa, an immigrant from Northern Cameroon. The movement opposed the Nigerian government for breeding and harboring corrupt officials whom the movement viewed as "infidels." The activities of this group terrorized the entire city of Kano and such activities spurred the Kano State government to go after the group. In 1982, the federal government banned the activities of the group in the country as a whole. There were more religious riots reported in Kano after the Maitatsine Movement was banned. In these riots, Christian Churches were burned by Muslims and the riots spread to Zaria and Kaduna. Contrastingly, Muslims and Christians in Southern Nigeria have had good relationships with each other; both sects have respected each other's way of life and have lived harmoniously amongst each other. Indeed, Northern Muslims should emulate such relationships, because it is what the country needs to move forward.

There is a dictum that says whenever human beings solve one problem they create another. This statement is true in the Nigerian context, as it is also true for most countries. We should remember that Northern leaders had initially advocated for a strong regional structure, a sort of confederacy, fearing that Southerners would dominate the central government, when the idea of a strong national government was proposed by the NCNC and later by General Aguiyi-Ironsi's administration that sought for the unification of the country. The North rejected the idea on the ground that it lacked Western educated Civil Servants. Unfortunately, when the North took control of the central government, Northern leaders abandoned the regional structure they once advocated for and embraced a strong national government philosophy, which enabled them to nationalize almost every aspect of the Nigerian life. By doing so, they gave more responsibilities and more powers to the central government.

Today, Northern leaders are expressing frustrations and anger because they see the North as not being as influential as it was in the 1960s, 1970s, 1980s, and the 1990s, when Northern leaders were in the driver's seat or dictating the country's agenda. To their utmost dismay, they never thought that the day would come when they would no longer be in control of things for this long; this scenario worries them a lot. Northern leaders are worried that they are no longer relevant or profiting from the central government they built-up because of the new political dispensation in the country that called for: 1) the division of the country into six political zones, which weakens the so-called Northern majority; 2) a rotational presidency to deny the North its monopolization of power in the country; and 3) the outlawing of military coup in the country, a move that would deny the North its effective instrument of power. Northern leaders never knew that building a Northern hegemony through the central government would backfire.

While a few Northern leaders benefited enormously from the hegemony, a majority of Northerners were left behind to fend for themselves, leading to the massive poverty in Northern Nigeria. Critics have identified the endemic poverty prevailing in Northern Nigeria, as one of the sources fueling the recent religious violence that has engulfed the North. Indeed, the recent religious violence in Northern Nigeria is a culmination of frustration and anger resulting from massive poverty and unfounded perception that the North is gradually losing power at the center. Because it is difficult to stage a successful military coup in today's Nigeria due to the general public awareness of such dynamics and dilemma, religious violence is now seen as an effective weapon to disrupt the smooth running of the country. The recent expressions of frustration, anger, and deprivation in Northern Nigeria produced a group of Islamic militants known as Boko Haram, who are terrorizing citizens living in the North-Eastern part of the country. The group has been bombing Christian Churches and schools and has killed thousands of innocent people, especially Christians and Southerners, in pursuit of the group's religious agenda, which include: 1) making Nigeria an Islamic country; 2) hatred for Western education; and 3) disruption of Goodluck Jonathan's administration, the second democratically elected president from the South since Nigeria became an independent country.

It is unfortunate that many Northern leaders have come to tolerate the violent activities of Boko Haram since the armed group came into existence in 2002. Northern leaders have not spoken out publicly in condemnation of Boko Haram's attempt to undermine the national security interest of the country, and the huge number of innocent lives the armed group have wasted in its campaign against the Federal Government of Nigeria. Only a few of these leaders have spoken out after the Emir of Kano, Alhaji Ado Bayero and his family were attacked by members of this armed group—an attack that left four people dead. The few leaders who spoke out did so because they realized that Northern leaders were no longer safe or immune from being attacked by this group if a personality like the Emir of Kano was not spared in the ensued violence. What the attack on the Emir translates to, is that "the chicken has come home to roost."

Another lesson to be drawn from the Emir's attack is that Northern leaders can no longer remain aloof or complacent, while lives of innocent Northern Muslims and Southern Christians are wasted by Boko Haram. In commenting on the Emir's attack, General Babangida described the incident, as "a wake-up call to all." He questioned the motives behind the attack and demanded to know "what the perpetrators stood to gain by attempting to kill an Emir who is nearing 80 years." In his usual manner, Babangida described the embattled Emir as "one traditional ruler who does not seek favour from those in government and outside it and who, over the years, had been able to live an exemplary life to the admiration of all."

As a result of the threats facing the country, General Babangida called on the Federal Government of Nigeria to exploit the option of dialogue with the insurgent groups in order to arrest the prevailing drift in the country's national security. While advising against the use of force as a means of bringing the conflict to finality, the Minna-born Army General concluded with the following remarks:

> The use of force has proven to be inadequate and ineffective to checkmate this ugly trend. We must, therefore put hands together to find a more rewarding and meaningful end to this security concern. Dialogue is my number one preference in this regard. Government must also encourage positive discourses among its political appointees delivered with respect and rendered in temperate language to soothe the mood of the nation. Language of force will not help us in our strong determination to address this insecurity problem. We must engage ourselves constructively and in a manner that puts the interest of the country far and above other partisan consideration (Babangida, 2013).

Another Northern leader who spoke out in reaction to the attack on the Emir and his family was the former governor of Kano State, Senator Kabiru Gaya, who lamented that the country was in trouble over the assassination attempt on the Emir of Kano, noting that "incessant attacks by faceless gunmen in Kano State was impeding business there."

The Honorable Senator reminded Nigerians about the consequences of insecurity. He regretted that this is happening at a time when "the country is wooing investors to address youth unemployment," and concluded that insecurity was "becoming a clog in the wheel of progress" (Makinde, 2013).

The attack on the Emir of Kano has, indeed, awoken the moral consciousness of Northern leaders over the insecurity engulfing the North-East region of the country—an insecurity caused by Boko Haram's callous crusade, aimed at destabilizing the country. After the assassination attempt on the Emir of Kano, a summit tagged as "Development, Peace, and Unity" was summoned in Kano by the Northern Development Focus Initiative (NDFI). Its purpose was to discuss the prevalent issues facing the region, including the multi-faceted security challenges unleashed by Boko Haram. Speakers at the conference concurred that the security challenges confronting the country were being localized as a problem of the people of the North East geo-political zone with little or no commitment by the federal government to resolve the crisis in the interest of peace and development (Muhammad, 2013).

Although the three-day summit was largely attended by retired military officers of Northern extraction, retired technocrats, some politicians, and artisans, key but vital Northern leaders stayed away from the summit. According to the *Vanguard Nigeria Newspaper* article (2013), the key Northern leaders who were invited to the summit, but stayed away included the country's Vice President, Namadi Sambo, the three former Heads of State, Gen. Yakubu Gowon, Gen. Ibrahim Babangida, and Gen. Abdulsalami Abubakar. Others were the Senate President, Sen. David Mark, the country's former Vice President, Atiku Abubakar, and the Speaker of the House of Representatives, Rep. Aminu Waziri Tambuwal.

It was regrettable that these leaders shunned the peace summit in Kano, when the nation had waited patiently to hear the collective condemnation of Boko Haram's violence from Northern leaders, other thinkers and stakeholders alike, and had eagerly awaited news of how they planned to assist the federal government in resolving the crisis for the good of all.

Although these leaders may have had reasons for staying away from the summit, their absence from the Summit was not the best option, when an issue of such national significance (insecurity challenges) had been placed on the agenda of the Summit. This singular issue should have propelled them to attend the conference for the sake of peace and stability of the country. The absence of these leaders from the summit has left many mixed messages.

On the one hand, it says that these leaders do not care about the stability of the country, or that they don't realize the seriousness and implications of the problem at hand, or that they are not aware of the huge number of innocent souls being wasted by Boko Haram's menaces. On the other hand, their absence gives the impression that Northern leaders are part of the problem and not part of the solution, since some leaders in the North have been accused of being sponsors of Boko Haram.

It is unconscionable and regrettable that Gen. Yakubu Gowon, who had always boasted that the reason he took Nigeria to war was to "keep Nigeria one," has kept silent. Collectively, he and his Northern colleagues have kept deafeningly silent in face of the Boko Haram mayhem. They have done little to preserve the national security interest of the very country they (Northern military leaders) ruled for several decades; done little to prevent the country from drifting apart. Northern leaders have remained aloof and failed to offer concrete solutions on how to rescue the country from Boko Haram's violent actions. Although a few of these leaders have made brief comments on Boko Haram's criminality and violence, the nation still wants to hear loud and clear, their collective condemnation of the group and how the country can overcome the security threats posed by this group. The country is looking to them for input and guidance.

It is obvious that if these barbaric acts were perpetrated against Northern interests by another ethnic nationality in the country, for example the Igbos, the war drum beats that would be coming from the Northern circles would be precise, loud and clear. By now, the might of the Federal Government of Nigeria would have been unleashed on the said group and such carnage would have been justified with the famous slogan that says "to keep Nigeria one is a task that must be done." The integrity and sincerity of Northern leaders are now being called into question in the case of Boko Haram, and the country is yet to see their negative reactions to the threat posed by this armed gang.

Because a few Northern military officers, the country's first Prime Minister and the first Premier of the Northern region were assassinated by the January 15, 1966 military coup plotters, who were purported to be Igbo military officers (a coup which many Nigerians condemned), over eighty to one hundred thousand innocent Igbo lives, and the lives of other Southerners were wasted in Northern Nigeria in retaliation. Today, more innocent Igbo lives are being wasted by Boko Haram; however, no single retaliatory action has been taken by Ndigbo.

The bogus justification for the July 29, 1966 military countercoup led by Northern military officers was built around the theme of "Igbo domination" of the country, but today, Northern leaders have failed to acknowledge that the North profited the most from the Nigerian Project.

For instance, the North was heavily favored by British colonial policies during the colonial era, at the expenses of the other two Southern regions. The North had more representatives in the National Assembly than its Southern counterparts. In the military, the North had more foot soldiers and fewer military officers than its Southern counterparts, who had more officers and fewer foot soldiers. Since independence, the North has dominated the country's governance; therefore, why should Northern frustrations and anger be directed at Jonathan's administration at this time when the North benefited the most from the Nigerian Project?

The Information Minister, Labaran Maku, expressed similar sentiment highlighted above in a *Vanguard Nigeria Newspaper* article of January 25, 2014, where he repelled accusations made by his fellow Northerners, who described Jonathan's administration as anti-North, one that has done little and nothing to develop the North. Reacting on the allegation of Northern marginalization by the Jonathan administration, Maku reminded Northern politicians that since independence, Northern region has ruled the country for a longer period of time than any other region and has enjoyed utmost support and cooperation from all sections of the country, so it is only ideal for the North to reciprocate the gesture by supporting the people of South-South to complete their natural tenure of two terms for the first time in history.

To make his points succinctly clear, Maku was quoted in the article as saying that:

Since independence, we have more Northerners ruling Nigeria and people not causing trouble because we were ruling. Whenever we were president whether military head of state or civilian, the Southerners did not say let there be war because some northerners are ruling or let us raise a religious war or let's create confusion in the country. We ruled and ruled and they cooperated with us (Elebeke, 2014).

The Information Minister then went on to debunk the myth that President Jonathan has done nothing to develop the North since he became the president of the country. He noted that of the thirteen Universities created by Jonathan's administration so far, ten are located in the North as a deliberate policy to expand access to education and develop the human capacity that is desperately needed in the North. The Minister also went on to list other projects the Jonathan administration has executed in the North, which include the following: 1) the construction of over 100 Almajiri schools; 2) dredging of River Niger; 3) construction of Baro and Lokoja seaports; 4) construction of standard gauge rail-line from Abuja to Kaduna which will eventually link up to Kano; 5) restoration of train services from Lagos to Kano; 6) construction of a power plant in Kaduna; 7) dualisation of Maiduguri-Kano road; 8) revamping of agriculture; 9) construction of Oweto Bridge in Lokoja to link Benue and Nasarawa States; and 10) reactivation of Kaduna Refinery (Elebeke, 2014; Isenyo, 2013).

Another Northerner who took issue with President Jonathan's Northern critics is the former Jigawa State governor, Sen. Saminu Turaki, who described Jonathan's administration as one that upholds social justice and fairness in the country. The Honorable Senator asked the North to stop blaming President Jonathan for its perceived problems, saying that the North was its own greatest enemy. He told his Northern brethren that the people from South-South, the president's political zone, had treated him and his associates better than his fellow people, adding that the people that destroyed the North are Northerners, not Southerners (Dangida, 2014).

Although the collective condemnation of Boko Haram's criminality by Northern leaders was long overdue given their years' of silence on the group's violence, the courtesy visit to President Jonathan by the Northern Traditional Rulers Council (NTRC) in April of 2013 was both a welcome and encouraging development. The purpose of the Council's visit led by Sultan of Sokoto, Alhaji Sa'ad Abubakar, III was to present the president with a position paper on how best to tackle Boko Haram's violence. The Council Secretary, Alhaji Najeem Adamu, the Emir of Kazaure, told the Nigerian Press that their visit to the president was to discuss the state of the nation and the security challenges facing the country. The Emir further noted that the position paper, which the NTRC presented to the president, had strategies, which include the use of dialogue, as a means of obtaining sustainable peace in the country. Prior to the NTRC's visit to Aso Rock, the Sultan of Sokoto, Alhaji Sa'ad Abubakar, III had already asked the Jonathan administration to grant amnesty to members of Boko Haram.

In his defense for amnesty for Boko Haram, the eminent Islamic spiritual leader was quoted as making the following remarks:

> We want to use this opportunity to call on the government, especially Mr. President, to see how he can declare total amnesty for all combatants (Boko Haram) without thinking twice. That will make any other person who picks up arms to be termed a criminal. If amnesty is declared, it will give so many of those young men who have been running and hiding to embrace that amnesty. Some of them have already come out, because we have read in the papers that some have already come out. Even if it is only one person that denounces terrorism, it is the duty of the government to accept that person and see how he can be used to reach out to others. It is left for the government to use that person, evaluate him and see whether he is genuine or fake. These are some of the things we are pushing for, yet people will be saying that we are not doing anything as Muslim leaders in the north. No! We are doing much more than what any other person has done. And I want to commend you all. We will continue to do more despite criticisms (Binniyat, 2013).

Nigerian of all persuasions must pause and reflect on the fatherly advice the former military Head of state, Gen. Muhammadu Buhari, has offered the nation on issues concerning the on-going carnage that is ravaging the country and how the fight against terrorism in Nigeria is being conducted. General Buhari had not said much about Boko Haram's violent acts against the nation until recently. It took the Nyanya bomb blast, where seventy-two precious lives were wasted (murdered) and hundreds injured to get the retired Army General to open up to the nation. Like other men and women of good conscience, Buhari could no longer sit idly by while the carnage continued to consume precious lives of innocent Nigerians. In reacting to the Nyanya bomb blast, the Katsina-born Army General told the nation that what it lost on that day was irreplaceable, noting that the number 72 seemed like just another grim tally among the death statistics that have become all too common, but what occurred on that day was much more than that.

As a result of the grief and suffering directly experienced by those Nigerians who were victims of the Nyanya bomb blast and the over hundred schoolgirls abducted in Chibok, Borno State, Buhari (2014) passionately advised and cautioned the Nigerian nation to really stop and take notice of where evil was leading the country. In light of this sad moment and driving his point home, the former military head of state and the 2015 President-elect made the following touchy remarks:

> The abduction of over one hundred schoolgirls is unacceptable, condemnable and saddens me greatly. We cannot allow these merchants of death to make us numb to the tragedy they manufacture. Those who were killed were not

merely numbers on a page. They were human beings, made of flesh and blood, body and soul like all the rest of us. They were someone's fathers or mothers, brothers or sisters. They had parents; they were someone's children. They were husbands or wives, neighbouring friends and colleagues. They had dreams and hopes. They were loved and they loved others in return (Buhari 2014).

To make Nigerians understand that violence of any sort does not pay, Buhari went on to highlight some human characteristics that Nigerians have in common and why the unity of the country must and should not be compromised. Most Nigerians, according to Buhari, share the same aspirations; seek an improved fate for their children and hope to leave them a better life; want to work and live in dignity and respect; want a life of peace and harmony with their neighbours regardless of religion, ethnicity or background; seek prosperity not poverty; seek brotherly understanding, not strife; and seek peace, not bombs. Violence and war always lead to loss of precious lives, grief, and suffering.

Sounding prophetic, the Katsina State-born Army General has these words to say:

No matter our religion or place of birth, we all bleed and are wounded the same way by injustice. Decency runs through the teachings of each religion and ethnic group that comprise the people of Nigeria. We may have our differences, but the vast majority of Nigerians stand united against the appalling violence committed in Nyanya and other places. These acts have no place in Nigeria. Those who commit them have no place in our country. The perpetrators may look like human beings. They may have limbs and faces, like the rest of us, but they are not like us. In killing innocent people, they have become inhumane. They live outside the scope of humanity. Their mother is carnage and their father is cruelty. They have declared war against the people of Nigeria. They have shown that they do not want to liberate the people. They want to kill them. Yet, with all the energy of their evil and ignorant hatred, they shall fail. The good people of Nigeria shall triumph. Such a wicked mission shall not succeed. We have gone too far in our journey to nationhood and endured too much to allow these terrible acts to divert us. Not only have these agents of death killed innocent people, they also abducted over 100 young women from their school. Why abduct schoolgirls? Whatever they plan, they should be ready to face the wrath of Nigerian people. They should release these young girls unharmed. Anything else would be an abominable crime. We all must take close heed at this moment and recognise the severity of what is upon us. A small minority seeks to bring the nation to its knees through terror. Thus, we must stand tall and united. We can ill afford to allow their crimes to go unpunished (Buhari, 2014).

Before Buhari's advice to the nation became public, some Northern leaders, including Murtala Nyako, the governor of Adamawa State, had openly accused Jonathan's administration of orchestrating genocide in the war against terror by colluding with backers of Boko Haram to perpetuate the conflict in the North. The governor and his kind blamed Jonathan's administration for being "responsible for all the security challenges in the country, including the insurgency, oil theft, kidnapping for ransom and armed robbery (Daniel, 2014). Governor Nyako's stern accusation of the administration has caught the attention of many well-meaning Nigerians who concluded that if the governor did not tone down his rhetoric; such outbursts are inclined to incite dissentions in certain quarters, which could endanger the country's national security.

Blaming the Jonathan administration for its inaction on Boko Haram's terror will not justify Northern leaders' indifference to the plight of the victims of Boko Haram and the criminality of the group. If Northern leaders feel that President Jonathan is using Boko Haram's onslaught to blackmail them, which is not the case, it is because they have not mustered enough courage to condemn the group's violence. Secondly, if President Jonathan reacts the way they want him to, which is to unleash the "military might of the nation" on Boko Haram, this very forum, the Northern Elders Forum, will be the first group of Northerners to accuse the president of committing genocide against the Northern people, and this is corroborated by its recent threat to drag the former Chief of Army Staff, Lt. Gen. Azubuike Ihejirika to the International Criminal Court in The Hague.

Let it be known that the granting of amnesty to Boko Haram, which some Northern leaders have asked for, is the easiest thing to do, but there is more to it. For amnesty to be granted to this group, Northern Muslims must denounce group violence against law abiding citizens and foreigners living in Northern Nigeria. Nigerians of all persuasions are tired of Northern violence. Whenever a group in Northern Nigeria has an ax to grind with its political leaders or with the federal government, innocent citizens, who are in no way part of the problem, or who through no fault of theirs, always become the target of terror.

You cannot convert the whole nation to your religious faith by force of arms. Let your religious doctrines and practices speak for themselves. People should be allowed to make their choices freely and without intimidation. It is the peoples' inalienable right to make such a determination. Gone are the days when force of arms is used to convert people into religious faiths and beliefs.

Let it be known as well that before Boko Haram's menaces, there was a group from the Niger Delta known as MEND that threatened the country's national security, when the group openly declared a shooting war against the Nigerian government over the group's perceived injustice against the riverine people of the Niger Delta. The group protested vehemently against oil pollution of its creeks and communities, and the lack of economic and social development in the area, given the fact that the bulk of the country's oil revenues are generated from the area. The oil companies operating in the region, including the federal government and their surrogates became the group's target, but common sense prevailed when the federal government struck a deal with the militants, offering them amnesty, technical and human skills, and the development of infrastructures in the impoverished areas of South-South political zone.

MEND's violent activities were directed towards its enemies that happened to be the Multinational Oil Corporations, and the Nigerian military. In spite of the fact that the country's oil policies that adversely devastated the Niger Delta area were initiated and implemented by Northern Army Generals who ruled the country for several decades, members of MEND never targeted innocent Muslims from the North and never used religion and Islamic (Arabic) education, as bases to justify their course of action. They targeted foreign oil workers instead for ransom and vandalized oil companies' installations. The group went into a shooting war with the federal troops who came to protect the installations and to ensure that oil shipments were not interrupted. These were the facts.

Unfortunately, some Northern leaders have come to equate Boko Haram's violent activities with those of MEND—a claim that distorts the truth. The goals of MEND were not to make Nigeria a Christian nation nor did the group call for the abolition of Islamic education in the country, as Boko Haram called for the Islamization of the country and abolition of Western education.

Second, the group did not demand that Northerners living in Southern Nigeria should relocate to the North, as Boko Haram did. Third, the group did not bomb Moslems' mosques in Southern Nigeria nor kill Muslims, as members of Boko Haram are doing in the North.

Fourth, MEND did not pose a threat to Northern leadership during those years the North was in total control of the country, as Boko Haram is today undermining Jonathan's administration. Fifth, members of MEND accepted the amnesty deal offered to them by the Federal Government, while members of Boko Haram out rightly rejected any amnesty deal offered to them by the Federal Government, claiming that the federal government has no legitimate right to grant the group such an amnesty; rather, it is the group (Boko Haram) who should grant the federal government an amnesty. What a claim!

If members of Boko Haram had gone after those who are directly responsible for their state of impoverishment, hopelessness, and despair, who happen to be Northern political leaders, including Northern Army Generals who dominated the country's leadership for several decades, their cause would have gotten support from outside the North, mainly from the South.

Members of Boko Haram lost legitimacy in the eyes of many Nigerians, when they injected religious rhetoric to their cause and targeted poor Christians and Southerners who are also victims of misrule in their own respective political zones or regions; these are people who are also impoverished by their own political leaders in the South.

How Overzealous and Power Hungry Politicians Contribute to Group Violence and Insecurity in Nigeria

The most important thing poor Nigerians everywhere must understand is that there is a war raging among the so-called elite class in the country, who are competing for political power and domination. It is a war once described by our famous African political genius, Kwame Nkrumah of Ghana, as "class struggle." Power hungry seekers from both political zones in the country have always been scheming for power, influence, and control. This group of people cannot succeed at their game without relying heavily on poor people, whom they use as pawns or tools to gain access to the corridor of power. When they get there, they forget the very poor people who saw them through. Power hungry seekers are good at manipulating the poor because they know full well that the poor are gullible, vulnerable, and easily deceived. Because of these short-comings, power hungry seekers in Nigeria use the poor for a variety of things: the poor are used as political thugs; the poor are used in rigging elections; they are used in assassinating political opponents; and the poor are used in destabilizing governments, when power hungry seekers are dislodged from power.

The advice from the Honorable Speaker of the Federal House of Representatives, Rep. Aminu Waziri Tambuwal, to the Nigerian youths was noble, refreshing, and a welcoming change in Nigeria's political discourse. In his goodwill message to the Northern Youth Wing of the Christian Association of Nigeria--a message delivered on his behalf by his advisor on legal and legislative matters, Chili Adangwa, during the group's two-day annual conference, held in Kaduna in September of 2013, the Speaker told the youths to resist the urge of being used as political thugs during elections, especially as the 2015 elections draw nearer. The Honorable Speaker encouraged the Nigerian youth to always demand from politicians who would turn them into political thugs and use them to disrupt elections in the country that they use their own children to lead the squad. While emphasizing on tolerance and harmony among the various divisions within the country, the humble Speaker was quoted as saying:

> I make no pretensions of the high incidences of unemployment of our youth and concomitant disposition to violence as an expression of frustration; I am nonetheless, persuaded that violence is not a helpful alternative, rather constructive effort at addressing the issue...I am willing to partner with individuals or group propagating ideals that seek to promote tolerance and harmony among the various divides within the nation (Alabelewe, 2013).

The Honorable Speaker was right and he spoke truth to power. Nigerian politicians are using vulnerable youths in the country to ferment violence and mayhem of all sorts; thereby, putting the youth's lives and the lives of other law abiding citizens in harms' way just for selfish political ambitions, while their children are sent away to various Ivy

League Schools abroad, where they lavish the ill-gotten wealth their parents stole from the country's treasury. If vulnerable youths in the country would heed to the Speaker's noble advice, perhaps elections in Nigeria would be free from violence and fair elections could be obtainable.

Power hungry seekers always play on the emotions of the poor. They would have the poor believe that their current state of poverty or despair was caused by another entity or by the poor themselves for not doing much to uplift themselves from poverty (blaming the victim syndrome). Political leaders always defend their misguided policies that lead to the impoverishment of the poor. For example, in Northern Nigeria, poor Northerners have been indoctrinated by their leadership to believe that as far as the country's governance is concerned, it is the birthright of the people of Northern Nigeria to rule, and that the country's head of state must always be a Northern Muslim. Many poor Northerners have come to believe these claims to be true. This kind of thinking explains why Northern poor are quick to get upset and turn to violence whenever a Northern political candidate of Islamic sect is defeated in a national election. Second, poor Northerners have been told repeatedly that the reason Southerners are migrating to the North at a high rate, is to take away their jobs from them. Many poor Northerners believe this to be true and, should any little misunderstanding between the two parties occur, poor Northerners usually turn such a situation into violence; thereby, inflicting pains and emotional tremor on their Southern brethren. At times, they demand that Southerners should go back to their region of origin. From all indications, Northerners would prefer foreigners; say folks from India or Pakistan to execute the jobs that could be done by their Southern neighbors. This way of thinking does not promote national unity.

Given these misconceptions, misinformation, and the brainwashing of the Northern poor who are in most cases the youth, Alhaji Gambo Ibrahim Gujungu, the president of a group of Northern Youths known as the Arewa Youth Forum (AYF), weighed in to set the record straight. Alhaji Gujungu must be applauded for summoning the courage to call a spade a spade and for speaking truth to power. Speaking on behalf of his members, he indicted Northern political leaders for not showing enough interest in tackling regional challenges that would pave the way for peace and development. In articulating the views of Northern youths, Alhaji Gujungu was quoted as making the following provocative remarks:

> We are disappointed that since the upheavals in the region started and is slowly crippling the economy of the region, those that are said to be representing the region have not deemed it necessary to meet and find a lasting solution to the impasse. As youths from the North, we are not only disappointed but we also feel let down by those that we toiled for to occupy the exalted positions they are now enjoying today. We are worried that instead of working for the good of the people, these leaders are busy pursuing a personal agenda to the detriment of

all. It is in view of this that we call on leaders of the North at different levels, governors, senators, ministers, lawmakers at the state, national levels, commissioners and even those at the local government level to join hands with the Vice President, Namadi Sambo, who is the political leader of the North and tackle the problems in the region....We use this opportunity to call these leaders to put their personal ambition behind them and work for the good of the North as the youths and other well-meaning individuals are watching what is happening and will take necessary action when the time is right. AYF wants to call persons like the Katsina State Governor, Shehu Shema that Arewa Youths are disappointed that instead of staying in Katsina to attend to the needs of the people the governor is now more prominent in Abuja and Niger Delta. AYF is calling on those in the league of the Katsina Governor to have a rethink as after all is well and done, power resides with the people and no matter what the supposed godfathers think, the Nigerian people will one day decide their own fate (Daniel, 2013).

In echoing the sentiment expressed by the AYF president, the Niger State Governor, Muazu Babangida Aliyu, blamed the prevailing poverty and underdevelopment in the Northern part of the country on past Northern political leaders whom the governor claimed had ruled the country since 1960. He further noted that the current outcry over the high level of poverty in the North by Northern leaders meant that the people of the region had been deceiving themselves over the years despite their easy access to political power at the center.

The governor blamed the people of the North for refusing to demand what he referred to as "quality service" from their leaders, reminding them that until the people begin to ask for better service, Northern leaders will continue to mess up. The outspoken governor was also quoted as saying the following:

> When you wait and take things for granted just because you have a leader from a particular place and he also takes things for granted and begins to mess up, and you do not demand for good leadership, that is the situation that we are in and how we ended up....Till today, even with the realization of our past mistakes, we still have problems everywhere because people still think they can run away from the general problem since nobody cares. And even if you steal money, there are times when money becomes ordinary papers without value. Today, there is the realization that some past Northern leaders have not done quite well when they had the opportunities of ruling the country (Ogiji, 2013).

The Niger State governor insisted that Northerners and, indeed, every Nigerian must henceforth demand for quality leadership and good governance on a daily basis from their leaders with the view that the leaders would be put on their toes to do the right things. The governor's remarks resonate with many Nigerians. This is the same view most Nigerians have about their leaders regardless of the political zones they may have come from.

In Southern Nigeria, especially in the South-East Zone, the poor are made to believe by their political leaders that their source of impoverishment came from the Central Government dominated by the North. Southern political leaders have always used terms like "marginalization of the region" by federal government dominated by Northern oligarchy, as reasons the South East Zone is abandoned, impoverished, or left out in the scheme of things. Propaganda of this kind creates animosities in both camps. Most poor people tend to believe this falsehood because it is coming from leaders they respect, admire, and cherish. Political leaders from both regions of the country have failed to tell their poor citizens how they (the leaders) have contributed in making their lives a living hell. They have failed to let the poor know the amount of revenues they collect each month from a federal allocation account meant for the social and economic wellbeing of their citizens. Leaders from both regions of the country have failed to make the public know how much of these amounts they spent on empowering their poor masses and how much of these amounts they laundered into their offshore bank accounts.

There is also a great divide between Northern poor and their Southern brethren in understanding the political intrigues hatched by power hungry seekers. The Southern poor are more sophisticated than their Northern counterparts when it comes to dealing with the issue. Most Southern poor are not willing to sacrifice their limited time or their precious lives for any political leader, who does not care for their wellbeing for that matter. They truly believe that most political office seekers are corrupt, selfish, arrogant, overbearing, and cannot be trusted. It is only during electoral campaigns that some of these poor people gravitate toward political office seekers. Their rationale is simple: to grab whatever they can from these political vultures. The Southern poor know full well that once a power seeker gets elected and steps into an office that is the last time they will ever see or hear from him/her.

The poor know that once in office, the power seeker will have nothing to do with them anymore. He/she will no longer be reachable either by telephone or in person. The Southern poor understand that once these politicians take up offices, they build a wall of separation between them and those individuals who worked tirelessly in their campaigns. In realizing these dynamics, the Southern poor do not want to waste their precious time depending on these political vultures. Once elections are over, the poor go on living their lives as usual and do not depend on them for handouts because they know that such handouts will never come their way.

The mindset of Northern poor is quite different. They believe that their political office seekers, once they are elected, will deliver the goods as promised. They get frustrated when they discover that they have been lied to, manipulated, and deceived by the very leaders they once trusted, cherished, and admired. At this point, instead of directing their anger and frustration at these leaders, they turn such anger and frustration on innocent people, who have nothing to do with their pains, misfortune, and disappointments.

Instead of fighting each other, poor Nigerians must understand when the "invisible hands" are at work or who their real enemies are. They must understand who is fueling this division among them and what he/she stands to gain? Poor Nigerians must understand that the war in Nigeria today is not a war between North and South, but a war between rich and poor; it is an economic war—a war based on who controls the country's wealth and resources.

The poor must, therefore, realize that they need each other if they are to withstand the onslaught of the rich and famous in the country. They cannot allow themselves to be divided because that is exactly what the rich want to see—a weak and fragmented group. The slogan of poor Nigerians must always be, "united we stand divided we fall." This is the time when poor Nigerians from all walks of life whether Igbos, Yorubas, Hausa-Fulani, Ijaws, etc. must come together and unite their forces to fight for inclusion and equal justice for all.

It is saddening to note that while poor Nigerians are killing each other in defense of their regional political leaders and their religion, the very leaders who ferment divisions among the poor meet frequently in Abuja and elsewhere in the country to socialize and strategize on how to hold on to power in perpetuity. Whenever and wherever this elite class gather to conduct their business, their ethnic-nationality and their religious affinity become irrelevant, but in their respective political zones, they promote and encourage division and hatred among their poor, blaming the poor's misfortunes on others; thereby, refusing to take responsibility for what they have done to the poor in Nigeria. As Pope Francis once said "a country is measured on how it treats its poor." The game plan of the elite class in Nigeria is to exploit the country's resources for its own benefit and, whatever happens to the poor is left to the poor.

These political leaders are succeeding because they are using the old playbook of the British colonial authorities who stayed in power for so many years in Nigeria. These famous British colonial tactics included the doctrines of divide and rule and indirect rule. By favoring one segment of the Nigerian populace at the expense of others, the British colonial administration was able to sustain itself in power for the many years it ruled the country (1861-1960).

One hundred years of rule was a long time and the reason the colonial government was able to govern this long was because the indigenous opposition against it was divided, weakened, and could not speak with one voice. It is said that a divided house will never stand. The concept of us versus them is what is in play here, and the poor in Nigeria must understand this trend and devise an effective means to counter it.

Poor Nigerians must understand the game plan and unite their forces for their own betterment. In a democracy, nothing is handed out freely to anybody. Poor people must, therefore, be prepared to stand up and fight to protect their inalienable rights; otherwise, their God-given rights will be relegated to the back burner. Let it be known that the author of this discourse does not condone violence, as a legitimate means of seeking redress. Rather he believes that intensive pressure through nonviolence should be brought to bear on governments to do the right things, as we have seen throughout human history of what became of those oppressive, unresponsive, and unproductive governments that failed to yield to common sense.

Mass Movement: A Balancing Force in Nigeria's Democracy

If democracy is to gain root in Nigeria, the Nigerian people must wake up from their slumber and organize themselves into effective civil organizations (pressure groups), whose objectives are to ensure that those in power govern well and will be held accountable for their actions. It is time for Nigerians to seriously embrace the philosophy or principles of social movements. Civil organizations are needed to ensure that those in power fulfill their campaign promises. If you vote in an election and fail to monitor what those you voted for are doing in office, the tendency is that they will not fulfill the promises they made to you during their electioneering campaign. This is human nature at its best. Civil organizations are an important element in any democratic process; they are the balancing force. Power is not given out freely whether in a democratic or authoritarian society, because those in power do not want to extend the privileges of power or the opportunities that go with power to everyone in the society.

Members of the ruling class like to monopolize power if they are allowed by the people to do so. Nigerians must not forget that power belongs to them (the people) and that the Nigerian government derives its legitimacy from the people through: 1) their obedience to the laws enacted by the legislative branch of the government; 2) payment of their taxes and other fines to sustain government's functions; and 3) enlistment into the country's armed forces in the defense of the country from external enemies. When the people refuse to honor these obligations, the government ceases to function because it has lost its legitimacy to govern.

If a majority of Nigerians feel that "good governance," which is an embodiment of the rule of law, accountability, transparency, equal opportunity for everyone, is lacking in the country, it is the people's right and duty to demand those things from their governing elite who may be reluctant to implement them, as Governor Babangida Aliyu alluded above. Power is taken away from those in office who do not want to exercise it to the benefit of all citizens. It means, therefore, that if elected officials fail to yield to popular demand, it is the right and duty of the people to use their voting power to overthrow such officials from the corridor of power.

Regrettably, this scenario only works where elections are free, fair, and peaceful, but not where elections are rigged or bought. Where elections are rigged or bought, the aggrieved people always resort to violence if they see violence as the only and the last option available to them to address the wrong done to the "General Will" of the people by stolen elections. When violence erupts as a result of stolen elections, the unpopular regime that rigged itself into office may resort to repressive measures to legitimatize itself and quell the people's anger and rage aimed at the regime. To counter these circumstances, formidable oppositions are critical and may prevail if such oppositions have the following characteristics of an effective organization: 1) a huge numeric strength or a sizable membership; 2) having an effective and able leadership (a charismatic leader); and 3) having adequate resources both in terms of revenue and human capital. Citizens can also use civil organizations to mobilize against their ruling class when they feel disempowered or denied the opportunities to advance economically, socially, and politically.

There are abundant examples where people's power or mass social movements have brought positive changes in human history. Given the ugly history of African Americans in the United States of America, for example, Barack Obama's presidency would not have been possible if it were not for the activities of Civil Organizations in that country, which fought aggressively against racial inequality and other socio-economic injustices and eventually broke those barriers. Some of these Civil Organizations in America are worthy of mention, and they included the Southern Christian Leadership Conference (SCLC), once led by the late Moral Leader, the Rt. Rev. Dr. Martin Luther King, Jr.; the National Association for the Advancement of Colored People (NAACP) once led by W.E. B. Dubois, the Universal Negro Improvement Association (UNIA) led by Marcus Garvey, the National Urban League now led by Marc Haydel Morial, the Student Nonviolent Coordinating Committee (SNCC) led by John Lewis, the Rainbow Push Coalition led by Jesse Jackson, the Nation of Islam now led by Louis Farrakhan, the Congress of Racial Equity (CORE), the National Action Network led by Rev. Alfred Charles, Jr. now known as "Al Sharpton," the Dream Defenders led by Phillip Agnew, and other Civil Rights Organizations.

In addition to these Civil Organizations were individual Americans, who had contributed in a profound and instrumental way, to the liberation of African Americans from the inhumane conditions they had been subjected to by mainstream America; conditions that had dominated the country's political system for centuries. These brave Americans included: Booker T. Washington, Frederick Douglass, John Brown, William Lloyd Garrison, Harriet Tubman, Sojourner Truth, Rosa Parks, Nat Turner, Malcolm X, Thurgood Marshall, Philip A. Randolph, Stokely Carmichael, Paul Leroy Robeson, Amiri Baraka, Joseph Lowery, Harold George "Harry" Belafonte, Jr., Danny Glover, Corner West, Julius Chambers, and a host of others both dead and alive.

Before the emergence of these organizations and individuals, African Americans were never viewed as human beings or equal to their white counterparts; they were viewed and referred to as "slaves, property, or Three-Fifth of a person." On a daily basis throughout those turbulent years, African Americans were treated inhumanely and were not respected as human beings, as the Dred Scott case of 1857 made crystal clear. It was in this case, *Dred Scott v Sandford*, that the US Supreme Court legally assigned the label of inferiority status on African Americans. In rendering the majority opinion in the case, Justice Roger Brooke Taney noted that "blacks were not considered (and were not intended to be considered) citizens under the Constitution, They could not claim any of the rights and privileges the Constitution guaranteed and secured to citizens of the United States." He went further to say that "blacks had never been regarded as a part of the people or citizens of the United States or supposed to possess any political rights which the dominant race might not withhold or grant at their pleasure" (Napolitano, 2009: 60).

From Dred Scott's decision to other relevant US Supreme Court decisions on racial issues, the American Courts became important instruments that helped to legalize and institutionalize racism and inequality in America. In the case of *Plessey v. Ferguson* (1896), for example, the Court agreed with the general notion held by a majority of white Americans that African Americans were from an inferior race. Consequently, when it established the "doctrine of separate but equal," the court ruled that the two groups should be separated from one another along color or racial line. From this landmark decision, African Americans were systematically discriminated against and excluded from the country's economic, social, and political processes. They were segregated and discriminated against by "Jim Crow Laws" in all aspects of the American life: from school segregation, housing, in the work place, to the ballot boxes, in spite of the passages of several Amendments to the US Constitution, most of which, were passed specifically to address past injustices aimed at the African American community.

These famous and remarkable Amendments to the US Constitution included: 1) the Thirteenth Amendment—an Amendment that abolished slavery in the United States. The Amendment was adopted in 1865; 2) the Fourteenth Amendment, which was a reaction to the US Supreme Court ruling in the Dred Scott case. It granted citizenship rights to the newly freed African slaves and other individuals who are to be born in the United States' territories, and whose parents may not be citizens of the United States. Other provisions built into the Amendment included:

      a) The privileges and immunity doctrine;
      b) Due process; and
      c) The equal protection clause.

The Amendment was adopted in 1868; and 3) the Fifteenth Amendment, which extended voting rights to African Americans who were once denied this right on the grounds that they were not citizens of the United States, as proclaimed in Dred Scott's decision. The Amendment was adopted in 1870 (The Constitution of the United States, 2005).

Once again, these landmark Amendments wouldn't have been possible if it weren't for the activities of the Civil Rights Organizations of those eras and the activities of progressive members of Abraham Lincoln's Republican Party, who were bent on changing the country's ugly history of racial discrimination, emanating from human vices, such as hatred, the passion to oppress others, and xenophobia (fear of the unknown). Despite these Amendments to the US Constitution, the forces of evil and darkness persisted, especially in the Southern States, where the Fifteenth Amendment was seriously undermined and circumvented. For several decades, such circumvention of the Fifteenth Amendment denied eligible African American voters the right to vote and to be voted for.

Here are some of the strategies most Southern States adopted to undermine the provisions of the Fifteenth Amendment to the US Constitution: 1) having all-white primaries, where white candidates were the only nominees to vie for vacant political seats; African Americans were never allowed to participate in these primaries, fearing that blacks' participation could lead to the nomination of some black candidates for political offices; 2) a literacy test was introduced to force black voters to read a section or two of the state constitution or any other reading materials the State may deem appropriate for black voters. Failure to pass the reading test would automatically disqualify the individual from voting. The irony of this saga was that, at the time, it was a crime to educate a Negro because in these Southern States, laws forbade Negro education, as Frederick Douglass noted in his narratives. The refusal to educate Negroes, at the time, was borne out of fear among slave owners who contended that Negro education would instigate revolt against the system of slavery; 3) poll tax was instituted to disenfranchise black voters; before they would be allowed to vote, they had to produce evidence showing that they had been paying their taxes.

This is another contradiction the African Americans had to endure. Since the first set of black people were brought to Jamestown, Virginia, in 1619, African Americans had never worked for themselves; they were brought to America against their will to work in plantations owned by white farmers, where African slaves did not receive an income from their labor. From 1619 till the emancipation proclamation in 1865, many African Americans were labeled as property of their slave masters and had no freedom to earn an income. How could they be asked to pay taxes when they did not earn any income? And 4) the grandfather clause was also put in place to prevent black voters from exercising their constitutional rights, which were granted to them by the Fourteenth and Fifteenth Amendments. This clause demanded that the newly freed African slaves should prove that their grandfathers had been voting in the past. How possible could this be, considering most African slaves had never voted before in any elections because they were not regarded as citizens of the United States, according to the US Supreme Court decision on Dred Scotts' case?

Given the circumvention of the Fifteenth Amendment, freed black slaves, now citizens of the United States were still denied the right to vote—the very right they were entitled to under the Fifteenth Amendment of the US Constitution. This flagrant violation of the US Constitution by Southern states was totally ignored by the US government until the Civil Rights Organizations of the 1950s and 1960s mobilized their members for positive action through non-violent means. Members of this movement staged mass rallies and protests in most Southern states, notably in Selma and Montgomery, Alabama,

Mississippi, Louisiana, and what became known as the "March on Washington D.C" in 1963. The Civil Rights Movement embarked on several tactics or strategies, such as the "bus boycotts and sits-in," to call to question the moral consciousness of a nation that prided itself as a beacon, champion, and protector of democracy and human rights, and a nation that always claims that "We hold these truths to be self-evident: That all men are created equal; that they are endowed by their Creator with certain unalienable rights; that among these are life, liberty, and the pursuit of happiness..." But, as we know, the architect of this famous Declaration of American Independence, Thomas Jefferson, was himself a slave owner.

With these activities and other social turmoil that consumed the governance of the country, in the 1960s, the US Congress passed two landmark Civil Rights Acts: the Civil Rights Act of 1964, and the Voting Rights Act of 1965.

The social turmoil that consumed the governance of the country in the Sixties included: 1) the massive war demonstrations against the Vietnam War; 2) the ugly police incident that took place at the Democratic National Convention (DNC) in Chicago in 1968; and 3) the assassinations of President John F. Kennedy, James Meredith, Martin Luther King, Jr., Malcolm X, and Robert Kennedy to mention just a few. The Civil Rights Act of 1964 has a provision known as Title VII, which called for Equal Employment Opportunity (EEO) with respect to public sector jobs and outlawed racial, religious, and gender discriminations in hiring. The Act also created a Commission known as the Equal Employment Opportunity Commission (EEOC), to monitor discriminatory practices in the public sector job market.

The Voting Rights Act of 1965 was enacted to remove voting barriers, such as those instituted by Southern States that denied African Americans the right to vote and to be voted for. Under Section 5 of the Voting Rights Act, the law made it difficult for states to deny citizens the right to vote. Unfortunately, Sections 4 and 5 of the Voting Rights Act were recently challenged in Court by the Shelby County authorities in the state of Alabama, who asked the US Supreme Court to overturn those Sections; reminding the Court that with the election of President Barack Obama, as the first African American president, voting discrimination has no place in the country's political process and; therefore, Sections 4 and 5 of the Voting Rights Act were outdated and should be eliminated.

On June 25, 2013, the US Supreme court ruled by a vote of five to four, agreeing with the Shelby County authorities' premise that voting discrimination in America is no longer in existence and, as such, the Court struck down section 4 of the Voting Rights Act, which many Civil Rights leaders and scholars claimed to be crucial to section 5, the very section the Shelby County authorities had asked the Court to declare unconstitutional. Section 4 of the Voting Rights Act is very crucial because it is the section that sets the formula that will be used in determining which state and local jurisdictions comply with section 5 preapproval requirement or what most Civil Rights scholars referred to as the preclearance principle.

By declaring section 4 unconstitutional, section 5 of the Act has seriously been weakened. This means that there is no longer a mechanism in place to prevent states with a history of voters' disenfranchisement from enacting such laws. The removal of the preapproval requirement or the preclearance principle has now rendered section 5 of the voting Rights Act irrelevant, unless and until the US Congress passes a new law to determine who should be covered by it. Thus, the Court ruling has emboldened Southern states or other states in the Union to resort to the old ways of discriminating against minority population at the polling booths.

It is also important to highlight here roles the US courts played in revising past discriminatory laws in the United States. For example, in the early 1950s and 1960s, the US Supreme Court, under the leadership of Chief Justice Earl Warren, began to dismantle Jim Crow laws, especially in areas of school segregation and police misconduct, which were major problems at the time. With the 1954, *Brown V. Board of Education* Case, the issue of segregation in public schools was put to rest.

Other achievements made by mass movements throughout the Third World included the dislodgement of colonialism and oppressive regimes in places where such policies existed. Most oppressed people everywhere used these formidable movements to dislodge their oppressors. We have seen these struggles taking place throughout the world, especially in the Third World nations.

Without these mass movements, colonialism and other oppressive regimes would not have been defeated in most cases. In spite of the terror unleashed on indigenous people by oppressive regimes, the oppressed have never been deterred from mobilizing themselves for "positive action."

The massacre at Amritsar, India on April 13, 1919, came as a result of Indians' protestation against the British draconian colonial rule. The massacre was ordered by Brigadier-General, Reginald E. H. Dyer to deter further protests against British colonial rule in India.

But, this act of barbarism could not accomplish its intended objective; rather, it intensified the resolve of Indians to continue with their quest for self-determination. This singular act of man's inhumanity to man (cruelty) strengthened Mahatma Gandhi's noncooperation movement to gain more Indian support and sympathy, which the movement mobilized for the emancipation of India. With this massive support and resilience, British colonial rule in India was brought to its knees in 1947.

It was a similar situation in Soweto, South Africa, where Black students were massacred for vigorously protesting against the introduction of Afrikaans' language as a medium of instruction in local schools. The Students' Action Committee, which later became known as Soweto Students' Representative Council, the African Teachers' Association of South Africa, the Black Consciousness Movement, and a majority of the black population in South Africa rejected the Decree on the grounds that it was the language of the oppressor.

Those concerned favored English and Native languages over the Afrikaans' language. Consequently, on June 16, 1976, the students took to the streets of Soweto to oppose the Apartheid law. In response to these protests, the Apartheid regime security apparatus unleashed its military might on the protesting students, killing over 700 of them and wounding an estimated number of four thousand.

In 1977, Steve Biko, the leader of Black Consciousness Movement in South Africa, was killed by the Apartheid security officers while he was in detention. The Soweto massacre and Biko's death sparked world-wide condemnation of the White Minority Regime in South Africa, and these massacres led to the demise of Apartheid. These events swelled the membership of the African National Congress (ANC). With this massive support, the ANC, an organization labeled as both communist and terrorist by Great Britain and the United States of America, vigorously mobilized and campaigned world-wide to dismantle the White Minority rule in South Africa. In 1994, the Apartheid regime was finally brought to an abrupt end, when the first ever multiracial election was held in the country, and from that moment, the ANC took over the governance of the country.

Nigeria had similar stories where several groups in Nigeria came together to confront British draconian rule. Nigeria wouldn't have been freed from the chain and yoke of colonialism if it weren't for the efforts made by Herbert Macaulay, the Nigerian Youth Movement, the Zikist Movement, the Aba Women's Riot of 1929, and the Nigerian Labor Movement led by Michael Imoudu, whose leadership orchestrated the famous General Strike of 1945 that weakened the British resolve and paved the way for more political reform and accommodation in the country.

Nigerians are also very familiar with how the National Democratic Coalition's (NADECO) activities ended the military and political career of Gen. Ibrahim Babangida following his regime's annulment of June 12 1993 election—an election which a majority of Nigerians proclaimed to be the most clean, free, and fair election ever conducted in the annals of Nigerian political history. The group also made governing very difficult for the Abacha regime before his sudden death. All the above illustrations are essential factors that demonstrate the effectiveness and importance of Civil Organizations in any country. For a positive change to take root in contemporary Nigeria, Nigerians must embrace the philosophy of social movement and must use it effectively to address social injustices that exist in the polity. This is the most legitimate means of bringing political pressure to bear on a governing elite rather than resorting to military coups or armed struggles.

PART FOUR

WAYS TO ACHIEVE GOOD GOVERNANCE IN NIGERIA

Chapter 7

A NEW VISION FOR NIGERIA

Having thoroughly examined "the trouble with Nigeria" and issues facing Nigerians daily, and having carefully and meticulously provided brief chronological events that have contributed immensely in shaping Nigeria's history, it is adequate and proper at this juncture, to articulate the way forward for Nigeria. This new vision is a must, if the country is to strengthen its corporate existence, which at the present moment, is on a shaky ground due to poor governance. The goal should be to achieve good governance in Nigeria and enhance its national unity and identity, to broaden and strengthen the country's political, social, and economic forces, to prevent the disintegration of the country, and to promote social justice for all, the country's governing elites, the Nigerian business community, the Nigerian intelligentsia community, the Nigerian criminal justice community, the Nigerian traditional rulers, the Nigerian civic and religious organizations, other stakeholders and, indeed, the totality of the Nigerian people must join hands together to ensure that the Nigerian Project is preserved and nurtured. These socio-political actors must recommit and rededicate themselves through positive actions and not by mere words to make the above claims and assertions a reality.

Over the years, Nigerians have allowed their great country to drift into oblivion because of their lack of patriotism, greed, and selfishness. There is no time to spare any longer. Now is the time for all hands to be on deck. Simply put, now is the time for Nigerians to decide whether they are going to live side by side with one another, as one indivisible people, who share a common destiny and identity and, as people living under one sovereign entity, or as people willing to live separately in different sovereign nations. This is the choice Nigerians have to make. The Jonathan administration must be applauded for listening to the voices of reason in the country by creating the national platform (the sovereign national conference), where issues of national significance were adequately addressed. Men and women of goodwill concluded that the best instrument to address those national concerns was the sovereign national conference that was convened on March 17, 2014, in Abuja, the nation's capital.

Given the enormous crises in the polity, which emanated mainly from faulty political structure, unhealthy ethnic and religious rivalries, the indifference to the poor, and the massive looting of public funds, the call for a sovereign national conference is an important step forward in addressing these national issues once and for all, rather than sweeping them under the rug, as was the case in the past. The years of Boko Haram's egregious atrocities, especially the abduction of over two hundred schoolgirls in Chibok, Borno State that generated a worldwide outcry and condemnation, have really exposed the weakness and vulnerability of the Federal Government of Nigeria to combat the group's violence and its efforts to destabilize the country. This, indeed, is a wake-up call for the country's governing elite and other stakeholders that the peaceful and smooth governing of the country will no longer be the same. If Boko Haram's criminality is not dealt with precisely and cautiously, the group's activities have the potential of breaking the country apart. That is the ultimate goal of the group and its sponsors. Most of Boko Haram's demands are not acceptable and will not be tolerated by the people of Southern Nigeria; the insistence on such demands can only lead to the dissolution of the country if the group's violence and demands persist and if no solution is found.

However, well-meaning Nigerians do not think that the disintegration of the country is imminent nor the best option available. Those clamoring for the breakup of the country have failed to realize that Nigerians traveled this path in the past, when the country was on the verge of collapse. To save the Union, the country went into a bloody Civil War (1967-1970), which took over two million lives and damaged properties worth billions of naira. As a result of this war, many Nigerians, especially those of Igbo extraction, lost their homes and land properties in some parts of the country, under an obscure name known within the Nigerian circle, as an "abandoned property." Indeed, one would think that the devastating nature of the war would have taught Nigerians a great lesson, especially to the power elites in the country, who stand to lose the most if the country descends into another Civil War or breaks up; but apparently, the ruling class does not seem to have learned from those mistakes that took the country to war.

The breaking up of Nigeria into different nations is not the best option or solution. It will not be the panacea that will cure the social ills that confront the Nigerian people. Breaking up the country will not eliminate all forms of discrimination and injustice that precipitated the crises, nor will it empower the poor politically and economically. Clamoring for the dissolution of Nigeria is just a way to dodge or evade the real problems facing the country. Nobody has actually predicted the aftermaths of secessions, because such undertakings do not always turn out well as most people expect. Let us take a cue from history.

Take South Sudan, for example, an entity that was carved out of Sudan in 2011, as a new Republic after so many years of embroilment in a Civil War with Northern Sudan. The people of South Sudan are mainly Christians by religion and have common African roots in their genes, but these common attributes did not stop them from being at war with each other. Whoever expects a country that is barely four years (2011-2014) old to go into a shooting war against itself after spending forty years fighting a war of liberation against Northern Sudanese Muslims of Arab extraction?

The same scenario applies to Nigeria. The country descended into a Civil War, six years after it gained its political independence from Great Britain. No one was certain that a series of secessions would not occur in Nigeria if the country was dissolved. For example, in the Republic of Biafra, no one would have predicted with certainty that the new Republic would remain peaceful if it had succeeded in its quest for secession from the Nigerian Union, given the realities on the ground today. Ndigbo are too familiar with the malicious and discriminatory policy state governments in Igbo land introduced against Igbo government workers, and this policy has made some Igbo people wonder whether these leaders were the very Igbo people who fought a common enemy collectively during the said Civil War.

Since the creation of states in the country after the Civil War, some governments in Igbo land had demanded that their government officials who were non-indigenes of the states should vacate their positions and move back to their respective states of origin. Those individuals who did not respond to this "draconian law" lost their government positions as a result. This is not the kind of policy that promotes the very slogan (the unity and cohesion of the Igbo nation), which many of those who favor such an unjust law always evoke today in their public statements to arouse the Igbo sentiments. Generally speaking, this kind of behavior has made some people, including the author of this discourse, to doubt the survivability of the Biafran state had Ndigbo succeeded in their quest for secession.

The instabilities in the former Soviet Republics, such as Ukraine, Georgia, and Moldova, where the suppression of ethnic Russians in those former Soviet Republics has precipitated the Russian Federation's current military interventions, is an indication that secessions have not always turned out to be the way they were intended. Whoever expected that Moslem countries like Iraq, Yemen, and Syria would ever engage in a sectarian war against each other because of religious dogma: Shia Islam as against

Sunni Islam? One should also look at the outcomes of the Arab Spring or Arab Awakening that spread throughout the Middle East in 2011, starting with the Tunisian uprising. As one can see, these revolutions have been hijacked by military oligarchies, especially in Egypt, where a democratically elected government of the Muslim Brotherhood led by Mohamed Morsi was toppled by the Egyptian military. In Libya, for instance, after the toppling of Muammar Gaddafi by a NATO assisted revolt, the country is now governed by several armed militias in different provinces, thereby making the central governing body irrelevant. These scenarios are lessons that nations must learn and understand before calling for the dissolution of a country.

Secession does not guarantee instant stability, peace and harmony, nor promotes social justice and economic empowerment. These are things people have to achieve collectively through meaningful and peaceful dialogue and negotiations. Dialogue and negotiation may be a long and painful process, but they are worth engaging in, if nations must move forward to achieve stabilization, peace and prosperity. Every nation in the world has its own peculiar or unique problems, just as human beings do. The difference is how nations handle their problems. Some nations handle their problems much better than others.

The best way to solve a nation's problems is by confronting them immediately when they crop up, rather than sweeping them under the rug or pretending that all is well and expecting that somehow these problems will eventually go away with time. It is important to note here that national problems are not adequately solved on the battle field. War should always be the last resort. War is only inevitable when common sense fails to yield to reason.

Nations with a diverse society must learn how to effectively manage their diversity for the good of all. They should not view their diversity as a "divine curse," but as a blessing. The United States of America, for example, does not openly discriminate against those whom it admits into the country as long as the new arrivals are willing to respect the laws of the country. There are thousands, if not millions of Nigerian natives, who are living in the United States and who are doing extremely well in various professions of their choosing.

They are doing very well because of the opportunities the country has created to empower its diverse population. Because of the hopeless situation in Nigeria, many Nigerians are leaving the country for other parts of the globe, especially for North America and Europe, where the standard of living and opportunities to succeed in life are provided and enhanced. These are comforts the Nigerian government cannot guarantee to its own citizens.

Realizing that strength is generated from diversity, the United States government found a way to accommodate and energize its diverse population for the good of all. Today, the country is a formidable world power because of the human capital and dynamism its diverse population brings to bear. Nigerians can draw enormous strength from its own diversity, as the United States of America, Brazil, and South Africa have done.

In spite of their past racial discriminations, the United States and South Africa have repositioned themselves, as viable countries and major players in the global system. Today, the United States is welcoming more people from various racial groups to its shores and empowering them by creating opportunities for them; thereby, making them productive and contributing members of society. Nigeria can equally achieve this feat if the country's leadership and other stakeholders believe that Nigeria is worth preserving and dying for. To avert the disintegration of the country and to attain global preeminence, Nigeria must treat its diverse population with respect and fairness. This means that no preferential treatment should be given to any entity in the country.

The achievement of this aspiration calls for a new attitude, a new thinking, and a new vision that are forward looking and positive. Nigerians must realize that some of the country's current policies are no longer working and; consequently, such policies have no place in the new Nigerian political dispensation. It is always said that wise people learn from their mistakes and find solutions to them, while fools perish because they don't learn from their mistakes. Nigerians must realize that their strength lies in their unity. It is on this obvious fact that Gen. Ibrahim Babangida based his thought provoking advice, which he made known in one of his dialogues with the Nigerian press. These are pieces of advice that must be considered and taken seriously if Nigeria is to be rescued from disintegrating. Below are the pieces of advice proffered by the Niger State-born Army General:

> Nigeria is precious enough to be saved. It deserves an investment of our time and resources to make Project Nigeria a success. But the starting point has to be an admission that we need to fix things. We need a new mindset about the Nigerian project. Let us start off by admitting the mistakes of the past. Right policies have at times been wrongly implemented. Temporary solutions have often turned into permanent policies, even though the problems they were designed to address have long been solved. The issue of the principle of federal character needs to be revisited. In a multi-ethnic, multi-cultural and multi-religious nation, the principle of Federal Character is a sensible one and there is no alternative to it. Each national group must be given a feeling of belonging.... We must admit that sacrifices have been made and sacrifices will continue to be made for the survival of this Nigerian project. In the past, maybe there has not been sufficient recognition of the fact that those making these sacrifices have grievances which should have been addressed. Maybe in the past, there had not been sufficient recognition of the fact that each national group has legitimate fears and grievances. Some of the mistakes of the past have now come to haunt us. But let me make one thing clear. Not all these mistakes were made out of callousness or bad faith or malice (Odiogor and Kumolu, 2013).

Unfortunately, General Babangida had the opportunity to unite the country on solid grounds, but he failed for three major reasons: 1) the admission of Nigeria into the OIC without due consultations, thereby, injecting religion into the Nigerian polity; 2) the annulment of the June 12, 1993 election; and 3) the blocking of the release and implementation of the Oputa Panel report, which he successfully pulled through by instituting a court injunction. These three events have turned out to be the biggest mistakes the Niger State-born Army General made during his reign as the country's military head of state, and history will not forgive him for those costly mistakes.

Although Babangida was part of the problem, he has now come to acknowledge and accept the mistakes he and others made while they were in office. This is a good start and a bold move. No changes can be made unless past mistakes are acknowledged, and no progress can be made unless those who made those mistakes are willing to embrace new approaches that will correct those mistakes of the past. Therefore, Nigerians must find it in their hearts to forgive him for mistakes that were made in the past, including during his own regime.

On the other hand, President Obasanjo must also share the blame for playing along and for not challenging the court injunction barring the release of the Oputa Panel report. It was a national disgrace to deny Nigerians the Commission's report, which cost the country millions of Naira to obtain and prepare, including the amount of time invested in gathering the necessary information needed through several public hearings conducted for that purpose. The Oputa Panel otherwise known as the Human Rights Violations Investigation Commission (HRVIC) was modeled after South Africa's Truth and Reconciliation Commission (TRC).

The Commission was established by President Obasanjo's administration on June 14, 1999, and the Commission was headed by Justice Chukudifu Akunne Oputa of blessed memory. The Panel was charged with the responsibilities of establishing the cause, nature, and extent of human rights violations in particular to: the assassinations and attempted killings between January 15, 1966 and May 28, 1999; to identify perpetrators (individuals or institutions); to determine the role of the state in the violations; and to recommend means to pursue justice and prevent future abuses. It was said that the Commission was initially asked to investigate the period from 1984 to May 1999, covering four military regimes, but this period was later extended back to 1966, the year of Nigeria's first military coup following independence (United States Institute of Peace, 1999).

On a cautionary note, if Nigerians cannot sustain the Nigerian nation and cannot nurture it as their precious commodity, or as a country worth dying for, then, there is no need to keep pretending that Nigeria exists while it is gradually dying and disappearing from the world radar.

The choice of whether Nigerians will live side by side with each other in harmony and peace is for them to make. If they decide collectively to dissolve the corporate entity called Nigeria, let it be done amicably without shedding more blood. Nigerians are tired of killing one another for things that do not matter. They should borrow a leaf from the former federated state of Czechoslovakia that dissolved itself into two separate states on January 1, 1993, becoming Czech Republic and Slovakia. This was done without malice or rancor. The people of Czechoslovakia parted their separate ways when they decided collectively that they could no longer live together as one entity. The dissolution went on without people losing their lives; it was done amicably and was peaceful.

There are other examples where nation-states fell apart when the component parts of the states could not successfully unite their forces. The former Union of Soviet Socialist Republics (USSR) fell apart in 1991 when the fifteen Republics making up the Union decided to go their separate ways. The dissolution was done amicably and without rancor. Here are the fifteen Republics and the years they were admitted as members of the USSR: Armenia, 1922; Azerbaijan, 1922; Byelorussia, 1922; Estonia, 1940; Georgia, 1922; Kazakh, 1936; Kirghiz, 1936; Latvia, 1940; Lithuania, 1940; Moldavia, 1940; Russian Federation, 1922; Tajik, 1929; Turkmen, 1924; Ukraine, 1922; and Uzbek, 1924 (*Wikipedia, the free Encyclopedia*, 2014).

If Nigerians come to the conclusion that the unity of the country is far greater and more important than regional, ethnic, and religious interests, then, they must work collectively to unite the country for the good of all Nigerians. For Nigeria to be resuscitated from its enduring problems and revive its once envious vibrancy and vitality, Nigerians must embrace the principle of good governance, which can only be achieved through the following elements of nation building:

Revitalization of Nigerian National Unity

The national unity of a country is always viewed as a thread, string, or glue that binds all societal fabrics or forces together for the sole purpose of strengthening the society's resolve; thereby making such a society a formidable and indestructible entity. Whenever these threads are cut loose because of poor governance resulting from ineffective leadership, such situations often lead to alienation, anger and frustration, violence and instability. These social vices often lead to a lack of nationalism or patriotism that is so central to a nation's cohesiveness and unity. When a nation's unity is broken, the center will no longer hold, and if the center does not hold, conflicts of all sorts will ensue and things will eventually fall apart, and that makes the country ungovernable. In today's Nigeria, the country's national unity is fragile and in shamble because the interests of ethnic nationalities and religious affiliations in the country supersede the country's overall national interest. The national unity of a country is not promoted or nurtured when one ethnic nationality continues to dominate the country's leadership and does not want to share power with other sections of the country, or when corruption in all forms, including political patronage and nepotism are allowed to dominate the nation's psyche.

When a country cannot provide adequately for its citizens the basic necessities of life, such as jobs, food, shelter, education, health care, a secured and peaceful environment, how can anyone expect the people to be patriotic and be willing to defend the country's national interest? In Nigeria, many people are deprived of these basic social welfare amenities.

As a result, the country is experiencing a "brain drain syndrome," where many Nigerians are leaving the country in greater number than ever, to other countries around the world in search of these basic social needs because the Nigerian governments at federal, state and local levels are not adequately providing those basic needs to their citizens.

This is a clear demonstration that Nigerian government operatives are not fulfilling their civic obligations to the Nigerian people, as representatives of the people. These kinds of behavior undermine the country's national unity. The only way Nigeria's national unity can be strengthened and energized is when the following principles of good governance are injected into the Nigerian polity:

Injecting Transformational Leadership into Nigeria's Polity

The problem with Nigeria, as Prof. Chinua Achebe of blessed memory rightly pointed out, is the problem of leadership. With the exception of few leaders, Nigeria has not been lucky to have leaders who made a positive difference in the lives of ordinary Nigerians. To change this perception or trend, Nigeria needs transformational leaders in all ramifications. This is so true if the country is to overcome its leadership problem and revitalize its national unity. Transformational leadership is the brand of leadership that will positively transform the lives of individuals in the country.

According to Northouse (2004), a transformational leadership is a leadership process that is concerned with emotions, values, ethics, standards, and long-term goals, and includes assessing followers' motives, satisfying their needs, and treating them as full human beings. It involves an exceptional form of influence that moves followers to accomplish more than what is usually expected of them. Charismatic and visionary leaders are important elements of transformational leadership (p.169). A transformational leadership will afford the country the necessary leadership quality that is so central to the revitalization of Nigeria's national unity.

Below are the leadership qualities that most Nigerians will expect from their leaders if the country is to move forward for better things. For example, Nigerians deserve leaders who can initiate, develop, and carry out significant changes in the country that will transform the lives of ordinary Nigerians for good. They want leaders who will empower them and nurture them in change.

They want leaders who will raise their consciousness and get them to transcend their own self-interests for the sake of others. Nigerians want leaders who will become strong role models for the country with a highly developed set of moral values and a self-determined sense of identity. Nigerians want leaders who are confident, competent, articulate, and who can express strong ideals. They want leaders who will listen to the people and are not intolerant to opposing viewpoints. They want leaders whom they can trust and believe in. More importantly, Nigerians are desperately in need of leaders who will create a vision that emerges from the collective interests of various individuals and units within the country.

Nigerians want leaders who will act as change agents and who will initiate and implement new directions within the country. They want leaders who are social architects and who will help direct and shape the emerging political culture of the country. Transformational leaders will help citizens know their roles and understand how they are contributors to the greater purpose of the country. Additionally, Nigerians want leaders who will be sensitive to how their leadership affects the lives of ordinary Nigerians. Nigerians deserve leaders who understand that they have a moral responsibility to treat citizens with dignity and respect, as human beings with unique identities. Nigerians want leaders who understand that they are in a special position, where they have a greater opportunity to influence others in significant ways.

Like health professionals who provide a vital service, Nigerians want moral leaders who know that they have a responsibility to serve them in ways that are beneficial to them and not harmful to their welfare. Nigerians do not want leaders who are self-centered, but leaders who integrate one's self or vision with others in the country. Nigerians want leaders who are concerned about issues of fairness and justice and make it a top priority to treat all citizens in an equal manner. Nigerians want good and honest leaders who will lead by examples. Nigerians want leaders who know that dishonesty brings with it many objectionable outcomes and, more importantly, dishonesty creates distrust. "When leaders are not honest, others come to see them, as undependable and unreliable. People lose faith in what [irresponsible] leaders say and stand for and, consequently, their respect for leaders is diminished. As a result, the leader's impact is compromised because others no longer trust and believe in the leader" (Northouse, 2004: 314).

To avoid the disintegration of the country, as predicted by both domestic and foreign critics, in 2015, the country's ruling class must change course and embrace public policies that will promote good governance. Nigeria cannot continue with policies of the past that are leading the country to the brink of collapse. It can no longer be a society where abuse of power and corruption are perpetrated and nurtured. Nigerians can no longer tolerate a situation where the ruling class sees itself as above the law of the land; where it cannot be held accountable for its actions; where its activities cannot be transparent; where it favors one ethnic nationality at the expense of others; and where it governs as if the Nigerian government is an alien institution, one that is no longer seen as "the government of the people, by the people, and for the people."

It is obvious that the newly emerging governing elites in the country have elevated themselves above every other Nigerian. Members of the governing elite in Nigeria see themselves as neocolonial masters who rule as outsiders. Their attitude and mindset have shown that they are not in touch with realities in the country. They are too far removed from the sufferings of the masses. Like their former British colonial counterparts, they are becoming more oppressive, arrogant, materialistic and wasteful. They do not come to power to serve the Nigerian people, but to enrich themselves by appropriating "the wealth of the nation" to themselves, and to their relatives and friends at the expense of millions of ordinary Nigerians. While the seventy percent (70%) of Nigerians are languishing in abject poverty, the one percent that makes up the country's ruling class are well off and doing extremely well. They are well-off because they are sharing the nation's wealth among themselves; and using their privileged positions in government to buy off the nation's assets for less than their monetary values through an economic slogan known as privatization.

In the words of Woody Guthrie, an American singer and poet, who in his famous lyrics called on the human conscience of his country's power elites, reminding them that "this land of ours is made for you and me?" Unfortunately, the Nigerian ruling class has forgotten the true meaning of Guthrie's famous slogan, which denotes that Nigeria, as an entity, belongs to everyone who resides in it, that the country's natural resources should be used equitably for the good of every Nigerian, and that no preferential treatment should be given to anyone, no matter that person's socio-economic status in the country. Drawing from Guthrie's main thesis, every Nigerian has an equal stake in what the country has to offer. This is how national consensus and consciousness are formed and built. If Nigerian government operatives want a United Nigeria, they must remember that the country in which they govern belongs to them and to those they rule. Being in a position of power does not give policymakers more leverage than average citizens.

The Nigerian governing elite must be reminded that the legitimacy of their power comes from the Nigerian people. Therefore, they should not take advantage of their office to rob the country of its scarce and precious resources, which are desperately needed for the enhancement of the well-being of the Nigerian people. As the endemic corruption which plagued the country has slowed down its progress and development, the reversal of such a trend will be difficult to achieve if the country's endemic corruption is not halted or minimized.

To rescue Nigeria from disintegrating, the author of this discourse recommends a new vision, a new thinking or a new mindset for the country. Many Nigerians of goodwill have come to conclude that the Nigerian Project is a precious commodity that must be saved and preserved and, as a result, such a passionate conclusion deserves adequate consideration by those in power. If the country falls apart because of lack of good governance and committed leadership, the negative impact of such disintegration will be felt strongly across the West African region and across the entire continent of Africa. It will be a disaster of the greatest magnitude. But, if Nigerians get it right this time, such a rescue effort will definitely raise the country's profile and strengthen its resolve. It will enhance the country's status among the comity of nations, both regionally and globally. Such a high profile will enhance the country's national unity; it will bring about a lasting peace and stability, where quality of life of the Nigerian people can be nurtured and protected. If the country can overcome its overwhelming problems that suffocated its advancement and progress over the years, Nigeria may, through this renewed spirit and vigor, play a pivotal role in leading the Black World to prosperity, as many had anticipated in the past.

Creating Adequate Opportunities to Enhance Nigerians' Social and Economic Well-being

Nigeria can no longer afford to have governments that cannot provide adequate opportunities for their citizens' social and economic mobility or advancement. Creation of opportunities for citizens' well-being, including their safety are paramount reasons why governments are created.

Governments establish socioeconomic programs, such as quality and affordable education and health care; and they also create jobs and security apparatus for the purposes of promoting and enhancing the well-being of their citizens. As previously noted in several sections of this book, the implementation of these vital socioeconomic programs have virtually been lacking in Nigeria, because the Nigerian governments are absolutely playing politics with the welfare of the Nigerian people.

Take education; for example, how can Nigeria compete globally in terms of science and technology and in job creation without having a highly educated manpower? How can Nigerians reap the benefits of democracy or be able to sustain it when they are denied adequate and quality education?

Nigeria's global competiveness hinges on the quality of education its people acquired, but as we know it, this is zero because of what has been done to Nigerian education. Since the introduction of privatization scheme in Nigeria, the country's educational system has been decimated through government's neglect and lack of funding. This neglect and underfunding have often led to industrial strikes and lockouts, which make students' timely graduation highly impossible.

The former Governor of Anambra State, Peter Obi, has laid the blame of the country's educational deterioration on political parties for not having a definite framework for Nigeria's educational sector. He made his observation known to journalists during the Founder's Day Lecture held in Lagos on September 18, 2014, in commemoration of the 105th anniversary of King's College, Lagos. In that speech, Gov. Peter Obi of All Progressive Grand Alliance Party (APGA) indicted the country's political parties that have been in power, since the demise of military dictatorship in the country, for toying with Nigerian education. The former Chairman of APGA's Board of Trustee, but now a new member of the PDP, was vividly quoted, as saying:

> Today, I do not think any party in Nigeria has a vision about education; that is the truth. I am a politician and I belong to a political party but I can tell you that there is none that has a plan and I can back this up with the statistics of the result of West African Senior School Certificate Examination (WASSCE).... When Tony Blair (ex-United Kingdom Prime Minister) was campaigning, he emphasized education and when he got there, he dealt squarely with the issue of education. Here we promise one thing when we are campaigning but deliver another thing when we are in office. One of the reasons why Nigeria's standard of education is low is not because of lack of funds but the government's inability to effectively monitor the usage of funds which goes into the pockets of third parties instead of the schools that need them (Akinkuotu, 2014).

Given the above situations, a high priority must be given to Nigerian education if the country is to compete globally and if Nigeria is to become self-reliant and/or self-sufficient. It is unconscionable to keep using foreign expertise to extract Nigeria's mineral resources, or build its roads and bridges, when such tasks can be performed by Nigerians if they are given the necessary and adequate training that is required for such jobs. Recalling President Jonathan's indictment of the Nigerian Universities for producing graduates who lack relevant preparations and skills, the response of this author to such a rhetoric blame is, why wouldn't Nigerian universities produce such a large number of graduates who lack relevant preparations and skills, when Nigerian governments (federal, state, and local) have turned their back on Nigerian education, as Gov. Peter Obi alluded above?

Nigeria's lackadaisical attitude towards its educational sector has forced many well-to-do parents in the country to send their children to foreign institutions of higher learning. The Nigerian governments' nonchalant attitudes toward education have turned many potential school-goers to look the other way. The millions of Naira spent annually by Nigerian parents in educating their children abroad would have been invested in the country's economy, if the Nigerian educational system was well entrenched. Such revenues would have strengthened Nigeria's educational sector. By allowing the country's educational system to deteriorate drastically, as it has, Nigeria is losing on many fronts, while these foreign institutions are benefiting tremendously from monies coming from the Nigerian students. Because of the neglect of Nigeria's education, the country is also experiencing a mass exodus of its brilliant minds in the educational profession to foreign shores, where education is a top priority. Many of these Nigerian professionals in these foreign countries will not want to return to Nigeria for many reasons--issues which have not been properly addressed by Nigerian policymakers. Some of these unaddressed issues include: poor salaries and fringe benefits; lack of social amenities, including a poor health care system, lack of constant supply of electricity, and insecurity.

There is no way Nigeria will advance economically and militarily with an unhealthy population. In addition to an educated work force, a country's economic growth and military preparedness and strength depend solely on how young and healthy the country' population is. This is another sector where the Nigerian government has done a poor job; it has neglected its health sector to the point where it will take decades to undo the harm done to the Nigerian health care industry. The recent outbreak of Ebola virus in Guinea, Sierra-Leone, Liberia, Senegal, Nigeria, and Mali, where over twenty-four thousand Africans are infected and over eleven thousand deaths have been recorded, has, indeed, exposed the inadequacy and ineffectiveness of the health care sector in the West African region. The huge number of lives lost as well as those infected is a clear indication that most African governments are incapable of coping with this deadly disease, because they failed to invest adequately in their citizens' health care programs for many decades. Many are dying from this virus because there are no preventive measures put in place to combat the disease, and governments in this region never anticipated that the outbreak of this virus would be deadly, as it has proven to be. However, this is not an excuse for not doing more to keep the Africans healthier.

The virus is a wake-up call for governments in Africa not to take the health care of their citizens for granted. It also means that African governments should take more proactive measures than reactive ones, when it comes to the health of their citizens. Indeed, it is absurd that a disease of this nature will force the Federal Government of Nigeria to inject $6.1 million into the country's health sector to implement a Special Intervention Plan to contain the Ebola virus. This program should have been in place before now, in anticipation of such an outbreak, given the fact that the African continent is prone to infectious diseases. The said fund was earmarked for the establishment of the following items: additional isolation centers; case management; contact tracing; deployment of additional personnel; screening at borders; and the procurement of required items and facilities (Finley, 2014).

Like the educational sector, the health industry in Nigeria is undermined by government's neglect and underfunding, which was masterminded by the IMF Structural Adjustment Program. Because of this program, quality health care in the country has become a luxurious commodity, only to be purchased or made available to those who can afford it.

As a result of government underfunding and neglect, Nigerians are dying by the thousands annually of diseases that are curable, preventable, and manageable. Consequently, Nigerians are witnessing unprecedented number of affluent Nigerians, including government officials and politicians seeking medical attention abroad, where billions of Naira of both private and public funds are spent annually. In assessing Nigeria's health care sector, as the country celebrates its fifty-five years of independence, the former president of the Nigerian Medical Association (NMA), Dr. Osahon Enabulele, was quoted as saying the following:

> At fifty-four, Nigeria's health care system is still being undermined by the poor political commitment to health and the health care needs of Nigerians, by the country's top political and public office holders. The health sector is also still blighted by poor budgeting for health at federal, state, and local government levels. This has not been helped by the absence of constitutionally justifiable health rights for Nigerians and the frequent recourse to foreign medical care by Nigeria's top political and public office holders. Now Nigeria loses $800 million each year in capital flight to other countries because of medical tourism....At fifty-four, Nigeria is yet to witness massive investments in health research. The Ebola pandemic and the glaring absence of proactive research efforts by African countries, including Nigeria to develop a preventive vaccine or a drug cure for Ebola Virus Disease since its first outbreak in 1976, is a clear testimony of the poor priority for health research (Olokor and Adebayo, 2014).

The costs of seeking medical attention abroad are funds that would have been invested in the country's economy to boost its health industry, rather than using such huge sums of revenues to boost foreign economies. This behavior does not make economic sense whatsoever; neither does it promote self-reliance and/or self-sufficiency.

Like the country's educational sector, the health industry is marred by industrial strikes and layoffs. Nigeria cannot compete globally when this caliber of professionals are not satisfied with their jobs, partly because of poor conditions of service and lack of respect to the medical profession, as the attitudes of the country's governing elite have shown over the years. These negligent attitudes toward the country's medical profession has forced many experienced physicians, nurses, pharmacists, and other health professionals to leave the country in an unprecedented number to foreign countries, where people's health is a top priority.

The Nigerian governments (federal, state, and local) must not forget that quality and adequate education and health care are essential tools in a nation building effort and; therefore, such social programs must be treated as "human right" issues in Nigeria. These programs must be made available and accessible to everyone who needs them. No one should be denied or deprived of these vital programs simply because of that person's socio-economic status in the country.

Job creation is of great importance in order to minimize the hardships and agony that joblessness inflicts on people. Job creation should be made Nigeria's top priority, as the World Bank ranks the country third on the world poverty index. Speaking at the

IMF/World Bank Spring Meeting in Washington D.C., United States of America on April 10, 2014, the World Bank President, Jim Yong Kim, noted that "Nigeria is one of the top five countries that has the largest number of poor." According to Kim, India ranked first with 33 % of the world's poor, China ranked second with 13%, Nigeria ranked third with 7%, Bangladesh ranked fourth with 6%, and the Democratic Republic of Congo ranked fifth with 5%. Kim concludes that "these five countries are home to 760 million of the world's poorest population" (Gabriel, 2014). As it has been generally acknowledged, poverty is induced due to lack of employment opportunities.

As previously noted in several sections of this book, massive unemployment in the country has forced many skilled and unskilled Nigerians to migrate to countries in Europe and North America, where they have sought a decent livelihood. It is also said that countless Nigerians did not make it to their final destination alive, especially those entering Europe through Morocco and Libya. At these entry points, many Nigerian migrants lost their lives at sea, whilst others did not survive the hostile environment and climate of the Sahara Desert. Those who made it to their final destinations were not all that lucky either. Many of these people were arrested and deported upon arrival because of inadequate or forged traveling documents, whilst others ended up in prisons for various crimes ranging from drug trafficking, human trafficking to property and other violent crimes. As a result of these criminal activities, the perception held in many host countries where Nigerians reside is that Nigerians are shady characters, people who cannot be trusted. Furthermore, because of this negative perception, Nigerians traveling abroad, regardless of their socio-economic status in the society, are often subjected to intensive scrutiny and ridicule.

To overcome this ugly image, the Nigerian government must create incentives and an enabling environment that will promote job creation in the country so that these young and able-bodied Nigerians can stay home and provide for themselves those same comforts they desperately seek abroad. Unfortunately, this aspect of government's function is seriously lacking in Nigeria at the present time and hardly enough is being done to improve the situation.

An enabling environment entails building new infrastructures and making sure that such infrastructures are maintained frequently. The building of infrastructures and their constant maintenance is one of the ways most governments around the world create jobs for their citizens. For example, no country's economic base will flourish without adequate and constant electricity, good road and railway networks, clean and running water, an effective communications network, well-equipped and maintained schools and hospitals, well-equipped and maintained airports and seaports, shopping malls, and other social amenities like sport stadiums and other recreational centers, public libraries, art theaters, and cinemas, to name just a few.

The construction and constant maintenance of these infrastructures create construction jobs for citizens searching for income generating opportunities. Construction jobs will do a lot of good for the country. For instance: they will enhance the living standard of citizens;

they will provide the much needed technical skills; they will generate income for government through taxes and; most importantly, they will stimulate the economy.

To encourage optimum employment in the country, the Nigerian governments must embark on a vocational training or job training programs that will enable many Nigerians youth to acquire the necessary technical skills they will need to fend for themselves. The Nigerian governments must understand that tertiary education is not meant for everybody; therefore, the uneducated persons must be encouraged to become contributive and productive citizens. This means that roadside mechanics, wielders, carpenters, plumbers, masons, electricians, fashion designers, traders, and others must be given some basic training to enhance their skills and knowledge base, training that is desperately needed if these uneducated persons are to fulfill their God-given potentials and talents. It is this author's considered opinion that no individual survives economically in today's digital world without adequate technical and human skills, acquirable through formal training and/or education.

It is also an obvious fact that government alone cannot create jobs. Individuals, groups, and private corporations are said to be major job creators, especially in the capitalist countries. For this obvious reason, incentives must be given to these entities to encourage them to do what they do best, which is job creation. Based on this simple fact, the Nigerian government should endeavor to provide the following incentives to indigenous business people, including sole proprietorships, partnerships, and corporations doing business in the country: 1) granting them tax holidays; and 2) providing subsidies to indigenous industries doing business in the following areas: agriculture, mining, and high tech industries. By the same token, the governments must ensure that these industries are protected from foreign competitors. This is how the country can build up its economic base and become self-sufficient and self-reliant.

In addition, the "minimum wage" of the Nigerian working poor must be increased every five years to meet the rising cost of living. Although the author of this book is not an economist, one thing is certain and that is, putting more money in the hands of those who are likely to spend it, enhances the economic growth of the country. The more money the poor have at their disposal, the more likely they will spend it. This is another way of creating jobs. Business owners will like to expand their businesses with profits realized from such a booming economy. The expansion of businesses entails hiring of more people. It is heartbreaking, when the country's policymakers argue blindly that the country cannot afford to raise the minimum wage of the Nigerian working poor, but they keep raising their own salaries and bonuses. The question is where are these policymakers getting the money to pay for the increase of their salaries and bonuses, when the country cannot afford to raise the minimum wage of the poor working class? It is very unfortunate that it takes national industrial actions or strikes to force the Nigerian governing elite to increase the minimum wage of the working poor in the country.

Nigerian government must understand that, while the Western world is preaching "free trade" and "privatization," it secretly subsidizes its local industries and prevents foreign corporations from acquiring businesses it considers essential to its national interest. The time has come for Nigeria to reconsider its commitment to the economic principle of the Chicago School of Economics, which the Nigerian government operatives have come to embrace.

The school's theory of "trickle-down economy" has failed woefully; even in the United States of America where it fails to fulfill its promise of creating economic prosperity for everyone. Instead of creating prosperity for all, the supply-side economic theory benefits only a few individuals; and decimates the middle class; thereby creating more poor people than the founders of the school had anticipated.

As chief architects of the IMF and World Bank, do you know that major Western countries forbid the borrowing nations of the Fund and the Bank from subsidizing businesses, education, and health care, while these Western nations provide these services virtually free to their citizens? In the United States of America, for example, education is mainly a state government responsibility, primary and secondary education are free, while at the university level, tuition is subsidized by state governments. In addition, there is a federal government program known as the "Pell Grant" designed to assist the children of the poor who are attending American Universities and Colleges. This program pays the students' full tuition and pays the cost of their textbooks, provided such students stay in school and maintain a cumulative grade point average of 2.0 every semester for the four year duration, or as the case maybe. There are other incentives available to US College and University students such as:

- Different scholarship and grant programs;
- Government students' guaranteed loans;
- Assistantship and fellowship programs for graduate students; and
- Various students' work and mentorship programs made available to needy students.

Similar programs are also made available to American students attending Private Colleges and Universities.

Education and health care in Canada are virtually free. The same thing applies to education and health care in most European countries. In Europe, education and health care are free to everybody, especially in France and in the Scandinavian countries (Finland, Norway, and Sweden). These incentives go to show how serious and committed Western governments are to the health and education of their citizens. They invest much money in their children's education and health care. This explains why the Western countries are more progressive on all fronts than their Nigerian counterparts. These incentives enhance the living standard of those who live in the Western world, an idea Nigeria has to borrow if she wants to enhance the living standards of her poor citizens.

The establishment of a new global bloc known as the BRICS nations (Brazil, Russia, India, China, and South Africa) was conceived because of the Chicago School of Economics' draconian economic policies, which are directly implemented by the IMF and the World Bank. These harsh policies have forced the BRICS nations to agree in principle to create a new Global Development Bank for the newly emerging world economies. As previously noted, the

IMF/World Bank conditionality imposed on borrowing nations has inhibited these nations from developing economically and, such policies have usurped the sovereign rights of these borrowing nations from determining their own future and destiny.

It is refreshing to know that the IMF/World Bank will have a strong competitor once the BRICS' Development Bank is up and running. In this case, the borrowing countries will now have a choice, something they never enjoyed under the IMF/World Bank hegemony.

The Nigerian governments must also ensure that any economic relationship agreement to be made between Nigeria and foreign investors must be based on reciprocity and/or on mutual respect and equity, and should not be based on a master-servant relationship. Nigeria will no longer tolerate a situation where Nigerian workers are exploited for the good of others, or where they are viewed as "hewers of woods and drawers of water." To attract foreign investors, the governments must ensure that adequate infrastructures, financial institutions like ethical banking and insurance, good governance, and adequate security are in place. Without the existence of these vital instruments or institutions, most foreign investors will not like to do business in the country. Foreign investors like any business person anywhere in the world will only invest in countries where there is stability, where corruption is not endemic, where rule of law means what it says, and where investors can derive huge profits from their investments.

Having said the above, the Nigerian government should strive to attract foreign investors in areas, where indigenous corporations do not have a "comparative advantage." On the other hand, the governments should work assiduously to ensure that indigenous businesses gain some advantages so that the country can truly become independent and self-reliant. The government must unequivocally communicate to investors both foreign and domestic that a good business climate is always a win-win situation for both parties (the government and investors). While the government assure foreign investors of their corporations operating freely without having the fear of being nationalized and that they will keep and repatriate their profits back to their home countries at any time of their choosing, foreign investors on the other hand will assure the Nigerian government that they will provide the country with meaningful and steady employment, including the much needed training to enable the Nigerian work force excel in those jobs. Additionally, foreign investors will assure the government that part of their yields will be reinvested in community projects that will empower members of those communities, where they do business.

The Nigerian governments must also understand that the insecurity of the country (like the Boko Haram menaces and other high crimes) will repel foreign investors from the country, and that a situation of this nature will lead to joblessness and endemic poverty which, in turn, contributes to the hopelessness and despair of many Nigerians. People who are mostly affected by these economic woes are young Nigerians, who often find themselves in this predicament. A situation of this nature forces many of these young people to gravitate towards crime of all sorts. The vulnerability of poor young Nigerians is often manipulated by shameless politicians and crime syndicates who have no human conscience and who use these vulnerable youngsters to hatch their dirty games and machinations. These vulnerable young men and women are often used by drug and human traffickers to execute their illicit trade, while power hungry politicians use these young vulnerable people to rig elections and have them pose as thugs and assassins.

The joblessness and endemic poverty in Nigeria should never have been an issue in an economy said to be the biggest in Africa and one of the fastest growing in the world. This sad experience should not have been the case in a country, where the number of planes in the presidential air fleet is said to be the largest in Africa and larger than the size of the presidential air fleets in some Western countries. Nigerian youths should not be experiencing hopelessness and despair in a country, where cabinet ministers are said to be spending millions and billions of Naira of public funds to acquire personal exotic cars and to hire private jets for personal use. This should not have been the case in a country, where the salaries and bonuses of lawmakers are said to be the highest in Africa and higher than in most European countries. This neglect should not be happening in a country where billions of Naira are frequently looted by those in government and siphoned abroad. Generally speaking, the Nigerian youth and the population at-large have been betrayed by the country's governing elite who have not provided adequate social and economic opportunities for their citizens' enhancement and well-being. This is a trend that must be changed for the good of all.

Minimizing the Importance and Relevancy of Ethnicity and Religion in the Country's Polity

Ethnicity and Religion are the most divisive and destabilizing forces in countries where they exist or are at play. They are also sources of nationalism or patriotism. Religion, for example, is an ancient force that has continuously influenced world events. It plays a dual role in world politics. In one sense, it is the source of humanitarianism and pacifism. At the other extreme, religion is at the center of many bloody wars and social unrests. Ethnicity on the other hand, is seen by many as the main source of xenophobia, racism, stereotype, and bigotry. It is said that both ethnic and religious values are more firmly entrenched in most Third World cultures, and their impacts on politics, more profound. In places where ethnicity and religion are firmly entrenched, they literately dictate the political culture of those places. Ethnic and Religious rivalries are common in places where multi-ethnic and multi-religious bodies exist and if such rivalries are not properly handled, they are likely to cause serious conflicts between and among the competing bodies which, in turn, threatens the unity and the co-existence of a country, where such divisive forces are predominant.

Most world conflicts, whether in Ukraine, Syria, Palestine, Iraq, South Sudan, Central African Republic, Democratic Republic of Congo, Rwanda, Somali, Bosnia Herzegovina, or the 17th century Europe, have always been instigated by ethnicity and religion. As we see in Nigeria, ethnicity and religion dominated the political psyche of the country and have halted its full integration. Every national issue in Nigeria is seen through the prism of ethnicity and religion. This means that Nigerian Christians and Moslems and the Hausa-Fulani, Yoruba, and Igbo ethnic groups do not get along as well as they should or see eye to eye with each other.

It also means that there is less tolerance between these two dominant religions and among the ethnic groups in the country. The truth must be told: the Nigerian Moslems in Northern Nigeria have tried to impose their religious beliefs and dogma on non-Muslims living in that part of the country, especially upon the Northern Christians and Southern Christians residing in Northern Nigeria. Given this ugly situation, Nigeria has experienced several religious conflicts in the Northern part of the country that have claimed tens of thousands of lives and damaged properties worth billions of Naira, as the current Boko Haram atrocities have demonstrated.

It is important to note here that on no account should force of arms be used to convert people into a religious sect or body that people do not subscribe to. Let religious teachings speak for themselves. People should be allowed to make their choices freely without being coerced to embrace a religion they know nothing about. If your religious doctrines are as good as you claim; you don't use violence to increase your membership. Nigerians are intelligent enough to know the differences between various religious sects, and it is their inalienable right to decide for themselves what religious body or bodies they should belong to.

All religious bodies in Nigeria must be made to respect the rights of people to choose whatever religious body they want to belong. Average Nigerians know what is good for them. No religious body should use force to win converts or recruit members. What they should do instead is, persuade people to join their flocks by living and behaving according to the moral teaching of their religion, and not by terrorizing people in the name of religion.

You have to convince people to join your flock through persuasion by proving to them that your religious belief is suited for them and, then, allow them to make that determination of whether to join your flock or not. You cannot convert a whole country with different religious beliefs into one religion by means of force; it is highly impossible and unrealistic. Using force to convert people into a religious bloc was tried in the past and it was not successful. Why do people think it is possible to do so now, when it was not successful then?

Nigeria must desist from drifting onto the path of insecurity and destruction. The country must, at least, borrow a leaf from Europe and North America. People in these continents worked extremely hard to overcome their ethnic and religious differences, bigotry, and sexism. Although Europeans and Americans have different identities within their confines and boundaries, such differences (nationalities, languages and cultures, religious sects and denominations, ideologies, and sexual orientations) no longer matter so much to most people on these continents. To them, the differences are mere labels which mean absolutely nothing.

Today, many of these people see themselves and others, as people who deserve to live side by side with each other in peace and harmony. Having experienced two major catastrophic World Wars, Europeans in particular, see each other as people who deserve equal opportunity to develop their God-given potentials and talents; and they see each other as people originating from one source of divinity. After the two major World Wars in Europe, Europeans came to the conclusion that human progress and prosperity are not achievable through war and violence, but through peaceful co-existence. The respect for humanity, irrespective of the human differences, has become the cornerstone of International Humanitarian Law, which is also central to cultural diversity and conflict resolution strategies.

Having said the above, there is still residual racism and discrimination all over Europe and North America; however, these behavioral attitudes have been curtailed to a minimum. The author of this book recognizes the fact that a total elimination of ethnic biases and prejudice, stereotype and religious bigotry is impossible but what we see in Europe and North America today is the minimization of these divisive forces. The issues of ethnicity and religion no longer dominate the national debates in these continents, as they once did. Ethnic nationality and religion are no longer perceived as major divisive forces in Europe and North America, as they are in Nigeria today. What we see on those continents today is a de facto racism and religious xenophobia and not de jury racism and segregations that were once the case.

For Nigeria to enhance its political stability and economic growth, it must bring these divisive forces (ethnicity and religion) under control and minimize their effects. To achieve this uphill battle, the Nigerian government at all levels must in their public dialogues, call for the respect of persons and the toleration of human differences that exist among people and groups. Presently, many Nigerians lack these positive human attributes. The prevailing attitude in the country today is that people only respect and tolerates those who share similar ethnic identity, or those belonging to the same religious affiliation.

This kind of behavior has actually undermined Nigeria's national unity, as Gov. Adams Oshiomhole rightly pointed out in his August 2014 address, which was delivered at the swearing-in ceremony meant to honor the 2,787 Batch B members of the Nigerian Youth Service Corps posted to his state. The former national labor leader told the youth to build bridges of unity in spite of the challenges facing the nation, noting that the promotion of ethnic origin has led to more division and disunity among Nigerians. "Nigerians should regard themselves as one and members of any community in which they find themselves" (Aluko, 2014).

Ethnicity and Religion have contributed immensely to the mistrust existing between the various ethnic groups in the country. Nigerians of all persuasions must realize that their country is a multi-ethnic, multi-religious, and multi-cultural society. They must accept this reality and come to terms with it in a more positive manner. If Nigeria is to become a vibrant and envious nation, Nigerians must unite their forces for this common purpose.

They must not forget that the Nigerian Civil War was fought simply because of the mistrust on both sides, coupled with lust for power and egocentric attitudes exhibited by those who were directly responsible for the nation's affairs at the time. The war would have been prevented if there were respect, tolerance and trust among the major actors at the time. In this new dispensation, Nigerians must vow never to make that same mistake again. This time, they must go outside the box (the ethnic and religious divide) to embrace, appreciate, and celebrate their differences and to see their co-existence as an act of faith and destiny.

If the above-stated scenarios are not achievable, the ugly picture painted by Nobel Laureate, Wole Soyinka, about Nigeria descending into another Civil War will surely come to fruition and that will not augur well for the country. Speaking with the British Broadcasting World Service in London on January 10, 2012, the Eminent Professor of Art History, Theater, and Literature (playwright and poet) warned the Nigerian nation that the country was heading towards a Civil War because some political leaders in the country were spreading religious hatred and intolerance. In buttressing his point, the Ogun State-born Academician made the following thought provoking statements:

> When you have got a situation where a bunch of people can go into a place of worship and open fire through the windows, you have reached a certain dismal watershed in the life of that nation...There are people in power in certain parts of the country, leaders, who quite genuinely and authoritatively hate and cannot tolerate any religion outside their own. When you combine that with the ambitions of a number of people who believe they are divinely endowed to rule the country and who believe that their religion is above whatever else binds the entire nation together, and somehow the power appears to slip from their hands, then they resort to the most extreme measures....Youths who have been indoctrinated right from infancy can be used, and who have been used, again and again to create mayhem in the country (Soyinka, 2012).

To change this thought process, efforts should be made to bring Christian and Moslem leaders together in a forum where both religious leaders will work out modalities to achieve harmony and a peaceful co-existence of the two religious bodies and to use their influence in convincing their followers to preach more love than hate. Nigerian governments (federal, state, and local) must also use the media, schools, and other socializing agents within their disposal to promote positive images of Nigerians, the country at-large and, indeed, the continent of Africa. Nigerians must respect and tolerate each other's cultural values and belief systems since the country is a multi-ethnic and multi-religious society.

It is not in the country's national interest if a majority of Nigerians cannot speak other Nigerian languages fluently as they do with the English language or other foreign languages. The Nigerian government should strive to design a school curriculum that will make an average Nigerian student proficient in at least two Nigerian local languages, including the English language. In addition, cultural diversity and conflict resolution should be introduced, as a new curriculum in secondary and university education. These issues must be made a national priority, if the program is to succeed. This kind of policy, if properly implemented, will eliminate tribal sentiments that have dominated the lives of many, and fueled the hatred we now witness in the country.

Additionally, the Nigerian governments must encourage Nigerians to live, work, and seek political offices in any state of the federation without any constraint. It is understood that the 1999 Constitution has a provision for such a thing, but this policy has not been aggressively enforced, as Nigerians in certain regions of the country are constantly harassed and asked to go back to their states of origin or deported, as was the case in Lagos State, where the state government deported some people of Igbo extraction, whom the government described as idlers and social rejects. This kind of behavior does not promote national unity and cohesiveness. Nigerian leaders must be made to understand that the country's national interest is much bigger than individual ethnic or religious interests.

Citizens' Role in Achieving Good Governance in Nigeria

Citizens have much to say in the running of a government. They legitimize the existence and power of the governing class, meaning that the ruling class derives its authority and legitimacy from the people. Such acclamations entail that power belongs to the people. Citizens in a democratic state elect those who govern and they, in return, will obey the laws enacted by those whom they elected. Given this scenario, citizens are the embodiment of good governance. Citizens' major role in society is to ensure that those who are elected to service are executing their functions in accordance with the rule of law.

The rule of law implies that the law must be known to all and that no person is above the law of the land, no matter his/her position in government or in society. All public acts must be executed in accordance with the law and all changes in law and policy must be sanctified by the principles of the society. To ensure fairness, the rule of law maintains that all people should be treated equally. This means that the law should be applied equally and even-handedly, no matter who is before the bar of justice.

Literally, the rule of law implies that those in authority must govern by way of ensuring good governance, upholding the law and operating within the boundary of the law at all times. They should always stick to the game plan; they should never promise what they cannot deliver; and government operatives should learn to communicate effectively to the people.

The rule of law doctrine forbids deceptive acts (secrecy) of leaders; forbids the tyranny of the majority; forbids abuse of power by leaders; decries nepotism, bribery and corruption by public officials; forbids intolerance and lack of respect for humanity; and other social injustices. Those in authority must understand that power will be taken away from them when they fail to exercise it to the benefit of all citizens. It means, therefore, that when elected officials fail to yield to the "General Will" of the people, it is the right and duty of the people to use their voting power to overthrow such officials from the corridor of power.

Regrettably, this scenario only works where elections are free and fair, but where elections are rigged or bought, aggrieved people always resort to violence, as a means of righting the wrong done to the "General Will" of the people by stolen elections. When violence erupts as a result of stolen elections, the unpopular regime that rigged itself into office may resort to repressive measures to legitimatize itself and quell the people's anger and rage aimed at the regime. In exercising their constitutional rights, citizens can mobilize against their ruling class, if they feel they are denied and deprived the opportunities to advance economically, socially, and politically.

Another role of citizens in any democratic society is to hold their ruling class accountable for the actions it undertakes on behalf of the country, and to ensure that government's operations and activities are open and transparent. To achieve and sustain these aspects of government ethos or principles, the country must ensure that it has an educated citizenry who understand their constitutional rights; who overcome their ethnic and religious biases and hatred; and who refuse to be used by shameless politicians in rigging elections and assassinating political opponents.

The trouble with Nigeria, however, cannot be laid on the door steps of the ruling class alone. Some citizens, knowingly or unknowingly have helped, in many ways, to create these problems. Ethnic politics and religious intolerance are at the center of this divide.

These social vices are chiefly responsible for most citizens' failure to hold the Nigerian leaders accountable for their unpatriotic acts. Ethnicity and religion are chiefly responsible for the failure of most Nigerian citizens to demand openness and transparency from their national leaders.

Here is how the average Nigerian contributes to this ugly saga: Nigerians are too sectional and have always supported their national leaders along the ethnic or religious lines. They tend to follow their leaders sheepishly, not minding whether such leaders are right or wrong on national or regional issues.

For example, the people of Northern Nigeria will never condemn their national leaders publicly or privately for doing wrong things, even when such leaders are accused of abusing their offices, or accused of non-performing and incompetency, and/or engaging in unlawful practices such as, nepotism, bribery and corruption. Because of their ethnic and religious connections, the people of Northern Nigeria will quickly come to their national leaders' defense without looking into the merit of the accusation. Rather than doing so, most Northerners will blame the accusers and label them as anti-North or anti-Islam if the accusers are Non-Moslems and Non-Northerners.

Northern supporters will even go further to contend that such accusers were politically motivated. The story is the same throughout the country whether in South Western Nigeria or South Eastern Nigeria. This is the kind of behavior that polarizes the country and denies the people the right of speaking truth to power, or deprives them from speaking with one voice on national issues.

It discourages national unity and cohesiveness from growing and flourishing, and it promotes bad governance in the country. The support for national leaders based on ethnic or religious lines has become the prevailing norm in Nigeria because most Nigerians have come to accept this aspect of the country's political culture, which encourages and nurtures the illegal activities of the country's national leaders.

Decent and honest public servants in Nigeria are often smeared and vilified by their kinsmen for failing to participate in the massive looting of the country's treasury, unlike their crooked counterparts throughout the federation. These decent and honest public officials are neither valued by their people nor respected in their communities at-large. They are mocked and often ridiculed for doing their work the honest way. The culture of illegal wealth accumulation in the country has compounded the problem: it induces many public officials in Nigeria to use their public offices to enrich themselves at the expense of ordinary Nigerians. These shameless leaders who engage in the looting of public funds knew they would get away with their criminality without reproach or suffer any consequences as a result. They know that criminals are handsomely rewarded in Nigeria if they have the right connections in high places.

Generally, National Honors and Chieftaincy Titles should be used to reward meritocracy, especially to those honest and decent contributing members of the society but unfortunately, it is the professional or political criminals who are rewarded instead. You don't need to be a rocket scientist to know that rewarding criminal behaviors only ends up creating more criminals. Because many Nigerians are not asking the right questions or demanding to know where the sources of these crooked Nigerian public officials' wealth and riches are coming from, other shady characters in the country are delightfully joining the bandwagon by engaging in high crimes such as money laundering, kidnapping, armed robbery, and other forms of violent crime.

As it has become the normal practice in Nigeria, political criminals are rewarded in many ways: they are awarded National Honors or granted a presidential pardon or clemency for looting public funds and/or committing other high crimes. At the state and local government levels, such political criminals are equally rewarded by being elected into various political offices, as governors, members of the national and state assemblies, or local government chairpersons.

At the grass root or communal level, professional criminals are bestowed with distinctive chieftaincy titles by some of the unscrupulous traditional rulers. Additionally, some of the country's musicians should not be spared in the blame because they use their music lyrics and prowess to lavish praises on both professional and political criminals, portraying them as people who acquired their wealth and riches the honest ways.

The *Nigerian Punch Newspaper* article of September 16, 2014, drove this point home, when the apprehended armed robbers in Lagos told the Lagos State Police Command that they usually lavished the proceeds of their criminality on musicians who sang their praises at any party they attended (Aluko, 2014). When you reward and sing praises of criminals, you are only cultivating and breeding more criminals. Decency and honesty no longer mean anything in Nigeria. Getting wealthier or richer, no matter how one acquires it, is what prevails in the country. Public corruption and high crimes are now the order of the day in Nigeria. This is why many government officials in Nigeria cannot give proper account of their stewardship, and this is why things are not done openly.

Many Nigerians, including the author of this book, had always thought that the military coups that toppled democratically elected governments in Nigeria were hatched or conceived by overzealous military officers, but never knew that some highly placed Nigerians (civilians) were the major sponsors of most of these coups. This revelation came from a retired Army General and a former Federal Capital Territory Minister, Gen. Jeremiah Useni, who noted in the interview he granted to the *Daily Sun Newspaper* reporters, Iheanacho Nwosu and Fred Itua on April 6, 2014, that, "no coup in Nigeria took place without civilian interference. It's because they knew what they would gain" (Nwosu and Itua, 2014).

To buttress his point, the former Army General claimed that only three military officers served as ministers during those years of military dictatorships in the country, the rest of the ministers were all civilians. The Langtang-born Army General also stated that in the states, there was one military administrator and the rest were civilians. This revelation suggests that military coups in Nigeria would not have been successful had well connected civilians not involved themselves in the process.

The same conclusion or scenario applies to the rigging of elections in the country. If it weren't because of the urge of getting rich overnight, and if it weren't because of vulnerable civilians allowing themselves to be manipulated and bribed by shameless and power hungry politicians in the country to rig elections on their behalf, election fraud would not have been a major issue in Nigeria's electoral process. These politicians knew very well that without this dubious means, their chances of getting elected into the offices they sought would have been highly remote. To achieve their diabolic aims, shameless politicians have perfected the means of manipulating the outcome of elections. One such means is the use of vulnerable citizens, who are mostly the youth, some errant judges and police officers and, to a certain extent, some officials and staff of the Independent National Electoral Commission. These groups of citizens are bought to change the election results in favor of undeserving candidates.

The People's Democratic Party National Chairman, Alhaji Adamu Mu'azu, was right in his assessment of how members of the ruling class in Nigeria have exploited the vulnerability of poor Nigerians to their own advantage. In his Independence Day message, the PDP Chieftain was quoted as saying:

> Poor Nigerians fight themselves in a bid to protect the interest of politicians. Members of the ruling class whom the poor and helpless fight their cause are more united in achieving their political dreams....The disunity and division in our nation are more visible among the poor and the helpless. Even those who divide you are united. Unity is not in words, it is in action. Patriotism is not for the lips, it is shown by your actions. Reject their divide and rule methodology and Nigeria will remain one indivisible entity strong and glorious. Make few calls across borders, reach out today and reassure them of your love, respect, admiration and loyalty (Famutimi, 2014).

The PDP National Chairman also took issue with a commentary credited to the former Governor of Lagos State and the National Leader of APC, Asiwaju Bola Tinubu, who was quoted in an article, published by the *Nigerian Punch Newspaper* on October 7, 2014, for having said the following: "Nigerians should be prepared for change. We must rescue Nigeria from those set to cause it irreparable harm. The change I talk about is the only route to our deliverance from sixteen years of the PDP locusts. Nigeria is ours to keep and its democracy is ours to save" (Famutimi, 2014).

In reaction to Tinubu's call for unseating the ruling party from power, the PDP National Chairman told Nigerian youth not to fall for such an intrigue. He reminded the nation that "many young Nigerians have lost their lives in the process of being used by politicians to further their selfish interests." The former Bauchi State Governor out rightly condemned such a reprehensive action of the country's elite, whom he described as "old folks," blaming them for introducing the endemic corruption that is plaguing the country today and undermining its polity.

To overcome the country's depredations caused by power hungry and shameless politicians, the PDP Chieftain advised young Nigerians to distance themselves from these so-called advocates of revolution, who will not voluntarily lay down their lives in the process. In his humble advice to the Nigerian youths, the former Governor of Bauchi State had this to say:

If a politician asks you to lead a riot, a protest or a revolution when his children are in safety or abroad and you do so, who is the fool? Any politician who wants to achieve a revolution or a violent change but not willing to do so with his blood should be ignored. Do not allow politicians to use you for sacrifice or their selfish interests. Many ignorant young people have been used. They are dead now. Innocent Nigerians should refuse being used as pawns by politicians because in the process many of them are killed and later abandoned. Those killed during electoral campaigns or violence will never come back. They are victims and pawns used by politicians.... Young Nigerians must begin to outsmart politicians who deceive them using the bait of religion to actualise their selfish agenda. If a politician is sponsoring you to perpetrate Islamic extremism and he is a moderate Muslim himself, when you die and you discover there is no paradise or all the false promises of paradise for you. Who will you blame? If a politician wants to sponsor anyone for paradise or Islamic extremism, why not let him start with his children? May you become smarter than those deceiving you in the name of religion for their selfish ambition or desires? The counsel I offer to you here is free. We may never have another platform to do this but make use of it (Famutimi, 2014).

A behavior of this kind deprives popular or deserving candidates the opportunity to be elected. If the Nigerian citizens should refrain from being used to rig elections, unpopular or undeserving candidates will never be elected into any elective offices in the country.

If citizens refrain from assisting in rigging elections and being used as assassins and thugs, such an effort will definitely lead to good governance, because those who are duly elected by popular mandate will do the right things, believing that by doing so, their chances of being reelected in subsequent elections are much greater. It is a fact that unpopular or undeserving candidates, who stole elections through voting fraud, will not do the right thing, because their purpose of seeking a political office is not to serve the people honestly, but simply to use their positions in government to empty the national treasury or state treasury and secretly conceal their unlawful acts. These illustrations are how the Nigerian citizens, knowingly or unknowingly, have contributed in promoting and sustaining bad governance in the country.

To save Nigeria's nascent democracy and to achieve good governance in Nigeria, patriotic Nigerians should not allow themselves to be used in undermining the integrity of elections since elections are the only legitimate and acceptable means of electing people democratically. Nigerians citizens should not allow the unpatriotic and undeserving national leaders to use ethnicity or religion to polarize the country in order for them to remain in power in perpetuity.

Every Nigerian who is truly committed to good governance in the country must embrace and support transformational leaders irrespective of their ethnic origin or religious affiliation, and must support leaders who have genuine programs that will promote self-reliance, vibrancy, and the stability of the country. Nigerians should be mindful of the fact that no outside forces or individuals will solve Nigeria's problems better than the Nigerian people themselves. Nigerians should not give up fighting for the unity of the country. They should muster the courage to rescue Nigeria irrespective of the ugly trends prevailing in the country, and irrespective of the fact that the current leadership in the country does not care about what the ordinary Nigerians think or say.

The complacency and passivity in the country's affairs have contributed immensely in perpetuating bad governance in the country and, allowed one particular ethnic nationality to dominate the country's leadership. Nigeria's struggle for democracy, freedom, and social justice is not in isolation from other global struggles for self-determination. Nigerians should understand that if it were not for the sacrifices the country's Founding Fathers made during the struggle for independence, the rights most Nigerians are enjoying today would not have been possible. If they had folded their arms or had remained aloof and complacent on issues facing the nation, life would not have been more comfortable to most Nigerians, especially to the current Nigerian political class.

One other lesson to be drawn from this scenario is that many countries have gone through this dark path and bounced back. They did not invite other countries to come and resolve their internal problems like most Nigerians are asking other nations to rescue Nigeria from the hands of its non-performing leaders. The problem with most Nigerians is that they are free-riders who want others to fight their battles for them. Instead of asking other nations to intervene in their domestic affairs, they should adopt strategies similar to most other nations in resolving their own internal problems. If Nigeria is to be a stable and prosperous nation, which is the main goal of the country, Nigerians of all persuasions must join hands together to liberate the country from its internal and external enemies.

Nigerians know who these enemies are. A stable and prosperous Nigerian will foster self-sufficiency and self-reliance rather than being in continuous dependency on foreign powers. It will empower Nigerians economically, politically and socially and will force Nigerians to work together with other progressive African countries to unify the African states under one continental government, as was envisioned by Kwame Nkrumah of Ghana and other progressive members of the pan-African movement of the 1950s and 1960s.

The author of this book applauds Nigerians in Diaspora, especially those in North America and Europe, for their selfless efforts in raising the economic profile of Nigeria through their substantial remittances to the country. For example, the *Nigerian Tribune Newspaper* noted in its September 3, 2014, *News Headlines* that Nigerians in Diaspora remitted $10.40 billion in the first half of 2014. The Newspaper also said that in 2013, Nigerians abroad remitted a whopping sum of $20.77 billion; and these were remittances meant for families, friends and communities, medical missions and scholarships (Subair, 2014).

The sad story is that, while Nigerians in Diaspora are supporting the economic development of the country by remitting their hard earned money, the governing elite and their cronies are busy looting public funds and transferring such funds to their overseas' bank accounts, where such funds are being used to boost the economies of those recipient nations. Having said the above, Nigerians in Diaspora have more to do to ensure that good governance, equality and fairness, social justice, peace, economic prosperity and stability prevail in Nigeria. Nigerians in Diaspora must also ensure that those things (social amenities) that made their stay in their newly adopted countries more comfortable should also be made available in Nigeria. There is a great need for Nigerian professionals in the Diaspora to continue investing their resources and expertise, as they have been doing, in building a new Nigeria that will take its rightful place in the comity of nations. This cannot be done by foreign entities but by Nigerians themselves. This aspiration entails that all hands be on deck and it is a reminder that nobody can develop Nigeria other than Nigerians.

It is a heartbreaking to see the Nigerian governing elite traveling abroad frequently for various reasons without coming home with new ideas, ideas of changing the country for the better. Whilst in these foreign countries, especially in Europe and North America, they enjoy frequent power supplies, they drink clean and running water, they drive on good roads and highways, they receive adequate medical care and, of course, they send their children to these countries' Ivy League Universities and Colleges but, in Nigeria, these social amenities are neglected and abandoned. What a shame!

Finally, Nigerians must recognize and applaud the political awareness some Human Rights and other Civil Organizations, including the Nigerian Labor Unions, are providing to the country. These organizations' dedicated efforts in monitoring Nigerian government's activities and their speaking out against government's misconduct and misrule must be highly appreciated.

The socio-political and legal activities these organizations bring to bear are much needed in the country at this time, more than ever before, for several reasons: 1) holding government functionaries that have gone overboard, accountable for their actions and deeds; 2) sustaining and nurturing the country's nascent democracy; and 3) ensuring that good governance is achieved and sustained in the country.

Literally, social movements are true voices of the voiceless and they are the true change agents in societies. Government operatives in Nigeria have, for too long, been getting away with misconduct, misrule and betrayals. This is because of the complexities existing among Nigerians, but more so because the country lacks formidable social movements that will positively confront these government functionaries to make them discharge their duties in accordance with the law of the land. Nigerians should seriously embrace and encourage more of these social movements in the country for the good they provide to societies.

Restructuring of Nigeria's Political Institutions

Office-holding in Africa, including Nigeria, has been coveted as a major means by which politicians enhance their economic and social positions. Political offices in this continent have been a springboard for individual enrichment. Since independence, leadership positions in Nigeria have always been highly valued and priced, particularly because of the financial rewards such offices attract. At all levels of government, whether at national, state or local, the incumbents (office holders) are expected to earn high salaries, often many times higher than the earnings of peasants and workers, not taking into consideration their car allowances, housing subsidies and other emoluments. On top of these financial gains are the earnings generated from the use of public offices for private gain, which include such things as gains from award of contracts and licenses, and/or the diversion of public funds into private accounts.

Like in most other political settings, the Nigerian leaders who occupy these political offices are mostly men who are self-serving, over-bearing, unpatriotic, and above all, they are men who place ethnic and religious interests above Nigeria's national interest and security (Nigerian National Alliance, 1994). These leaders fail to recognize the obvious fact that, the supremacy of the Nigerian nation and the rights of its citizens are more sacrosanct (sacred) and also above ethnic and religious interests. The failure of Nigerian leaders to acknowledge this simple fact has led to frequent threats of secession often expressed in the country. It is, indeed, a sad situation to see a group of Nigerians suppressing and harassing other Nigerians.

Unfortunately and undoubtedly, the current Nigerian leadership has forgotten the consequences and changes that the Magna Carta of June 15, 1215; the American Revolutionary War of 1775-1783; and the Declaration of American Independence of July 4, 1776 brought on the British political history. The current Nigerian leadership equally has forgotten the consequences and changes the Haitian Revolution of 1791-1804; the French Revolution of 1789-1799; and the French Declaration of the Rights of Man of August 26, 1789 brought on the French monarchy and to his despotic regime. The current Nigerian leadership, of course, should be too familiar with the on-going Arab Spring or Arab Awakening that began in 2011. These famous revolts and documents were reactions to bad governance. They helped to mobilize and galvanize the British barons, clergies, and nobles; the people of the United States; the Haitian Slaves; and the French people, including the peasants, clergies and nobles to demand their emancipation and self-determination, equality, fraternity and liberty from their tyrannical rulers.

The reactions and mobilization of the oppressed in North America, France, and Haiti eventually ended British control of its North America colony, and the overthrow of the French monarchy, Louis the XVI. Led by Toussaint L'Ouverture (1743-1803), the Haitian Slaves freed themselves from the yokes of Emperor Napoleon Bonaparte of France and the French Bourgeois class (Plantation owners) in Haiti who enslaved the African Haitians. The Haitian Slave revolt has been described as the only successful slave revolt ever recorded in human history. The successful outcome of this revolt helped to end slavery in all French colonies.

Below are some of the phrases that galvanized the White settlers in the British North American colony to revolt against the British government for its obscured policy of "taxation without representation." The enshrined phrases in the Declaration of American Independence were drafted in June of 1776, and was ratified by the fifty-six delegates to the Continental Congress on July 4, 1776. Here is a brief passage of the famous Declaration of American Independence:

> We hold these truths to be self-evident: That all men are created equal; that they are endowed by their Creator with certain unalienable rights; that among these are life, liberty, and the pursuit of happiness; that, to secure these rights, governments are instituted among men, deriving their just powers from the consent of the governed; that whenever any form of government becomes destructive of these ends, it is the right of the people to alter or to abolish it, and institute new government, laying its foundation on such principles, and organizing its powers in such form, as to them shall seem most likely to affect their safety and happiness. Prudence, indeed, will dictate that governments long established should not be changed for light and transient causes; and accordingly all experience hath shown that mankind are more disposed to suffer, while evils are sufferable, than to right themselves by abolishing the forms to which they are accustomed. But when a long train of abuses and usurpations, pursuing invariably the same object, evinces a design to reduce them under absolute despotism, it is their right, it is their duty, to throw off such government, and to provide new guards for their further security.... (*An Excerpt from the Challenge of Democracy: Government in America*, 1989: A-1-A-3).

If the Nigerian leadership circle does not demonstrate good leadership capability and does not provide adequately for the Nigerian people sooner than later, the oppressed will have nothing to lose than to win their freedom and happiness. The country's governing elite should not under-estimate the "General Will" of the oppressed, simply because they are in control of the country's instruments of power. They must be reminded that nothing stops the oppressed from liberating themselves from the tyranny of their oppressor especially when they decide to do so. There will be no amount of military hardware the country's military may have under its possession, and there will be no amount of brutalization and torture the country's security agencies may inflict on the oppressed that will prevent them from achieving their inalienable rights to life, liberty, and the pursuit of happiness. It seems that the current Nigerian leadership is living in isolation or has failed to learn from the mistakes of other world tyrants who were deposed by their oppressed masses.

To avoid or avert the above sentiments from manifesting, Nigeria's political structure needs a serious reform or overhaul, giving the realities on the ground. For instance, the country's population, including the middle class, is growing much faster than anyone expected or anticipated. This means that the prevailing political structure cannot cope with these unexpected changes. The examination of Nigerian problems reveals several findings, but the most prevalent and enduring one is the defectiveness of the country's political structure which has led to an extreme power concentration at the national level and the endemic corruption it creates. The central government in Abuja enjoys enormous power and is causing serious tension in the country's polity. The extreme power concentration at the national level makes mockery of the Nigerian federalism. The central government has given itself too many responsibilities and with that, states are left with little or no responsibility.

The same situation is also seen at the state level, where local government affairs are dictated directly from states' capitals without much input from the local communities. Since the end of the Nigerian Civil War (1970 to present), state and local governments in Nigeria have never enjoyed "greater autonomy," as they should in any true federal structure. It should be noted that during the First Nigerian Republic (1960-1966), the four main regions in the country (Northern, Western, Mid-Western, and Eastern) at the time, enjoyed unprecedented autonomy. In diverse countries with federal structures, such as the United States of America and Canada, government powers are highly decentralized, while in Nigeria, an extreme power concentration exists at the national level, which suffocates the equitable power sharing formula between national and state governments

Like the United States, Nigeria is a multiethnic, multicultural, and multi-religious society, a country with a huge population. These attributions make the country a more complex society to govern. Nigerians had never wished these attributes on themselves (the amalgamation of Northern and Southern Nigeria in 1914). Rather, they were foisted on them by a foreign power that had no respect for the indigenous people's history and tradition. Since Nigerians have come to accept this reality as a way of life, they must not allow these attributes to further divide them. They must overcome these attributes, as the Americans overcame their own biases and prejudices. For a national unity to be sustained in any diverse society, such as Nigeria, the people must recognize that every nationality that makes up the country has its own interests and agenda. These divergent interests and agenda must be celebrated, respected, and protected at all times. No ethnic-nationality interest or agenda should supersede other ethnic-nationality interests or agenda. There should be no labels describing some groups of Nigerians as "majority groups and others as "minority groups." Nigerians must always be made to recognize the simple, but obvious fact that "there is strength in diversity."

Nigerians of all persuasions must be treated as "one indivisible people," meaning that every Nigerian must be accorded the same rights and opportunities and must be treated equally and fairly, with love, respect, and dignity, regardless of their socio-economic status, ethnicity, and religious affiliations. This is one way to avoid the alienation of groups in diverse societies. Whenever one ethnic nationality feels marginalized or deprived of equal opportunity to advance alongside with other nationalities within the country, conflicts will definitely ensue and if the conflict is not quickly rectified by the country's leadership, such emotions or sentiments can lead to social disorder or anomie.

To glue the social fabric of a society together, effort must be made by those in power to promote social justice that calls for inclusion and not exclusion. The governing elite in Nigeria must make sure that all ethnic nationalities in the country are winners. A situation where some ethnic nationalities win, and others lose, should be avoided entirely because such situations promote class struggle or ethnic rivalry and hatred, as structural or instrumental Marxists have observed. The win-loss syndrome, according to Marxist scholars, produces structural inequalities which on a sociological level, lead to gender, race, and class disparities. Whilst on a psychological level, the win-loss syndrome produces frustrations, repression, and alienation. These are sentiments being expressed in Nigeria today by some ethnic nationalities that feel deprived, alienated, and marginalized in spite of the creation of political zones and federal character mechanism that are in place to calm this kind of fear.

The creations of states, political zones, and federal character programs are not enough to calm the nerves, because current situations in Nigeria demand that state and local governments be given more political powers to empower and nurture ethnic nationalities' interests since members of these ethnical nationalities live in the states. To avoid further alienation, deprivation, and marginalization of these ethnic nationalities' interests and their advancement, more states should be created to accommodate these ethnic nationalities' interests and aspirations. The corporate existence of some of these organized ethnic militant groups, such as Boko Haram, the Movement for the Emancipation of the Niger Delta (MEND), the Movement for the Actualization of the Sovereign State of Biafra (MASSOB), the Movement for the Survival of the Ogoni People (MOSOP), the Movement for Survival of Ijaw Ethnic Nationality (MOSIN), and the Oodua People's Congress (OPC), is a clear indication that there is still unfinished business with ethnic-nationalities' rights in the country.

Ethnic nationalities in Nigeria must be given the opportunity to chart their own course, as long as such autonomy does not interfere with the laws of the federal and state governments. More state creation and granting of more autonomy to state and local governments will decentralize the enormous powers currently held by the national government. Decentralization of power in Nigeria will definitely lessen the class struggle, which is currently overheating the country's polity and will make Abuja less attractive to many politicians.

Decentralization of power in Nigeria will be one major way of accommodating the newly emerging national political actors in the country. Creating more political structures with responsibilities will loosen the frictions strangulating the polity. This means that the federal government will have to give up some of its powers. State governments will do likewise by giving more responsibilities to local governments. Abuja should no longer be seen as the only center of power and attraction. The same thing goes for state capitals; they should no longer be seen as the only centers of power and attraction. More division of labor and delegation of powers will open up the country's political system for more participants to join the political process. This must be done if a true federalism is to prevail in Nigeria.

Other areas that need serious reforms in the country's political structure are the political party systems and how political campaigns are financed. Nigeria has always maintained a multi-party system since it became an independent nation, but the country has not fully benefited from such a party structure, because of the intrigues it produces. The system allowed for the creation of several mushroom parties that were not viable enough to win a single seat in both national and state Assemblies. From the dozens of political parties that emerged during the Nigerian First Republic (1960-1966), only three of these parties dominated the political process of the country. None of these three dominant parties had a national outlook; they were regionally based, and were representing the three major regions that existed at the time.

The parties were: the Northern People's Congress (NPC), representing Northern Nigeria; the Action Group (AG), representing Western Nigeria; and the National Council of Nigeria and Cameroon, which later changed its name to National Council of Nigerian Citizens (NCNC), representing Eastern Nigeria. Because, none of the parties won a clear majority of seats in the National Assembly, NPC and NCNC had to go into alliance building to form the central government. Created on ethnic sentiments, these parties promoted and perpetuated tribal politics, which helped to intensify the disunity of the country. Instead of helping the country to grow politically and economically, the multi-party system brought enormous political upheavals on the country, which eventually led to the Civil War that devastated the country and slowed down the development of the country.

During the Nigerian Second Republic (1979-1983), the country adopted yet another multi-party system. Of the seven political parties that were created at the time, only three parties emerged as dominant parties. Of these three dominant parties, it was only the National Party of Nigeria (NPN) that had a fairly national outlook; it drew members from all regions of the federation. The other two parties, the Unity Party of Nigeria (UPN) and the Nigerian People's Party (NPP) had more regional leanings. Even with NPN's national outlook, it went into alliance with the NPP to form the national government because NPN did not have clear majority members to form the government. Once again, the center could not hold because the Nigerian political process at the time was marred by tribal sentiments, coupled with the massive corruption that ensued.

The abortive Nigerian Third Republic ushered in a party reform and other vital reforms meant to address the political problems facing the nation. As a result, a two-party system was introduced to address the issue of tribal politics that had torn the country apart. The creation of the National Republican Convention (NRC) and the Social Democratic Party (SDP) was to ensure that the country's political parties had a national leaning or flavor. Unfortunately, this experiment did not see the light of the day, because the Babangida administration that introduced the two-party system annulled the very election (June 12, 1993 election) that would have solidified the two-party system or the election where the effectiveness of the newly proposed two-party system would have been tested. With the cancelation of this election, the two-party system that brought Nigerians from all walks of life under these parties (NRC and SDP) died a natural death and the country went back to a multi-party system that did not do the country any good.

The Nigerian Fourth Republic (1999-present) reverts to a multi-party system, where dozens of parties were created. Like the Nigerian Second Republic, only one political party, the People's Democratic Party (PDP), among numerous other parties registered, has a national leaning, while both the Alliance for Democracy (AD) and the All Progressives Grand Alliance (APGA) have regional leanings. Because of its broad scope, the PDP was elected in 1999 to form the government. The party has been in power since then, winning the elections of 2003, 2007, 2011, but failed to retain power in 2015.

These election victories have not been won without controversies. The party has been accused of election fraud by its political detractors repeatedly. Since 1999, the ruling party has been in power with no serious opposition to challenge its supremacy, until lately, when some of these other non-performing political parties came together to form a new party now known within the Nigerian political arena, as the All Progressive Congress (APC). The parties that came together to form the APC, included: the Congress for Progressive Change (CPC); the Action Congress of Nigeria (ACN); the All Nigerian Peoples Party (ANPP); and some elements of the All Progressives Grand Alliance (APGA), led by the Governor of Imo State, Rochas Okorocha. The coalition party, the APC, is now the country's ruling party following its victory in the 2015 general elections.

From this scenario, it seems that the country is being governed by a one party-system, the PDP, which has been in power since 1999 without a formidable opposition to challenge its supremacy. The one party-system scenario will not be good for the country, given the country's diverse interests, and its political philosophy (democracy) which guarantees Nigerians' rights to choose. From these brief descriptions of the Nigerian political party system and its role in undermining the unity of the country, Nigeria should revert to a two-party system, because a two-party system will strengthen the opposition party and make it more viable to compete. Such a system will create an alternative choice for Nigerians, rather than having one political party dominating the country's political landscape which, in all ramifications, does not promote good governance.

As a new democracy, Nigerians must be cognizant of how political campaigns are financed and their ramifications on the political development of the country. Whenever you allow individuals to sponsor political candidates, the tendency of creating loopholes or situations where state treasuries can be mortgaged to the highest financial contributors as reward for sponsoring candidates into political offices, is very clear and evident. Nigerians are too familiar with the concept of "political godfatherism," where a few individuals will lay claim of ownership to states' treasuries simply because they financially sponsored the candidatures of those elected into various offices in the states, such as governors, state legislators, and local government chairpersons.

The impacts of political godfathers in Nigeria's political process were well articulated in a recent seminar organized by the EFCC, held on September 9, 2014, in Abuja. The discussions in the said seminar centered on various issues ranging from anti-corruption, fiscal responsibility to good governance for state government officials in Nigeria. In that seminar, the Chairman of the nation's anti-graft agency, Ibrahim Lamorde, lamented with disappointment at the low level of development witnessed throughout the thirty-six states of the federation.

The seasoned national law enforcer claimed that the level of development in those states is not commensurate with the huge amounts of allocation these states receive from the federal account. The EFCC boss went on to conclude that such lapses could be blamed on the "outright payment of huge sums of money to political godfathers."

The EFCC boss also identified other corrupt practices that are negatively impacting on the development of the states, in spite of the huge amounts of allocation these states receive from the federal account. The said corrupt practices include: "the inflation of prices; over-estimation of cost of projects (over invoicing); and ghost workers syndrome." The enduring consequences of these corrupt practices, as described by the anti-graft agency also include the following: "poor service delivery; inadequate infrastructure; poor management of public enterprise; bad governance; moral decadence and general underdevelopment" (Onyeocha, 2014). It must be noted here that the problem of political godfatherism in Nigeria is not peculiar to states only; it is also a major problem at the national level.

Given the EFCC assessment of state governments' inability to develop and deliver good governance in their respective states, nobody whether rich or poor, including organizations, corporations, and foreign entities, should be allowed to sponsor political candidates in Nigeria. Such a practice undermines the country's nascent democratic process and denies average Nigerians a voice in determining their future and destiny. To eradicate this ugly practice, political parties in the country should, under their banners, be the sole sponsors of candidates who are seeking political offices at national, state, and local government levels. They should be able to introduce a party disciplinary measure that will control their errant members.

When a political party sponsors its candidates to political offices, it will be very difficult for candidates to dump the party for other parties and still retain their positions in government. A party discipline will strip errant politicians of their positions when they decamp to a political party of their choice. This was the case, when a large number of PDP members, including its State Governors, its National Assembly members, its State Houses of Assembly members, and its Local Governments' Chairmen decamped to APC and still retained their seats in government. The story is the same in other parties; where their elected members decamped to the PDP and retained their seats. These politicians were able to decamp and keep their seats because they literally sponsored themselves with little or no assistance from their parties; therefore, their parties had no absolute control over them and, that prompted them to act the way they did without minding the actions their parties might take.

On the other hand, the Nigerian governments should always make funds available to duly registered political parties, during electoral seasons, in a way, to assist them in reducing costs of sponsoring candidates for political offices and other party expenses. Additionally, these governments should grant political parties free airtime in governments' owned Radio and Television Networks so that their political communications (political speeches, advertisements, and other campaign activities or materials) can be easily disseminated to the public with no cost to the parties.

As many Nigerians know, the financing of political campaigns by individuals has also led to the defrauding of many banks in the country. As previously noted in one of the chapters of the book, many Nigerian banks were liquated because some politicians borrowed huge sums of money from these banks for their political campaigns, but failed to pay them back. By the same token, a few others floated their own banks for political reasons, and such banks were used to rob customers' life savings. Thereafter, the banks were liquated. By these deceptive acts, the Bank Managing Directors, who now turned politicians, brought untold hardships on their customers. The irony of this saga is that, while these politicians are stealing from states' funds and from citizens to build their political empire, the country is paying dearly for their deceptions.

There was an article in the *Nigerian Punch Newspaper* on October 2, 2014, that drove this point home. The article told a story of how oil pipelines in some states in Nigeria are being vandalized by some individuals who desperately want to become politicians. According to the *Punch Metro* article, a self-proclaimed politician, named Wahab Junaid, was arrested by the Anti-Pipeline Task Force in the Obafemi/Owode Local Government Area of Ogun State for vandalizing a Nigerian National Petroleum Corporation pipeline. The self-acclaimed politician told the police that the purpose of his criminality was to raise money to contest for a political office in the 2015 elections. The purported politician was further quoted in the Newspaper article, as having made the following statements:

> I am an active member of a political party in this state [Lagos state]. So, when the slot for the House of Representatives was zoned to my area, my people nominated me to represent them. Since I know that I had a good chance of winning the election, I accepted. I was told to go and look for money to sponsor my campaigns.... In the course of looking for funds, a friend of mine, Ologe, who is also a vandal, informed me that the area was calm, and that I could come and lift some fuel and get money for my political ambition. I was waiting

with my tankers to lift the product when policemen arrested me. My enemies, who are bitter that I was anointed for the political position, betrayed me. Please forgive me and give me another chance. I am sorry and I promise that as soon as I am elected, I will assist the police in the war against pipeline vandalism. A full tanker could be bought for N1.5 million from vandals and sold for N3 million (Olufowobi, 2014)

Given all these facts, political campaigns in the country should neither be financed by individual candidates, nor their friends and relatives, or by groups, but the parties. It is logical that when political office seekers finance their own campaigns, the tendency for them to take money from political godfathers (lobbyists), or borrow money from banking institutions and from other sources, which they are unlikely to pay back, is apparent and will have enormous negative consequences on the system. It is certain that states' funds will be used to pay off the debts the moment these shameless politicians get elected into those offices. Nigerian electoral process should not be privatized if Nigeria is to sustain its nascent democracy and give every average Nigerian a voice. Nigerians should see what the lobbyists' money is doing to America's democracy.

Utilizing Commissions of Inquiries as Vital Instruments in Solving the Nations' Problems

Commissions of Inquiries are essential tools most governments around the world and Inter-Governmental Organizations (IGOs) use in addressing and rectifying problems that are of national and international significance. Governments are organic institutions operated and administered by human beings who, by their very nature, are bound to make mistakes or engage in illegal activities. Whenever national problems occur as a result of human fragility or delicacy, or as a result of natural disasters, most governments create Commissions of Inquiries consisting of bodies of men and women who are competent and well versed on the subject matter, to look into such problems. The missions of most Commissions of Inquiries are: 1) identifying problems in terms of time, location, and behavior; 2) providing analysis of the problems by answering who, what, where, when, how, and why questions; 3) responding to the problems by developing alternative problem-solving strategies or approaches and selecting the most appropriate alternative; and 4) assessing the actions taken by evaluating the response selected to determine its effectiveness. In the law enforcement field, this type of problem-solving technique or strategy is known as the SARA Model, meaning: Scanning; Analysis; Response; and Assessment (Cox et al, 2014: 158).

By the same token, the work of Commissions of Inquiries in a political sphere, is to determine whether or not the incident that led to the creation of the Commission is real and, if it is real, the Commission will then look into the underlying causes of the problem and provide analysis of what can be done to rectify the problem. Once this is done, the Commission will then recommend actions to be taken to address the underlying causes. The findings and recommendations of the Commission are then communicated directly to the appropriate authorities that created the Commission for immediate implementations. According to public policy analysts, the Commission's recommended actions could either be seen as problem identification, which leads to publicizing or outlining societal problems and expressing demands for government action, or such recommended actions could be seen as public policy formulation, which results in developing policy proposals that will resolve the issues and ameliorate the problems (Dye, 2002:32).

In most part, Commissions of Inquires, especially those designated as Truth and Reconciliation Commissions are instituted not only as truth-gathering, truth telling, and reconciliation, but also for other important purposes, such as alleviating victims' suffering, promoting trust, contributing to the consolidation of democracy, and helping to prevent future conflicts.

Based on this obvious fact, Truth and Reconciliation Commissions are strictly based on "restorative justice" ideology, whose main objective is to heal relationships between offenders, victims and the community. In the criminal justice field, restorative justice is also known as "the balance approach," which seeks to hold offenders accountable for their criminality by requiring the offenders to repay or restore victims' losses, such as reparation or restitution. Restorative justice calls for community protection by weighing both public safety and the least costly, least restrictive correctional alternative. Restorative Justice also promotes competency development by emphasizing remediation for offenders' social, educational, or other deficiencies when they enter the correctional system (Mays and Winfree, Jr., 2009:10).

On the other hand, International Criminal Court (ICC) and International Criminal Tribunals (ICT) are borne out of "retributive justice," whose aim is to find fault and punish the guilty. The ICC that came into effect in July of 2002 was a brainchild of the Rome Treaty of 1998. Both the ICC and International Criminal Tribunals of the Former Yugoslavia (ICTY), Rwanda (ICTR), and the Special Court for Sierra Leone are other examples of Commissions of Inquiries created by the United Nations Organization to try and prosecute government officials who are accused of committing egregious crimes, such as Genocide, War Crimes, and Crimes against Humanity (Daykeay, 2014; and Andreopoulos, 2005).

Examples of Truth and Reconciliation Commissions are numerous, and they include the following:

- The Ivory Coast Dialogue, Truth and Reconciliation Commission (CDVR) was constituted in 2011 to investigate a decade-old bloody political violence that marred the country following the presidential election victory of the opposition leader, Laurent Gbagbo in 2000;

- The Chilean National Commission on Truth and Reconciliation (known as Rettig Commission), was established in 1990 by President Aylwin to gather information about, and attempt to clarify, the many allegations of human rights violations during the Pinochet period. The basis of the truth, according to the Commission's founding decree, "will it be possible to satisfy the basic demands of justice and create the indispensable conditions for achieving an effective national reconciliation;"

- The Honduran Truth and Reconciliation Commission was created in 2010, as a result of the Guaymuras Dialogue: Tegucigalpa/San Jose Accord for the national reconciliation and strengthening of democracy in Honduras. It aims to clarify the events that occurred before and after the constitutional crisis of June 28, 2009, to identify actions that led to the crisis situation and provide the people of Honduras with fundamentals for preventing these events from occurring in the future;

- The Liberian Truth and Reconciliation Commission was established in 2005 under the Transitional Government, to promote national peace, security, unity and reconciliation by investigating more than twenty years of civil conflict in the country and to report on gross human rights violations that occurred in Liberia between January 1979 and October 14, 2003. Violations were defined by the Commission as violations of international human rights standards, crimes against humanity, war crimes, and any breaches of the Geneva Conventions;

- Commission on the Truth for El Salvador was instituted in 1992, to investigate serious acts of violence occurring since 1980 and the nature and effects of the violence and recommend methods of promoting national reconciliation;

- Truth and Reconciliation Commission of Canada was instituted on June 1, 2008, to create a historical account of human rights abuses in the Canadian Indian residential school system, help people to heal, and encourage reconciliation between aboriginals and non-aboriginal Canadians. The Commission was designated to host events across the country to raise awareness about the residential school system and its impact;

- South Africa Truth and Reconciliation Commission was created in 1995, to investigate gross human rights violations that were perpetrated during the period of the Apartheid regime from 1960 to 1994, including abductions, killings, torture. Its mandate covered violation by both state and the liberation movements and allowed the commission to hold special hearings focused on specific sectors, institutions, and individuals. Controversially, the TRC was empowered to grant amnesty to perpetrators who confessed their crimes truthfully and completely to the commission.

Sources: *Wikipedia, the free Encyclopedia*, 2014; *FAQ*, 2010; *United States Institute of Peace*, 1992, 1995 2010; Daykeay, 2014; Fioriti, 2014; and Weissbrodt and Fraser, 1992).

Other TRCs held around the world, included those of Argentina, Brazil, Colombia, Czech Republic, Ecuador, Fiji, Ghana, Guatemala, Haiti, Kenya, Morocco, Panama, Paraguay, Peru, Poland, Philippines, Solomon Islands, South Korea, Sri Lanka, East Timor, Uganda, and Ukraine (*Wikipedia, the free Encyclopedia*, 2014). Of all these Commissions, the South Africa's Truth and Reconciliation Commission, was so profound because it accomplished some of its intended goals and objectives which are, exposing the atrocities and the lies the racist state (the Apartheid system) propagated over the years against the true champions of democracy, equality, freedom and inclusiveness (the African National Congress and other progressive groups in South Africa), whose members paid the ultimate price with their lives, in their attempt to liberate the country from the racist elements. The South Africa White minority regime and its Western allies and supporters like the United State of America and the United Kingdom had, for decades, labeled the African National Congress and other progressive groups in the country, as Communist and terrorist organizations.

The Apartheid regime had repeatedly accused the ANC and these other progressive social movements in the country of working against the state, but the picture of whom the real terrorists were, emerged when the Commission began its work. As a result of the Commission's investigations, many South Africans, especially the White South Africans, discovered that the Apartheid state was not only a terrorist, but also an anti-democratic state. Although none of the White minority government functionaries who perpetrated these atrocities (crimes against humanity) went to prison for their criminality, revelations from the Commission hearings brought a measure of comfort to a majority of the Black South Africans who were victimized by the Apartheid system. The outcome of this exercise was rewarding, because it brought healing, reconciliation and a new chapter to most South Africans, especially to the former oppressed Black majority.

The South African experience (victims of the racist state having the opportunity or platform to confront their abusers, and the healing process that began after the TRC completed its work) was an experience Nigerians never had, when the findings and recommendations of the Human Rights Violations Investigation Commission (known as the Oputa Commission) were blocked and were never made public. Because of this fact, many Nigerians, especially those who were not born during the period of the investigation (between January 15, 1966 to May 28, 1999), were deprived of the privilege of knowing exactly what really happened during those turbulent periods in Nigerian history (periods during the Nigerian Civil War and military dictatorship that followed thereafter). What most of these people know today about these periods in question may have come from what they learned from the history books.

One indictment against the Nigerian government is that, it has an image of creating Commissions of Inquiries without implementing either in part or in full the recommendations those Commissions suggest. Apart from the Oputa Commission, there were other Special Task Forces, Committees or Summits that were created by the Nigerian government, whose recommendations were buried in the sand. One such example was the aborted Aburi

Summit in Ghana that met in Accra in 1967 to work out modalities that would prevent the country from breaking up, but the Summit's recommendations were never implemented by those who were in charge of the Nigerian military at the time.

The country descended into a Civil War because of the failure in implementing the accord agreed upon by parties involved in the negotiation. Another recent example of government failure in implementing the recommendations of a constituted Commission is the Petroleum Revenue Special Task Force, headed by Mallam Nuhu Ribadu, a task force created by the Jonathan administration to investigate the alleged endemic corruption that muddled the fuel subsidy regime. The Task Force submitted its recommendations to the administration in 2012, but those recommendations are yet to be acted upon until this day.

Many Nigerians have lost faith in their government's ability to utilize Commissions of Inquiries in solving the country's endemic problems. As a result of this, many Nigerians supported the call for a Sovereign National Conference, which has just concluded its deliberation. If the Nigerian government had been utilizing the services of these Commissions of inquiries in addressing national problems the way it should, there would have been no need to call for an expensive Sovereign National Conference which cost Nigeria tens of millions of Naira for assembling 492 delegates for over a three-month duration just to do what members of the National Assembly are hired to do. The purpose of Nigerians electing their representatives in both National and State Assemblies is to tackle the country's problems and address any constitutional issues that may serve as impediments to good governance and the country's developmental projects.

Take the United State of America, for example. The first time the country had its Sovereign National Conference was in 1787, when fifty wise men were assembled at the Independent Hall in Philadelphia, Pennsylvania to review the Article of Confederation. The reason for such a gathering in the state of Pennsylvania was to address the issue of a weak center (Confederacy) and the lack of cohesiveness and unity existing among the former Thirteen Colonies, which later became Thirteen States after the country obtained its Independence from Great Britain on July 4, 1776. Since that time, subsequent changes in the country's polity have been done through constitutional amendments, legislative process, case laws, and through the works of Commissions of Inquiries. It is important to underscore here that most findings and recommendations of Commissions of Inquiries have helped the US lawmakers to legislate; this is how crucial the works of Commissions of Inquiries have been in the United States of America.

Since the adoption of the US Constitution in 1789, there have been twenty-six Constitutional Amendments made thus far. The last Amendment to the US Constitution was adopted in 1971, which grants eighteen year olds the right to vote (Janda, et al, 1989: A13). Over the decades, the US government has created several Commissions of Inquiries to assist the government in addressing the numerous challenges facing the country, especially in the areas of police corruption and other misconducts. Such Commissions of Inquiries included: the National Commission on Law Observance and

Enforcement, known as the Wickersham Commission (1931); the President's Commission on Law Enforcement and Administration of Justice (1967); the National Advisory Commission on Civil Disorders, known as the Kerner Commission (1968); Cox Commission (1968); Knapp Commission (1970); the National Advisory Commission on Higher Education for Police Officers, known as the Sherman Commission (1978); the National Advisory Commission on Criminal Justice Standards and Goals (1973); Commission on Accreditation for Law Enforcement Agencies (1982); the Mollen Commission, (1990); and the Christopher Commission (1991) (Dempsey and Forst, 2014; Cox et al., 2014).

After the September 11, 2001, terrorist attacks on US soil where America's military and economic symbolisms (the Pentagon and the World Trade Center), were destroyed and over three thousand Americans and other nationals died, as a result of the attacks, the US government instituted a National Commission on Terrorist Attacks Upon the United States (better known as the 9-11 Commission), to investigate what happened, why it happened, and what could be done to prevent such attacks in the future. After a few months' deliberations, the Commission came up with its findings and recommendations, which were immediately implemented by the Bush administration. One of the Commission's findings was that there was communications break-down between various federal intelligence and law enforcement agencies. The Commission's report revealed that several federal agencies knew that some people of Arab extraction were planning to attack the United States but this vital information was not shared among the agencies that would have investigated such information until the execution of the attacks. It was learned that some of these individuals were learning how to fly aircrafts, but not how to land them.

Based on the analyses, the Commission recommended the restructure of the federal law enforcement and intelligence agencies, which led to the creation of the Department of Homeland Security (DHS) now housing twenty-two Departments and Agencies with a workforce of over 240,000 employees (*DHS Website:* http://www.dhs.gov). The Commission also recommended that an Office of the Director of National Intelligence (ODNI) be created. This recommendation led to the creation of Intelligence Reform and Terrorism Prevention Act of 2004 (IRTPA). President Bush signed the IRTPA into law on December 17, 2004 (*ODNI Website:* http://www.dni.gov/index.php/about/history). The duties of the ODNI, according to the 2004 Act include the following: 1) to serve as principal advisor to the President, the National Security Council, and the Homeland Security Council about intelligence matters related to national security; 2) to serve as head of the sixteen-member Intelligence Community; and 3) to direct and oversee the National Intelligence Programs (*ODNI Website:* http://www.dni.gov). This office was created on April 22, 2005 by the Bush administration. Since its creation, the following individuals have served as DNI under both Presidents Bush and Obama: 1) John Negroponte, (April 21, 2005 to February 13, 2007), serving under George W. Bush; 2) John Michael McConnell, USN (Ret.) (February 13, 2007 to January 27, 2009), serving under George W. Bush and continued with Barack Obama; 3) Dennis C. Blair, USN (Ret.)

(January 29, 2009 to May 28, 2010), serving under Barack Obama; 4) David C. Gompert (May 28, 2010 to August 5, 2010), serving under Barack Obama; and 5) Lt. Gen. James R. Clapper USAF (Ret.) (August 5, 2010 to present), serving under Barack Obama *(Wikipedia, the Free Encyclopedia, 2014; ODNI Website: http://www.dni.gov).*

The above narratives are examples of how a functional government integrates the findings and recommendations of Commissions of Inquiries into public policy formulations for the purpose of promoting good governance and enhancing democratic processes. The Nigerian government can no longer turn a blind eye on the importance of these Commissions or ignore their usefulness in public policy making. At fifty five years of Independence, Nigeria should not be relying solely on Sovereign National Conferences as the only legitimate instrument of solving national problems. For sure, Nigeria cannot afford to be paying the jumbo salaries and bonuses of the 471 (House of Representatives 362; and House Senate 109) members of the National Assembly, and the Office of the president, when their crucial work is being performed by another entity.

The reason this is happening is because the governing elite have failed to do the work they are hired to do. The National Assembly discharges its functions through Committees. How can the National Assembly legislate, when it keeps ignoring Committees' findings and recommendations? How can the president understand the mood of the country when his office refuses to honor the recommendations of the Commission his office created to assist him to deal with problems that may endanger the national security of the country if such problems are not tackled? It is unconscionable for a government to set up a Commission to investigate an issue of national importance and fail to act upon the recommendations put forward by the constituted Commission. Why waste the time and energy of the men and women who spent numerous hours, perhaps weeks and months, and public funds invested in the project in examining such issues, only to trash the reports of the Commission into a dust bin. Behavior of this kind must stop if Nigeria is to move forward for a better tomorrow. The Nigerian government should understand that Commissions of Inquiries are important tools that assist governments in making good decisions, and their relevancy on policy identifications and policy formulations cannot be underestimated or overlooked.

Making Self-Reliance a National Ethos

It is said that nations may be politically independent, but economically they are not. Economically, nations depend on each other for their survival. This notion is borne out of the interdependency theory, which explains that no country is an island to itself. However, there are times when nations must strive for self-reliance, especially when it comes to the issue of national security. Under such circumstances, nation-states should not place their safety and security in the hands of other nations. This is the reason why nation-states have defense forces to ensure that their territorial boundaries are not penetrated or violated by outside forces. Additionally, nation-states have internal security mechanisms that will curb disruptive behaviors that might endanger the peace of their societies.

What this means literally is that every country no matter its size must engage in activities that will enable it to promote self-help in order to avoid a situation where erupt or aggressive behaviors of other nations will undermine its territorial integrity and sovereignty. A nation cannot place its corporate existence purely in the hands of other nations and expect those nations to guarantee its safety and security without something in return. This is not the way it works on the world stage; it is "I for myself and God for us all." There is always a "quid pro quo" principle in place before a nation does something for another. A country must be self-sufficient militarily and economically, including being politically stable in order to avoid being on the peripheral. Without these factors, a country cannot strengthen and maintain its national security and cannot prevent other nations, especially the powerful ones, from taking advantage of such a nation.

As previously noted in some sections of this book, Nigerian government has never promoted or encouraged self-reliance in the country. It depends solely on foreign countries for virtually everything. Total dependency on foreign goods, for example, has caused many Nigerians to hate Nigerian-made goods; they see Nigerian-made goods as inferior products that have no value. This is why the country has become a dumping ground for foreign goods. Many Nigerians also prefer being who they are not; they are not proud of their existence as people with a rich history and culture. They promote foreign cultures at the expense of theirs. Because of this mindset, some Nigerian indigenous languages and cultures are becoming extinct. Nigerians are "copycats" who embrace the cultures of other people that do not recognize them nor respect them as equal human beings. The notion that Nigeria cannot do better (the inferiority mindset) is deeply responsible for the Nigerian upper and middle class frequently flying overseas for medical treatment, while at home, the Nigerian health industry is left to deteriorate. The same could be said about Nigerian education. These false images have become noticeable in the country, prompting the Jonathan administration to do something to minimize the damage. To reverse this trend, the administration came up with a program known as the "rebranding of Nigeria," an effort that neither went anywhere nor accomplished anything.

There are huge consequences for a nation that depends heavily on other countries for its survival, as Nigeria is now witnessing. The criminal activities of Boko Haram have, indeed, exposed the rot in the Nigerian military, leading to the country's weaknesses, vulnerability, ineffectiveness, and non-performance. The Nigerian Armed Forces, which the country spent tens of billions of Naira to build over the years, cannot dislodge or defeat Boko Haram, a rag-tag militant group that has destabilized the Northeastern part of the country and has seriously threatened to destabilize the whole country.

This is an institution that brags about the number of Army Generals, Navy Rear Admirals, Vice Admirals, and Air Marshals and Vice Marshals it has within its ranks, yet the Nigerian Armed Forces are unable to put Boko Haram out of business. The irony here is that many of these Generals, Admirals, and Marshals have not been battle tested, there are three main reasons the country's armed forces are unable to defeat the insurgents. First, many moles who pledged their allegiance and loyalty to the Boko Haram, and often sabotage the efforts made by the Nigerian military to engage the insurgents, have been detected among the Nigerian troops fighting Boko Haram in the Northeastern part of the country.

Unfortunately, many of the Nigerian soldiers who were reportedly killed by members of Boko Haram met their demise because of the intelligence the Islamic group received from these moles (military saboteurs). The clandestine activity of these military saboteurs prompted the President of the Church of Christ in Nations, Rev. Dachollom Datiri, to conclude that "the war against insurgency in the country cannot be won because of corruption and the existence of saboteurs in the military."

He claimed, as others have alluded to, that military saboteurs were frustrating the efforts to fight the Boko Haram insurgency and, that the Nigerian military had continued to show that it was incapable of stamping out insurgency in the country. This unpatriotic behavior makes one wonder as to whose interest and loyalty these soldiers (moles) are serving. These were soldiers who took oaths to defend the country from its enemies, but when "push comes to shove," they turn their back on the country and switch allegiance to the country's enemy.

Second, Nigerians have been reading from their daily newspapers about how some Nigerian troops are abandoning their locations and weapons and fleeing to neighboring countries like Cameroon for safety. There was a *Nigerian Punch Newspaper* article published on August 26, 2014, which claimed that 480 Nigerian soldiers fled into Cameroon following fierce fighting with Boko Haram (Soriwei, Nnodim, Idowu, 2014). Another *Nigerian Punch Newspaper* article published on November 3, 2014, reported that the Nigerian Army arrested six military commanders, including an injured Lieutenant Colonel for withdrawing their troops from Mararaba, Michika, Madagali, Mubi and Vimtim, when Boko Haram attacked these communities. The withdrawal of these commands from those communities, according to the Newspaper article, made it easy for the insurgents to gain the upper hand in those areas.

Third, the Nigerian armed forces are unable to defeat Boko Haram because they lack modern weaponry to fight such a sophisticated and formidable enemy. Sheikh Ahmad Abubakar Mahmud Gumi, a retired military officer, has this to say: "Boko Haram is getting empowered and protected, while the Nigerian Army is decaying." The retired army officer claimed that, "the reason the Nigerian army is decaying is because there is an internal force sapping the energy of the institution." To substantiate his claim that the huge military budgets meant to equip the Nigerian

Armed Forces with modern weaponry were embezzled by top military leaders, Ahmad Abubakar Mahmud Gumi was quoted, in *the Daily Sun Newspaper* article published on November 16, 2014, as saying the following:

> Historically, the Nigerian Army has been an avenue for siphoning billions of Naira by our Generals. All the money earmarked for weapons is stolen by our Generals. They are already intoxicated by it. It is like people dealing in cocaine, can you stop them? I could remember when the Infantry Divisions were converted to Mechanized Infantry Divisions; I was in the army myself, then. By that, it meant soldiers would no longer go on foot for operations, but move in Amoured Personnel Carriers (APCs). But in a whole Division, you find only three APCs and these three APCs were refurbished after the Second World War. But look at the billions of Naira that have been stolen in the past, in the name of equipping these Divisions. The truth is that there was never a truly full Mechanized Division (Omipidan, 2014).

Decades of looting the Nigerian Armed Forces funding have tremendously weakened the institution's resolve and ability to confront an adversary like Boko Haram militarily. If previous Nigerian administrations had utilized the appropriated military budgets to procure modern military weapons that the Nigerian armed forces desperately needed to confront an enemy like Boko Haram, the Jonathan administration would have cared less whether or not the US government sold its weapons to Nigeria to fight Boko Haram. The inability of the Nigerian military to defeat Boko Haram's insurgency has now emboldened the Islamic sect whose atrocities have spread beyond the Nigerian borders, making the conflict a regional one.

Boko Haram's mayhem has attracted the attention of four neighboring countries, which include Nigeria, Cameroon, Niger, and Chad. These countries have formed a military alliance to eliminate this terror group from their borders, and the country of Niger is expected to join the alliance for the same objective.

The inability of the Nigerian military to dislodge Boko Haram has also led to a blaming game by some members of the Jonathan administration and by some prominent Nigerians over the United States government refusal to sell its weapons to Nigeria to fight Boko Haram.

One of the Jonathan's administration's outspoken critics of the US government over the issue is the Nigerian Ambassador to the United States, Prof. Adebowale Ibidapo Adefuye. The Nigerian Ambassador claimed that the US government refusal to sell its weapons to Nigeria was frustrating Nigeria's war against Boko Haram. He argued that such refusal to grant Nigeria's request to purchase lethal equipment has impeded Nigeria's efforts "that would have brought down the terrorists within a short time." Prof. Adefuye was further quoted in the *Nigerian Punch Newspaper* article published on November 13, 2014, as saying the following:

Our people are not very happy with the content of America's support in the struggle against the Boko Haram sect. The terrorists threaten our corporate existence and territorial integrity. There is no use giving us the type of support that enables us to deliver light jabs to the terrorists when what we need to give them is the killer punch. A friend in need is a friend indeed. The true test of friendship is in the times of adversity....We find it difficult to understand how and why in spite of the US presence in Nigeria with their sophisticated military technology the Boko Haram sect should be expanding and becoming more deadly. At first, we had problems with the manner in which intelligence was being shared. The allegations that Nigeria's defense forces have been violating human rights of Boko Haram suspects when captured or arrested are not true. I am sad to inform you that the Nigerian leadership: military and political, and even the general populace, are not satisfied with the scope, nature and content of the United States' support for us in our struggle against terrorists (Eniola, 2014).

The above-articulated outrage was immediately refuted by the US Ambassador to Nigeria, James Entwistle, who claimed that "his country has not cut off military assistance to Nigeria." The US envoy further argued that his country has not reneged on its pledge to empower Nigeria in its fight against terrorism, claiming that his country has supported Nigeria in both training and logistics, a statement reechoed by the US Secretary of State, John Kerry, when he visited Nigeria on January 25, 2015. Kerry told his audience that the US stood firmly with the Nigeria government in its effort to defeat Boko Haram militarily. Additionally, the US Ambassador to Nigeria, told his Nigerian audience that his country has requirements on arms sale, which every country must meet before a deal is sealed. Nigeria, according to the Ambassador, did not meet the criteria for the sale of arms, but cautioned that such a failure should not be interpreted to imply that the US is cutting off military assistance to Nigeria.

The US government based its decision not to sell its modern weapons to Nigeria on the grounds that the Nigerian military violated the human rights of Boko Haram's suspects and the non-protection of civilians' lives in the combat areas it conducts its military operations. Furthermore, the US authorities claimed that their concerns were communicated directly to the Nigerian government and nothing changed. Consequently, the US government believes that the activities of the Nigerian military in the Northeastern Nigeria violate the US law (the Leahy Law on Human rights, 1997) that bans the sale of US lethal weapons or aid to countries whose military are accused of gross human rights abuses. In defending his country's decision not to sell to Nigeria the weapons it needs to fight the insurgents, the US Ambassador to Nigeria reminded Nigerians that defeating terrorism requires more than just military power. According to the seasoned diplomat, defeating terrorism in Nigeria requires addressing the following issues:

It requires protecting civilian populations despite the fact that terrorists don't. It requires working to develop impoverished areas where extremism takes root. It requires that education is accessible to all. It requires empowering a free and fair press to report openly and without fear of reprisal. And, perhaps most importantly, it requires engaging the growing youth populations that are being swayed towards terrorism due to lack of economic opportunities, education and distrust of government. It requires a comprehensive, whole-of-government approach (Iyatse, 2014).

Additionally, the spokesperson for the US State Department, Jen Psaki, defended her country's refusal to sell cobra helicopters to Nigeria, saying that Nigeria was free to buy fighter jets from any country. She went on to say that, "Nigeria has purchased helicopters that originated in countries other than the US and nothing in our decision prevents Nigeria from obtaining weapons and equipment from other countries" (Adepegba and Owuamanam, 2014).

The refusal of the US authorities to sell its weapons to Nigeria because of the alleged violation of the human rights of Boko Haram's suspects by the Nigerian military was not well received by some prominent Nigerians. For example, Nigeria's second military Head of State, Gen. Yakubu Gowon, took a swipe at the United States for refusing to sell its arms to Nigeria to fight the insurgency of the Islamic group, Boko Haram. In his own words, General Gowon concluded that America has never been Nigeria's friend. He went on to say that his regime had a similar experience with the US government during the Nigerian-Biafran War, which happened during his watch—a war that began in 1967 and ended in 1970. The longest serving military Head of State in Nigerian military history had this to say about Nigerian-US relations during the Nigerian Civil War:

> The same thing happened during the Civil War. The Americans refused to sell arms to us. I wanted them to help me with some modest aircraft so that I could chase out Ojukwu's [Col. Odumegwu Ojukwu] B52 or B56 as they called it. That was all I wanted; not to shoot it down but to chase it away so that it does not drop bombs and kill innocent people. But the Americans refused to help us and they even refused to sell us arms and ammunitions and the spare parts of the equipment that we got from them. And at the same time they [the Americans] were shipping aircraft and loads of arms and ammunition to Zaire. What sort of friends are they? You call them your friends and they say that they helping us to fight terror. We don't want their people [the Americans] to come and fight the war against Boko Haram for us but, at least we need the equipment.... During my time [as Head of State], I had to go the Russians to get the equipment we wanted in order to prosecute the war. If they cannot help us, they should allow us to go elsewhere and get what we want to ensure that we deal with this particular problem (Adepegba and Owuamanam, 2014).

The Nobel Laureate, Prof. Wole Soyinka did not want to see this outrageous remark made by Washington to go by without making his feelings known publicly. Like most Nigerians, he asked the United States to stop giving excuses on why it would not supply arms to Nigeria. He reminded the Americans that what Nigeria needs are not emergency relief materials, but support to win the war against terror. The Laureate was quoted in the *Daily Sun Newspaper* of December 3, 2014, as saying:

> Please, United States of America, could you please, overlook the arithmetical deficiency of governance and stop giving an excuse to this government for failing to protect us. We are trying to create, I hope, a situation where we do have conflict affected households. We do not need emergency relief supplies. We want to stop the displacement of humanity. So, please, just say that you will not supply arms to Nigeria and leave it at that. But don't say that instead you will send other things. That is not the issue at this critical moment for Nigeria. We are fighting a legitimate, a just war (Orji, 2014).

The emergency relief supplies Professor Soyinka referred to in his commentary are the humanitarian programs, intelligence, and strategic assistance the US government claimed to have delivered to Nigeria in an effort to address the underlying causes of terrorism in the country. According to the US authorities in Nigeria, the assistance focuses on Religious Freedom, civilian security, and the needs of the victimized communities, especially those in Northeastern Nigeria. The lists of the assistance delivered to the Nigerian government, according to the US authorities in Nigeria, included the following:

- The sum of $19 million provided to vulnerable and conflict-affected households in Nigeria.

- The sum of more than $7 million from the US Agency for International Development's (USAID) Office of Foreign Disaster Assistance to support health, water and sanitation services, and the delivery of emergency relief supplies and protection activities for women and children in North-eastern Nigeria.

- An additional sum of $7 million from the USAID /Food for peace to provide emergency food assistance.

- The sum of more than $5 million of the US Department of State to fund protection activities in the affected areas.

- The sum of more than $54 million in humanitarian assistance provided to Cameroon, Chad and Niger, targeting the refugee populations from the neighboring countries, including Nigeria.

- The sum of about $20 million to $30 million to fund a 'crisis response' program that administers basic education to internally-displaced persons and others affected by the violence in the North-east, including Bauchi, Gombe, and Adamawa states.

- A flagship program leading to a five-year education project that will strengthen the systems to provide greater access and learning for primary school children, principally in Sokoto and Bauchi, and other states of the North as conditions allow.

Source: *Nigerian Punch Reporters* (Adepegba and Owuamanam, 2014).

Another prominent Nigerian who disagreed with the US government's accusation that the Nigerian military was in violation of the human rights of civilians in the Northeastern part of the country, where military operations are on-going, was the former Nigerian External Affairs Minister, Prof. Bolaji Akinyemi, who argued passionately that "the Nigerian military has been fighting with one hand tied behind its back as the Northern establishment was until recently opposed to a military solution to the Boko Haram insurgents. Long after the objectives of the Boko Haram had been spelt out by them; there was still plenty of self-denial in appraising the Boko Haram."

What the distinguished Professor was referring to, was the unpatriotic attitude of the Northern establishment that condoned Boko Haram's atrocities and carnage during the group's initial stage of mayhem in Northeastern Nigeria. For example, when the Islamic group directed its anger and venom on Christians and Southerners in Northern Nigeria, the Northern establishment kept quiet and did not condemn such cowardly acts of violence. When the Federal Government of Nigeria took a military action against the group after it refused to accept an amnesty deal offered to it by the Nigerian government, the Northern establishment accused the Nigerian military of war crimes (ethnic cleansing and genocide) and threatened to take the Army Chief and a few other persons to the International Criminal Court in The Hague. When there were few Southerners and Christian targets in the North to attack, Boko Haram unleashed its anger and venom, this time, on fellow Muslims and their institutions.

These unspeakable acts of violence against Northern Muslims have gotten the attention of the Northern establishment who now realize that the "cancer tumor" (Boko Haram) they helped to create can no longer be controlled. It is affecting everybody in the area and knows no friend or foe. The inability of the Northern establishment to control the Islamic sect has prompted some elements of the establishment to urge Northern Muslims to unite against the elimination of the cancer. Boko Haram's recent attacks on Muslims and their institutions have also forced the establishment to sing a different tune. This time, they are accusing the Nigerian government of not doing enough to stop Boko Haram's mayhem. They accused the Jonathan administration of playing politics with Boko Haram's atrocities because the administration wants to win the 2015 Presidential election by all means necessary. The very establishment that accused the Jonathan administration of being anti-North, anti-Moslem, and an administration that committed genocide against the Northern people, is now urging the Nigerian government, "to take decisive actions that would portray the government as serious in its anti-terrorism crusade." They are saying this now because, "the chicken has come home to roost;" the bad seed they sowed for others is now hurting them.

In advancing his argument against the Americans' concerns over the human rights abuses committed by the Nigerian military, Prof. Bolaji Akinyemi was vividly quoted in the *Nigerian Vanguard Newspaper* article published on November 30, 2014, as making the following remarks:

> Continuing references to human rights violations by the Nigerian military will carry more credibility if they come from the Vatican which gave up fighting wars centuries ago, than from the United States whose favourite weapon, the drone, makes no distinction between civilians and combatants. I believe the term "collateral damage" was coined by Colin Powell to justify the often appalling civilian casualties that resulted from United States military activities abroad.... What the United States needs to do is to cut Nigeria some slack and stop irritating comments whether by scholars or diplomats (Akinyemi, 2014).

It is understandable if the United States government chooses not to sell its arms to the Nigerian government to combat Boko Haram's terror activities in the country. In general terms, the US government has the right to sell its military weapons to whomever it chooses, and Nigeria also has the right to buy weapons from any country of its choice. But, for the US government to use human rights violation of suspected Boko Haram's insurgents held in custody and the number of civilians killed in the combat areas of Northeastern Nigeria as a basis to deny its arms sale to Nigeria is purely hypocritical (double standard) and, at best, questionable, when the US government has, on many occasions, violated its own sacred laws that, "ban the sale of US lethal weapons or aid to countries whose military are accused of gross human rights abuses."

It is interesting to note how quickly the US government justifies its military operations abroad, especially when such operations involve huge civilian casualties. In justifying the huge civilian causalities resulting from US military operations in countries it invades, Washington always claims that, "nicety things happen in wars; that civilians are sometimes killed in wars and; that such ugly situations, are true nature of wars." The irony here is that the US authorities do not see "collateral damage" as a nature of war, when such acts are committed by other countries. For Americans, "collateral damage" or civilian deaths committed by another country during wars are gross human rights violations, which amount to war crimes or genocide. But such acts (collateral damage or civilian deaths) are seen as a normal phenomenon or a nature of war when committed by the US government. Truly, nicety things happen during wars, including human rights violations because war machines, including bullets, do not distinguish who the combatants are from non-combatants (civilians), just like Professor Akinyemi alluded above. This is why wars in general must be avoided if the human rights of innocent people are to be respected and preserved during wars.

Let's take the US war against global terrorism as an example. Such a military venture did not protect nor respect the human rights of civilians in places where these wars were being fought. Many innocent people have been indiscriminately killed by the US military tanks, F-16 fighter jets, cobra helicopters, and drones in places like Iraq, Afghanistan, Pakistan, Yemen, Somalia, and in some parts of Syria, where wars against global terrorism are raging, and these civilian casualties are viewed by the US authorities as "collateral damage" and not seen as human rights violations.

Most importantly, many people, both inside and outside the United States, believed the US government when it said that, "America does not torture," but a different picture emerged, when in 2014, a US Senate report on torture revealed that the CIA used torture techniques, known within the US intelligence community as "an enhanced interrogation technique and rendition program," to extract information (intelligence) from the so-called terrorists whom the US government accused of masterminding the 9-11 attacks on US soil on September 11, 2001. The report also revealed that the human rights of many of the individuals detained in US custody who had nothing to do with the incident of 9-11, were violated by the torture team.

Another irony to this saga is that the US government has been authorizing the sale of its arms to governments and groups around the world that violated the Leahy Law on Human rights. For example, the US government authorizes the sale of its modern weapons to the government of Israel, when Washington knew that such weapons were used in violating the human rights of the Palestinians in the occupied territories (West Bank, Gaza, and Golan Heights). Additionally, the US government has frequently used its United Nations Security Council's (UNSC) veto to block any UN measures that grants and legitimizes Palestinian's statehood—a move that would have curbed Israelis' flagrant violation of Palestinians' human rights. By the same token, the US government authorizes the sale of its weapons to the Egyptian government when Washington knew that such weapons were used in abusing the human rights of the Islamic Brotherhood whom the Egyptian government has repeatedly accused of trying to overthrow the Egyptian secular government.

The US government turned a blind eye to a military coup led by Gen. Abdel Fattah el-Sisi that ousted a democratically elected government in Egypt on July 3, 2013, a government headed by President Mohamed Morsi. It also turned a blind eye to other flagrant abuses and suppressions of political dissidents in Egypt, including the false imprisonment of journalists who were doing their job. The reason the US government compromised its laws and values in Egypt is because the state of Israel is fully supported and sustained with Egyptian energy and Egyptian military, including the Egyptian government headed by Hosni Mubarak and Abdel Fattah el-Sisi. The story is the same in Saudi Araba, Jordan, and Bahrain, where US weapons are often used to suppress the political aspirations of those people who are genuinely demanding the democratization of these countries.

Additionally, the US government had authorized the sale of its arms, in a program known as military aid assistance, to other Third World countries and such weapons were used in fomenting social unrests (Civil Wars), particularly in countries the US government perceived to have a Communist leaning. A case in point was Nicaragua, where the US government under President Ronald Reagan armed the Contras to overthrow a democratically elected government, the Sandinista government, headed by Daniel Ortega. The same experiences happened in places like Angola and in other parts of Southern Africa where US weapons were used by white minority governments to counter, disrupt, and defeat the aspiration of the African Liberation Movements in the region.

If the US government was truly committed and concerned about human rights protection of the oppressed and was interested in strengthening its democratic values in these regions of the world, Washington would not be providing white minority governments with arms to suppress the people from seeking political independence and freedom. If the US government was truly committed and concerned about human rights protection of the civilian population, Washington would not be invading independent countries under the pretense of what it terms as "regime change," because such military operations in those places and regions often violate the human rights of innocent civilians whom the US government claims to protect.

What we do know is that the US national interest has always trumpeted human rights and democracy; these values are often disregarded by the US government when its national interest is at stake. Whenever the US national interest is challenged, the protection and promotion of human rights and democracy are thrown overboard. What we have noticed is that the US government always hid behind the defense of human rights and democracy to escape the sledge hammer of International and Humanitarian Law whenever the enforcement of such a law does not favor US interest. The definition of International Law was best articulated by Abba Eban, an Israeli former Ambassador to the United States during the 1950s. In his own words, the preeminent Ambassador described International Law as, "the law which the wicked do not obey and which the righteous do not enforce" (Glahn, 1986:4).

The refusal of the US government to sell its Cobra helicopter to Nigeria in its effort to defeat Boko Haram militarily must be a wake-up call for the Nigerian government. Such a disappointment might make Nigeria realize that no country should rely solely on other countries for its own security and survival. The US State Department spokesperson, Jennifer Psaki, was absolutely right when she said that Nigeria was free to buy its fighter jets from any country of its own choosing. Blaming the US government for its refusal to sell its Cobra helicopter to Nigeria does not make sense at all. Nigeria is rich and old enough to have its own weapon manufacturing industry, at least, for the defense of its territorial integrity and the protection of its own national interest. This is what self-reliance means.

If the huge amount of money spent annually in procuring military hardware and other weaponry from other countries is invested in the local arms manufacturing industry, such a monumental effort would have made a tremendous impact on the nation's economy and on its national pride.

Nigeria should not be afraid to embark on a project of this nature; it makes economic sense, and it enhances and strengthens the country's national security. Additionally, it creates a meaningful job and enhances the skills of Nigerian workers. An industry of this nature will absorb many Nigerian engineers, chemists and other scientists who are graduating from Nigerian Universities and whose talents can be tapped and developed if such an industry exists. Nigeria is experiencing huge brain drains because this kind of industry does not exist. Individuals who have skills in weapon design and production are migrating to countries where such expertise and skills are highly needed. A creation of an arms industry will also lead to the creation of other industries like the iron and steel industry.

Nigeria cannot be industrialized without this vital industry. The establishment of the Ajaokuta Steel Industry by the Obasanjo regime in 1979 and commissioned by Alhaji Shehu Shagari's administration in the early 1980s, was to spur the nation's industrial growth, but unfortunately this vital industry has been neglected and mismanaged by many Nigerian administrations that did not understand the basic concept of the steel industry and its impact on a nation building effort. Because these administrations did not fully understand what the steel industry meant for the country's manufacturing base, they privatized the industry and allowed Indian companies to take ownership of it. This arrangement has seriously impeded the operation and completion of the Ajaokuta Steel plant; thereby delaying any hope of creating an arms manufacturing industry in the country and other related industries.

On a sad note, Nigeria's reliance on a petro economy has backfired since its largest oil importer, the United States, has stopped buying Nigerian oil. It is said that since the end of OPEC's oil embargo of the 1970s, the US government has been importing oil at the peak of 1.3 million barrels of oil per day from Nigeria until July of 2014, when the Obama administration ordered the stoppage of oil importation from Nigeria.

In defending the Obama administration decision to end US oil import from Nigeria, the White House Economic Council Director, Jeff Zients, noted that the US oil production has ramped up significantly by more than 50 percent to over eight and a half million barrels of oil per day. He further claimed that such a high turnout in local US oil production has now dramatically reduced US dependency on oil imports. It was the Director's considered opinion that the United States produces more oil than it imports (Akande, 2014).

Nigeria was warned repeatedly by many economic analysts that, depending on oil money as the only means of generating wealth for the country would be counterproductive, if the country does not diversify its economy. But, Nigeria's government never heeded this advice and never planned for the rainy day. They knew that a day like this would come, but they did nothing to prevent it from manifesting. This is, indeed, a big lesson for policy makers in Nigeria to learn that the huge sum of money generated from oil over the years should have been used to create other revenue generating sources for the country, but they decided to rely heavily on oil revenue instead.

Nigerian leaders should always think big and should operate outside of the box for most of the time. More importantly they should be more proactive and adapt to the changing environment. The austerity measures imposed on the country during the oil glut of the mid-1970s should have served as a great lesson. During that time, many Nigerians suffered economically as a result of the glut which came without a warning.

While the Obasanjo regime asked the Nigerian masses (the poor) to tighten their belts, the elite class loosened theirs. It is the poor who always suffer the most when there is an economic downturn, resulting from bad national economic policies and corporate greed. Nigerian leaders should do better in fulfilling the aspirations of their fellow country men and women. To do so, they must be flexible in their thinking and be more receptive to new ideas and changes. These are some of the expectations that most Nigerians demand from their leaders. The two above highlighted scenarios (the refusal of the US to sell its arms to Nigeria and the stoppage of US oil importation from Nigeria) should make the Nigerian leaders realize that there is a great need for the country to embrace self-reliance as a vital means of sustaining the country's social, political, and economic forces.

PART FIVE

A BLUEPRINT FOR ACTION

Chapter 8

POLICY IDENTIFICATIONS AND PROPOSALS

Notwithstanding the enormous challenges facing the country which, in most cases, are man-made, Nigeria has made some useful strides on many fronts since its existence as a nation. All the country needs now, is how to get Nigerians of all persuasions but, more so, the political class to assist the country in achieving greatness and taking its rightful place in the comity of nations. As noted in the introductory phase of this book, Nigeria has enormous potentials both in natural resources and in human capital, but the country's main problems are how to utilize these resources to enhance the quality of life of average Nigerians and, how to reposition the country to achieve global competitiveness, greatness, recognition, and respect. The question here is how will Nigeria truly become "the giant of Africa," a label often used to describe her? These socio-economic attributes cannot be achieved given the way the country is being governed presently. Nigeria can only accomplish these tasks by adopting a new strategy, approach, or orientation.

What the country desperately needs now in order to solidify its national unity, avoid disintegration; achieve global greatness and competitiveness, and enhance the quality of life of the Nigerian citizens, is simply to embrace Good Governance, which is the cornerstone of every modern society. Good Governance is achieved by recognizing and nurturing core human values and decencies, which include the following: civility and respect for humanity and other individual rights (such as freedom of speech, freedom of religion, and freedom of the press); an inclusive government; respect for the rule of law and due process of law; ensuring transparency; holding government operatives accountable for their actions. Good Governance guarantees the stability of a country. Generally, it calls for a shared responsibility.

Policy Identifications

Here are things that must be done to get Nigeria on the right track. From this extensive study, here are problems that pose serious threats or impediment to the country's stability and growth. Below are issues the study has identified as impediments to the country's stability and growth:

On the social realm, the study has identified the following problems causing hindrance to the sustainability of Nigeria's national unity, political stability, socio-economic growth and global competitiveness:

- Ethnic and religious intolerance;
- Non-government commitment to quality public education;
- Non-government commitment to quality public health care;
- No national institution created to harmonize the differences found amongst ethnic nationalities in Nigerian;
- Inadequate number of states to address the imbalance found amongst ethnic nationalities in the country;
- No provision for state and municipal police agencies in the country;
- No provision for state prisons and local jails in the country;
- Granting self-rule (Home Rule Charter) to local governments;
- Poor performance of Nigerian criminal justice and other security agencies; and
- Compulsory retirement of public servants from states not considered as their states of origin.

On the economic front, the study identified the following problems, as issues causing impediments to the country's economic growth and global greatness:

- Inadequate protection of bank customers' deposits;
- Massive unemployment for both skilled and unskilled workers in Nigeria;
- No government incentives for indigenous businesses and corporations;
- No administrative body to coordinate the activities of small and medium size indigenous businesses;
- Insufficient excellent quality infrastructures (no good roads and bridges, no good transportation network, airports and seaports, stadiums and recreation centers, no constant energy supplies, and telecommunication networks); and
- Too much dependency on foreign entities, which undermines the concept of self-reliance and self-help in the country.

On the political realm, the study identified the following problems, as issues hampering the country's national unity, political stability, and the country's global recognition and respect:

- Massive bribery and corruption in the public sector of the country;
- The misuse of the immunity clause by the offices of the president, governors, legislators, and local governments' chairpersons;
- No provision for a part-time legislature in both national and state assemblies, and local government councils;
- No provision for whistle-blowers in the system;
- No provision banning convicted politicians or government officials from active politics or from government posts;
- No provision for a two-party system in the country, rather than what the country has now, non-performing multi-party system;
- No provision banning individuals, groups, and corporations from financing political campaigns in the country;
- No provision banning political thuggery in the polity
- No provision banning the use of security officials in electoral processes
- Inadequate use of commissions of inquiries in solving national problems.

Policy Proposals

Based on the above identified problems or hindrances to the sustainability of Nigeria as a viable country, the study offers the following policy proposals as a means of avoiding further deterioration of the country's social, economic and political fabric. The above identified issues are issues many Nigerians are too familiar with and although some well deserving and meaningful Nigerians have touched on some of these, what this study tries to do is to lend support to those claims and to highlight the negative impacts these issues may have on Nigeria's polity if left unattended or unresolved. Whatever is proposed here may not be a cure-for-all but a building block to what may have existed before. The issues raised here are steps in the right direction, as nations' problems are not solved with a single bullet or solved in one day; solving a nation's problems has always been an on-going process. Below are policy proposals articulated in this study:

1. The study proposes that quality public education and health care in Nigeria be made a human right issue and be enshrined in the federal and state Constitutions as guaranteed free entitlements to all Nigerians.

Justifications for Proposing Policy #1

Quality public education and health care are the main pillars of any progressive society. No nation advances both politically and economically without educated and healthy citizenry. Countries do not develop nor does democracy flourish with ignorant people. The advanced countries, for instance, made their marks by embracing these vital social programs and refused to be governed by ignorance and superstition. Information Technology of the twenty-first century demands for an educated and healthy work force. Because of their unique importance in the scheme of things, progressive societies place high premium on quality education and health care above other priorities, by investing heavily in them and making them accessible to all citizens. The successful implementation of these high quality social programs provided by most governments was achieved through government subsidies or by making them free for all.

As noted in some sections of this book and as many Nigerians have come to acknowledge, quality public education and health care have not been accorded the priority they deserve in the country's scheme of things. Governments' lack of commitment to public education and health care has made these vital social programs a mockery in the country. Nigeria will not be a great country and will not compete globally as long as public education and health care remain neglected and relegated to the back burner. By making public education and health care a Constitutional issue, the federal and state governments will no longer undermine these important sectors of the economy, and will no longer rob the Nigerian people, especially the children, of the good life they must have. The country's workforce will double its output and grow healthier if public education and health care are given the priorities they deserve. Public education and health care will spur the Nigerian workforce to embark on human activities that will be beneficial to the people.

Making public education and health care a Constitutional issue will force both federal and state governments to pay adequate attention to these programs. Investing much in these programs and placing them at the top of governments' priority will definitely stabilize public education and health in the country. Such an effort will induce federal and state governments to intensify their involvement and commitment to these programs. Such an involvement and commitment will raise the quality and standard of these programs and will lower the tempo of industrial actions and lockouts that have marred these sectors for decades.

Implications of not implementing Policy Proposal #1

If governments' lack of funding and commitment to public education and health care persist, these vital social institutions will seriously fade away or deteriorate further. Teachers and staff in both institutions (education and health) will embark on more industrial strikes and lockouts. Such governmental non-commitment will force more Nigerian professionals from both institutions to migrate to advanced countries, where their skills and expertise are highly needed. More Nigerian children will be left uneducated and more Nigerians including the young and the old will die from preventable and curable diseases because of inadequate health care facilities, equipment, and lack of experienced health practitioners and professionals. It is unconscionable that the Nigerian governing elite are not concerned or worried about losing over twenty-five thousands of its medical professionals to the United States alone, and not those in Europe. There will be enormous consequences to bear if the Nigerian governments fail to address these debilitating problems.

Failure to address such endemic problems will encourage more well-to-do Nigerians to send their children to Ivy League institutions in North America and Europe. And more well-to-do Nigerians, including the political class, will be encouraged to travel abroad frequently for medical treatments. It makes good economic policy, if the huge amount of money that Nigerians are willing to pay for foreign medical services, is reinvested into the country's economy. It also makes good economic policy if Nigerian governments could adequately develop these social institutions. Such an effort will attract more foreigners to Nigeria for the same reason many Nigerians are attracted to advanced countries.

2. The study proposes that more legislation be enacted to strengthen the peace and stability of the country, given the current instability in some parts of the country.

a) The legislation should outlaw **ethnic and religious intolerance** that is destroying the social fabric of the country. While Nigerians should be allowed to practice any religion of their choice, they should not be allowed to use such a body to intimidate, coerce, degrade, or make mockery of other faiths. The legislation should persuade all Nigerians to embrace tolerance and respect of the differences existing among and in-between them.

b) Nigerians of all persuasions should be reminded that no Nigerian chooses to be born into a particular ethnic nationality. They must recognize that being born into a particular ethnic nationality is an act of God, and not by a personal choice. For this purpose, the legislation should outlaw the divisive concept of **majority versus minority** syndrome that has become a pervasive and prevailing norm in the country.

c) The majority-minority concept should not be tolerated and should be made a thing of the past, because it is divisive and polarizing. Nigerians should see each other as equals and as fellow citizens having the same rights and privileges. The legislation should remind all Nigerians that no particular ethnic nationality has the ownership of the country. Nigeria belongs to all of those who reside in it. The leadership of the country should not be a birth right of one particular ethnic nationality. This basic reality must be understood by all ethnic nationalities and religious bodies in the country.

d) To concretize the above-stated ideas and to bring them to a successful and logical conclusion, the legislation must create a **new Federal Ministry** that will ensure that peace and stability reign supreme in the country. The new Federal Ministry should be known or referred to as **the Federal Ministry of Peace**, whose duties shall be to bring together all ethnic nationalities and religious bodies in the country and seriously engage their stakeholders in a series of dialogues to determine empirically and systematically the underlying causes of ethnic and religious tensions in the country. It is also the focus of this Ministry to ensure that ethnic and religious intolerance will never again have a place in Nigeria's social circle.

e) It should also be the responsibility of the new Ministry to articulate programs like conflict resolution strategies, seminars and organized public lectures, and other rewarding incentives that will strengthen the co-existence of all the groups in the country. This Ministry must be a performing and engaging one. It must be well structured, well supported, and well equipped so that its missions and goals will be effectively and efficiently administered. This Ministry must be seen as the glue or thread that brings the country together.

f) The legislation should create more **states and local governments** to ensure that no ethnic nationality is marginalized or relegated to a minority status. The creation of more states in Nigeria should be based on ethnic and linguistic lines. Such an effort will give more voices to the voiceless and allow these groups of Nigerians to determine their own destiny and chart their course without being dictated to either from Abuja or from elsewhere about what to do. The creation of more states and local governments will eliminate the majority versus minority syndrome in the country. It will open up the country's political processes by encouraging mass political participation and grassroots' politics. The creation of more states and local governments will strengthen the national unity of the country, and will ensure the equitable distribution of the country's national wealth.

g) The legislation should broaden and strengthen **the image and performance of the Nigerian Criminal Justice System and other Security Agencies**. The Criminal justice system and other related security agencies are government institutions the political class uses in maintaining law and order and in maintaining peace and stability in the country. The Nigerian Criminal Justice institutions whose responsibilities include law enforcement, law interpretation, and the incarceration of those offenders who are convicted for violating the law of the land, are the true builders and protectors of the nation.

h) Because of the uniqueness of these institutions (the Nigerian Police, Courts, Prison, Nigerian Custom Service, Nigerian Immigration Service, Department of State Service, and other related security agencies in the country), the legislation must ensure that their public negative image, indiscipline, low morale, and poor performance are improved. The politicization of these institutions must be deemphasized. Ethnicity and religion should be deemphasized as a basis for the recruitment of personnel into these institutions. Recruitment and promotion of personnel should be based purely on meritocracy and not on mediocrity or on political patronage (whom you know). The legislation should elevate the career of these institutions to a professional one.

i) To professionalize these institutions, the legislation should ensure that officers and staff (personnel) of the Nigerian Criminal Justice System and other related security agencies are well-educated, with at least, a Baccalaureate Degree in a Social Science discipline, such as law, political science, criminology, psychology, sociology, in conjunction with courses in natural sciences like biology, chemistry, and physiopathology—courses leading to the study of Forensic Sciences.

j) The legislation should ensure that men and women of these institutions are well-trained, well-equipped, and well-paid to avoid being easily corrupted by members of the society. Training in these fields must be continuous and should be focused on the following areas: conflict resolution strategies, technical skills, human relations and interpersonal communication skills. The legislation should ensure that criminal justice and other security professionals are given, as part of their training program, a proper and adequate orientation that would enable them treat Nigerian citizens with dignity and respect, and uphold their constitutional rights. The legislation should ensure that **no Nigerian is detained beyond** the reasonable time-frame allowed by law without trial to determine the guilt or innocence of the accused person.

k) To adequately protect lives and property in Nigeria and to enable the Nigerian Criminal Justice professionals to discharge their constitutional responsibilities effectively, the legislation must **decentralize the Nigerian Police and Prison, and create state and municipal police agencies, including the creation of state prisons and municipal jails.** Given the realities on the ground (the increasing wave of crime and insecurity in the country), the Nigerian Criminal Justice System and other related security agencies have not been able to cope with the endemic security threats, crimes and violence plaguing the country. The reasons for the poor performance of the Nigerian Criminal Justice institutions are their highly centralized structures, the endemic corruption within these institutions, and lack of legislative oversight.

l) The **creation of state police and prisons, and creation of municipal police and jails** will give **state and local governments more responsibilities and autonomy**. The restructure will allow the federal government to concentrate fully on the protection of the country's borders, while it frees itself from the country's internal security, which state and local governments are well positioned to handle. With this new structure, the federal government should be in control of the country's armed forces, the Department of State Service, the Customs Service, the Immigration Service, and other related security agencies that the National Assembly may deem necessary to create. The federal government may intervene in state affairs when states abuse the constitutional rights of their citizens or when states call for assistance from the Central Government.

m) The legislation should give more autonomy to local governments by granting them the **Home Rule Charter** which, in essence, is referred to as a local government constitution. The Home Rule Charter will enable local governments in the country to set up their own system of self-government. It will afford them the opportunity to amend their governmental organization and powers to suit their needs. The Home Rule Charter will enable local governments to operate their own **Local Police and Jails** independently from state governments, but states will have the oversight legislative functions and can intervene in local government affairs when asked to do so. With the Home Rule Charter, local governments should be receiving their monthly or yearly allocations (appropriations) directly from the **Federal Account** and not from state governments, as is currently the practice.

n) Granting local governments a Home Rule Charter will make them more effective and efficient. It will make them more accountable than they have been. Such an arrangement enables Local Governments to conduct **frequent elections of their Chairmen and Councilor**s without states' intervention. The Home Rule Charter will accelerate the infrastructural development of local government areas, and will lessen the burdens placed on state governments. Unfortunately, all these efforts are stalled because of the **Dillon Rule,** a policy currently practiced in Nigeria.

o) In Nigeria, the Dillon Rule allows state governments to dictate whether or not local government elections should be held and in what form. It also allows state governments to be the custodian of local government allocations from the Federal Account—allocations some state governors and some states' House of Assembly members use for events other than their intended purposes. Originating from the United States of America, the **Dillon Rule** is used in interpreting state law when there is a question of whether or not a local government has a certain power.

p) The legislation should also outlaw the **arbitrary retirement of public servants, serving in states other than their own states of origin.** This behavior is becoming a serious problem in modern Nigeria, especially in the South East geo-political zone, where public servants who have been in the service for many years will be forced to retire simply because they are not born in the states they are currently serving in. Such an attitude creates bad blood among people and between the states involved. It leads to retaliatory action, which creates unnecessary tensions between those concerned. Generally, the policy is an unjust law and un-Nigerian. It must be stopped because it is endangering the country's national unity. No Nigerian should be barred from living and working anywhere he/she chooses to live and work within the geographical boundaries of Nigeria. This legislation should strengthen the residency question in the country.

Justifications for Proposing Policy #2

Based on the history of the country, this legislation is desperately needed. As indicated in several sections of this book, Nigeria is seriously becoming a fragile state. Nigeria is a keg of gunpowder waiting to explode. Its national unity is on a shaky ground as a result of disunity and mistrust existing between and among the various segments of the Nigerian society. While this is happening, the Nigerian governing elite are paying lip-service to the Nigerian project without showing serious commitment or dedication to its causes. What members of this elite group are interested in, is what they can get out of the system and not how to build an enduring and formidable society, where everybody can prosper. Presently and as noted above, there are some Nigerian ethnic nationalities that do not believe in the Nigerian dream because they feel marginalized. They do not believe that the Nigerian government is there for them. They don't even feel that they are part of the Nigerian project. There are some Nigerians who are not free to live and work where they reside. A feeling of this nature undermines the national cohesion and consensus of the country.

Life in Nigeria has become nasty, short, and brutal because there is a total breakdown of law and order in certain quarters. For example, there is an Islamic insurgency in Northeastern Nigeria that is terrorizing the people of the area and, such activities, are making life a "living hell" for the people of Northeastern Nigeria. Other Nigerians are also witnessing an increasing wave of crimes in their regions. Crimes like kidnapping, armed robbery, extra-judicial killings, political assassinations, looting of public funds, money laundering, drug and human trafficking are becoming too obvious in the country. These human activities are overheating the Nigerian polity and undermining law and order in the entire country.

The President-elect of the All Progressive Congress (APC), Gen. Muhammadu Buhari, brilliantly summarizes the security risks many Nigerians are confronted with today and the inaction of the government of the day in tackling the issue effectively. The President-elect, during his electoral campaign in the 2015 general elections, made the following remarks when he addressed the Nigerian Labour Congress during its 11th Delegates Conference, held on February 9, 2015:

> Our security situation in this country has never been so dire. Today, Nigerians have to endure, not just terrorist attacks in the North, but militancy in the Niger Delta; communal violence in the Middle Belt, cult wars in the South and Kidnappings, robberies and acts of thuggery throughout the country.... Many are left to fend for themselves. Those who turn to the police, the army or any other state security agencies usually have the means and personal connections to buy help and protection. Those who don't, simply move on, and resigned to fate. The bitter ones may form vigilante groups; others join mobs that dispense jungle justice on suspects and scapegoats alike. Too many believe they have nothing to lose, and everything to gain and the most alienated are easy prey for terrorists, militants, and thugs. This must change (Fagbemi, 2015).

Unfortunately, the country's security agencies charged with the maintenance of law and order and the promotion and protection of public safety are not well-equipped to handle these criminal activities. Consequently, most of these criminal activities go unresolved. By failing to confront these illegal activities with the intensity and adequate measures they deserve, such human activities have become the prevailing norm in the Nigerian society.

The governing elite in the country must understand that Nigeria is becoming more diverse, complex, and complicated due to many social factors, which include: population explosion; Nigeria having more educated and enlightened people; the rise of middle class individuals in the country; and more Nigerians becoming politically active.

For Nigeria to be vibrant, remain relevant, and engaged, it needs a holistic reform of the country's political system that will accommodate these newly emerging social trends. To achieve this aspiration, the country's political system must be decentralized if more room is to be created for this emerging political class that wants to come into the country's political theatre. Embarking on this effort will lead to the creation of more states, and more responsibilities given to state and local governments. Such an effort will empower every ethnic nationality in the country and strengthen the country's national unity.

Generally, the enactment of this proposed legislation into law will help to enhance the peace and stability that is desperately needed in today's Nigeria. An effort of that nature will make a majority of Nigerians feel good about themselves and their country. It will make them feel secure in themselves and will induce them to believe that they are part of the system; that their interests matter; and that there is something out there for them to cheer for. Nigeria has come of age, and disappearing from the world radar or from the world map is not an option. The country needs to be rescued and this legislation, if passed and implemented as it should, will definitely achieve that aspiration.

Implications of not implementing Policy Proposal #2

Doing nothing to address these lingering problems will definitely weaken the country's national unity as many indicators have shown. Doing nothing to strengthen the peace and stability of the country means the disintegration of the country, which will not do anyone any good. Allowing Nigeria to break-up will be devastating to the entire West African region, and will definitely slow down the socio-economic development of the breakaway states, as most political disintegrations or failed states do not go away quietly without schisms leading to armed struggles or armed conflicts (Civil wars) which, in most cases, destroy lives and property

Those frustrating the Nigerian unity have easily forgotten the devastating nature of the Nigerian-Biafran War and the ugly legacies it left behind. The Ibos of Nigeria know too well these effects, because after forty-five years of the war, they are still suffering from it. If no lesson has been learned from the Nigerian Civil War, let those clamoring for the dissolution of the Nigerian state take a good look at the devastation now taking place in Syria, Iraq, Libya, South

Sudan, Yemen, Ukraine and other war ravaging areas around the world. It will take these countries many years and huge sums of money to rebuild their infrastructures that are being destroyed in these wars.

Those clamoring for the disintegration of Nigeria (the anti-Nigerian unity) should not forget the human cost and suffering that people in these warring countries are experiencing, especially those individuals fleeing from the combat zones and not to talk of the number of deaths. There are grave consequences to pay if the country breaks up. No patriotic Nigerian will allow the Nigerian nation to disintegrate. This is why it is necessary for government operatives to pay attention to what the people have to say about their performance in office and try to make the necessary changes that will enhance and strengthen the governance of the country.

3. The study proposes that more legislation be enacted to boost the country's economy, in order to alleviate the human suffering, the economic woes, and security problems plaguing the country.

a) To boost the country's economy, legislation should be enacted to **strengthen the protection of bank customers' deposit accounts** that they have with the country's banking institutions. The legislation should stipulate, in strong and clear terms, the punishment to be handed down to owners of banks and their management team who use their vantage positions to misappropriate customers' lifetime savings and who have used such funds for other human activities, such as seeking political office or floating businesses and, thereafter, allowed their banks to go into liquidation without refunding the customers their deposits.

b) The nation's economy cannot grow or blossom if the banking industry, which is the cushion of any national economy, does not enjoy the confidence of its customers. In light of this, the legislation should enhance and strengthen banks' regulatory policies to prevent future Nigerian banks from defaulting or extorting money from Nigerians. The legislation should also be extended to the **Nigerian Stock Exchange (NSE)** to stabilize its market operations from being over quoted—an ugly experience many Nigerians encountered during the 2008-2009 economic meltdown that resulted in a massive loss of income by investors.

c) The legislation should strengthen the laws of the country's Apex Bank (the Central Bank of Nigeria) by authorizing the Bank to publish the names of Nigerians, irrespective of their socio-economic status in the country, who failed to repay the loan they received from banks. A specific time frame should be given to the defaulters to enable them meet up with their payments and if, after the expiration date, the loans were not repaid, the Apex Bank has no more option than to publish the names of defaulters and bar them from obtaining loans from other banks in the country. The enforcement of this provision of the law should send a strong message (deterrence) to future defaulters that they will not escape the hammer of the law if they fail to repay their bank loans. The execution of the law is also a way of ensuring transparency in the system and a way of holding loan defaulters accountable for their dubious behavior.

d) This legislation is desperately needed to enhance **the growth of indigenous businesses** in the country. The Nigerian economy needs the assemblage of many Nigerian investors and business people for it to grow exponentially. Although, governments create public sector jobs by employing public servants and building infrastructure, it is the business communities that create most of the private sector jobs. Since one of the primary goals of governments is to enhance the socio-economic wellbeing of their citizens, this legislation should ensure that federal, state, and local governments in Nigeria create incentives that will lead to the creation of more small and medium size businesses in the country.

e) In addition, the legislation should establish an **administrative body** (like Small Business Administration) that will coordinate the activities of these small and medium size indigenous businesses. It will provide adequate and continuous training on how to run a successful business venture, and provide these small and medium size businesses with grants and/or free interest-loans, with stringent requirements built into such grants and loan packages. Assisting small and medium size businesses to grow means more job creation and more revenue for the nation's economy

f) To demonstrate that the Nigerian government is serious and truly committed to reducing massive poverty, resulting from the country's huge unemployment level, the legislation should address the nation's **dilapidated infrastructure and the infrequency of energy supply.** These crippled and crucial elements are most unfortunately hampering business activities in the country. There is no way the Nigerian economy can grow without adequate infrastructure and a constant supply of electricity. These are the core factors of any economic growth or the brainchild thereof. No manufacturing base is possible when these essential elements of growth, including raw-materials are not made available.

g) No nation's economy can grow rapidly when that country's road and railway networks are in bad shape, when its bridges are falling apart, when it runs its businesses primarily on electric generators, or when it sold its vital iron and steel industry to a foreign entity (an Indian Company) that does not want to expand the industry because it does not want the iron and steel industry to compete globally with that of its home country.

h) No nation can create an optimum employment level when its economy depends solely on **a petro economy or on a single commodity**; and no nation can boost its petro-economy, when it does not have functional oil refineries for its domestic consumption, but relies on private marketers (the oil subsidy regime) who over-charge the government for the services they (private marketers) never provided.

i) The legislation should reduce to the barest minimum the **size of the Nigerian diplomatic missions around the world**. Nigeria has over stretched itself by trying to have an embassy in every country of the globe, not minding whether or not the country's resources can sustain such missions. Because of the country's limited resources, many of these missions have been poorly administered. Some of them have failed to achieve their intended goals and objectives: they have not adequately represented Nigeria's interests in their host countries and have failed to address the immediate needs and concerns of the Nigerian citizens living in those host countries. Having foreign missions in strategic countries where Nigeria's interests and her citizens' wellbeing will be best served, is highly recommended and encouraged. The amount of savings to be realized from this exercise (the downsizing of the Nigerian diplomatic missions) will be enormous and will definitely boost the nation's economy if those amounts are properly utilized.

j) The Nigerian leaders should borrow a leaf from the **American Founding Fathers** (George Washington, Alexander Hamilton, Thomas Jefferson, James Madison and others). These men refused to over stretch their young nation's resources beyond its borders during the nation's early history. The primary focus of the American Founding Fathers, at the time (the isolation era), was to stay home and build up (consolidate) their nation's infrastructure and economy. When it was time to engage other countries in a more formidable fashion, the country stepped up to the plate and, today, the United States of America is one of the most powerful and dominant countries on the face of the earth.

k) The United States of America was not exposed to all issues that had international ramifications just like Nigeria was when she gained her political independence. For example, the United States of America refused to join **the League of Nations (1919-1920),** but Nigeria joined the United Nations Organization immediately she became an independent nation in 1960. This was done without consolidating the country's economy and other forces of nation building. This is a lesson Nigerians must learn. It is never too late to adapt to changes. To achieve greatness, the Nigerian leadership must now begin to streamline or prioritize its human activities just like the Americans did.

l) The legislation should reintroduce **the mixed economic philosophy** that encourages governments to create economic ventures that provide essential services to citizens at a minimum and/or affordable cost. The legislation should articulate stringent policies and guidelines that will ensure that the operations of government businesses will be effectively and efficiently administrated, always taking into consideration the constructive criticisms brought against government parastatals by critics.

Justifications for Proposing Policy #3

Nigeria cannot maintain a steady economic growth, when a large number of its banks were liquidated due to fraud, non-compliance with the governing rules, the granting of toxic loans, and mismanagement of customers' deposits as was the case with the so-called "New Generation Banks" that emerged during the early 1980s and 1990s. Many of these liquidated banks' customers lost their lifetime savings and never received anything in return. This ugly experience created a lack of confidence in most Nigerian banks. It is unconscionable that the Nigerian tax payers had to rescue some of these defaulting banks, while a majority of owners of the liquidated banks escaped the sledge hammer of the law. The owners of these failed banks and their management teams were allowed to get away with the fraud without being forced to pay back the stolen money to their rightful owners.

The country's massive unemployment level is another major cause for alarm. Under normal circumstances, no government operatives would be reelected into political office with such huge numbers of unemployed in the labor force, as is the case in Nigeria. Most governments in Nigeria have, over the years, ignored this endemic problem. As it is rightly acknowledged in the book, the primary obligation of governments is to provide adequately for the wellbeing of their citizens by ensuring that able-bodied men and women have access to decent and meaningful employment. It is unconscionable to note that there are too many Nigerians living below the poverty line in an economy said to be the biggest in Africa. As a known fact, there are enormous consequences associated with massive unemployment. On a daily basis, Nigerians are experiencing numerous crime activities which the system is unable to cope with. Some unemployed youth in the country are engaging themselves in all sorts of crime, which include kidnapping, the illicit drug trade, and human trafficking. These young Nigerians are being recruited by terrorist groups like Boko Haram and other militant groups in the country because of their vulnerability due to lack of gainful employment. They are being used as political thugs to foment social unrest in the country; they are used in rigging elections and are used as political assassins by power hungry politicians who want to rule Nigeria at all cost. These vulnerable youth would not have been exploited or manipulated the way they have been, if they were gainfully employed or had some meaningful things to do.

The proposed legislation is very essential and highly needed at this time, because it reminds the Nigerian governments of their basic constitutional obligations, which they have ignored for years. Governments in Nigeria have always forgotten why they were constituted. They have shifted their functions to private entities since the emergence of privatization scheme in the 1980s. The privatization exercise in Nigeria is a decimal failure.

It is no longer an attractive proposal, because it does not carry everyone along. It creates two classes by making the rich richer and the poor poorer. Nigerians were told that privatization was the way forward and that it would enhance the quality of life of the average Nigerians. Since the privatization of most government parastatals, such as the Nigerian Airways, Power Holding Company of Nigeria, and the Nigeria Steel Industry, Nigerians are yet to see any positive outcome in these areas. For example, there are still major blackouts in most places in Nigeria since the PHCN was sold. The privatization scheme in Nigeria is a scam that a few privileged Nigerians and their foreign corporate friends have used to enrich themselves at the expense of the Nigerian masses.

Implications of not implementing Policy Proposal #3

Failure to address these economic problems in more objective ways would likely create more social problems for the country. Nigeria is a fragmented nation-state with many ethnic nationalities that have their own social agenda and militant groups that are ready to do battle with the National government. Nigerians are too familiar with these militant groups, which include Boko Haram that is now terrorizing Northern Nigeria and whose atrocities and mayhem contributed, in part, in forcing the country to postpone its 2015 national elections scheduled to be held on February 14 and 28, 2015 to March 28 and April 11, 2015. Other militant groups are the MASSOB, MEND, MOSOP, and the OPC.

These are self-serving groups, meaning that they are created to defend their ethnic national interests by any means necessary. Some of these groups are religious in nature and others are purely socio-economic and political. Some of them have engaged the Nigerian government militarily in order to address their economic concerns and social needs. While other militant groups have not engaged in violent acts, at the moment, they have the potential of doing so if and when the need arises.

These militant groups are heavily supported both financially and morally by some powerful members of their respective ethnic nationalities whose personal identities are hidden from the Nigerian public. The activities of these militant groups are also gaining the attraction of youth in their respective regions because of the massive unemployment and other social ills plaguing the country. These are problems Nigerian governments have not adequately addressed. They are making the Nigerian youth restless, creating a situation that coincides with a popular saying, "an idle mind is a devil's workshop." If the status-quo remains the way it is without any meaningful reforms like those suggested above, the possibility of the country disintegrating is very high given the uncertainty and realities of things in the country.

4. *The study proposes that more legislation be enacted to minimize the tempo of using political offices, as a means of accumulating personal wealth, a vice leading to the looting of the nation's treasury.*

a) The legislation must ensure that **the immunity clause** granted to the offices of the presidency of Nigeria, state governors, local governments' chairmen, members of the national and state assemblies, and members of local government councils, as Chief Executive Officers and Legislative Officials of the three levels of government in Nigeria should be withdrawn immediately after they leave office. Removing such a clause should enable the country to prosecute members of the political class for an abuse of office during their tenure in office.

b) It is important that every political office holder in the country be held accountable for his/her deeds while in office. Political office holders who betray the sanctity of their offices by using such a privilege to enrich themselves or abuse the constitutional rights of citizens should not be shielded by the immunity clause. The country should no longer tolerate a situation where political office holders use their offices (privilege) to accumulate personal wealth or intimidate others, especially political opponents and get away with such a heinous crime.

c) The legislation should eliminate the secrecy and unaccountability clause attached to **the security vote** appropriated to the Nigerian president and state governors and the **constituency allowance** appropriated to the Nigerian legislators. These appropriations (the security vote and constituency allowance) have become recipes for corruption. They have been abused and misused and, more importantly, they are not accounted for. The security vote and constituency allowance were established to address certain specific problems facing the nation. Unfortunately, while the issues to be addressed by these appropriations continue to escalate, the cost of their funding keeps increasing on a yearly basis.

d) The security vote is meant for addressing security problems in the states and at the federal level, while the constituency allowance is meant for members of national and state legislatures to address peculiar issues within their respective constituencies. Because of their secret nature, these appropriations are not accounted for; meaning that Nigerians do not know how much of this money is authorized every year by the legislative arms of the federal and state governments, and they (Nigerians) do not know how much of these allocations are spent annually on what they are meant for. It also means that there is no legislative oversight built into these appropriations.

e) Given the importance of these appropriations due to the security threats and increasing wave of violent crimes in Nigeria, and given the need for legislators to remain in constant touch with their constituencies so as to address significant problems confronting the constituencies, these appropriations **(the security vote and constituency allowance)** should form part of the national and state annual fiscal budgets, where the use of such allocations should be subjected to legislative scrutiny at both federal and state levels, and the expenditures of these allocations be made a public record.

f) The governing bodies in Nigeria should be reminded that these allocations **(the security vote and constituency allowance)** are the people's money and, therefore, the allocations and expenditures of these programs should be made public, where every Nigerian who is interested in knowing how these appropriations are spent will have easy access to such a record. If the security vote and the constituency allowance are to be continued, they should no longer be executed under secrecy. Nigerians have the right to know how these funds are spent, and those in charge of these funds must give an annual account of them.

g) The legislation should reduce the size of the **presidential air fleet to two planes from its current number of eleven.** The Nigerian economy cannot sustain such a huge fleet, when millions of Nigerians are dying of hunger and starvation, and when many Nigerians are unemployed. Nigeria's political class cannot continue to live lavishly on public funds, when their brethren are impoverished and cannot make ends meet. The billions of Naira spent annually in maintaining these aircrafts could be used to create a common good for all.

h) The legislation should reduce to the barest minimum the **humongous life pension entitlements, severance allowances, and other outlandish allowances, such as** (Hardship, Constituency, Furniture, Newspaper, Wardrobe, Recess, Accommodation, Utilities, Domestic Staff, Entertainment, Personal Assistants, Vehicle Maintenance, and Leave)   allocated to Nigerian Presidents, Vice-Presidents, and Federal Lawmakers; and State Governors, Deputy Governors, and State Lawmakers. These entitlements and severance allowances were misguidedly authorized. The recent 300 percent rise in the severance allowances for the out-going President, Vice-President, Non-Returning Federal Lawmakers, President's Cabinet (Ministers and Aides), articulated by the Revenue Mobilisation, Allocation and Fiscal Commission (RMAFAC) is unacceptable given the dire circumstances of the country's economy.

i) State governments should roll back some of the **outlandish pension entitlements and allowances** they appropriated to their political class. In some states, for example, Governors, Deputy Governors, and State Lawmakers are entitled to private buildings bought and paid for by public funds. They and their family members are entitled to free medical care. They are entitled to annual paid holidays or vocations. They are entitled to house maintenance and new furniture bought every two years. They are also entitled to new vehicles purchased every three years including their maintenance.

j) This legislation should ensure that the Nigerian political class should sacrifice just as other Nigerians are bearing the brunt of their poor governance and their ostentatious lifestyle. Members of this class should be made to understand that the country's economy cannot sustain their outlandish lifestyle, which is unbearable and unacceptable. They cannot appropriate to themselves what belongs to all Nigerians. Members of this class do not need to be told that their greedy lifestyle has a direct link to the conflict and violence that is plaguing the country. This indifference must stop.

k) The legislation should also strip the legislative body in both federal and state governments of their full-time status and make them **part-time legislatures**. Nigeria, at this time, does not need a full-time legislative body that has few legislative duties to perform. What is being done in both national and state governments now in one year can be done in three or six months. As we see in Nigeria, these legislative bodies have not adequately addressed the endemic problems (corruption, insecurity and violent crimes, unemployment, lack of adequate education and healthcare programs, dilapidated infrastructures, and lack of constant electricity supplies) facing the Nigerian masses since the inception of the Nigerian Fourth Republic sixteen years ago (1999 to present).

l) Using part-time legislatures should save the country enormous revenues from the **jumbo salaries, pension entitlements severance allowances, and other allowances** currently paid to these legislators for doing so little. Such revenues should be used in funding Nigeria's ailing education and health programs; they also could be used in rehabilitating Nigeria's dilapidated infrastructures, which include federal and state roads and bridges, railways, seaports, airports, electricity, and other communication networks.

m) Since Nigeria has fully embraced the American legislative and judicial processes, it is appropriate and necessary that the country's governing elite take a look at the historical transition of the US Congress (the national legislative branch). If Nigeria wants to be as successful as the United States has been, the country has to take steps similar to the ones Americans took to get them where they are today. The governing elite should remember that "Rome was not built in a day." Below is a brief historic background of **part-time legislatures in the United States of America:**

n) From 1789 to 1815, members of US Congress could not afford to stay year-round in Washington because they were paid so poorly. Senators and representatives made just a few dollars a day. In 1815, they began receiving $1500 a year salary. In 1855 that doubled. By 1935, they were making $10,000 a year. But most members of Congress still needed day jobs. Even into the 1960s, "members of Congress were out of session about as much as they were in, and they had almost no personal and committee staffers assigned to them unless they were senior and powerful. It was not until the 1970s that members of Congress began seeing their positions as year-round commitments" (Seipel, 2010). The same was the case in many of the states in the United States, where part-time legislatures were optimally utilized.

o) The use of part-time legislature is not a new phenomenon, as some members of the Nigerian National Assembly have claimed. As noted above, the United States went through this process earlier in its history to meet the needs of the time. Nigeria should cut its coat according to the size of its cloth, meaning that the country cannot overspend its income. The full-time legislature can be revived when the country can afford such a huge venture and when the country becomes more complicated and complex than it is at the moment.

p) Currently, the full-time legislature is too expensive to maintain and cannot be justified when millions of Nigerians cannot afford one square meal a day and when millions of Nigerians are dying annually due to lack of adequate health care. This legislation should allow Nigerian legislators to seek other jobs on the side to compensate for the revenue losses they will incur for not being employed as full-time legislators. Nigerians should be reminded that running for political office is a voluntary exercise. No Nigerian is forced against his/her will to run for any political office. Doing so, is a personal decision.

q) The legislation should **limit the term** of every legislator in the country to **two consecutive terms** to coincide with those of the national president, state governors, and local government chairmen, who are constitutionally limited to serve only eight years in the same office if reelected for the second term. This is one way to curb corruption in the public sector. If an elected politician does well to the satisfaction of the people during his/her first-term in office, such a person may be rewarded for a second term to continue, so as to enable the individual to complete his/her good work, but after the expiration of his/her second term, he/she should allow another person to continue the political process.

Justifications for Proposing Policy #4

From the analyses provided in some chapters of this book, it was noted that the reason most Nigerians want to be in politics, whether or not they have what it takes to be productive politicians, is the notion that politics in Nigeria is attractive and lucrative. Most Nigerian politicians have come to see politics as an easy access of getting rich in a twinkling of an eye. This statement is not far from the truth when one looks at what is happening on the ground. First and foremost, political office seekers in Nigeria are virtually poor before getting into the country's political theater or arena, but after a year or two in office, one starts noticing great changes around them.

With time, their conspicuous lavish lifestyle begins to manifest or emerge. While in office, their main focus or priority is to build big mansions with gold bathtubs and other fanciful decorative items that may be worth millions if not billions of Naira. The other thing they seek the most while in office is the acquisition of various types of exotic bullet proof automobiles. By the same token, these politicians are attracted to investing in lucrative businesses, such as luxurious hotels, real-estate, and shopping malls. Businesses of these types are channels looters of public funds use to hide their ill-gotten wealth from the Nigerian public. They also use foreign offshore banks to shield their loots from the public by transferring such funds to their foreign bank account, where such funds are kept under secret codes only known to the looters.

Another area that is dragging many Nigerians into politics is the jumbo salaries, pensions, bonuses, and severance allowances these politicians award themselves. Nigerians have been witnessing the rate at which elected officials in the country are raising their salaries, allowances, bonuses, and pensions without taking into consideration the state of the nation's economy and the living conditions of average Nigerians. It has been revealed that several state Houses of Assembly in the country have passed laws to quadruple the pensions of their former governors and deputies. According to Aziken and Oke (2015) of the *Vanguard Nigeria Newspaper,* Lagos State is one of the states in the nation whose State House of Assembly enacted a law approving humongous pension entitlements to its governors and deputies. Other states having similar laws include Edo, Gombe, Oyo, Rivers, and Kwara (Aziken and Oke, 2015).

In Lagos State, for example, the approved pension entitlements or benefits include the following:

- One hundred percent (100%) of annual basic salaries of the incumbent governor and deputy;

- One residential house in Lagos and another in the Federal Capital Territory, Abuja;

- Three cars, two backup cars and one pilot car for the ex-governor every three years, two cars, two backup cars and one pilot car for the deputy governor every three years;

- Three hundred percent (300%) of annual basic salary every two years for furniture;

- Ten percent of annual basic salary for house maintenance;

- No limitation for domestic staff, which will include cook, steward, gardener who also shall be pensionable;

- Free medical treatment for ex-governor and deputy and members of their families, not just spouses;

- Two DSS security officers, one female officer, eight policemen for the ex-governor, one DSS security officer and two policemen for the ex-deputy governor;

- Twenty-five percent (25%) of annual basic salary for the ex-governor and deputy governor's Personal Advisor (PA);

- Thirty percent (30%) of annual basic salary for car maintenance;
- Ten percent (10%) of annual basic salary for entertainment;
- Twenty percent (20%) of annual basic salary for utility;
- No limitation for number of drivers who shall be pensionable; and
- No amount of money was specified for severance gratuity.

Source: *Vanguard Nigeria Newspaper* Reporters (Emmanuel Aziken and Gbenga Oke, 2015)

A *Punch Nigeria Newspaper* article published on April 29, 2015, also reveals that in the recent Remuneration Package put together by the Revenue Mobilization, Allocation and Fiscal Commission, the outgoing President, Goodluck Jonathan, Vice-President, Namadi Sambo, non-returning Federal Lawmakers, Ministers and Presidential Aides will collect N3.24 billion as severance allowances (Amaefule, Olokor, and Adesomju, 2015).

The article indicated that the President, Vice-President, the affected (76) Senators and (290) members of House of Representatives, (42) Ministers and presidential aides, numbering 133 will each received 300 percent increase on their annual basic salaries in severance allowances. By this raise (300% increase) the *Punch Newspaper* noted that the President whose annual basic salary was N3, 514, 705 received N10, 544, 115 in severance gratuity after he left office on May 29, 2015. The Vice-President whose annual basic salary was N3, 031,572 received N9, 094, 717 in severance gratuity.

The article went on to say that the 76 Senators who did not return to the National Assembly either because they did not stand for election or because they lost their bids to return collectively received N462, 019, 200 at the end of their tenure, which expired on June 5, 2015. With the 300 percent raise on their basic annual salaries, each Senator received N6, 079, 200 in severance allowance, while the 290 members of House of Representatives who did not return to the 8th National Assembly were paid N1, 727,134, 875 collectively. From this amount, each of these House members received N5, 955,637 as severance allowance (Amaefule, Olokor, and Adesomju, 2015).

The forty-two (42) Ministers in Jonathan's administration collectively received a total sum of N253, 967, 212, which N188, 455, 200 went to the Senior Ministers collectively, while N65, 512, 012 went the Ministers of State. Of the total amount (N188, 455, 200) for Senior Ministers who were thirty-one (31) in numbers, each received N6, 079, 200 in severance allowance. Of the total amount (N65, 512,012) for Ministers of State who were eleven (11) in numbers, each received N5, 872, 740.

The Presidential aides numbering 133, comprising of special advisers, senior special assistants and special assistants collectively received N775, 207,125. It was reported that out of these 133 aides to the President, twenty-three (23) of the aides worked directly with the president as special advisers and 110 aides worked with the Vice-President, the First Lady (Patient Jonathan) as special advisers designated as either senior special assistants or special assistants to the President. With their 300 percent increase on their annual basic salary, each of these aides received N5, 828, 625 in severance allowance (Amaefule, Olokor, and Adesomju, 2015).

Let it be known to all that this severance gratuity is a one-time payment. It is a voluntary sum paid in return for the services the out-going president, his vice-president, his cabinet ministers and aides, and non-returning national lawmakers rendered to the nation. The severance allowances are not part of their pensions, nor are they part of their salaries, security votes, constituency allowances, furniture allowances, Newspaper allowances, wardrobe allowances, recess allowances, accommodation allowances, utility allowances, domestic staff allowances, entertainment allowances, personal assistance allowances, vehicle maintenance allowances, and leave allowances which are humongous in nature. Given all of these, the author of this book has these noble questions to ask: How this huge amount of money (N3.24 billion) can be justified when many of these individuals have only been in office for a short duration? Where is the money to pay for these misguided allowances coming from when the country cannot meet-up with its socio-economic obligations to its people? Where is the money to pay for this huge appropriation coming from when many Nigerians are leaving the country in a large number for other countries in search of a better life simply because there are insufficient jobs available to them? Why is the Nigerian political class indifferent to the plights of ordinary Nigerians? Why are they impoverishing their own people unnecessarily? Why are they misusing the authority bestowed on them by the Nigerian populace to do better for the country? And why do they lack moral consciousness?

It is only in Nigeria, where the office of the president acquires as many as eleven aircrafts to its fleet when millions of Nigerians, especially the Nigerian children go to bed hungry. The Nigerian politicians spend huge sums from public funds annually to enhance their living conditions, when Nigerian educational institutions at various levels are ill-equipped, ill-funded, and inadequately staffed. This is happening when many Nigerians are dying on a daily basis from preventable diseases because Nigerian hospitals lack adequate facilities, equipment, drugs, and experienced medical staff. These are the politicians who argued against paying the average Nigerian work-force a decent minimum wage they deserve. These are the politicians who will turn round and blame the government for spending so much and creating a waste in government. They will never accept the fact that it is their greedy behavior and insatiable appetites that are making the Nigerian governments inefficient and non-performing. It is, indeed, their culture of greed and insatiable appetite that is overheating the country's polity.

This culture of greed and insatiable appetite or consumption would not have persisted or flourished if it were not for the loopholes built within and around the political structures, which allow public office holders to manipulate those institutional weaknesses to their own advantage. To minimize the tempo of using political offices to accumulate personal wealth, a vice leading to the looting of the nation's treasury, the Nigerian governing elite should take a critical look at the above proposed solutions dealing with the problem.

Political office holders in Nigeria should know, first and foremost, that they are public servants and using their political offices to enrich themselves at the expense of ordinary Nigerians is a flagrant violation of the ethics of their profession. Nigerian politicians should know that they were not forced by anyone or at gun point to run for political offices. The decision to offer oneself for a political office is personal and voluntary. If Politicians' interior motive (the driving force) is to get rich overnight, then politics should not be the profession for them. They should seriously consider going into private businesses, where they can make the type of money they have in mind. They should not convert public funds into personal property.

To bring this greedy behavior to a halt, the above proposed suggestions should be instituted in order to make politics in Nigeria less attractive. When Nigerian politicians' current jumbo salaries, pensions, severance allowances and bonuses, including their security votes and constituency allowances are slashed, they may not want to run for political offices in the future, if the incentives that attracted them to seek these offices are curtailed.

Limiting legislators' tenure of office and making them part-time legislators may also discourage many of them from seeking political office. Politicians should understand that they cannot use their offices as a source for wealth acquisition. Removing the immunity clause will enable the country to prosecute errant and corrupt public officials. Prosecuting corrupt politicians after they leave office will send a strong message to others that "you can run, but you cannot hide." It will also send a strong message to those errant and corrupt politicians that they are not above the law of the land.

Nigeria, at this time, needs selfless public servants who want to serve their country with respect, pride, honor and dignity. Nigeria needs public servants who will leave moral legacies that will withstand the test of time. At this critical time in the country's history, Nigeria does not want leaders who do not care about the wellbeing of its people, as Eke (2015) rightly articulated in his article titled "Nigeria, A Republic, Not Criminal Paradise," where he noted the following:

> The business of Government in a republic [which Nigeria is], should be the welfare and rights of the people and, whenever a republic fails to prioritise the interest and welfare of the people and put the interest and welfare of a group or organization over and above that of the people, such a

government has failed and such a country cannot claim to be a republic, in the true sense and meaning of the word. Educating Nigerians to understand that the government is established to serve them and that they should be vigilant to know, when those in power are misusing their power for selfish ends. It is their civic duty in a democracy to change such a behavior (Eke, 2015).

The above-proposed measures are articulated because Nigerians do not want to see the distribution of their national wealth being top-heavy. They do not want to see the leaders getting everything, while ordinary Nigerians are getting nothing. Nigerians do not want to see political offices in Nigeria becoming too attractive. They want to see these offices become less attractive so that it can attract only those politicians who are willing to serve. As it has been generally acknowledged, a majority of Nigerian politicians are in politics because of the easy access political offices provide them in looting public funds, which are executed in different ways. A majority of these politicians are not in politics to transform the country or the lives of ordinary Nigerians. As far as they are concerned, their self-interest is paramount and more sacrosanct than improving the socioeconomic wellbeing of average Nigerians, which absolutely means nothing to them.

Implications of not implementing Policy Proposal #4

The failure to respond accordingly to the frustrations and anger of many Nigerians against the governing elite's inaction toward their plight may lead to the deterioration of the country because these frustrations and anger are becoming louder and clearer on many Nigerian streets. For too long, these resentments have been ignored by many administrations in Nigeria. Making politics attractive in Nigeria has overheated the polity and has created a culture of corruption and impunity in the system. Such a culture has led to a looting of public funds.

The use of political offices to accumulate personal wealth has also led to electoral fraud in Nigeria. Overzealous and power hungry politicians rig elections and, sometimes, create violence in order to gain access to the corridor of power. They see political offices as their only means of survival or as a "meal ticket." Because of their desperation to be in the corridor of power, these overzealous and power hungry politicians are willing to do the unthinkable even if it means exterminating (killing) their political opponents or crushing anyone standing in their way to election victory.

This is the situation Nigeria finds itself in today. Therefore, if the country does not reform itself by implementing some of the above-proposed measures, Nigerians will continue to die in the hundreds whenever there are elections in the country, as seen in past elections, where violence overtook the conduct of those elections and, thereby, making them not free and fair. If these measures are not seriously considered and instituted, there will be a rise in corruption and other crimes, unemployment, and insecurity will quadruple. The country's growth and advancement will stagnate and massive poverty will become the order of the day.

5. The study proposes that more legislation be enacted to minimize the frequent occurrences of corruption and the impunity in which this graft is committed by politicians and other public officials.

a) To robustly combat corruption in Nigeria, this legislation should establish a protective measure or mechanism for **whistle-blowers** in the system. If the Nigerian governing elite are serious about curbing corruption as they claim they are, whistle blowers should be made part of the machinery in the fight against corruption. The enactment of this provision into law will not necessarily mean the end of corruption in Nigeria, but it will surely slow down the momentum or tempo. Whistle blowers are desperately needed in the system in order to link perpetrators directly to the crime. It is logical that before going public, whistle blowers would have sufficient and impeccable evidence that may lead to the conviction of the errant politician or the public official in question.

b) This measure is extremely important because if public officials are aware that a member of their inner circle, such as their personal secretaries, personal assistants, family members, friends and colleagues, may expose their illegal activities, they will be cautious when engaging in such illegal activities for the fear of being exposed and, perhaps, humiliated publicly. By the same token, if close associates of a corrupt public official do not have government protection (safe net), such individuals may not come forward to reveal or testify against that public official concerning his/her illegal dealings out of fear of losing their lives.

c) The legislation should guide against the abuse of this law by whistle blowers who may use the law for witch-hunting. Before granting such a protection, and before making such an accusation public, the evidence of the case linking the purported corrupt public official to the crimes must be credible and must withstand courts' scrutiny. The identities of collaborating witnesses must be protected as well.

d) The legislation should also strengthen the effectiveness of **the Economic and Financial Crimes Commission (EFCC)** and the **Independent Corrupt Practices and Other related Offenses Commission (ICPC)** by giving them much broader responsibilities and powers to discharge their significant duties and functions. If the Nigerian government is serious about fighting political corruption, bribery, gratification, graft and abuse or the misuse of office, advance fee fraud, money laundering and other financial crimes, and to ensure that public officials are not living above their means, these important Commissions should be restructured, empowered adequately, well-funded, and well-equipped. The missions of these Commissions should be clearly defined in order to avoid overlap, confusion, and ambiguity.

e) These Commissions should be made an independent body, whose leaders will be elected by the Nigerian electorates for four years and will be eligible for reelection for another four years after which they will no longer serve in this capacity. This means that after their two consecutive terms in office, they may seek political office elsewhere. The leaderships of these Commissions will no longer be an appointive position. Those offering themselves to serve in this capacity must be men and women of impeccable character, who are well versed in the country's legal system and have had substantial years of experience in law enforcement functions, especially in the areas of arrest, investigation, and interrogation.

f) The two agencies should be housed under one umbrella, to be known as the **Commission against Corrupt Practices** and led by **three elected officials** who will choose among themselves the **Director-General of the Commission**, while the other two elected officials serve as Directors of ICPC and EFCC respectively. The Director-General of the Commission will oversee the entire management of the two agencies, while the two Directors head each of the agencies. This means that Directors of ICPC and EFCC will report directly to the Director-General of the Commission, who also reports to the Nigerian electorates. The three elected officials of the Commission should jointly hire a Legal Advisor to head the Legal and Prosecutorial Department of the Commission. Additionally, the leadership of the Commission should hire the heads of Arrest and Investigatory Department, and Human Resources Management. The same structure should be replicated at the state level, where they perform similar functions and duties, include making sure that local government appropriations (funds) are utilized by local government officials for what they are meant for, and not to be usurped by state governments, as is currently the case.

g) The minimum educational requirement for entry-level staff of the Commission should be a Bachelor Degree in Social Science fields, especially in Law, Political Science, Psychology, Sociology, Criminology, Criminal Justice, Forensic Accounting, etc. The Agency appropriation should be subjected to a legislative oversight at both federal and state levels, and their expenditures made public for all to see. The legislation should impress upon the **Commission against Corrupt Practices,** that it must publicize its list of arrestees and their charges—those prosecuted and those yet to be prosecuted, those convicted and those acquitted for no wrong doing. Such publications should cause other Nigerians who are nursing the ambition of engaging in any form of corruption to refrain from such thinking, because using one's public office to loot the nation's treasury would no longer be tolerated in Nigeria.

h) The legislation should ban **convicted politicians or public servants** from active politics or from government posts for that matter. The country should not be rewarding criminals, because doing so encourages more criminal activities. Presidential or Governorship pardon or clemency should not be granted to convicted politicians or public servants who used their privileged offices to rob the country of its limited resources. If Nigeria is to curb corruption and other crimes in the country, politicians and public servants convicted for criminality should serve the maximum sentence for the crime they committed. That will send a strong message to others that crime does not pay. This may not deter others from committing crimes but, definitely, it will minimize the commission of crimes in the country.

i) The legislation should ensure that **all corrupt charges brought by the graft agencies before sitting judges should be fully disposed on a timely fashion**. The judiciary has been allowing many of the accused state governors and other corrupt politicians to evade prosecution. Nigerians are aware of many state governors who were accused of looting their state treasuries and gotten away with the crime. They are also aware that once court bails are granted to these individuals by the adjudicating judges, nothing else will be heard about the cases. Literally, that will be the end of those charges, and the accused are allowed to walk freely without reproach.

j) The legislation should demand that adjudicating judges should **establish a time table or a time-frame** when corrupt charges brought before them are finalized. It is said that justice delayed is justice denied. Nigerians have the right to know the truth and, such a truth should not be hidden from them. A judicial malpractice of this nature should have no place within the Nigerian judicial circles. It is a malpractice that should not be tolerated because it encourages and nurtures a culture of impunity and corruption. It must be brought to a halt if corruption among public officials and others is to be discouraged and/or minimized.

k) Granting of bails to the accused individuals without the full prosecution of the charges is tantamount to a denial of justice to the Nigerian people. For **transparency sake**, the legislation should demand that all sitting judges should disclose publicly the disposition of all corrupt charges brought before them so that the Nigerian people will know exactly who (public official) is charged and for what crime, who is convicted, who is acquitted, who is awaiting trial, and the time frame to bring the charge/s to finality.

Justifications for Proposing Policy #5

As the author of this book has rightly pointed out in various sections of the book, the desperation and the inordinate quest to be in politics and the impression it creates as a viable means of getting rich quick, has contributed in attracting many Nigerians into the field of politics, where many have, indeed, become wealthy overnight. Because many of these politicians are never prosecuted when they are caught in the act of corruption, the illegal activity has become a household name in the country. Instead of punishing those persons (politicians) who engage in corruption severely, they are handsomely rewarded. You send a wrong message to the country when you grant a presidential pardon to a politician who was convicted for looting public funds after serving a few years in prison. By the same token, you send a wrong message to the country when you award some former military heads of state who were widely known for looting public funds, with the nation's highest honor. By doing this, you are telling the public that, indeed, crime pays. If those persons who took oaths to serve the country are caught in the web of corruption and they are not punished for their wrong doing, then corruption will become pervasive and will continue unabated. This explains why no sector or institution in Nigeria is immune from corruption, not even the churches, mosques, public sector or private sector, and schools, such as colleges or universities to mention, just a few. As highlighted in chapter 5 of this book, corruption in Nigeria has devastating consequences, which have hindered the development and growth of the country.

Corruption has been identified by many Nigerians of all walks of life, as one of the major problems facing the country and, consequently, the APC Presidential candidate, General Buhari (rtd.), during the 2015 electoral campaign promised to rid the country of corruption. Given his track record in the fight against corruption, when he was a military Head of State, Nigerians overwhelmingly voted for him in the 2015 presidential election, where he was declared the President-Elect, thereby, making him the country's fourth Executive President during the country's Fourth Republic (1999 to present). Patriotic Nigerians should not allow him to solve this endemic problem alone; they must join hands with him in removing this cancerous tumor that is destroying the country's social fabric. This book has articulated some measures that will minimize the frequent occurrence of this endemic problem. It is now up to the country's governing elite to seriously consider the proposed measures, if the elite class wants to bring this unpatriotic behavior (corruption) to a halt.

Implications of not implementing Policy Proposal #5

The consequences of doing nothing to combat corruption and other identified problems facing the country will be enormous and grave if these problems are allowed to continue unabated. If nothing concrete is done to minimize the effects of corruption in Nigeria, the country is doomed. The violence that will ensue, as a result, will be far worse and much greater than the violence unleashed so far by Boko Haram. Nigeria may be facing similar fate as the "Arab Spring," which manifested in countries, such as Egypt, Syria, Yemen, Iraq, and other war-torn regions of the world like Afghanistan, Somali, and South Sudan. Nigeria should not wish a situation of this kind on herself, but if nothing is done to reform, the "Nigerian Spring or Awakening" may not be averted and that will mean the disintegration of the country. This is the time to begin repairing the damage done to the Nigerian nation; it is never too late to embark on those reforms.

6. *The study proposes that more legislation be enacted to strengthen Nigeria's electoral process in order to minimize the frequent occurrences of electoral malpractices in the country*

a) Nigerians should not forget that the legitimacy of government is derived from the people. Therefore, all governmental powers belong to the people. People's power is expressed through open, free and fair elections. The expressed powers of the people (the General Will of the people) are then entrusted to a popular political party that will transform the lives of the people into something that is much better than ever before. When the ruling party (government/administration) fails to live up to its promises, it is the right of the people to remove such a party from governing through a democratic means (electoral politics) and replace it with another entity (party) that will guarantee their life, liberty, and the pursuit of happiness

b) To ensure that open, free and fair elections exist in Nigeria, which has never been the   case; this legislation should ban **individuals, groups, and corporations from financing political campaigns** in the country. If these entities are allowed to finance the country's political campaigns, they will dictate and control the country's agenda solely for their own benefits and not for the benefit of average Nigerians. Driven by profit motives and the urge to control government activities, **political godfathers** (campaign financers) will use this means to generate huge returns from their investments.

c) Literally, this means that national and state budgets will be used in servicing the debts political office seekers borrowed from their political godfathers to finance their campaigns. A trend of this nature will definitely undermine the improvement and enhancement of the socioeconomic wellbeing of the Nigerian people. Nigerians have seen how a large chunk of federal and state governments' annual appropriations meant to fund social and other programs that benefit the poor are often used to pay off the borrowed debts elected officials owe to their political financers. When political godfathers are not paid in cash, they are usually rewarded with government contracts. In most cases, these contracts are sub-contracted to other entities (sub-contractors) who then execute the contracts, after political godfathers (middlemen) have received their (ten percentages) commissions. Because of this double dealing, the contracted jobs are always poorly done due to lack of adequate funding and because of this intrigue; the rich get richer and the poor get poorer. Consequently, the country becomes the loser because its development plan stagnates and is delayed indefinitely.

d) When politicians sponsor their own political campaign out of their pockets, there is a tendency or likelihood that they will use government funds to recover the expenditures they incurred during their campaigns. To overcome this ugly situation, the legislation should demand that all registered political parties in the country **fund the campaign of their candidates,** rather than allowing individual candidates to fund their own campaigns. Nigeria should learn from the American experience, where campaign money coming from private sources is seriously threatening or undermining the American democracy. Too much money in politics does not give a voice to the voiceless.

e) When individuals are allowed to finance their own campaigns, the **party hierarchy loses control** of what party members should do and how they should act. When party members fund their own campaigns and get themselves elected, they are most unlikely to be loyal to the party on whose platform they got elected. They are likely to shift allegiance to another party, at a time of their choosing.

f) Decamping from one political party to another, and legislators and governors retaining the seats they won under the banner of the party from which they are departing, have created some legislative problems, which need a constitutional remedy. Before the 2015 general elections, Nigerians witnessed a mass exodus of members of the National and State Assemblies, and some state governors decamping from the ruling party, the People's Democratic Party (PDP), to the opposition party, the All Progressive Congress (APC) and vice versa. Because of this shift, the PDP that had majority members in the National Assembly became a minority party after most of its members, including the Speaker of the House of Representatives, moved to the opposition party, the APC. This move also created some disturbances that interrupted the functions of the National Assembly for weeks. This event, once again, reminded Nigerians of the political crises that abruptly brought Nigeria's First Republic (1960-1966) to a halt.

g) Given the current political trend in the country, this legislation should ban politicians from **shifting allegiance from one political party to another.** But, if they do, they must **first resign officially from the party and relinquish any elected seats or positions they occupy,** at the time, to the party on whose platform or banner they got elected to those seats or positions. It is the right of the party through its protocol to nominate a member or members to fill the vacant seat or seats created by the decamping legislator/s. The same scenario applies to a state governor who decamps from the party that put him/her into an office.

h) To assist registered political parties in Nigeria minimizes the burden of financing their candidates' campaigns and to enhance party discipline within parties' organizations, the legislation should demand that federal and state governments **subsidize the parties finances and allow them equal air time** in using federal and state media networks to disseminate their messages to the public during political campaign seasons.

i) There were **sixty-three (63) registered political parties in Nigeria** that vied for the political offices during the 2011 elections, and since the birth of Nigeria's Fourth Republic (1999--present), the PDP has been the ruling party in the country with little or no challenges coming from these numbers of parties. With the emergence of the new opposition party, the APC (coalition of a few parties), the PDP's prominence and dominance have been seriously questioned and challenged, as the 2015 election outcomes have shown.

j) Given the obvious fact on the ground, the legislation should create **a two-party system** for Nigeria rather than having a **multi-party system** that has helped in making Nigeria a **one-party state**. Since these mushroom parties do not have a political clout in the National Assembly because of their small number of members in the National Assembly, and since the country has, by default, come up with two strongest parties, it is time for these other mushroom parties to fall behind any of these parties (PDP and APC). This is one way to strengthen party politics in Nigeria, it is a way to promote and nurture good governance since no political party will ever monopolize power in the country, and a two-party system will help to minimize the effects of religiosity and ethnicity in the country.

k) To ensure smooth elections in the country, one that will be free from rigging and violence, the legislation should ban the **use of thugs from the polling stations during elections.** By the same token, political campaign and distribution of money to voters by parties' representatives at **the polling booths** on the day of elections should be banned outright. Such practices amount to buying votes and they undermine the integrity of elections in determining the people's choice.

l) The legislation should also outlaw the use of **law enforcement officials and the military** from polling stations, except during party rallies, where they may be needed to provide adequate security. To minimize vote rigging in the country, political thugs and law enforcement officials, including the military should stay away entirely from the polling stations. The legislation should impose a heavy penalty on political parties that employ thugs and law enforcement officials, distribute money and ask people to vote for their party candidates at the polling stations during elections. Any political party that employs thugs, uniformed officers, gives out money to voters and asks them to vote for its candidates in polling stations, snatches ballot boxes, intimidates voters, **Independent National Electoral Commission's (INEC) officials**, or party opponents, stuffs illegal ballot papers, deliberately delays and diverts electoral materials during elections must forfeit the votes cast on its candidates' behalf in polling stations, where such violations occurred.

m) The law should mandate all political parties to educate their members and supporters on the significance of these issues, and the INEC should use the mainstream and social media consistently to remind the parties of their obligation to educate the public, especially the youth and party members about the consequences of being used by politicians as thugs to disrupt elections and cause mayhem.

n) The legislation should make it as a mandate that the only entities to be seen at polling stations around the country during elections should be **voters, officers and staff of the INEC.** The law should make it crystal clear that the INEC is the only body authorized to conduct elections in the country. For INEC to gain legitimacy and trust among the Nigerian electorates, the legislation should broaden the roles and powers of the organization. It should make it crystal clear that the leadership of the INEC should be an elective position with no party affiliation and not an appointive one. The legislation should ban the INEC from using paid volunteers to conduct elections. The organization should be empowered to recruit and train its own permanent staff for election purposes and heavy penalties imposed on staff with shady characters.

o) If INEC is to be truly independent (neutral), its budgets should be appropriated by the National Assembly and should not be coming from the Office of the President that appoints the Commission's leadership. One of the new roles of the INEC is to ensure that local government elections are **conducted at the same time the Governorship and State House of Assemblies' elections are conducted.** Local Government Elections should no longer be left in the hands of State Governments because many state governors have abused this privilege. Instead of giving the local people (people at the grassroots) the opportunity of choosing their Local Government Chairmen and Councilors, some state governors handpick these individuals and create what they term as an **Interim administration,** thereby, usurping the people's right to choose. This kind of behavior is undemocratic.

Justifications for Proposing Policy #6

Elections in Nigeria have not been free, fair, and open. Election malpractices have been major sources of Nigerian political crises since the country gained her political independence from Great Britain in 1960. Generally speaking, elections are one of the democratic means of getting people into political offices and positions. Since it is impossible for every citizen of a country to assemble together in a place to deliberate on the welfare of their country, a representative assembly is created to allow citizens to elect or appoint a few numbers of people among themselves to represent their interests in the assembly. This is what makes modern electoral process very unique and attractive. Those persons who are elected into these positions (national, state, and local government legislators, national president, state governors, and local government chairmen) are then responsible for the governing of the country. They set the policy agenda, control government's revenues, and decide how these funds are to be spent.

Unlike military rule, no politician comes into a democratically constituted government without being democratically elected. Since individuals can no longer shoot their way into power, elections are now the only means of getting people into government positions. Because the electoral process is not as easy as a military dictatorship, politicians who want to be in power at all cost and by all means necessary, have to devise illegitimate means of circumventing the sanctity and integrity of elections. Their overall intention is to cheat their way into power, just like the military personnel use the barrel of their guns to achieve power. Politicians who indulge themselves with these kinds of shady behaviors are never interested in serving the country and its people adequately, but only interested in accumulating personal wealth.

Because of the intention they had for going into politics, which is to loot public funds, and because they knew that they would not be successful at the polls due to their unpopularity among voters, shady politicians always resort to election rigging, which can be achieved through various means, such as:

- Buying of votes at polling stations;
- Stuffing of ballot boxes with illegal ballot papers;
- Snatching of ballot boxes from polling stations, the collation centers, or while being transported to the collation centers;
- Illegal thumb printing;
- Deliberate delays and diversion of electoral materials,
- Intimidation of voters, INEC officials, and opponents at polling stations and at the collation centers; and
- Falsification of results.

The constant electoral malpractices in Nigeria has given the country a black eye in the comity of nations, but Nigerians whom, according to Andrew Harding (2015), a BBC African correspondent, are fighting back with "social media, fingerprinting scanners, and an army of young volunteer observers armed with mobile phones have all played their role, as they have done in other recent African elections, in limiting the possibilities of ballot stuffing and other shenanigans."

To minimize the adverse effects of electoral malpractices in Nigeria, the author of this book has come up with various measures, as you have read, that can be taken to address this endemic problem facing Nigeria's electoral process. It is definitely up to the Nigerian people and their governing elite to embrace the proposed measures and implement them, if they are serious and interested in eliminating or minimizing the adverse effects of these electoral malpractices in the country. Politics in Nigeria should be seen as a sport and not as warfare. There is a lot to gain from having the real choice of the people in office rather than having the wrong ones running the country. There is nothing wrong in contesting and winning elections, but to win, you must win clean without cheating.

Implications of not implementing Policy Proposal #6

The quest for using politics for personal wealth acquisition must be discouraged. One way to achieve this is by making election fraud impossible. The anxiety elections generate in Nigerian cannot be underestimated. During elections, there is always a high degree of fear of violence and panic and, as a result, most

Nigerians do not know what else to expect the next time around. Because of election anxieties in Nigeria, many foreigners are eager to leave the country as quick as possible because they are afraid of violence erupting. The economy is also brought to a halt because the free movement of people and goods are restricted as a result of the insecurity elections may generate. These are major problems Nigerians are confronted with during elections. Election anxieties and the violence it generates will continue unabated if nothing concrete is done to curtail electoral malpractices in Nigeria. The Nigerian governing elite should not forget that Boko Haram's mayhem intensified after the 2011 elections, when those in Northern Nigeria felt that Gen. Muhammadu Buhari's presidency was stolen at the polls. Nigerians have suffered dearly for this perception and, a repeat of such will be catastrophic for the country. The lesson of the past should not be swept under the rug, but must be used to transform the future.

Chapter 9

CONCLUSION

The Way Forward

Nigeria, like most Third World countries, has many endemic problems hindering its progress and advancement. As identified in the book, these endemic problems include: lack of national consciousness (unity), resulting from bad governance, ethnic and religious intolerance; civil war and decades of military dictatorship (grabbing power through the barrel of the gun), resulting from ethnic dominance and hegemony; insecurity (youth restiveness, crime and violence), resulting from massive unemployment; vast dependency on foreign countries, resulting from colonial legacy; non-utilization of commissions of inquiries in solving issues of national significance, resulting from lack of political education and strong political institutions; decades of defective political institutions, resulting from over concentration of power (a highly centralized federal institution) in Abuja; and election fraud, resulting from desperation and inordinate quest for political power and accumulation of personal wealth.

The empirical examination of the above-stated problems, in terms of how they evolved, why they still exist, and the inability of the Nigerian government in solving them, reveals that members of the Nigerian ruling class are more interested in maintaining their lavish lifestyles than transforming the lives of average Nigerians, given the country's enormous strategic natural resources. The facts on the ground also show that those (the ruling class) who are responsible for steering the affairs of the country are not deeply interested in empowering ordinary Nigerians economically, because making the necessary and needed changes in the system may jeopardize their chances of getting ahead. Consequently, greedy Nigerian officials want to keep things the way they are because the status-quo benefits them tremendously. Given the status-quo, members of the ruling class have concluded that why "fixing things or reinventing the wheel" when things are not broken. The general belief in Nigeria is that members of the political class will care less about the plights of ordinary Nigerians as long as their welfare and those of their immediate family members and cronies are met and secured. This scenario explains why the above-enumerated problems still persist.

As an organic entity, Nigeria is capable and able to transform itself into a formidable and envious society if visionary, selfless, transformational, nationalistic and patriotic leaders can be found to take their rightful place in the governance of the country. To right the wrong done to the Nigerian nation by those who have, in the past, steered its affairs, the author of this book has painfully and meticulously articulated some measures that can be used to overcome some of the problems enumerated above. The institutionalization of these measures will definitely lead to the achievement of good governance in Nigeria, a dream to which many Nigerians are desperately seeking. Some of these proposed measures have been openly expressed by various writers and opinion makers in Nigeria. To a certain degree, some provisions of the report of the recently concluded National Sovereign Conference that met in 2014 are reflected in the proposed policies outlined in Chapter 8 of this book.

Nigerians are, indeed, desperately yearning for positive changes in the polity and the emergence of the APC in the 2015 general elections, as the new ruling party in the country, is a testimonial fact that Nigerians do not want to see non-performing politicians or a political party in control of the country's governance. Nigerians are gradually awakening to the political reality in the country. They have realized that failure to hold politicians accountable for their deeds while in office will always undermine good governance.

The implication of the APC electoral victory both at the national level and in many states of the federation on March 28 and April 11, 2015, is to let non-performing politicians and their political parties know that their days in politics are numbered and that from now on, it is no longer going to be "business as usual." Nigerians are definitely looking for leaders and parties that will transform their lives for the better.

By this singular act from the Nigerian electorates (voters), it seems that the era of selfishness, over-bearing, impunity, and looting of public funds is coming to an abrupt end. If the proposed measures articulated in this book are implemented, they will definitely eliminate these vices (impunity, massive corruption, and self-centeredness) from the country's polity. The measures will move the country forward and will make it compete globally and, thereby, restore its envious image as "the giant of Africa."

Nigeria must regain its lost glory, because many in the Black World are still looking upon her to provide the able leadership needed for the Black world to move forward. The articulation of this exercise (research study) is the author's own contribution in making Nigeria a better place, where coming generations of Nigerians can live comfortably in peace and harmony and be able to fulfill their God given potentials. A better Nigeria will definitely eliminate the massive migration and the "brain drain" the country is currently experiencing because of bad governance, which has plagued the country for years.

Appendices

Nigeria's Presidents / Heads of States and Vices   [1960 – Present]

Presidents / Heads of State   *Period*

1. Dr. Nnamdi Azikiwe (Governor General)   1st Oct. 1960 – 1st Oct. 1963
    Sir. Abubakar Tafawa Balewa; (Prime Minister)

    Dr. NnamdiAzikiwe (President)   1st Oct. 1963 – 16th Jan. 1966
    Sir. Abubakar Tafawa Balewa; (Prime Minister)

2. Gen J.T.U Aguyi Ironsi (Military Head of State)   16th Jan. 1966 – 29th July 1966
    Brig. Babafemi Ogundipe (Chief of Staff, Supreme Hq.)

3. Gen. Yakubu Gowon (Military Head of State)   1st Aug. – 29th July 1975:
    Vice Admiral Joseph Edet Akinwale Wey, (Chief of Staff, Supreme Hq.)

4. Gen. Murtala Ramat Muhammed (Military Head of State) 29th July 1975 – 13th Feb. 1976:
    Gen. Olusegun Obasanjo (Chief of Staff, Supreme Hq.)

5. Gen. Olusegun Obasanjo (Military Head of State) 13th Feb. 1976 – 1st Oct. 1979
    Maj. Gen. Shehu Musa Yar'Adua (Chief of Staff, Supreme Hq.)

6. Alhaji Shehu Shagari (President)   1st Oct. 1979 – 31st Dec. 1983
    Dr. Alex Ifeanyichukwu Ekweme (Vice President)

7. Maj. Gen. Muhammadu Buhari (Military Head of State) 31st Dec. 1983 – 27th Aug. 1985
    Brig. Babatunde Idiagbon (Chief of Staff, Supreme Hq.)

8. Gen. Ibrahim Badamasi Babangida (Military President) 27th Aug. 1985 – 26th Aug. 1993
    Commodore Ebitu Ukiwe (Chief of General Staff; 1985 -1986),
    Admiral Augustus Aikhomu (Chief of General Staff; 1986-1993)

9. Ernest Shonekan (Head of Interim National Government) 26th Aug. – 17th Nov. 1993

10. Gen. Sani Abacha (Military Head of State)   17th Nov. 1993 - 8th June 1998
    Lt. Gen. Oladipo Diya (Chief of General Staff)

11. Gen. Abdulsalami Abubakar (Military Head of State) 8th June 1998 – 29th May 1999
    Vice Admiral Mike Okhai Akhigbe (Chief of General Staff)

12. Chief Olusegun Obasanjo (President)   29th May 1999 – 29th May 2007
    Alhaji Atiku Abubakar (Vice President)

13. Umaru Musa Yar'Adua (President)   29th May 2007 – 5th May 2010
    Dr. Goodluck Ebele Jonathan Vice President)

14. Dr. Goodluck Ebele Jonathan (Acting President, Acted for Umaru M. Yar'Adua who was indisposed due to ill health)   9th Feb.2010 – 6th May 2010

15. Dr. Goodluck Ebele Jonathan (President)   6th May 2010- 29th May 2011
Arc. Namadi Sambo; (Vice president)

16. Goodluck Jonathan (President)   29th May 2011 - 28th May 2015
    Arc. Namadi sambo (Vice president)

17. President Muhammdu Buhari   29th May2015 -to date
    Prof. Yemi Osinbanjo

Reference List

Abayomi, Amaka and Ikenna Asomba. (2012, November 29). Prof. Anibeze: Give Top Priority to Teacher's Welfare, *Vanguard Nigeria.* Retrieved on November 30, 2012, from http://www.vanguardngr.com/2012/11/give-top-priority-to...

Abby, Wakama. (2007, November 20). Siemens Bribery Scandal: Nigerian President Orders Probe. Retrieved on August 24, 2010 from http://www.itnewsafrica.com/2007/11/siemens-bribery-scandal-niger...

Abdullahi, Bello (n.d.) Banks Consolidation and N25bn Recapitalization: Another Perspective. *Gamji.Com.* Retrieved on February 27, 2012 from http://www.gamji.com/article6000/NEWS6057.htm

Abioye, Oyetunji. (2013, October 23). Presidential Fleet Larger than Three Domestic Airlines. *PunchNigeria.Com.* Retrieved on October 24, 2013, from http://www.punchng.com/news/presidential-fleet-larger-than-three-domestic-airlines...

About the United States Department of Homeland Security. (2003, March1). *DHS Website.* Retrieved on November 2, 2014, from http://www.dhs.gov/about-dhs

Aborisade, Sunday. (2013, February 24). Most Nigerian Billionaires are Corrupt—Akinyemi. *Punch Nigeria.* Retrieved on March 24, 2013, from http://www.punchng.com/news/most-nigerian-billionaires-are-corrupt-akinyemi

Achebe, Chinua. (1983). *The Trouble With Nigeria.* Enugu, Nigeria: Fourth Dimension Publishing Company.

Adebayo, Bukola. (2013, January 16). Hypertension, Now Killing Young Nigerians—Experts. *Punch Nigeria.* Retrieved on January 17, 2013, from http://punch.www.punchng.com

Adebayo, Bukola. (2011, October 12). Nigerians Spend N2.5 billion Yearly on Medical Trips to India. *NigeriaWorld.com,* Retrieved on October 12, 2011, from http://odili.net/news/source/2011/oct/12/802.html

Adefaka, Bashir. (2011, December 10). I Used to Help OBJ Get Access to Abacha and Diya— Bode George. *Vanguardngr.Com,* Retrieved on December 11, 2011 from http://www.vanguardngr.com/2011/12/i-used-to-help-obj-get-access...

Adeoye, Akinola O. (2009). Godfatherism and the Future of Nigerian Democracy. African *Journal of Political Science and International Relations* Vol. 3 (6), pp.268-272.

Adepegba, Adelani and Owuamanam, Jude. (2014, November 30). Boko Haram: America not

Nigeria's Friend, Says Gowon. *Punch Nigeria.* Retrieved on December 2, 2014, from http://www.punchng.com/news/boko-haram-america-not-nigerias-friend-says-gowon/

Adepegba, Adelani. (2014, February 4). Policeman Who Demanded Dollar Bribe Faces Dismissal. *Punch Nigeria.* Retrieved on February 4, 2014, from http://www.punchng.com/.../policeman-faces-dismissal-over-dollar-bribe/

Adepegba, Adeline. (2013, January 22). Minister, IG on Collision Course over Police Funds. *Punch Nigeria,* Retrieved on January 23, 2013, from http://www.punchng.com/news/minister-ig-on-collision-course...

Aderinokun, Kunle. (2008, June 26). Bankole: Obasanjo Release $13.5 Billion for Unidentified Projects. *Thisdayonline.com,* Retrieved on June 26, 2008, from http://www.thisdayonline.com/nview.php?id=115221&printer_friendly=1

Adetayo, Olalekan. (2012, November 3). Oronsaye, Oti, Ribadu Fight Openly Before Jonathan. *PunchNigeria.Com,* Retrieved on November 5, 2012 from http://www.punchng.com/news/oronsaye-oti-ribadu-fight-openly-

Adeyemi, Babalola (2011). Bank Failure in Nigeria: A consequence of Capital Inadequacy, Lack of Transparency and Non-performing Loans. *Banks and Bank System* Vol. 6 Issue 1, 99-109.

Adewole, Lanre. (2012, October 19). EFCC Arraigns Man Arrested With $7 Million Cash Today. *Nigerian Tribune,* Retrieved on October 20, 2012 from http://tribune.com.ng/index.php/news/49482-efcc-arraigns-man-arres...

Adewole, Lanre. (2012, October 22). EFCC Arrests Two Cash Couriers with $107,000. *Nigerian Tribune,* Retrieved on October 23, 2012, from http://tribune.com.ng/...efccarrests-two-cash-couriers...107000--

Adewole, Lanre. (2012, December 20). EFCC Nabs another Cash Courier with $130,000 at Mallam Aminu Kano International Airport, Kano. *Nigeria Tribune,* Retrieved on December 21, 2012, from http://tribune.com.ng/news2013/index.php/en/component/k2/item/...

Adisa, Taiwo. (2014, April 21). Insurgency: Middle Belt Leaders Threaten to Quit ACF; Say Forum Has Failed to Prevent Killing of Northern Minorities; Give June 30 Deadline. *Nigerian Tribune,* Retrieved on April 23, 2014, from http://www.tribune.com.ng/news/latest-news/item/3786-insurgency-middle-belt-leaders-th...

Adisa, Taiwo. (2012, October 23). Nigerian Diplomats in Europe, Americas Stranded: Use

Ghanaians as Fronts to Secure Accommodation, as Federal Government Owes them Salaries and Allowances. *Nigerian Tribune,* Retrieved on October 25, 2012, from http://tribune.com.ng/index.php/lead-stories/49642-nigeria...

Agande, Ben. (2013, October 9). Jonathan Promises Special Intervention Fund to Establish More Hospitals. *Vanguardngr.Com.* Retrieved on October 9, 2013, from http://www.vanguardngr.com/.../jonathan-promises-special-intervention-fund-to-establish-more-hospitals...

Agbakwuru, Johnbosco and Joseph Erunke. (2014, January 23). Ihejirika: Ndigbo to Head to ICC Over Biafra Massacre. *Vanguard Nigeria.* Retrieved on January 24, 2014, from http://www.vanguardngr.com/.../ihejirika-ndigbo-head-icc-biafra-massacre/

Agbakwuru, Johnbosco and Joseph Erunke. (2013, October 26). Senate Justifies N150billion Annual Budget for NASS. *VanguardNigeria.Com.* Retrieved on October 28, 2013, from http://www.vangardngr.com/.../senate-justifies-n150-billion-annual-budget-for-nass...

Agbakwuru, Johnbosco, Joseph Erunke, and Levinus Nwabughiogu. (2013, August 21). N1 Trillion Expenditure: NASS to come up with Accurate Figure--Maccido. *VanguardNigeria.Com.* Retrieved on August 21, 2013, from http://www.vanguardngr.com/.../n1trn-expenditure-nass-tocome-up-with-accurate-figure...

Akande, Laolu. (2014, December 21). Nigeria: Why We Stopped Buying Nigeria's Oil, By White House. *allAfrica.com.* Retrieved on December 23, 2014, from http://allafrica.com/stories/201412220407.html

Akasike, Chukwudi. (2013, October 2). Honour Agreement with ASUU, Group Tells FG *Punchng.Com,* Retrieved on October 2, 2013 from http://www.punchng.com/news

Akasike, Chukwudi. (2012, November, 16). Federal Government to Float National Carrier with Thirty Aircrafts. *Punch Nigeria.Com,* Retrieved on November 16, 2012, from http://www.punchng.com/business/business-economy/fg-to-float...

Akinkuotu, Eniola. (2013, March 19). Senators Are Worse Than Robbers—Suspects. *Punch Nigeria.* Retrieved on March 26, 2013, from http://www.punchng.com/metro/senators-are-worse-than-robbers-suspects

Akinkuotu, Eniola. (2014, September 19). No Political Party has Plan for Education--Peter Obi. *Nigerian Punch.* Retrieved on September 20, 2014, from http://www.punchng.com/politics/no-political-party-has-plan-for-education-peter-obi/

Akinkuotu, Eniola. (2012, October 21). EFCC Arrests FAAN Official with N218 Million at

Airport. *Punch Nigeria,* Retrieved on October 23, 2012, from http://www.punchng.com/2012/10/12efcc-arrests-faan...

Akinyemi, Bolaji. (2014, November 30). Why Irritating Comments from America Should Stop. *Vanguard Nigerian.* Retrieved on December 2, 2014, from http://www.vanguardngr.com/2014/11/irritating-comments-america-stop-prof-akinyemi/

Akoni, Olasunkanmi and Monsur Olowoopejo. (2012, October, 23). Bad Roads: Citizenry, Motorists at the Mercy of Gridlock, Bandits. *Vanguard Nigeria,* Retrieved on October 23, 2012, from http://www.vanguardngr.com/2012/10/bad-roads-citizentry...

Alabelewe, Abdulgafar. (2013, September 17).Let Politicians' Children Lead If You must be Thugs, Tambuwal Tells Youths. *Daily Sun.* Retrieved on September 17 2013, from http://www.sunewsonline.com/.../let-politicians'-children-lead-if-you-must-be-thugs...

Alaneme, Erasmus. (2010, November 1). Nigeria: Siemens Bribery Scam—EFCC to Arraign Suspects Thursday. *Daily Champion,* Retrieved on August 24, 2012 from http://allafrica.com/stories/20101030609.html

Alarape, Akeeb. (2012, September 23). David West: What Nigerians Don't Know about IBB, Buhari's Oil Industry Management. *Daily Sun Nigeria,* Retrieved on October 11, 2012, from http://sunnewsonline.com/new/politics/what-nigerians-don't-know-ab...

Alawiye, Ademola. (2014, January 30). Politicians Hide Fortunes in Real Estate, Hospitality Sectors. *Punch Nigeria.* Retrieved on January 30, 2014, from http://www.punchng.com/.../politicians-hide-fortunes-in-real-estate-hospitality-sectors

Albanese, Jay S. (2011). *Transnational Crime and the Twenty-first Century: Criminal Enterprise, Corruption and Opportunity.* Oxford, London: Oxford University Press.

Alechenu, John. (2013, December 21). I Was Forced to Pay Godfather N10 million Monthly as Anambra Governor—Mbadinuju. *Punch Nigeria.* Retrieved on December 23, 2013, from http://www.punchng.com/.../i-was-forced-to-pay-a-godfather-n10m-monthly-asanambra-governor-mbadinuju/

Alexander, Michelle. (2012). *The New Jim Crow: Mass Incarceration in the Age of Colorblindness.* New York: The New Press.

Aluko, Banji. (2014, August 8). Oshiomhole: Ethnic Origin Concept, Cause of Disunity. *Nigerian Tribune,* Retrieved on August 10, 2014, from http://www.tribune.com.ng/news/news-headlines/item/12804-ethnic-origin-concept-cause-...

Aluko, Olaleye. (2014, September16). Musicians Sing Our Praises--Robbery Suspects. *Punch*

Nigeria. Retrieved on September 17, 2014, from
http://www.punchng.com/metro-plus/musicians-sing-our-praises-at-parties-robbery-suspects/

Amaefule, Everest, Olokor, Friday, and Adesomoju, Ade. (2015, April 29). Jonathan, Sambo, Others to get N3.24 Billion Severance Pay. Punch Nigeria. Retrieved on April 30, 2015, from   http://www.punchng.com/news/jonathan-sambo-others-to-get-n3.24billion-severance-pay...

Amaefule, Everest, Fidelis Soriwei, and John Alechenu. (2012, October 14). Presidency to Spend N654.02 Million on Generators. Punch Nigeria, Retrieved on October 14, 2012 from http://www.punchng.com/news/presidency-to-spend-n654-02m-on-ge...

Amaefule, Everest. (2012, September 26). Federal Government to Sell Power Firms to Elumelu, Otedola, Others. *Nigeria World,*
Retrieved   on   September   26,   2012   from
http://odili.net/news/source/2012/sep/26/831.html

Ameh, John. (2013, August 22). Ask RMAFC to Slash Our Wages--Reps. *PunchNigeria.Com.* Retrieved on August 23, 2013, from http://www.punchng.com/news/Ask-RMAFC-to-Slash-our-wages-Reps...

Ameh, John and Oluwole Josiah. (2012, October 11). Budget: Education, Defense, Police Get Lion's Share as President Jonathan Proposes N4.9 Trillion for 2013, *PunchNigeria.Com.* Retrieved from
http://www.punchng.com/news/budget-education-defense-police-get...

Amodu, Taiwo. (2012, October 19). Power Distribution: Governors Reject Bid Winner. *Sunnewsonline.Com,*
Retrieved on October 19, 2012 from
http://sunnewsonline.com/new/national/power-distribution-govs-reje...

Andreopoulos, George J. (2005). Genocide, War Crimes and Crimes against Humanity. In Mangai Natarajan (Editor), *Introduction to International Criminal Justice* (pp. 265-270).

Anumihe, Isaac. (2012, September 26). IBB Group Buys Shiroro Plant. *Daily Sun Nigeria,* Retrieved on September 26, 2012 from http://sunnewsonline.com/new/national/transcorp-to-pay300m-for-ug...

Attack on Emir of Kano, A Wake UP Call—IBB. (2013, January 21). *Daily Sun Nigeria,* Retrieved on January 22, 2013, from http://sunnewsonline.com/new/cover/attack-on-emir-of-kano-a...

Ayittey, George B. N. (1992). *Africa Betrayed.* New York: St. Martin's Press.

Aziken, Emanuel and Oke, Gbenga. (2015, April 14). Buhari to Move Against Pension for Ex-

Governors. *VanguardNigeria.com.* Retrieved on April 16, 2015, from http://www.vanguardngr.com/2015/04/buhari-to-move-against-pension-for-ex-governors...

Babangida, Ibrahim Badamasi. (2013, January 21). Attack on Emir of Kano, a Wake-up Call. *Daily Sun Nigeria,* Retrieved on April 3, 2013, from http://sunnewsonline.com/new/cover/attack-on-emir-of-kano-a-wake-up-call-ibb

Balogun, Wole. (2014, January 3). For Human Traffickers, It's a Bad New Year. *Daily Sun Nigeria.* Retrieved on January 5, 2014, from http://sunnewsonline.com/new/cover/human-traffickers-bad-new-year

Bartollas, Clemens. (1997). *Juvenile Delinquency.* 4th Ed. Boston: Allyn and Bacon.

Bello, Bashir. (2013, September 13). Kaduna Assembly Stops Allowances, Overseas' Medical Treatment for Ex- Governors, Deputies. *Guardian Nigeria.* Retrieved on September 15, 2013, from http://www.ngguardiannews.com/.../132653-kaduna-assembly-stops-allowances-overseas-medical-treatment-for-ex-governor-deputies

Bennis, Phyllis. (2006). *Challenging Empire: How People, Governments, and the UN Defy US Power.* Gloucestershire, Great Britain: Arris Books.

Binniyat, Luka. (2013, March 6). Declare Total Amnesty for Boko Haram, Sultan of Sokoto Tells Jonathan. *Vanguardngr.Com.* Retrieved on March 7, 2013, from http://www.vanguardngr.com/declare-total-amnesty-for-boko-haram-sultan-...

Binniyat, Luka. (2012, August 28). Buhari: Corruption Came into Petroleum Sector During Babangida, Obasanjo, and Jonathan Era.*Vanguadngr.com,* Retrieved on August 30, 2012 from http://www.vanguardngr.com/2012/08/buhari-blames-insurity-on1...

Boese, Wade. (2004, May). NATO Expands, Russia Grumbles. Arms Control Association. Retrieved on April 10, 2014, from http://www.armscontrol.org/print/1553

Bribery Scandal: Siemens to Pay Nigeria N7 billion in Damages. (2010, November1). *Pointblanknews.com.* Retrieved on August 24, 2012 from http://www.pointblanknews.com/News/os4189.html

Buhari, Muhammadu. (2014, April 22). Nyanya Bomb Blasts and the Fight against Terrorism in Nigeria. *Daily Sun Nigeria.* Retrieved on April 24, 2014, from http://sunnewsonline.com/new/?p=60776

Buhayar, Noah. (2012, August 31). Hurricane Isaac May Cost Insurers $2 Billion, AIR Says *Bloomberg News*, Retrieved on November 10, 2012, from http://www.bloomberg.com/news/print/2012-08-31/hurricane-isaac-...

Chiakwelu, Emeka. (n.d.). Nigeria Payment of Foreign Debt: The Largest Transfer of Wealth in

Modern   Time.   *Gamji.Com.*   Retrieved   on   February   11,   2014,   from
        http://www.gamji.com/article8000/NEWS8358.htm

Chief of the Defense Staff (Nigeria) (2014, July 2). *Wikipedia, the Free Encyclopedia*. Retrieved
        on   November   12,   2014,   from
        http://en.wikipedia.org/wiki/Chief_of_the_Defense_Staff_(Nigeria)

Chicago School of Economics: Definition and Meaning (2010). *BusinessDictionary.com,*
        Retrieved on December 12, 2012, from
        http://www.businessdictionary.com/definition/Chicago-school-of-ec...

Christensen, John. (2007). Dirty Money: Inside the Secret World of Offshore Banking. In Steven
        Hiatt (Ed.), *A Game as Old as Empire: The Secret World of Economic Hit Men and the
        Web of Global Corruption* (pp.41-68). San Francisco: Berrett-Koehler Publishers.

Chronicles of Command. (n.d.). *Nigerian Navy Official Website*. Retrieved on November 11,
        2014, from http://www.navy.mil.ng/Chronicles-of-command

Cole, George F., Christopher E. Smith, and Christina Dejong. (2015). *The American System of
        Criminal Justice.* 14th Ed. Stamford, CT: Cengage Learning.

Cole, George F. and Christopher E. Smith. (2010). *The American System of Criminal Justice.*12
        Ed. Belmont, CA: Wadsworth, Cengage Learning.

Colonial Constitutions of Nigeria. (2007, January 1). *Citizens for Nigeria.com*, Retrieved on
        December 5, 2012, from
        http://www.citizenfornigeri.com/library/politicial/55-colonial-consti...

Combs, Jerald A. (1986). *The History of American Foreign Policy.* New York: Alfred A. Knopf.

Cowry Research Desk (2009, June 30). *Nigerian Banking Report: Following the Progress of
        Nigerian Banks in the Last Ten Years.* Cowry Asset Management Limited.

Cox, Steven M., McCamey, William P., and Scaramella, Gene L. (2014). *Introduction to
        Policing*, 2nd Ed. Thousand Oaks, California: Sage Publications, Inc.

Crisis of the Nigerian Academy. (2012, December 6,). *The Guardian Nigeria Editorial Board
        Commentary,*   Retrieved   on   December   7,   2012,   from
        http://www.ngrguardiannews.com/index.php?option=content&...

Daka, Terhemba. (2012, November 10). Nigerians in Diaspora to Remit N4.7 Trillion. *The
        Guardian   Nigeria,*   Retrieved   on   November   11,   2012,   from
        http://www.ngrguardiannews.com/index.php?option=content&...

Dangida, Aliyu. (2014, February 20). Don't Blame Jonathan for Your Woes, Turaki Tells North

Vanguard   Nigeria   Retrieved   on   February   28,   2014,   from
      http://www.vanguardngr.com/.../don't-blame-jonathan-woes-turaki-tells-north

Daniel, Soni. (2014, March 30). Nyako to Jonathan: Your Government Responsible for Rising
      Terrorism in the North. *Vanguard Nigeria.* Retrieved on March 31, 2014, from
      http://www.Vanguardngr.com/.../nyako-jonathan-govt-responsible-rising-terrorism-
      north

Daniel, Soni. (2013, April 2). Northern Leaders to Jonathan: Stop Using Boko Haram to
      Blackmail   us.   *Vanguardngr.com,*   Retrieved   on   April   3,   2013,   from
      http://www.vanguardngr.com/.../northern-leaders-to-jonathan-stop-using-b...

Daniel, Soni. (2013, January 17). Nigeria Immigration Service: Rose Uzoma's Sack:
      Recruitment Turns Awry as Fate of 4, 560 Employees Hang in Balance. *Vanguard Nigeria.*
      Retrieved on January 18, 2013, from
      http://www.vanguardngr.com/rose-uzomas-sack-recuritment-turns-awry-as-f...

Daniel, Soni. (2012, September 21). Oil Subsidy Scam: CAC Hides Suspects'
      Files.*Vanguardngr.com,*   Retrieved   on   September   22,   2012,   from
      http://www.vanguaedngr.com/2012/09/oil-subsidy-scam-cac-hides-s...

Daykeay, Emmanuel Bravy. (2014, May 14). Truth and Reconciliation Commission in Liberia:
      Analysis of the Prospects and Challenges Faced by the Government of Liberia. *The Game
      Changers-Human Rights Movement for Liberia, West Africa.* Retrieved on September 30,
      2014, from http://gamechangersofliberia.com/2014/05/15/truth-and-reconciliation...

Dempsey, John S. and Forst, Linda S. (2014). *An Introduction to Policing,* 7th edition. Clifton
      Park, New York: Delmar Cengage Learning.

Director of National Intelligence. (2014, August 5). *Wikipedia, the Free Encyclopedia.* Retrieved
      on   October   20,   2014,   from
      http://en.wikipedia.org/wiki/Director_of_National_Intelligence

Duru, Peter and Onyegbadue, Amamdi. (2013, November 1). Nigeria: Federal Government yet
      to Release N100 Billion to Universities, Say ASSU. *Vanguard Nigeria* Newspaper,
      published   in   *allAfrica.Com.*   Retrieved   on   November   3,   3013,   from
      http://www.allafrica.com/stories/201311010297.html

Dye, Thomas R. (2002). *Understanding Public Policy.* 10th Ed. New Jersey: Upper Saddle
      River, Prentice Hall.

Ebegbulem, Simon. (2013, October 24). Oshiomhole Accuses Police of Aiding Electoral

Malpractices. *Vanguard Nigeria.* Retrieved on October 25, 2013, from http://www.vanguardngr.com/.../oshiomhole-accuses-police-aiding-electoral-malpractices/

Edeh, Suzan. (2013, September 20). No Going Back on ASUU Demand--ATBU Chapter Chairman. *allAfrica.Com,* Retrieved on September 21, 2013, from http://www.allafrica.com/stories/201309201215.html

Edike, Tony. (2014, January 22). Ihejirika: Anglican Bishop of Enugu Warns Northern Elders. *Vanguard Nigeria.* Retrieved on January 22, 2014, from http://www.vanguardngr.com/.../ihejirika-anglican-bishop-warns-northern-elders/

Edike, Tony. (2012, January 30). Jonathan Decries Poor Ratings of Nigerian Universities, *Vanguardngr.com,* Retrieved on January 31, 2012, from http://www.vanguardngr.com/2012/01/jonathan-decries-poor...

Efforts to Save Nigeria's Indigenous Languages Intensifies. (2014, March 4). *Nigeria World.Com,* Retrieved on March 5, 2014, from http://odili.net/news/source/2014/mar/4/3.html

Eke, E.O. (2014, March 27). Nigeria, A Republic, Not Criminal Paradise. *NigeriaWorld.Com.* Retrieved on March 30, 2015, from http://nigeriaworld.com/feature/publication/eke/032715.html

Elebeke, Emmanuel. (2014, January 25). Since Independence More Northerners Ruled Nigeria, People Didn't Cause Trouble-Maku. *Vanguard Nigeria.* Retrieved on January 27, 2014, from http://www.vanguardngr.com/.../since-independence-northerners-ruled-nigeria-people-didn't-cause-trouble-maku

Eley, Tom. (2008, September 26). Chrysler 1979: Lessons from an Early Corporate Bailout *WSWS.org,* Retrieved on October 10, 2012 from http://www.wsws.org/tools/index.php?page=print&url=http://...

Emejo, James. (2012, October 17). Abdulsalami, Offor-Backed Firms Win DSICO Bids *Thisdaylive.com,* Retrieved on October 17, 2012 from http://www.thisdaylive.com/articles/abdulsalami-offor-backed-firms...

Emewu, Ikenna. (2011, October 28). I Listed 500 Nigerians Who Stole Government Funds and Nothing Happened—Nzeribe. *Daily Sun Nigerian.* Retrieved on November 1, 2011, from http://www.sharpedgenews.com/index.php/interviews/243-i-listed-5...

Enogholase, Gabriel. (2014, January 20). Federal Government Places Restriction on Foreign Medical Trips by Government Officials. *Vanguardngr.Com,* Retrieved on January 21, 2014, from http://www.vangaurdngr.com/.../fg-places-restriction-on-foreign-medical-trips-by-government-officals/

Eniola, Toluwani. (2014, November 13). US Frustrating Nigeria's War against Boko Haram—

FG. *Punch Nigeria.* Retrieved on November 14, 2014, from http://www.punchng.com/news/us-frustrating-nigeria's-war-against-boko-haram-fg

Eteghe, Daniel. (2012, November 26). Two Suspected Air Passengers Arrested With US$2,073,160 AT Murtala Mohammed International Airport. *Vanguardngr.com,* Retrieved on November 26, 2012, from http://www.vanguardngr.com/2012/11/2-suspected-air-passengers...

Evangelii Gaudium, Apostolic Exhortation of Pope Francis (2013). Addressed to the Bishops, Clergy, Consecrated Persons and the Lay Faithful on the Proclamation of the Gospel in Today's World. Retrieved on February 17, 2014, from http://www.vatican.va/holy_father/francesco/apost_exhortations/documents/papa-francesc...

Eze, Sylvanus, Agborh, Alphonsus, and Oruya, Suzy. (2014, March 11). Second Niger Bridge: My Sincere Promise Now a Reality--Jonathan; Federal Government Invests N40 Billion on Project. *Nigeria Tribune.* Retrieved on March 14, 2014, from http://www.tribune.com.ng/index.php/news/top-stories/items/1120-2nd-niger-bridge-my-sin...

Fabiyi, Olusola and Oluwole Josiah.(2012, February 6). Federal Government to Spend N3.1Billion on Obasanjo, Others in 2012 *Punch Nigeria,* Retrieved on February 6, 2012, from http://www.punchng.com/news/fg-to-spend-n3.1bn-on-obasanjo...

Fagbemi, Soji-Eze. (2015, February 10). Despite $32.88 Billion Defense Budget, Jonathan Cannot Tame Boko Haram—Buhari Tells Workers. *Nigeria Tribune.* Retrieved on February 11, 2015, from http://www.tribune.com.ng/news/news-headlines/item/29068-despite-32-88bn-defense-budget...

Falola, Toyin. (2009). *Colonialism and Violence in Nigeria.* Bloomington, Indiana: Indiana University Press.

Falola, Toyin and Heaton, Matthew M. (2010). *A History of Nigeria.* New York: Cambridge University Press.

Famutimi, Temitayo. (2014, October 7). Muazu Tackles Tinubu Over Calls for Revolution. *Nigeria Punch.* Retrieved on October 8, 2014, from http://www.punchng.com/i-punch/muazu-tackles-tinubu-over-calls-for-revolution...

Famutimi, Temitayo. (2014, October 3). Nigerians Are Missing my Late Father--Abacha's Daughter. *Nigeria Punch.* Retrieved on October 5, 2014, from http://www.punchng.com/i-punch/nigerians-are-missing-my-father-abacha's-daughter/

Famutimi, Temitayo. (2013, December 30). Policemen Live Like Refugees in Dilapidated

Barracks. *Nigeria Punch*. Retrieved on December 30, 2013, from http://www.punchng.com/.../policemen-live-refugees-in-dilapidated-barracks/

FAQs: Truth and Reconciliation Commission of Canada. (2010, June 14). *CBC News.* Retrieved on October 13, 2014, from http://www.cbc.ca/news/canada/faqs-truth-and-reconciliation-commission...

Ferrara, Peter. (2011, May 5). Reaganomics v Obamanomics: Facts and Figures. *Forbes Magazine,* Retrieved on September 22, 2012 from http://www.forbes.com/sites/peterferrara/2011/05/05/reganomics-v...

Fioriti, Joris. (2014, September 30). Ivory Cast Truth Commission Testimony Ends. *Yahoo News.* Retrieved on September 30, 2014, from http://news.yahoo.com/ivory-coast-truth-commission-testimony-ends...

Folasade-Koyi, Adetutu. (2013, September 19). Mark begs China to Release 490 Nigerian Prisoners. *Nigeria Daily Sun Newspaper*. Retrieved on September 19, 2013, from http://sunnewsonline.com/.../mark-begs-china-to-release-490-nigerian-prisoners...

Folasade-Koyi, Adetutu. (2013, March 5). Cash-for-Job Scam: Senate Indicts 13 Federal Ministries, Agencies. *Nigeria Daily Sun Newspaper*. Retrieved on March 6, 2013 from http://sunnewsonline.com/cash-for-job-scam-senate-indicts-13-federal-mimis...

Folasade-Koyi, Adetutu and Omolehin, Tunde. (2012, April 18). Pension Fraud Probe Latest: My Account Was Used to Steal N30bn—Clerk….Task Team Uncovers 73,000 Ghost Pensioners. *Nigeria Daily Sun,* Retrieved on April 18, 2012 from http://odili.net/news/source/2012/apr/18/517.html

Finley, J.C. (2014, August 8). Nigeria Declares State of Emergency in Response to Ebola Outbreak. *UPI*, Retrieved on August 10, 2014, from http://www.upi.com/Top_News/World_News/2014/08/08/Nigeria-declares-state-of-emerg...

Gabriel, Omoh. (2014, April 11). Nigeria, Third on World Poverty Index--World Bank. *Vanguard Nigeria,* Retrieved on April 11, 2014, from http://www.vanguardngr.com/2014/440695

Gabriel, Omoh. (2012, February 13). Unemployment, a Ticking Time Bomb. Vanguard Nigerian.Com, Retrieved on February 14, 2012, from http://www.vanguardngr.com/2012/02/unemployment-a-ticking-timebomb

Gabriel, Omoh and Emma Ujah. (2012, November 2). Don't Waste Your Oil Money, IMF Warns Federal Government. *VanguardNigeria.Com,* Retrieved on November 3, 2012, from http://www.vanguardngr.com/2012/11/don't-waste-your-oil-money-imf

Gershoni, Yekutiel. (2001). Common Goals, Different Way: The UNIA and the NCBWA in

West   Africa—1920-1930. *Online   Journal   of   Third   World   Studies,* http://findarticles.com/p/articles/mi-qa38321/is-200110ai-n8959678...

Gilbert, Daniel. (2012, February 24). KBR Ex-Chief Says Ambition, Ego, Alcohol Fueled Bribes. *Wall Street Journal .Com*, Retrieved on March 3, 2012 from http://online.wsj.com/article/SB10001424052970204778604577241...

Glahn, Gerhard Von. (1986). Law Among *Nations: An Introduction to Public International Law*, 5th Ed. New York: MacMillan Publishing Company.

Grandin, Greg. (2006). *Empire's Workshop: Latin America, the United States, and the Rise of the New Imperialism.* New York: Metropolitan Books

Halliburton: US CEO gets 30 months in Jail for Bribing Nigerians (2012, February 24). *Vanguardngr.Com,*   Retrieved   on   March   3,   2012   from http://www.vanguardngr.com/201202/halliburton-us-ceo-gets-30-mo...

Halting Medical Tourism. (2014, March 4). *Daly Sun Newspaper*. Retrieved on March 4, 2014, from http://sunnewsonline.com/news/?p=54006

Hanser, Robert D. (2013). *Introduction to Corrections*. Thousand Oaks, CA: Sage publishers

Harding, Andrew. (2015, April 2). What Does Buhari Victory Mean for Africa? *BBC.com.* Retrieved on April 4, 2015, from http://m.bbc.com/news/world-africa-32158860

Harris, Robert. (2003). *Political Corruption: In and Beyond the Nation-State.* New York: Routledge Press.

Hiatt, Steven. (2007). Global Empire: The Web of Control. In Steven Hiatt (Ed*.), A Game as Old as Empire: The Secret World of Economic Hit Men and the Web of Global Corruption* (pp.13-29). San Francisco: Berrett-Koehler Publishers.

Hurricane Katrina Refief.com (n.d.) *FAQs,* Retrieved on November 10, 2012 from http://www. http://www.hurricanekatrinarelief.com/faqs.html

Hurricane Sandy Estimated to Cost $60 Billion (2012, October 31). The Associated Press, *Business Time,* Retrieved on November 10, 2012, from http:/business.time.com/2012/10/31/hurricane-sandy-estimated-to-co...

Hurricane Sandy Recovery. (2012, November 2*). USA.gov,* Retrieved on November 11, 2012, from http://www.usa.gov/Topics/Wealther/Hurricane/sandy.shtml

I Did Not Grant Waiver for Armoured Cars-- Okonjo-Iweala. (2013, November1).

VanguardNigeria.Com.   Retrieved   on   November   3,   2013,   from
http://www.vanguardngr.com/.../didn't-grant-waiver-for-armored-cars-Okonjo-
Iweala...

Idoko, Clement. (2014, January 3). We Rescue Nigeria's Education from Bretton Woods'
     Jugular Grip--ASUU: Commends Federal Government on Payment of Lecturers' Salary
     Arrears.   *Nigeriaworld.Com.*   Retrieved   on   March   5,   2014,   from
     http://odili.net/news/source/2014/jan/3/609.html

Ilallah, Musa. (2008, September 3). Siemens Bribery Scandal and Senator Aminu's Indictment
     Nigeria   Village   Square,   Retrieved   on   August   24,   2012   from
     http://www.nigeriavillagesquare.com/index.php?view=article&catid...

Illegal Immigrants: Saudi Arrests 562 Nigerians--Envoy. (2013, November 25*). Vanguard
     Nigeria.* Retrieved on November 25, 2013, from
     http://www.vanguardngr.com/.../illegal-immigrants-saudi-arrests-562-nigerian-
     envoy...

Isenyo, Godwin. (2013, December 11). Maku Lambasts Northern Leaders Over Development.
     Punch   Nigeria.   Retrieved   on   December   11,   2013,   from
     http://www.punchng.com/.../maku-lambasts-northern-leaders-over-development/

Isiguzo, Ikeddy. (2011, August 18). Abacha Did What You Wanted Him to do—IBB *Vanguard
     Nigeria.*   Retrieved   on   August   8,   2011,   from
     http://www.vanguardngr.com/2011/08/abacha-did-what-you-wanted-him-to-do-ibb/

It is wrong to Underfund EFCC. (2013, October 29). *PunchNigeria.Com.* Retrieved on October
     30, 2013, from http://www.punchng.com/editorial

Iyatse, Geoff. (2014, October 15). US Has not Refused Nigeria Military Assistance—Envoy.
     Punch Nigeria. Retrieved on October 17, 2014, from
     http://www.punchng./news/us-has-not-refused-nigeria-military-assistance-envoy

Janda, Kenneth, Berry, Jeffrey M., and Goldman, Jerry. (1989). *The Challenge of Democracy:
     Government in America* (2nd edition). Boston: Houghton Mifflin Company.

Jonathan, Allison-Madueke and the Ribadu Report (2012, November 2). *Punch Nigeria Editorial
     Commentary,*   Retrieved   on   November   3,   2012,   from
     http://www.punchng.com/.../jonathan...madueke-and-the-ribadu-report-

Jonathan Laments Lack of Adequate Skills Among Nigerian Graduates. (2013, October 23).
     VanguardNigeria.Com.   Retrieved   on   October   25,   2013,   from
     http://www.vanguardngr.com/.../jonathan-laments-lack-of-adequate-skills-among-
     nigerian-guadates

Josiah, Oluwole. (2013, March 7). Northerners Hold 83 Percent of Oil Blocks—Senator. *Punch

Nigeria. Retrieved on March 7, 2013, from http://www.punchng.com,news

Josiah, Oluwole. (2012, October 26). Nigerian Embassies to Fuel, Maintain Generators with N200 million. *PunchNigerian.Com,* Retrieved on October 27, 2012, from http://www.punchng.com/news/nigeria-embassies-to-fuel-maintain...

Kegley, Jr. Charles W. and Wittkopf, Eugene R. (1996). *American Foreign Policy* (5th edition). New York: St. Martin's Press.

Kern, Kathleen. (2007). The Human Cost of Cheap Cell Phones. In Steven Hiatt (Ed.), *A Game as Old as Empire: The Secret World of Economic Hit Men and the Web of Global Corruption* (pp.93-112). San Francisco: Berrett-Koehler Publishers.

Komisar, Lucy. (2007). BCCI Double Game; Banking on America, Banking on Jihad. In Steven Hiatt (Ed.), *A Game as Old as Empire: The Secret World of Economic Hit Men and the Web of Global Corruption* (pp.69-91). San Francisco: Berrett-Koehler Publishers.

Lasswell, Harold D. (1948). *Power and Personality.* New York: Norton Publishers.

Lawal, Iyabo and Musari, Abosode. (2012, April 13). Loot Recovered by Pension Task Force Hits N182bn. *The Guardian Nigeria,* Retrieved on April 16, 2012 from http://odili.net/news/source/2012/apr/13/16.html

List of ASUU's Demand that Triggered the Strike. (2013, September 21). *Osun Defender.* http://www.osundefender,org/?p=107249

Makinde, Bankole. (2013, January 24). Nigeria is in Trouble—Senator Gaya. *Tribune Nigeria,* Retrieved on January 24, 2013, from http://tribune.com.ng/.../3782-nigeria-is-in-trouble-senator-gaya-

Mays, G. Larry and Winfree, Jr. L. Thomas (2009). *Essentials of Corrections* (4th edition). Belmont, CA: Wadsworth.

Mbeki's Damming Verdict on Nigerians (2013, November 24). *Punch Nigeria Editorial.* Retrieved on November 25, 2013, from http://www.punchng.com/editorial/mbekis-damming-verdict-on-nigerians/

Mikairu, Lawani and Daniel Eteghe. (2012, November 21). Customs Arrests Passenger with

$320,000 at Lagos Airport. *Vanguard Nigeria,* Retrieved on November 21, 2012, from http://www.vanguardngr.com/2012/11/customs-arrests-passenger...

Monthly 200 Nigerian Girls are trafficked to Russia for Prostitution--Envoy (2013, November 21). *Vanguard Nigeria Newspaper.* Retrieved on November 21, 2013, from http://www.vanguardngr.com/.../monthly-200-nigerian-girls-are-trafficked-to-russia...

Muanya, Chukwuma. (2013, September 5). 3, 936 Nigerian Doctors Practise in UK. *The*

Guardian Nigeria. Retrieved on September 2013, from http://www.ngrguardiannews.com/.../131930-3-936-nigerian-doctors-practise-in-uk

Muhammad, Abdulsalam. (2013, January 25). Gowon, Babangida, Sambo, Others Shun Peace Summit in Kano. *Vanguard Nigeria,* Retrieved on January 25, 2013, from http://www.vanguardng.com/2013/01/gowon-babangida-sambo-others

Musari, Abosede. (2012, October 20). EFCC Freezes N16 Million Account in Bermuda. *The Guardian Nigeria,* Retrieved on October 23, 2012, from http://theguardianmobile.com/readNewsItem1.php?nid=8005

Napolitano, Andrew P. (2009). Dred Scott's Revenge: *A Legal History of Race and Freedom in America.* Nashville, Tennessee: Thomas Nelson Publishing Inc.

NAPTIP on the Sale of Babies. (2014, January 25). *Nigerian Tribune* Retrieved on January 27, 2014 from http://www.tribune.com.ng/.../31612-naptip-on-the-sale-of-babies-html

Nigeria: Africa's New Number One. (2014, April 12). *The Economist.Com.* Retrieved on January 5, 2015, from http://www.economist.com/node/21600685/print

Nigeria Becomes Africa's Largest Economy. (2014, April 6). *Aljazeera.Com.* Retrieved on July 3, 2014, from http://www.aljazeera.com/news/africa/2014/04/nigeria-becomes-africa's-largest-economy...

Nigeria Ranked Among World's Poorest Competitive Countries. (2013). *Vanguard Nigeria.* Retrieved on September 6, 2013, from http://www.vanguardngr.com/.../nigeria-ranked-among-world's-poorest-competitive-countries...

Nigeria Settles Paris Club Debt. (2006, April 21). *BBC News.* Retrieved on February 11, 2014, from http://news.bbc.co.uk/2/hi/business/4926966.stm

Nigerians Abroad Remitted N400 billion Home in One Year—World Bank. (2008, April 7). *Nigeria Tribune,* Retrieved on April 7, 2008, from http://odili.net/news/source/2008/apr/7/613.html

Nigerian Army Chronicle of Command: Past and Present Chief of Army Staff. (n.d.). *Nigerian Army Official Website.* Retrieved on November 15, 2014, from http://army.mil.ng/Chronicle-of-Command.html

Nigerian National Alliance. (1994). *Blueprint for Democracy in Nigeria.* Chicago: NNA Publication.

Nnodim, Okechukwu. (2012, November 16). Sanusi: $11 Billion Cash Taken Abroad Through

Nigerian Airports. *PunchNigeria.Com,* Retrieved on November 16, 2012, from http://www.punchng.com/...cash-taken-abroad-through-nigerian...

Nnochiri, Ikechukwu. (2014, January 10). Retiring High Court Judge Gives Reasons for High Level Corruption in Judiciary. *Vanguard Nigeria.Com,* Retrieved on January 11, 2014, from http://www.vanguardngr.com/retiring-high-court-judge-gives-reasons-of-high-level-corruption-in-judiciary/

Nnochiri, Ikechukwu. (2013, October 5). Politicians, Traditional Rulers Offer US Bribe, Says Retiring Supreme Court Justice. *Vanguard Nigeria.Com* Retrieved on October 6, 2013, from http://www.vanguardngr.com/.../politicians-traditional-rulers-offer-us-bribe-says-retiring-s-court-justice/

Nnochiri, Ikechukwu. (2012, April 23). Pension Scam: Seven Bureau de-Change Operators Used to Loot N38bn, EFCC Tells Court. *Vanguardngr.com,* Retrieved on April 24, 2012 from http://odili.net/news/source/2012/apr/23/324.html

Nnochiri, Ikechukwu. (2012, August 29). Ezekwesili: Nigeria Loses $400 Billion to Oil Thieves. *Vanguardngr.com,* Retrieved on September 22, 2012 from http://www.vanguardngr.com/2012/08/nigeria-loses-400bn-to-oil-thi...

Nnochiri, Ikechukwu. (2012, November 16). Contract Scam: How Ex-Works Minister Diverted N75 Billion, EFCC Tells Court. *VanguardNigeria.Com,* Retrieved on November 16, 2012, from http://www.vanguardngr.com/2012/11/contract-scam-how-ex-works...

Northouse, Peter G. (2004). *Leadership: Theory and Practice.* 3rd Ed. Thousand Oaks, California: Sage Publications, Inc.

Nwachukwu, Obinna E. (2000, September). *An Evaluation of the Impact of Privatization Programme on Government Owned Enterprises in Nigeria: A Case Study of the Union Bank of Nigeria Plc. and the National Oil and Chemical Marketing Plc.* Unpublished Manuscript, University of Nigeria Research Publication (PG/MBA/98/20956).

Nwogu, Success. (2012, September, 9). Nigerians Spend N160 billion Annually on Educations in Ghana—Babalakin. *Punch Nigeria,* Retrieved on September 10, 2012 from http://www.punchng.com/news/nigerians-spend-n160bn-annually-in...

Nwogu, Success. (2012, October 28). State Universities: Okojie Blames Governments for Underfunding. *Punch Nigeria,* Retrieved on October 29, 2012, from http://www.punchng.com/education/state-varities-okolie-blames...

Nwosu, Iheanacho, and Fred Itua. (2014, April 6.). Gen. Useni: Civilians behind Military Coups. *Daily Sun Nigeria,* Retrieved on April 7, 2014, from http://sunnewsonline.com/new?p=58836

Nwosu, Iheanacho. (2012, October 25). The Problem with South East Roads, By House Works

Committee. *Daily Sun Nigeria,* Retrieved on October 25, 2012, from http://sunnewsonline.com/new/politics/the-problem-with-seast...

Obineche, Chidi. (2012, October 22). Gov. Okorocha: My Life is Full of Struggles. *Daily Sun Nigeria,* Retrieved on October 22, 2012, **from** http://sunnewsonline.com/new/politics/my-life-is-full-of...

Odiogor, Hugo and Kumolu, Charles. (2013, February 1). How to Avoid Nigeria's Breakaway in 2015--IBB. *VangardNigeria.Com* Retrieved on February 2, 2013, from http://www.vanguardngr.com/2013/02/how-to-avoid-nigerias-breakaway-in-2015-ibb

Oduahgate: Lagos Denies Requesting for N255 Million BMW Cars. (2013, November 1). *VanguardNigeria.Com.* Retrieved on November 3, 2013, from http://www.vanguardngr.com/.../Oduahgate-Lagos-dissociate-self-from-importation...

Office of the Director of National Intelligence: Leading Intelligence Integration. (2004, December 17). *DNI Website.* Retrieved on October 20, 2014, from http://www.dni.gov/index.php/about/history

Official: 131 Nigerian Deportees from Saudi Arabia Arrive in Abuja. (2013, December 31). *Punch Nigeria.* Retrieved on January 2, 2014, from http://www.punchng.com/news/131-nigerian-deportees-from-sarabia-arrive-in-abuja-official/

Ogbodo, John-Abba. (2013, January 22). Rot at Police College: Senate, EFCC to Probe Ministry, Formations. *NigeriaWorld.com,* Retrieved on January 23, 2013, from http://odili.net/news/source/2013/jan/22/8.html

Ogedengbe, Alex. (2009, June 15). Nigerian Refineries: History, Problem, and Possible Solutions. *Businessdayonline.com,* Retrieved on August 28, 2012 from http://www.businessdayonline.com/NG/index.php/oil/3203-nigerian-r...

Ogiji, John. (2013, April 11). Blame Poverty in North on Past Leaders, Says Aliyu. *Nigeriaguardiannews.com,* Retrieved on April 12, 2013, from http://www.ngrguardiannews.com/index.php?option=com-content&view=article&id=118580:blame-poverty-in-north-on-past-leaders-says-aliyu&catid=1:national&Itemid=559

Ogundele, Kamarudeen. (2013, September 13). Judiciary Aids Corrupt Nigerians--Ribadu. *Punch Nigeria.* Retrieved on September 15, 2013, from http://www.punchng.com/news/judiciary-aids-corrupt-nigerians-ribadu/

Ojo, Jide. (2014, January 8). Another Presidential Jet for Nigeria, not again. *Punch Nigeria.*

Retrieved on January 9, 2014, from
http://www.punchng.com/opinion/another-presidential-jet-for-nigeria-not-again/

Oke, Gbenga. (2013, March 22). The Mistakes Rotimi Williams and I Made about Nigeria's
Constitution—Nwabueze. *Vanguard Nigeria.* Retrieved on March 22, 2013, from
http://www.vanguardngr.com/.../the-mistakes-rotimi-williams-and-i-made-about...

Oke, Tayo. (2012, October 22). CBN's Renewed Attack on the Scourge of Money Laundering.
Punch   Nigeria.Com,   Retrieved   on   October   23,   2012   from
http://www.punchng.com/opinion/cbns-renewed-attack-on-the

Okeke, Christian. (2012, December 10). We Will Expose Nigerian Treasury Looters—Swiss
Government: Says Abacha's Son Still Wanted in Switzerland, Public Office Holders with
Loot in Swiss Banks in Trouble. *NigeriaWorld,* Retrieved on December 10, 2012, from
http://odili.net/news/source/2013/dec/10/602.html

Ola, Idowu. (2012, October 20). The Presidential Scholarship Scheme for Innovation and
Development (PRESSID): Matters Arising. *Nigeriaworld.com,* Retrieved on October 23,
2012, from http://nigeriaworld.com/articles/2012/oct/201.html

Oladipo, Olaolu. (2012, June 16). Money Laundering: US Freezes Nigerian Embassy's
Accounts. *Leadership Nigeria,* Retrieved on October   25,   2012,   from
http://www.leadership.ng/nga/articles/2012/06/16/money...

Olokor, Friday and Bukola Adebayo. (2014, October 1). Nigeria at Fifty-four: Ex-NMA
President Decries State of Public Hospitals. *Nigerian Punch.* Retrieved on October 2, 2014,
from   http://www.punchng.com/health/nigeria-54-ex-nma-president-decries-state-of-
public-hospitals/

Olokor, Friday. (2012, November 9). EFCC Arrests Two with $238,858. *PunchNigeria.Com,*
Retrieved on November 9, 2012, from
http://www.punchng.com/news/efcc-arrests-two-with-238858-

Olufowobi, Sesan. (2014, October 2). Politician Vandalises Pipeline to Raise Campaign Funds.
Nigerian   Punch.   Retrieved   on   October   2,   2014,   from
http://www.punchng.com/news/politician-vandalises-pipeline-to-raise-campaign-
funds...

Olukoya, Olayinka. (2013, September 5). Awo Remains Nigeria's Greatest Leader--Ex-
lawmaker. *Nigerian Tribune* Retrieved on September 5, 2013, from
http://www.tribune.com.ng/.../20816-awo-remains-nigeria's-greatest-leader-ex-
lawmaker...

Ojogo, Donald. (2012, May 9). How North Cornered Nigeria's Oil Blocs Revealed Eighty

Percent of Ownership of the Nation's Oil Reserves is in the Hands of Some Influential Northerners: South-South in Battle Royale over Oil. *Nigeria Tribune,* Retrieved on March 9, 2012 from http://odili.net/news/source/2012/mar/9/601.html

Omipidan, Ismail. (2014, November 16). Superpowers Backing Boko Haram –Sheikh Abubakar Gumi. *The Daily Sun.* Retrieved on November 17, 2014, from http://sunnewsonline.com/new/?p=91208

Omoigui, Nowa. (2007, October 27). Military Rebellion of July 29, 1975: The Coup Against Gowon—Part 4. *Dawodu.com,* Retrieved on September 8, 2012 from http://www.dawodu.com/omoigui41.htm

Omonobi, Kingsley. (2013, February, 12). Jaji Attack: Maj. Gen. Isah Had Prior Information— Ihejirika. *Vanguard Nigeria.* Retrieved on February 12, 2013, from http://www.vanguardngr.com/.../jaji-attack-maj-gen-isah-had-prior-information...

Onyekakeyah, Luke. (2013, December 3). The Niger Bridge Agony at Christmas. *Nigerian Guardian.* Retrieved on December 4, 2013, from http://www.ngrguardiannews.com/index.php/opinion/columinist/139981-onyekakeyah-the-niger-bridge-agnoy-at-christmas...

Onyeocha, Ugochukwu. (2014, September 10). States Development Not Commensurate With Heavy Allocation, Lamorde Fires Governors. *Daily Times Nigeria.* Retrieved on September 22, 2014, from http://dailytimes.com.ng/article/states-development-not-commensutate-with-heavy-allocation-lamorde-fires-governors/

Onuba, Ifeanyi. (2011, September 1). Foreign Medical Treatments Cost Nigeria N30 billion Annually—Okonjo-Iweala. *Nigeria World,* Retrieved on September 1, 2011, from http://odili.net/news/source/2011/sep/1/814.html

Opara, Enyioha. (2014, March 3). Northern Governors to Abolish Fees in Secondary Schools. *Punch Nigeria.Com.* Retrieved on March 4, 2014, from http://www.punchng.com/news/northern-govs-to-abolish-fees-in-secondary-schools/

Opara, Stanley. (2012, October 18). Electricity Firms' Bid Result Disappointing—Obi. *PunchNigeria.Com,* Retrieved on October 20, 2012, from http://www.punchng.com/business/business-economy/electricity-firm...

Orji, Ndubuisi. (2014, December 3). Soyinka to US: We Don't Need Excuses. *The Daily Sun,* Retrieved on December 4, 2014, from http://sunnewsonline.com/new/?p=93786

Osaghae, Eghosa E. (1998). *The Crippled Giant: Nigeria Since Independence*. Bloomington, Indiana: Indiana University Press.

Otti, Sam. (December, 11). 8,000 Nigerians Rots in Foreign Prisons, Says Dabiri-Erewa.

Nigeriworld.com.   Retrieved   on   December   11,   2013,   from http://odili.net/news/source/2013/dec/11/524.html

Our Primary Healthcare Rotten, lost--NMA boss. (2013, September 25). *Nigeria Daily Sun Newspaper.* Retrieved on September 25, 2013, from http://sunnewsonline.com/.../our-primary-healthcare-rotten-lost-NMA-boss/

Oyebode, Akin. (2012, September 19). What We Have To Do About Corruption. *Nigerian Guardian   News.Com,*   Retrieved   on   September   19,   2012   from http://www.ngrguardiannews.com/index.php?view=article&catid=38...

Oyedele, Damilola. (2012, November 18). Nigeria: Assessment Report Indicts Varities' Governing Council, Principal Officers. *ThisDay Newspaper,* Retrieved on November 18, 2012, from http://allafrica.com/stories/201211180444.html

Oyesina, Tunde. (2013, November 7). Awo Instrumental to Development of Western States-- Clark.   *Nigeria   Tribune*   Retrieved   on   November   7   2013,   from http://www.tribune.com.ng/.../25727-awo-instrumental-to-development-of-western-states-clark

Oyesina, Tunde. (2012, April 21). Pension Scam: How Ghost Names Were Used to Siphon N80 Million—Investigation. *Nigeria Tribune,* Retrieved on April 23, 2012 from http://odili.net/news/source/2012/apr/21/614.html

Oyesina, Tunde. (2010, November 23) $17.5 Bribery Scam: FG Withdraws Corrupt Charges Against   Siemens   Nigeria   Tribune,   Retrieved   on   August   24,   2012   from http://tribune.com.ng/index.php/news/13780-175m-bribery-scam-fg-w...

Owuamanam, Jude. (2014, November 18). Corruption, Saboteurs in Military Killing Anti-Terror War– Cleric. *Nigeria Punch.* Retrieved on November 19, 2014, from http://www.punchng.com/news/corruptio-saboteurs-in-military-killing-anti-terror-war-cleric...

Padgett, Tim. (2012, August 24). Twenty Years after Hurricane Andrew, Storm Costs and Ideology Loom over Florida. *Swampland Time,* Retrieved on November 10, 2012, from http://swampland.time.com/2012/08/24/20-years-after-hurricane-an...

Paul, Ron. (2008). *The Revolution: A Manifesto.* New York: Grand Central Publishing.

Perkins, John. (2006). *Confessions of an Economic Hit Man.* New York: Penguin Group.

Popoola, Nike. (2014, March 27). Business Executives Scramble for Kidnap Insurance Cover. *Punch Nigeria.* Retrieved on March 28, 2014, from **http://**   www.punchng.com/business/business/business-executives-scramble-for-kidnap-insurance-cover

Poverty in the Midst of Growth. (2013, December 20). *Nigeria Daily Sun Newspaper Editorial.*

Retrieved   on   December   21,   2013,   from
http://sunnewsonline.com/new/editorial/poverty-midst-growth/

Reeve, Simon. (1999). *The New Jackals: Ramzi Yousef, Osama Bin Laden and the Future of Terrorism.* Boston: Northeastern University Press.

Republic of the Soviet Union. (2014, July 10). Wikipedia, the free Encyclopedia. Retrieved on July 17, 2014, from http://en.wikipedia.org/wiki/Republics_of_the_Soviet_Union

Sampson, Anthony. (1999). Mandela: The Authorized Biography. New York: Vintage Books

Samuel, Idowu. (2012, December 10). Akpabio Best Awo, Zik Disciple—Primate Ola Makindle. *Nigerian Tribune,* Retrieved on December 10, 2012, from http://www.tribune.com.ng/news2013/index.php/en/component/k2/...

Sanusi, Lamido Sanusi. (2010, February 26). The Nigerian Banking Industry: What Went Wrong And the Way Forward. *A Convocation Lecture Delivered at the Bayero University, Kano to Mark the Annual Convocation Ceremony of the University.*

Schmalleger, Frank. (2014). *Criminal Justice: A Brief Introduction.* 10th Ed. Upper Saddle River, New Jersey: Pearson Education, Inc.

Seipel, Arnie. (2010, October 28). Hey, Congress: Keep Your Day Jobs. *National Public Radio,* Retrieved on February 18, 2015, from http://www.npr.org/2010/12.28/132294306/hey-congress-dont-keep...

Shadare, Wole. (2013, September 6). 361 Nigerians Deported In Two Months. *The Guardian Nigeria.* Retrieved on September 9, 2013, from https://ngrguardiannews.com/index.php/news/national-news/132112-361-nigerians-deporte...

Siollun, Max. (n.d.). The Inside Story of Nigeria's First Military Coup--Part 2. *Gamji.Com.* Retrieved on April 19, 2014, from **http://www.gamji.com/article6000/News6574.htm**

Siollun, Max. (2009). *Oil, Politics, and Violence: Nigeria's Military Coup Culture* (1966-1976). New York: Algora Publishing Company.

Smiley, Tavis and Cornel West. (2012). *The Rich and the Rest of US: a Poverty Manifesto.* Carlsbad, CA: Smiley Books

Soniyi, Tobi. (2012, November 30). Court Dismisses $12.5Billion Gulf Oil Windfall Suit. *ThisDayLive,* Retrieved on December 1, 2012, from http://www.thisdaylive.com/articles/court-dismisses-12-5bn-gulf-oil

Soriwei, Fidelis. (2014, March 5). Pension Thief Loses Hotel to Federal Government. *Punch*

Nigeria, Retrieved on March 6, 2014, from http://www.punchng.com/news/pension-thief-loses-hotel-to-fg...

Soriwei, Fidelis, Allwell Okpi, and Leke Baiyewu. (2012, October 28). Ribadu Report: Sack, Prosecute Oil Minister—Labour, SNG, Others. *PunchNigeria.Com,* Retrieved on October 29, 2012, from http://www.punchng.com/news/ribadu-report-sack-prosecute-oil

Soyinka, Wole. (2014, March 2). The Canonisation of Terror. *Vanguardngr.com.* Retrieved on March 3, 2014, from http://www.vanguardngr.com/2014/03/canonisation-terror-wole-soyinka/

Soyinka, Wole. (2012, January 10). Nigeria Heading for Civil War. *Vangardngr.com.* Retrieved on January 11, 2012, from http://www.vangaurdngr.com/2012/01/nigeria-heading-for-civil-war...

Stiglitz, Joseph E. (2003). *Globalization and Its Discontents.* New York: W.W Norton and Company

Stone, Oliver and Kuznick, Peter. (2012). *The Untold History of the United States.* New York: Gallery Books.

Subair, Gbola. (2014, September 3). Nigerian in Diaspora Remitted $10.40 Billion in First Half Of 2014. *Nigerian Tribune.* Retrieved on September 4, 2014, from http://www.tribune.com.ng/news/news-headlines/item/15010-nigerian...

Subair, Gbola. (2012, October 17). Sale of PHCN: Abdulsalami Beats Tinubu, Otudeko, Wins Four Power Distribution Companies in Ikeja, Eko, Ibadan, and Yola: As Federal Government Rakes in N197 Billion from Sales. Nigeria Tribune, Retrieved on October 17, 2012 from http://tribune.com.ng/index.php/lead-stories/49324-sale-of-phcn-abdu...

Taiwo-Obalonye, Juliana. (2014, January 2). What Obama told me About Nigeria-Jonathan? *Nigeria Daily Sun.* Retrieved on January 2, 2014, from http://sunnewsonline.com/new/cover/obama-told-nigeria-jonathan/

Taiwo-Obalonye, Juliana. (2012, November 16). Second Niger Bridge Now to Begin in 2013, *Nigeria Daily Sun.* Retrieved on November 16, 2012, from http://sunnewsonline.com/...2nd-niger-bridge-now-to-begin-in-2013

The Former Chiefs of Air Staffs (n.d.). *Nigerian Air Force Official Website.* Retrieved on November 12, 2014, from http://airforce.mil.ng/former_cas

The Military Top Brass: From Inception to Date. (2013, January 9). *The Ambrose Ehirim Files.*

Retrieved   on   November   11,   2014,   from
http://ambroseehirim.blogspot.com/2013/01/the-military-top-brass-f...

The Mother of Revolution and Crime is Poverty (Aristotle). (2007, September 24) *Ultimate GP Blog*. Retrieved on November 26, 2013, from
http://golden-panther-blogspot.com/2007/09/mother-of-revolution-and-crime-is.html

The Trouble with Nigerian Universities (2012, December 13). *Nigeria Punch Editorial Board Commentary*. Retrieved on December 15, 2012, from
http:// www.punchng.com/.../the-trouble-with-nigerian-universities

Tukur, Sani. (2013, September 27). Why Kill Ironsi and Installed Gowon-- Lt. General Jeremiah Useni.   *Premium   Times   Nigeria*. Retrieved   on   September   28,   2013,   from
http://www.premiumtimesng.com/.../145535-interview-killed-ironsi-installed-gowon-jeremiah-useni.html/

Tuman, Joseph. (2003). *Communicating Terror: The Rhetorical Dimension of Terrorism*. Thousand Oaks, California: Sage Publications.

Tunisia Repatriates 90 Nigerians, Including 14 Minors. (2013, September 11). *Punch Nigeria Newspaper*. Retrieved on September 11, 2013, from
http://www.punchng.com/news/africa/tunisia-repatriates-90-nigerians-including-14-minors/...

Truth Commission: El Salvador. (1992, July 1). Commission on the Truth for El Salvador. *United   States   Institute   of   Peace*. Retrieved   on   September   30,   2014,   from
http://www.usip.org/publications/truth-commission-el-salvador

Truth Commission: Nigeria. (1999, June 14). Human Rights Violations Investigation Commission. *United States Institute of Peace*. Retrieved on May 6, 2014, from
http://www.usip.org/publications/truth-commission-nigeria

Truth Commission: Honduras 2010. (2012, February 9). Truth and Reconciliation Commission. *United   States   Institute   of   Peace*. Retrieved   on   October   11,   2014,   from
http://www.usip.org/publications/truth-commission-honduras-2010

Truth Commission: South Africa. (1995, December 1). Commission of Truth and Reconciliation. *United   States   Institute   of   Peace*. Retrieved   on   September   30,   2014,   from
http://www.usip.org/publications/truth-commission-south-africa

Truth and Reconciliation Commission (2014, September 27). *Wikipedia, the Free Encyclopedia*. Retrieved   on   October   11,   2014,   from
http://en.wikipedia.org/wiki/Truth_and_reconiliation_commission

Tutu, Desmond. (1994).*The Rainbow People of God: The Making of a Peaceful Revolution*. New York: Doubleday Publishing Company.

Ubabukoh, Ozioma. (2014, March 10). APC Says Jonathan is Toying with Ndigbo. *Punch*

Nigeria.Com. Retrieved on March 11, 2014, from http://www.punchng.com/news/apc-says-jonathan-is-toying-with-ndigbo/

Uche, Chibuike U. (2011, June). British Government, British Businesses, and the Indigenisation Exercise in Nigeria. *Paper presented at the ECAS 4 Conference.*

Ujah, Emma. (2013, August 22). Ezekwesili Challenges Federal Legislators to a Public Hearing On Their Pay. *VanguardNigeria.com.* Retrieved on August 23, from http://www.vanguardngr.com/.../ezekwesili-challenges-federal-legislators-to-a-public-hearing-on-thei-pay...

Umez, Bedford Nwabueze. (2002, January 7). Liberating African Mind (LAM): Belief and The Future of Africa. Naija Mall [Online]. Available: wysiwyg://6/http://NAIJAMALL.COM/News/Ngr/Articles/BeliefAndTheFuture.html

Umoru, Henry and Shaibu Inalegwu. (2012, April 17). N26bn Police Pension Funds Traced to First Bank, Fidelity, UBA, Others. *NigeriaWorld* Retrieved on April 18, 2012 from http://odili.net/news/source/2012/apr/17/339.html

Uwasomba, Chijioke. (2013, September 5). Why Does ASUU Always Go on Strike? *allAfrica.Com,* Retrieved on September 6, 2013, from http://www.allafrica.co,/stories/201309101008.html

Uwechue, Peter. (2010, December 23). Halliburton Scandal: Six Nigerians to Face Trial. *Nigeriansreportyournews.Com.* Retrieved on March 3, 2012 from http://nigeriansreportyournews.com/index.php/newsprintblog?index...

USA.gov. (2012, November 2). Hurricane Sandy Recovery. Retrieved on November 11, 2012, from http://www.usa.gov/Topics/Wealther/Hurricane/Sandy.shtml

Usigbe, Leon, Nnabuife Collins, and Fagbemi, Soji-Eze. (2014, March 18). Immigration Recruitment Tragedy: Jonathan Queries Moro, Parradang….Human Rights Commission to Investigate Applicants' Death. *Nigeria Tribune* Retrieved on March 18, 2014, from http://www.tribune.com.ng/.../immigration-recruitment-tragedy-jonathan-queries-moro-parradang...human-rights-commission-to-investigate-applicants-death/15

Usigbe, Leon. (2012, October 30). NCP Approves 15 Power Generations and Distribution Companies. Nigeria Tribune Newspaper. Retrieved on October 2012, from http://tribune.com.ng/index.php/complete-business-package/50084

Usim, Uche. (2012, November 9). Customs Arrests Passenger with Undeclared $137,435 at Airport. *Daily Sun Nigeria.* Retrieved on November 10, 2012, from http://sunnewsonline.com/new/national/customs-arrests-passenger...

Wali, Abdallah. (2013, January 12). 100 Nigerians Languish in Moroccan Prisons, Says

Ambassador. *Nigeria Vanguard.* Retrieved on January 13, 2014, from http://www.vanguardngr.com/.../100-nigerians-languish-in-moroccan-prisons-says-ambassador

Walker, Samuel and Charles M. Katz. (2011). *The Police in America: An Introduction,* 7th Ed. New York: McGraw Hill.

Waziri, Farida. (2011, September 6). Influential Nigerians Killing Anti-Corruption War. *Punch Nigeria Newspaper.* Retrieved on September 6, 2011 from http://odili.net/news/source/2011/sep/6/840.html

Weisenthal, Joe. (2013, November 26). The Pope Just Punished One of the Most Powerful Critiques of Modern Capitalism that You Will Ever Read. *Business Insider.* Retrieved on February 17, 2014 from http://www.businessinsider.com/the-pope-on-the-financial-system-inequality-money-2013-...

Weissbrodt, David and Fraser, Paul W. (1992). [Review of the book Report of the Chilean National Commission on Truth and Reconciliation by National Commission on Truth and Reconciliation]. *JSTOR: Human Rights Quarterly,* Vol. 14, No 4, 601-622.

Why Nigerians Study in Ghana--Okojie. (2013, September 3). *PunchNigeria.Com.* Retrieved on September 4, from http://www.punchng.com/education/why-nigerians-study-in-ghans-okojie/

Zepezauer, Mark and Arthur Naiman. (1996). *Take the Rich off Welfare: The Real Story Series.* Chicago: Common Courage Press/LPC Group.

Zhang, Qingming. (n.d.). *America's Response to Energy Demand of China and Sino-US Relationship in the 21st Century: A case Study of Failed Mergers and Acquisitions between China National Offshore Oil Corporation and Union Oil Company of California.* Unpublished manuscript, Auburn University.

Index

D

E

O

About the Author

Dr. **Christian Chukwuma Onwudiwe** is currently teaching Criminal Justice at Youngstown State University, Youngstown, Ohio, USA. Prior to accepting his new position at Youngstown State University, he taught Political Science at Xavier University of Louisiana, New Orleans. He earned his Doctoral Degree in Political Science from Howard University, Washington, D.C., his M.A. in Social Sciences and B.A. in Political Science and History from Southern University and Agricultural and Mechanical College, Baton Rouge, Louisiana. He obtained his second M.A. in Criminal Justice from Southern University at New Orleans, Louisiana.

Dr. Onwudiwe is also working on several other manuscripts, two of which are nearing completion and expected to be published soon.

His research and professional interests are in the areas of Political Integration, Third World Politics, Foreign Policy of Major Powers, International Relations, Transnational Crime, and the Administration of Justice.

Upcoming Titles:

- Global Terrorism: Why Have Some Western Countries, Especially the United States of America Become Targets of Terrorism

- A United States of Africa: An Idea Whose Time Has Come.